T0318244

Routledge Revivals

Turkic Oral Epic Poetry

Originally published in 1992, *Turkic Oral Poetry* provides an expert introduction to the oral epic traditions of the Turkic peoples of central Asia. The book seeks to remedy the problem of non-specialists' lack of access to information on the Turkic traditions, and in the process, it provides scholars in various disciplines with material for comparative investigation. The book focuses on "central traditions" of this region, specifically those of the Uzbeks, Kazakhs, Karakalpak's, and Kirghiz and looks at the historical and linguistic background to a survey of the earliest documents, portraits of the singers and of performance considerations of genre, story-patterns, and formulaic diction, and discussions of "composition in performance", memory, rhetoric and diffusion.

Turkic Oral Epic Poetry

Traditions, Forms, Poetic Structure

by Karl Reichl

Routledge
Taylor & Francis Group

First published in 1992
by Garland Publishing Inc.

This edition first published in 2018 by Routledge
2 Park Square, Milton Park, Abingdon, Oxon, OX14 4RN
and by Routledge
711 Third Avenue, New York, NY 10017

Routledge is an imprint of the Taylor & Francis Group, an informa business

© 1992 Karl Reichl

Publisher's Note
The publisher has gone to great lengths to ensure the quality of this reprint but
points out that some imperfections in the original copies may be apparent.

Disclaimer
The publisher has made every effort to trace copyright holders and welcomes
correspondence from those they have been unable to contact.

A Library of Congress record exists under LCCN: 92016726

ISBN 13: 978-0-8153-5776-6 (hbk)
ISBN 13: 978-0-8153-5779-7 (pbk)
ISBN 13: 978-1-351-12378-5 (ebk)

Preface to the Reprint 2017

This book was written to familiarize the reader with the world of Turkic oral epic poetry, the vibrant oral tradition of a great number of Turkic-speaking peoples, extending over a vast area from Turkey to Xinjiang in western China and Yakutia in eastern Siberia. Much of the book was written during my visiting professorship at Harvard in 1990, where Albert Lord was a frequent interlocutor. Soon after its publication, Metin Ekici, then a doctoral student of the University of Wisconsin at Madison, now Professor of Turkology at Ege University in Izmir, proposed translating the book into Turkish. The Turkish translation was published in 2002 and is now in its third printing. In 2008 a Russian translation was published in the series "Issledovaniya po fol'kloru i mifologii Vostoka" (Studies in the Folklore and Mythology of the East) of the Russian Academy of Sciences, and in 2011 a Chinese translation came out in the series "Folkloristic Studies" of the Chinese Academy Social Sciences. While these translations enjoy great popularity and are all still in print, the original has long been out of print. A reprint makes the English version again accessible, and I am most grateful to Routledge for making this possible.

Since the original publication there have been changes in various Turkic oral traditions and there have been advances in the field of Turkology. These changes, however, only impinge marginally on the argumentation of the book. This study of Turkic oral epic poetry is both introductory and descriptive in orientation, bringing together various oral traditions that share a common linguistic and cultural heritage, and analyzing them within a theoretical framework indebted to Oral Theory. What has changed since the 1980s and early 1990s, when the research for this book was conducted, can be summarized under two headings: 'death and revival' and 'editions and editorial projects'. In the past years a number of epic singer-narrators mentioned in this book have died and in some cases with their death oral traditions came to an end. Among the singers I have recorded are the Karakalpak *baqsï* Genžebay Tilewmuratov (d. 1997) and the Karakalpak *žïraw* Žumabay Bazarov (d. 2006), whose *Edige* appeared in 2007 in a bilingual edition.[1] The Kazakh *aqïn* Šeriyazdan Soltanbay-ulï from Xinjiang died in 2005. In 2014 two Kirghiz singers from Xinjiang died: Mämbet Sart (better known in later years under the name of Sart-aqun Qadïr), whose version of the epic *Qurmanbek* I was able to record a second time in 2011, and the great *manasčï Džüsüp*

---

[1] *Edige. A Karakalpak Oral Epic as Performed by Jumabay Bazarov*, edited and translated by Karl Reichl. FF Communications 293 (Helsinki, 2007).

Mamay, whose *Manas* I am in the process of translating.[2] With Žumabay Bazarov the last traditional Karakalpak *žïraw* has passed away. There is, however, a group of young epic singers (*žïraws*), who are eager to keep the tradition alive, although they have learned their art from books and recordings rather than in the traditional way by word of mouth from a master singer. Similar revivals can be observed in other Turkic-speaking regions, for instance in Yakutia, where the renewed performance of epics has also been stimulated by the inscription of the Yakut oral epic on UNESCO's Intangible Cultural Heritage List in 2008.

In all Turkic-speaking areas there have been remarkable advances in editing and publishing the oral epic heritage since the early 1990s. In Kyrgyzstan the festival "Manas 1000" was celebrated in 1995 and in its wake the voluminous versions of the *Manas* cycle by the great Kirghiz singers Saġïmbay Orozbaqov and Sayaqbay Qaralaev have been published in their entirety. In Uzbekistan a similar national festival, called "Alpāmiš 1000", was held in 1999, and the most accomplished version of this epic (by the singer Fāzil Yoldāš-oġli) was published with an unabridged text and a scholarly Russian translation in the same year.[3] Between 2004 and 2014 a hundred volumes of Kazakh folklore texts, mostly epics, were published in a series entitled *Babalar sözi*, "the words of the forefathers". Similar editorial projects, aiming at a much fuller publication of the epics preserved in the various archives than hitherto attempted, have also been undertaken in other areas, in Azerbaijan, Tatarstan, Bashkiria, Yakutia and elsewhere. There is also more audio and video material available; an excellent source of Central Asian music, including the music of epic, is the website of *The Music of Central Asia*, edited by T. Levin, S. Daukeveya and E. Köchümkulova.[4]

There is no denying that the book could be updated bibliographically[5], and there are, of course, many more questions that can be asked about the oral epics in the Turkic-speaking world, but to ask and attempt to answer these questions is the material for a new book.

Bonn, July 2017

---

[2] *Manas in the Version of Jüsüp Mamay*, translated by Karl Reichl. Xinjiang Manas Research Centre Publications. 2 vols. (Beijing, 2014-2015).

[3] *Alpamyš. Uzbekskij narodnyj geroičeskij ėpos*, edited by T. MIrzaev and translated by M. Abduraximov (Tashkent, 1999).

[4] Bloomington, IN, 2016. See http://www.musicofcentralasia.org.

[5] I have provided an up-to-date account, with bibliographical references, of the various Turkic oral epic traditions in the relevant entries of the *Encyclopedia of Turkic Languages and Linguistics*, edited by Lars Johanson, Éva Á. Csató et al. (Leiden: Brill, forthcoming).

TURKIC ORAL EPIC POETRY
Traditions, Forms,
Poetic Structure

Karl Reichl

GARLAND PUBLISHING, INC. • NEW YORK & LONDON
1992

Library of Congress Cataloging–in–Publication Data

Reichl, Karl.
    Turkic oral epic poetry : tradition, forms, poetic structure / Karl Reichl.
        p.   cm. — (The Albert Bates Lord studies in oral tradition ; vol. 7)
  (Garland reference library of the humanities ; vol. 1247)
    Includes bibliographical references and index.
    ISBN 0-8240-7210-3 (alk. paper)
    1. Epic poetry, Turkic—Asia, Central—History and criticism. I. Title.
  II. Series. III. Series: Garland reference library of the humanities ; vol. 1247.
  PL28.2.R45   1992
  894'.3—dc20   92-16726
                                             CIP

General Editor's Foreword

The purpose of the Albert Bates Lord Studies in Oral Tradition, as of its companion the journal *Oral Tradition,* is to bring before an interdisciplinary constituency essays, monographs, and collections that, in focusing on one or more oral or oral-derived traditions, offer insights that can be useful for investigators in many of the more than one hundred language areas now influenced by this field. Thus the first six volumes have treated, in order, orality and the Hebrew *Mishnah* (Jacob Neusner), *Beowulf* and shamanism (Stephen Glosecki), the Hispanic ballad (Ruth Webber, editor), the ballad tradition of "Count Claros" (Judith Seeger), memorization and the Middle English romances (Murray McGillivray), and Marcel Jousse's *The Oral Style* (Edgard Sienaert and Richard Whitaker, translators). Future books in this series will include studies of Beowulf and the Bear's Son folktale, African trickster tales from Togo, modes of identification in Homeric epic, and a collection of articles on a variety of areas for Alain Renoir. The overall aim is to initiate and to sustain conversations among scholars who, because of the categories according to which we are segregated in modern academia, seldom if ever have a chance to talk to one another. With this goal in mind, we extend a warm invitation to new voices to join the conversation—both as readers of these and other volumes and, hopefully, as authors with contributions to the ongoing discourse.

This seventh volume in the Lord series, Karl Reichl's Turkic Oral Epic Poetry, answers a longstanding need by providing an expert introduction to the oral epic traditions of the Turkic peoples of central Asia. It was in fact this set of traditions, particularly the Kirghiz, in which Milman Parry was initially interested as he contemplated extending his theory of traditional oral composition from its textual base in Homer to a fieldwork demonstration of how actual epic bards compose orally. Since

General Editor's Foreword

political complications prevented Parry and Albert Lord from pursuing central Asian traditions, following in the footsteps of Wilhelm Radloff,[1] they journeyed instead to the former Yugoslavia (a historical irony of considerable proportions) to investigate the unlettered tradition of Serbo-Croatian epic. This change in plans was of enormous import for the comparative study of oral traditions, since it would now be the South Slavic, and not the central Asian, epos that would serve as the model for a far-reaching new theory that over the next fifty to sixty years would have a significant and permanent impact on so many different language areas. In the meantime, as Reichl points out, the Turkic traditions did not receive the comparative, international attention for which Radloff had argued, and which Parry had planned to devote to their study.

The present volume seeks to remedy the problem of non-specialists' lack of access to information on the Turkic traditions, and in the process to provide scholars in various disciplines with material for comparative investigation. Professor Reichl's credentials for the undertaking are distinguished and unique: first trained as a medievalist with primary interest in Old English, he has done extensive fieldwork in Turkic-speaking areas of the former Soviet Union and China and is also a member of the same Bonn Seminar on Central Asia founded by Radloff. He focuses on the "central traditions" of this region, specifically those of the Uzbeks, Kazakhs, Karakalpaks, and Kirghiz, with some attention as well to the epic poetry of the Turkmens, Azerbaijanians, Turks (of Turkey), Altaians, Tuvinians, Yakuts, and Bashkirs. Reichl's account is chiefly descriptive, proceeding through a historical and linguistic background to a survey of the earliest documents, portraits of the singers and of performance, considerations of genre, story-patterns, and formulaic diction, and discussions of "composition in performance," memory, rhetoric, and diffusion. The result is a thorough and splendidly organized tour through some of the world's most important, but least understood, oral epic traditions, one for which scholars in many fields will be grateful.

I might close this preface on a personal note. When in 1986 I first told the late Albert Lord of the pending inauguration of a series in his honor and asked whether he had any thoughts concerning possible directions or contributions, the very first project he mentioned was a book on Turkic oral epic by Karl Reichl. Now, some six years later, that suggestion takes tangible shape as the seventh volume in his series, and I know he would be very pleased indeed.

John Miles Foley

Center for Studies in Oral Tradition
University of Missouri-Columbia

Notes

1. Especially important for Parry was Radloff's *Proben der Volkslitteratur der nördlichen türkischen Stämme*, vol. 5: Der Dialect der Kara-Kirgisen (St. Petersburg: Commissionäre der Kaiserlichen Akademie der Wissenschaften, 1885). An English translation of the preface is available in *Oral Tradition*, 5 (1990): 73-90. On Radlov's influence on Parry, see John Miles Foley, *The Theory of Oral Composition: History and Methodology* (Bloomington: Indiana University Press, 1988), pp. 10-13.

Contents

viii   *Contents*

Preface

Although a book on Turkic oral epic poetry needs no apology, such a book coming from a medievalist calls at least for an explanation. While still a student in Munich I bought a book with the title *Der Sänger erzählt: Wie ein Epos entsteht.* It was A. B. Lord's *The Singer of Tales,* which had only just come out in a German translation. It made fascinating reading and first revealed to me the relevance of living oral epic poetry for the study of medieval epic poetry, in particular of works such as *Beowulf* or the *Chanson de Roland,* epics which have come down to us in written form but betray their origin in an oral milieu. The path to Central Asia was opened for me only later when I discovered that the Bavarian State Library possessed a complete set of Radloff's *Proben der Volkslitteratur der türkischen Stämme.* Radloff's translations, in their charming, antiquated German, introduced me to a world of heroism and passion, romance and adventure, marvel and magic, which has held me spellbound ever since. The parallels to medieval narrative were obvious and seemed worthy of further exploration. It has been a long way since then, and on the way I met fellow-travelers, medievalists like me who had already studied Turkic oral epic poetry from a comparative point of view and on whose work I could build, standing, in the words of Bernard of Chartres, like a dwarf on the shoulders of giants. Although, in the end, I did not write a comparative study of Turkic oral epic poetry, the medievalist perspective will nevertheless be clear to the reader, in the types of questions asked as well as the general methodological orientation of the book.

In the course of doing research for this book I have become indebted to many people and institutions. The German Research Foundation (DFG) gave me grants for a number of extended research trips to Central Asia, both in the former Soviet Union and in China. The German Academic Exchange Organization (DAAD) sponsored a visiting professorship at the University of Nukus in Karakalpakistan. I have repeatedly been the guest of the Uzbek Academy of Sciences and the Chinese Academy of Social Sciences. Among the native scholars who have helped me with my research, I would like to express my gratitude in particular to Tora Mirzaev, head of the Folklore Department of the Uzbek Academy of Sciences in Tashkent, and to Professor Qabïl Maqsetov, formerly of the Karakalpak Branch of the Uzbek Academy of Sciences in Nukus, now at Nukus University. I have received much encouragement for my work on Turkic oral epic poetry through my membership in the Research Group on Central Asia at the University of Bonn, and I am grateful to Professor Walther Heissig for asking me to join the *Sonderforschungsbereich*. I am also grateful to Professor John Miles Foley for inviting me to write this book for the "Albert Bates Lord Studies in Oral Tradition."

My special thanks go to Professor John Stevens of the University of Cambridge and to Professor A. T. Hatto of the University of London for having made many valuable and thought-provoking comments on the manuscript of my book and for correcting a number of errors, inaccuracies, and stylistic infelicities. For imperfections that remain, I am solely responsible. Since the time when I was his student in Cambridge, Professor Stevens has encouraged me to see the literature of medieval England in a wider perspective, and I am grateful for his more than professional interest in my work. Professor Hatto has supported me in my study of Turkic oral epic poetry since we first met at the second *Epensymposium* in Bonn in 1979, and his advice has not only been of profit for this book but has also enriched my research into Central Asian oral epic poetry in general. I would finally like to record my gratitude to the late Professor A. B. Lord, whose closer acquaintance I was privileged to make during my time as a visiting professor at Harvard. His *Der Sänger erzählt* has had a decisive influence on my work, and I feel honored that my study of Turkic oral epic poetry will appear in a series bearing his name.

Karl Reichl

Introduction

Be Homer's works your study and delight,
Read them by day, and meditate by night;
Thence form your judgement, thence your maxims bring,
And trace the Muses upward to their spring.

Pope, An Essay on Criticism

The Homeric poems have not only had a profound influence on Western literature, from Virgil to James Joyce and beyond, their continued study has also deepened our appreciation of epic and heroic poetry in general. The world of the *Iliad* and the *Odyssey*, this "wide expanse... That deep-browed Homer ruled as his demesne" (Keats), has become a familiar world for the Western reader, guiding him when he first approaches epic traditions other than that of Ancient Greece. But while a knowledge of the *Iliad* and the *Odyssey* might help us in the understanding and interpretation of both Western and non-Western epic poetry, the study of contemporary or near-contemporary traditions of oral epic poetry can also throw light on the Homeric poems themselves. Turkic oral epic poetry was brought to the attention of comparativists as early as 1885 when Wilhelm Radloff pointed out the relevance of Kirghiz epic poetry to the Homeric question in the preface to the fifth volume of his monumental *Proben der Volkslitteratur der türkischen Stämme Süd-Sibiriens*:

> I believe that the dispute about the "Homeric question" has led to such irreconcilably opposing views mainly because none of the factions has understood — or could indeed understand — the true essence of the *aoidós*. The singer of Kirghiz epic poetry is a perfect example of an *aoidós*, as the Homeric songs themselves describe him.[1]

---

[1]Radloff 1885: xx; for a recent translation of Radloff's preface to the Kirghiz volume into English see Radloff 1990. — References are by author/editor and year; when two dates are given, the first date stands for the edition used, the date in

Neither the "analysts" nor the "unitarians" have, however, taken up Radloff's suggestion to settle their dispute by a close study of Kirghiz oral epic poetry. Quite apart from Homeric scholars like U. von Wilamowitz-Moellendorff, who have denied the legitimacy of comparing the *Iliad* or the *Odyssey* to oral epics such as those collected by Radloff, the references to Radloff's material in Homeric scholarship are generally slight and superficial. E. Drerup included Kirghiz epic poetry in his survey of oral epics, as does M. P. Nilsson in his discussion of the origin and transmission of epic poetry, but neither seems to have made any close study of the texts edited by Radloff.[2] When in the 1930s the "Homeric question" was finally tackled by investigating a living tradition of oral epic poetry, it was not possible for Western scholars to do any field work on the Turkic traditions in Central Asia. Milman Parry and Albert B. Lord turned to Yugoslavia instead, but they were both aware of the importance of Turkic material for the study of the "Homeric question," as is shown by several references to Kirghiz and Turkic epic poetry in their writings.[3]

   Although Radloff's material was seriously studied by some Western scholars, in particular by H. M. and N. K. Chadwick in the third volume of their *Growth of Literature* (1932-40) and by M. Bowra in his comparative treatment of the heroic epic (1952), the mass of material collected and edited in this century has remained a largely untapped source for Western comparativists. Victor Žirmunskij has written a bibliographically updated appendix to a reprint of Nora Chadwick's survey of Turkic ("Tatar") epic poetry, but most of the texts and studies he quotes have remained unknown to all but a few specialists.[4] With some notable exceptions, the situation has not much changed since the days of A. N. Veselovskij, who, in a course of lectures held in 1881, criticized Western scholars for their lack of first-hand acquaintance with genuine oral poetry and hence their proneness to treat medieval popular epic poetry solely in terms of written literature:

brackets for the original publication; for full bibliographical details see the bibliography at the end of this book.

[2] See Drerup 1920; Nilsson 1933: 184ff.

[3] See Parry 1971 [1932]: 329, 334; Lord 1960: 281; compare also Lord 1987a.

[4] Chadwick, Zhirmunsky 1969. For short surveys of Turkic oral epic poetry in a Western language see Boratav 1964; Hatto 1965; Başgöz 1978a.

> Western scholars, who are very little acquainted with living epic poetry, involuntarily transfer questions of purely written literary criticism to questions of popular poetry in the older period . This is the fault of the whole criticism of the *Nibelungenlied* and partly the criticism of the Homeric epics.
>
> (Veselovskij 1940: 622)

There is nevertheless today a growing number of scholars who have become interested in oral epic poetry, and there seems therefore to be room for a book on Turkic oral epic poetry in a Western language. As will become evident in the following chapters, however, the variety of Turkic epic traditions and the sheer volume of recorded texts forbid an exhaustive treatment of Turkic oral epic poetry in a monograph of the given scope. The present study can therefore be no more than introductory. In writing this book I have been greatly indebted to the work of Turkologists and comparativists, and this indebtedness will be duly recorded in the references to the work of Western, Russian, and native scholars.

The point of departure for the following analysis and discussion of the Turkic oral epic is the conviction that — in Nilsson's words — "a comparative and empirical study of all existing epics is the only method for attaining a better understanding of the origin and development of Greek epics,"[5] and, I would add as a medievalist, of those medieval epics for which an "oral background" can be assumed. Nilsson has the origin and development of the Homeric epics and other poetry rooted in oral tradition in mind. It is, however, not only the historical, but more importantly also the aesthetic aspect which is at stake here. For the appreciation of a classical or medieval epic poem which is surmised to have originally flourished in an oral milieu, though (necessarily) extant only in writing, it is of prime importance to know what distinguishes a work of oral verbal art from a work of written literature. There is a significant difference between interpreting the Anglo-Saxon *Beowulf* as the work of a learned poet who uses Germanic legend to write an epic inspired by Virgil's *Aeneid* (or who writes perhaps even some kind of Christian allegory in a Germanic garb) and seeing the epic as the work of an oral poet, intended to be performed in a context of oral story-telling like that evoked in *Beowulf* itself when the *scop* tells the tale of

[5]Nilsson 1933: 185.

Finnsburh (lines 1063ff.).   In his *Preface to Paradise Lost* C. S. Lewis
stressed this intentional aspect of a work of art:

> The first qualification for judging any piece of workmanship from a
> corkscrew to a cathedral is to know *what* it is — what it was intended
> to do and how it is meant to be used. After that has been discovered
> the temperance reformer may decide that the corkscrew was made for
> a bad purpose, and the communist may think the same about the
> cathedral. But such questions come later. The first thing is to under-
> stand the object before you: as long as you think the corkscrew was
> meant for opening tins and the cathedral for entertaining tourists you
> can say nothing to the purpose about them.
>
> (Lewis 1942: 1)

The term "intentionality" is a loaded term, and it is perhaps less controversial to use a different theoretical approach. Lewis' dictum that
a "piece of workmanship" is what it is by virtue of "how it is meant to
be used" can be expressed also in structuralist terms: a work of art is
a work of art not by virtue of some intrinsic characteristic but rather by
virtue of the rules which regulate its use. In order to understand a text
one must therefore know the conventions behind it, the rules that
regulate its use, or, to employ yet a different theoretical metaphor, the
code in which it is transmitted. It is with the code of oral poetry that
this book is ultimately concerned. But although the motivating forces
behind this study of Turkic oral epic poetry come from comparative
literature and literary theory, the orientation of the book is descriptive
rather than theoretical and comparative. The book is basically conceived as a descriptive analysis of Turkic oral epic poetry (with references to contiguous oral traditions), or rather of certain traditions and
certain features and problems of Turkic oral epic poetry. The parallels
with other epic traditions will, of course, be obvious to the compara-
tively-minded reader; I will, however, not pursue these parallels systematically in this book.

The focus of the book will be on what I term the "central traditions."
By "central traditions" of Turkic oral epic poetry I mean the epic
traditions of the Uzbeks (and Uighurs), Kazakhs, Karakalpaks, and
Kirghiz. These are also the peoples among whom my own field work
has been conducted. By subsuming these traditions under one heading
I do not want to imply that they form a homogeneous group; there are
marked differences between the various members of this group, and the
Kirghiz tradition in particular occupies a special position. Apart from
these central traditions I will touch upon a number of traditions on the

western and eastern fringes of what used to be called Western and Eastern Turkestan, i.e. on the epic poetry of the Turkmens, Azerbaijanians, and Turks of Turkey to the west and southwest of Central Asia proper and on the epic poetry of the Altaians and Tuvinians further east. Occasional references will also be made to other traditions more marginal to this central area, such as that of the Yakuts in northern Siberia or of the Bashkirs south of the Urals. Chapter One will provide some basic information on these and other Turkic peoples, on their languages and cultures.

Before some background information on the Turkic world is offered, a few general remarks on the terminology employed in this book might be helpful. A number of native terms like *dastan* or *baxši* will be found in my discussion of Turkic epic poetry. The meaning of these words is explained at their first occurrence; for the reader's convenience, however, a glossary of these terms will be found at the end of the book. It will be remarked that some of these terms, as well as personal and geographical names, occur in varying forms. Instead of *dastan* the reader will, for instance, also come across the forms *destan, dāstān,* or *dästan.* Variations of this kind are due to dialectal variations among the Turkic languages; these variations should not, it is hoped, impair the readability of the text. In the use of both native and English terms I have tried to be as consistent as possible. As far as English spellings of native names and terms are in common use, I have preferred these to transliterated forms.[6] I hence employ the spelling "Kazakh" rather than "Qazaq," which would be more correct according to the transliteration and transcription system used in this book. It should be noted that the Kazakhs were called "Kirghiz" in the 19th century and the Kirghiz "Kara-Kirghiz." I haved indicated deviations from modern usage in quotations from Radloff and other authors. Sometimes more than one English form is in use, such as "Turcoman," "Turkmen," or "Turkmenian"; I use "Turkmen" when referring to both the language and the people and "Turcoman" only in quotations when this word occurs in an English text.

In order to avoid confusion, the distinction between "Turkish" and "Turkic" has been carefully maintained throughout the book. "Turkish" refers to the language of the Turks of Turkey; older forms of Turkish

---

[6]The Russian terms *rajon* and *oblast'*, denoting administrative districts, have been translated as "district" and "province," respectively.

(before Ataturk's language reforms in the 1920s) are generally referred to as Ottoman or Ottoman Turkish. "Turkic," on the other hand, refers to the language-group to which Turkish belongs; it is a general term like "Germanic" as opposed to "German." No knowledge of a Turkic language is assumed on the part of the reader. All quotations from Turkic texts will be translated into English, and the linguistic and stylistic peculiarities of the texts analysed will be clarified for the non-specialist to the extent that their understanding is essential for my general argument. Unless indicated otherwise, all translations are my own. I have tried to translate the quotations from Turkic epic poetry fairly literally, preserving, however, English idiom as far as possible.

One further group of related words can easily lead to misunderstandings, and my use of them should be taken note of: "Altai" denotes the geographical area of the Altai Mountains in Central Asia; "Altaian" denotes the people living in and around the Altai and the group of closely related Turkic languages and dialects they speak; "Altaic" denotes a (proposed) language-family consisting of the Turkic, the Mongolian and the Tungusic languages (see Chapter One, pp. 25f.).

Finally, a few comments on my use of the terms "version" and "variant" are called for. According to Žirmunskij and other Russian and Central Asian scholars there is a difference between "variant" and "version."[7] The various texts performed by a singer are considered performances of his variant. We have hence a singer A's variant of the epic of *Alpamïš*, a singer B's variant of this epic etc. Related variants can then be grouped together into a version. We can there distinguish between the Uzbek version of *Alpamïš*, the Kazakh version of *Alpamïš* and so on. Although this distinction is useful when discussing the relationship between different texts of an epic across a wider area (see Chapter Ten), I will not follow this terminological usage here and use both terms interchangeably. The distinction between "variant" and "version" is not commonly made in Western literary studies, nor is it followed by all Russian and Central Asian scholars.

---

[7] See Žirmunskij 1960; Mirzaev 1968: 25-30; Putilov 1988: 137ff.

A Note on Transcription and Pronunciation

Before going into a more detailed description of the main Turkic-speaking tribes and their history in Chapter One, I will end this brief introductory chapter with a note on transcription, transliteration, and pronunciation.[8] For Russian I have adopted the international transliteration system, normally favored by linguists, rather than the English system of transliteration (hence writing "Ščerbak" instead of "Shcherbak" etc.).[9] For Chinese (occurring only in the bibliography) I have used the Pinyin transliteration system. For the various Turkic languages I have mainly followed the transcription system employed in the *Philologiae Turcicae Fundamenta*,[10] with the exception of Turkish (of Turkey), which is quoted in the official modern orthography. Other Oriental languages, such as Arabic and Persian, have been transliterated in the form customary among linguists. Many Arabic and Persian words have entered the Turkic languages; when transcribing Turkic texts they have been rendered in their Turkic form and no attempt has been made to restore their Arabic form.[11]

In transcribing or transliterating Turkic texts my main concern has been for clarity and consistency. I have therefore attempted to use the same system for all Turkic languages, all of which (with the exception of Turkish) are today written in non-Latin alphabets, as far as an official orthography exists. In the former Soviet Union all Turkic languages are

---

[8]By "transliteration" the rendition of one script by another, such as the Cyrillic by the Latin, is meant; by "transcription" the rendition of an oral text in writing is meant. Both occur in the following, as some of my examples come from printed editions and manuscripts, some from tape-recorded texts.

[9]If a Russian name also appears in a different form in a publication in English or another Western language, I have generally left the Russian form of the name and put the non-Russian form in brackets in the bibliographical references, writing e.g. Žirmunskij [Schirmunski]. The same applies to Turkic names, which often appear in a Russian form in publications from the former Soviet Union. Here the first name given is the Turkic name, the name in brackets the Russian form (e.g. Äwezov [Auezov]).

[10]Deny et al. 1959-64.

[11]Thus I transliterate the word for storyteller, *qïssaxān*, in the Turkic manner, rather than according to the Arabic and Persian roots of this word (< Arabic *qiṣṣa* + Persian *xwān*).

at present written in a modified version of the Cyrillic alphabet, although in some Central Asian republics the spread of the Arabic alphabet is noticeable. In China the Turkic languages are written in a modified form of the Arabic alphabet; the attempts at introducing a Latin script have not been successful. My transcriptions are "broad transcriptions," i.e. they are phonemic rather than phonetic. A number of nuances which the linguist would expect to find in a Turkological work have been ignored.[12] This applies in particular to the transcription and transliteration of Uzbek and Uighur. In the writing of Uzbek and Uighur (in Cyrillic and Arabic) no distinction is made between a close and an unrounded /i/-sound, a basic distinction in the Turkic languages (see below). This is due to the loss of vowel-harmony in these languages, at least in the standard varieties (see Chapter One). In spoken Uzbek and Uighur the /i/ is very often an unrounded /i/-sound; but as the laxness of this vowel is not regulated by the laws of vowel-harmony, I have adopted the practice of native orthography of symbolizing all /i/-sounds by <i>.

The following remarks are offered as a rough guideline to pronunciation.

— Apart from the cases discussed below, consonants are pronounced like their English equivalents, vowels like their Italian or Spanish equivalents.

— Long vowels are written as <ā> (also <â> and <aa>), <ē> (also <ee>), <ī> (also <î> and <ii>), <ō> (also <oo>), <ū> (also <û> and <uu>), <öö>, <üü>, and <ää>. The values of <ā>, <ē>, <ī>, <ō>, and <ū> correspond

---

[12]In Turkmen, for instance, the sibilants, transliterated as <s> and <z>, are pronounced as dental fricatives. In Karakalpak an initial /e/ is pronounced as [ye], an initial /o/ as [uo]. Variations also occur in the pronunciation of the development of Old Turkic /y/ in an initial position. In standard Kazakh and Karakalpak this sound is a [ž], but in many Kazakh and Karakalpak dialects it is a [dž]; even more variation is encountered in the development of Old Turkic initial /y/ in the various Altaian dialects. I have marked dialectal traits only in exceptional cases (see pp. 238ff.).

roughly to those they have in Italian or Spanish; for <ö>, <ü>, and <ä> see below.[13]

— In Uzbek, Persian, and Tajik words <ā> stands for a dark vowel as in English *ball*.

— The Turkic languages have an unrounded, central /i/-sound, transcribed as <ï> and written as <ı> in Turkish; its sound can be approximated by pronouncing German <ü> or French <u> without rounding one's lips.

— The rounded vowels <ö> and <ü> are pronounced roughly like their German equivalents, as in German *schön* and *München*, respectively.

— <ä> stands for an open /æ/-sound as in English *at*. The difference between an open and a closed /e/ sound has, however, not been expressed systematically, in particular not in the case of Turkic languages in which this distinction is not phonemic; here <e> can stand for both an open and a closed vowel.

— Consonants have approximately their English values, but the following conventions and exceptions should be noted:

— The voiceless and voiced sibilants as in English *shoe* and *rouge* are transcribed as <š> (= Turkish <ş>) and <ž> (= Turkish <j>), respectively.

— The voiceless and voiced affricates as in English *chin* and *jump* are transcribed as <č> (= Turkish <ç>) and <dž> (= Turkish <c>), respectively.

— The /r/ is trilled in the Turkic languages.

---

[13]In accordance with native orthography, I have symbolized long vowels by doubling the letter rather than by using the macron when transcribing/transliterating Kirghiz, Yakut, Altaian, and Tuvinian. The graphemes <â>, <î>, and <û> are mostly confined to Persian and Arabic loan words in Turkish.

— The velar nasal as in English *sing* is transcribed as <ŋ>.

— The velar voiceless fricative as in Scottish *loch* is transcribed as <x>, its voiced counterpart is transcribed as <ġ>. The latter is written <ğ> in Turkish; in Standard Turkish it is virtually unpronounced, with, however, compensatory lengthening of the preceding vowel.

— The semivowel /y/ as in English *you* is transcribed as <y>.

— The consonantal value of the sound transcribed as <w> is in Turkic words generally that of a labiodental fricative as in English *vat*, in Arabic and Persian words that of a bilabial fricative or labiovelar semivowel as in English *web*. After vowels, as e.g. in Uzbek *Rawšan*, it stands for a vowel or semivowel (compare the /au/-sound in English *bough*).

— Rarely some additional symbols are used in the transcription of Turkic texts:

— <d'> in the transcription/transliteration of Altaian and Yakut texts symbolizes a palatal /d/, partly realized as an affricate; compare the pronunciation of /d/ + /y/ in English *would you*.

— <ð> in the transcription/transliteration of Bashkir symbolizes a voiced dental fricative as in English *they*, <θ> a voiceless dental fricative as in English *thin*.

— <a'> in the transcription/transliteration of Tuvinian symbolizes a pharyngealized ("throaty") vowel.

— <ă> in the transcription/transliteration of Chuvash symbolizes a reduced vowel (ï, o).

— <ç> in the transcription/transliteration of Chuvash symbolizes a palatalized sibilant (sy, zy).

— As to the transcription/transliteration of Arabic and Persian words the following points should be noted:

— Silent <w> in Persian words is transliterated by <ẉ>.

— In Arabic words the so-called emphatic consonants are symbolized by a dot beneath them (e.g. <ṭ>). The dot is also used to mark the emphatically pronounced /h/: <ḥ>.

— <'> symbolizes in Arabic words the *hamza*, a weak glottal stop.[14]

— The Arabic ᶜ*ain*, a guttural stop pronounced with a tightened larynx, is symbolized by <ᶜ>.

---

[14] This is not to be confused with the use of <'> in the transliteration of Russian words, where it denotes palatalization.

Chapter One

The Turkic Peoples:

Backgrounds and Contexts

Arabī asl, fārsī šekar,
hindī namak, turkī honar.

Arabic is the root, Persian is sugar,
Hindi is salt, Turki is art.

These lines, attributed to one of the greatest Central Asian poets of the late Middle Ages, Mīr Ali Šīr Navā'ī (1441-1501), reflect not only the poet's pride in his own language, but also the multilingual context of the Turkic world. Ali Šīr Navā'ī wrote in Chaghatay, the predecessor of Modern Uzbek and Modern Uighur, a language which had come, like Turkish, under the strong influence of Arabic and Persian. The Persian and Arabic element in many Turkic languages is, of course, due to the fact that most speakers of Turkic idioms belong to the Islamic world. But this is not true of all Turkic-speaking peoples. The Yakuts of northern Siberia were at the beginning of this century still mostly shamanists, the Karaims in Lithuania and the Ukraine profess the Jewish faith, the Gagauz in Bulgaria and Moldavia are Christians, and the Tuvinians in the Altai Mountains were until recently Buddhists. All the Turkic languages spoken by the various Turkic peoples,[1] whatever their cultural and religious milieu, do, however, despite external influences from other languages, form a comparatively homogeneous language-family with well-defined structural traits. There is

---

[1]The expression "Turkic peoples" is to be understood as short for "Turkic-speaking peoples."

no space here for an extensive discussion of linguistic structure; information on the most characteristic features of the Turkic languages can, however, be found in the section on the Turkic languages at the end of this chapter.

Beginnings

The earliest documents in a Turkic language are runic inscriptions, of which the most important were found in the valleys of the Orkhon and the Yenisei rivers (see Figure 1, p. 29). These inscriptions date from the beginning of the 8th century A.D. onwards and record the warlike feats of various Turkic *qaǧans*, or rulers, of the Second East Turkic Empire (which flourished from about 680 to 740). They have been set down as a record as well as a warning for future generations; as the memorial inscription for Prince Kül puts it: "See these writings and learn a lesson!"[2]

The history of the Turks is, of course, older than the earliest documents in Turkic. The nomadic society depicted in the inscriptions is certainly not that of a people in the first stage of its ethnogenesis. The Turkic world had already undergone a fairly complex tribal fragmentation as a result of centuries of migration, conquest, defeat, and assimilation. This earlier history can only be reconstructed with the help of non-Turkic chronicles and annals, in particular the works of Chinese historiography. The ethnic and linguistic identification of peoples like the Hiung-nu (Eastern Huns; 2nd century B.C.) is, however, more than problematic, as is their relationship to the later Western Huns and the precise linguistic make-up of Attila's troops.[3] It is tempting to speculate

[2]Quoted from Tekin 1968: 263. On the dating of the runic inscriptions see Kononov 1980: 14ff., 19-20.

[3]There is a fairly extensive literature on the early history of the Turkic peoples, but many points remain unresolved. Detailed studies of the Old Turkic empire (6th to 8th c. A.D.) are Kljaštornyj 1964 and Gumilev 1967; the classic study of the nomadic empires of Eurasia from the Scythians to the Mongols is Grousset 1952; for surveys of Turkic history in Central Asia see Spuler 1966; Menges 1968: 16-55; Hambly et al. 1969; Kwanten 1979; Sinor 1990; an older study of the history of the Turkic peoples is Barthold 1962. On the Hiung-nu see Sinor 1990: 118-49; on the language of the Huns see Benzing 1959. — The early history of the various peoples of Central Asia is also extensively treated in the Academy histories of the various Central Asian republics (Uzbekistan, Kazakhstan, Kirgizia etc.).

that the two singers at Attila's court, seen by the Byzantine historio-
grapher Priskos on his embassy to the Huns in A.D. 448, were singing
in Turkic. His report would then be the first historical reference to
Turkic praise poetry.

> When evening came on torches were lighted and two barbarians
> stepped forth in front of Attila and recited poems which they had
> composed, recounting his victories and his valiant deeds in war. The
> banqueters fixed their eyes upon them, some being charmed with the
> poems, while others were roused in spirit, as the recollection of their
> wars came back to them. Others again burst into tears, because their
> bodies were enfeebled by age and their martial ardour had perforce to
> remain unsatisfied.
>
> (Chadwick 1932-40: I, 575-576)

But quite apart from the fact that these singers might have been Goths,
as Germanists like to suppose, it is far from certain that the retainers
of Attila's court spoke a Turkic idiom.[4]

Whatever the precise linguistic affiliations of the "northern barbarians" who have posed an ever-present threat to the Chinese from
time immemorial, and whatever the genetic relationship between the
Turkic, Mongolian, and Tungus languages, there can be no doubt that
all these peoples have similar origins if not a common origin in north-
east Asia and that they are culturally very close in their early stages of
societal development as hunters of the taiga. This cultural proximity
applies also to the later stages of Turks and Mongols as nomadic
peoples, roving over the steppes of Eurasia.

This is not the place to retrace the history of the Turkic peoples, but
it is important to realize, when discussing Turkic oral poetry, that it
does not exist in a timeless void, but is intimately connected to the
complex and diverse historical development of the Turkic tribes and na-
tions. There is a certain correlation between the various types and
forms of Turkic oral epics and their respective "historical depth." We
find among certain Turkic peoples such as the Altaians, Yakuts, and
Tuvinians epic poetry which is deeply imbued with shamanistic ideas
and has its historical roots in the archaic world of northern Asia.[5] This

---

[4]On the identification of the two "barbarians" performing at Attila's court as
Goths see Chadwick 1932-40: I, 576; Heusler 1943: 113-114; on their identification as
Turks see Žirmunskij, Zarifov 1947: 8. Compare also Hatto 1965: 115.

[5]For a short sketch of this world see Johansen 1959; for a more detailed survey
see the articles in Fitzhugh, Crowell 1988.

type of poetry must be seen in connection with the epic poetry of other
Siberian peoples, such as the various Tungusic and Palaeo-Asiatic
peoples, including the Ainu of northern Japan. At the other end of the
historical scale, so to speak, we find the oral epic poetry of the Islamized Turks such as the Ottoman Turks (the Turks of Turkey), the
Uzbeks, and the Uighurs, who have come heavily under the influence
of Persio-Arabic literacy and literature. Here oral and literate traditions cannot always be separated into independent strands; their symbiosis has resulted in particular forms and modes of oral epic poetry.
The most widespread genre of this type of epic poetry is the love-
romance; its typical form is the mixture of verse and prose (see Chapter
Five).

The World of the Nomad

The central core of Turkic epic poetry is formed by the epic traditions
of peoples such as the Kazakhs, the Karakalpaks, and the Kirghiz. It
is in their epic poetry that we encounter the best reflection and
expression of the world of the Central Asian nomad, a world in which
many Turkic tribes have lived from the time Turkic peoples first
appeared on the historical scene until fairly recently, in some cases until
now. This world had its historical apogee in the time of the Mongolian
expansion in the 13th and 14th centuries, the most powerful *empire des
steppes*.[6] The "heroic time" of the oral epic of the nomadic Turks is the
time of their freely roaming over the steppes of Central Asia, as in the
days of the Golden Horde (13th to 15th c.). Historically, a number of
epics typical of this group reflect, however, a later era, the time of the
tribal wars between the Western Mongols and the Turks (16th to 18th
c.).

Nomadism in the Eurasian steppes predates the putative origins of
the Turkic world by many centuries. The oldest extensive description
of a Eurasian nomadic tribe is Herodotus' account of the Scythians in
the fourth book of his *Histories* (5th c. B.C.). He characterizes them as
"pastoralists" (*nomádes*), warlike horsemen with barbarian customs such

[6]See Grousset 1952.

as head-hunting, horse-sacrifices, and drinking fermented mare's milk.[7] Although head-hunting is no longer practiced, fermented mare's milk (called *qïmïz*) is still a delicacy among the Central Asian Turks. William of Rubruk, the Franciscan friar who traveled to Mönke's court in Karakorum in the years 1253 to 1255, has left us a detailed description of how *qïmïz* was prepared among the Tatars of the South-Russian steppe.

> Cosmos, that is mare's milk, is made in this way: they stretch along the ground a long rope attached to two stakes stuck into the earth, and at about nine o'clock they tie to this rope the foals of the mares they want to milk. Then the mothers stand near their foals and let themselves be peacefully milked; if any one of them is too restless, then a man takes the foal and, placing it under her, lets it suck a little, and he takes it away again and the milker takes its place.
>
> And so, when they have collected a great quantity of milk, which is as sweet as cow's milk when it is fresh, they pour it into a large skin or bag and they begin churning it with a specially made stick which is as big as a man's head at its lower end, and hollowed out; and when they beat it quickly it begins to bubble like new wine and to turn sour and ferment, and they churn it until they can extract the butter. Then they taste it and when it is fairly pungent they drink it. As long as one is drinking, it bites the tongue like vinegar; when one stops, it leaves on the tongue the taste of milk of almonds and greatly delights the inner man; it even intoxicates those who have not a very good head. It also greatly provokes urine.
>
> (Dawson 1955: 98-99)

He has also given us a vivid picture of their nomadic way of life:

> And so on the third day after leaving Soldaia [on the Crimea] we came across the Tartars; when I came among them it seemed to me as if I were stepping into some other world, the life and customs of which I will describe for you as well as I can.
>
> The Tartars have no abiding city nor do they know of the one that is to come. They have divided among themselves Scythia, which stretches from the Danube as far as the rising of the sun. Each captain, according to whether he has more or fewer men under him, knows the limits of his pasturage and where to feed his flocks in winter, summer, spring and autumn, for in winter they come down to the warmer districts in the south, in summer they go up to the cooler ones in the north. They drive their cattle to graze on the pasture lands without water in winter when there is snow there, for the snow provides them with water.
>
> The dwelling in which they sleep has as its base a circle of interlaced sticks, and it is made of the same material; these sticks converge into

---

[7] *Histories*, IV.2 (fermented mare's milk); IV.64ff. (head-hunting); IV.72 (horse-sacrifice); see Godley 1920-25: II, 200/201; 260/261ff.; 270/271ff.

a little circle at the top and from this a neck juts up like a chimney; they cover it with white felt and quite often they also coat the felt with lime or white clay and powdered bone to give it a more gleaming white, and sometimes they make it black. The felt round the neck at the top they decorate with lovely and varied paintings. Before the doorway they also hang felt worked in multicoloured designs; they sew coloured felt on to the other, making vines and trees, birds and animals.

(Dawson 1955: 93-94)

This description could actually come from the great Turkologist of the 19th century, Wilhelm Radloff, who has given us a detailed and precise account of the Central Asian Turks in the ethnographic record of his travels among them.[8] The felt-yurt is still the dwelling of the nomadic or semi-nomadic Turks of Central Asia, conforming, despite regional variations, to the general pattern outlined by Rubruk.[9]

Nomadism is a form of life conditioned by economic necessities; as raisers of livestock the nomads have to move their animals to different pastures during the different seasons of the year. Their economically conditioned mobility has been enhanced from early times by the use of horses.[10] From the first millenium B.C. we encounter horsemen on the Eurasian steppe. How important the horse was to the Scythians is shown by Herodotus' report of a horse-sacrifice at the death of a nobleman (IV.72), a practice confirmed by archeological finds and later encountered also in the Turkic world. The Scythians and Sakas have left us pictorial representations of horses and riders; famous are their beautiful gold-ornaments, such as the "flying horse" from the Issyk kurgan (barrow) in southeast Kazakhstan, dating from the 5th or the 4th c. B.C.[11] "For the Kirghiz [= Kazakh]," writes Radloff, "the horse is the embodiment of all beauty, the pearl of the animals. He loves his horse more than his beloved, and a beautiful horse often tempts an

[8]See his *Aus Sibirien*; Radloff 1893.

[9]For the description of a Kazakh yurt see Radloff 1893: I, 457ff.; on Kazakh yurts see also Mukanov 1979; on Karakalpak yurts see Ždanko, Kamalov 1980: 27-57; on Kirghiz yurts see Dor 1975; on the different constructions of the yurts used by the nomadic Turks see also Basilov, Zirin 1989: 97-101. For a historical survey see Vajnštejn 1976.

[10]For a detailed account of nomadism among the Tuvinians see Vajnštejn [Vainshtein] 1980, in particular pp. 83ff.

[11]See Basilov, Zirin 1989: 33; on the "animal art of the steppes" see also the appendix to Grousset 1952: 623-637.

honest man to theft. Horse-theft is considered a kind of heroic deed, while the theft of other animals provokes only contempt. A Kirghiz is very loath to leave his riding horse to the use of another."[12] It is hardly surprising that in Turkic epic poetry the horse plays a role on a par with that of the hero and his companions (see Chapter Nine, pp. 296ff.).

Despite the importance of nomadism in the cultural and historical development of the Turkic peoples, it must be emphasized that one of the most important early medieval sedentary civilizations in Central Asia was also Turkic, namely that of the Uighurs, who flourished in Eastern Turkestan (the Tarim basin of present-day Chinese Xinjiang) between the 8th and the 14th centuries. The Uighurs, whose aristocracy was Manichean while the population was mostly Buddhist, have left a rich literary heritage.[13] Among the Uighur manuscripts which have come down to us there is one work which merits our attention here, the fragment of an epic on Oġuz (Oghuz) Qaġan from the 13th century (or possibly later). Another work originating in the Tarim basin is also of importance in this context, a Turkic dictionary, written between 1072 and 1078 by a member of the Karakhanid dynasty, Maḥmūd of Kashgar, which contains numerous illustrations from oral poetry, also from epic poetry. These works will be discussed in greater detail when it comes to putting Turkic oral epic poetry into its historical perspective (see Chapter Two).

The Turkic Peoples of Central Asia

In stressing the variety and diversity of Turkic epic poetry, a number of peoples and languages have been mentioned. It might be useful at this point to give a short survey of those peoples whose epic traditions will be dealt with in this book (see Figures 2 and 3, pp. 30-31). My main emphasis will be on the epic poetry of the Uzbeks, the Karakalpaks, the Kazakhs, and the Kirghiz. The Uzbeks live predominantly in Uzbekistan; they are also found in northern Afghanistan and in

[12]Radloff 1893: I, 441.

[13]On Old Turkic literature see Gabain 1964; on Old Turkic epic poetry see Chapter Two.

northwestern China. Their language belongs together with Modern
Uighur to the central group of Turkic languages, languages which have
developed from the Turkic dialect spoken and written at the courts of
the Karakhanid rulers in the 11th and 12th centuries (Bālāsāghūn,
Kashgar, Samarkand, Bukhara). Modern Uighur is spoken mostly in
Xinjiang by the Uighurs, the largest linguistic minority of "Chinese
Turkestan." The speakers of these two closely related languages have
been under the influence of Iranian languages (Persian and Tajik) for
centuries; in some areas (such as Bukhara or northern Afghanistan)
Turkic-Iranian bilingualism is the rule. Although the speakers of Uzbek
and Uighur are the typical city-dwellers of Central Asia and boast of a
rich literary heritage, oral epic poetry is nevertheless cultivated both
among the Uzbeks and among the Modern Uighurs of Eastern Turkestan (whose name is, incidentally, of recent date and is possibly a
misnomer, insofar as their direct descent from the earlier Uighurs is
doubtful). It came as something of a surprise when the serious recording of Uzbek epic poetry, which only started in the 1920s, uncovered a
flourishing tradition of oral epic poetry, in particular among the nomadic and semi-nomadic Uzbeks, the so-called Kipchak-Uzbeks.

From the 11th century onwards the Turkic Kipchaks roamed over the
vast steppes between the Caspian Sea and the Aral Sea, an area which
was called after them *Dešt-i Qïpčaq*, the steppe of the Kipchaks. From
medieval Russian sources the Kipchaks are known as Polovtsians; it was
against the Polovtsians that Igor Svyatoslavich led his ill-fated military
campaign, of which the celebrated *Lay of Igor's Campaign* tells. In the
13th century Batu, Chingis Khan's grandson, extended Mongolian power
over the territory occupied by the Kipchaks as well as into Eastern
Europe and founded the khanate of Kipchak, the realm of the Golden
Horde, with Saray on the Volga as its capital. Kipchak was in fact the
language of the Golden Horde, a language from which Modern Tatar,
Kazakh, and Karakalpak, as well as a number of smaller Turkic
languages, are descended.[14] At the end of the 14th century the khanate
of Kipchak collapsed under the attacks of Timur and finally disin-
tegrated into several smaller khanates. The khanates of Kazan and of

---

[14]The precise descent of these Turkic languages and their relationship to one
another as well as to other Turkic languages is disputed; see also below on the Turkic
languages.

Astrakhan lasted into the middle of the 16th century, the khanate of the Crimea even into the 18th century.

Further east Timur had erected the second Mongolian Empire, with Samarkand as his capital. Timur's realm was, however, of short duration, and decay set in after his death in 1405. In Transoxiana, the land east of the Oxus (Amu-Darya), a new power came to the fore in the second half of the 15th century, the Uzbeks under Muḥammad Shaibā- nī. Uzbek rule in Transoxiana (Arabic *māwarā'-an-nahr*, "the land beyond the river") resulted in three Turkic khanates, that of Khiva (the ancient Khwarezm), of Bukhara, and of Kokand. These khanates con- tinued well into the 19th century, when they finally became incor- porated into the Russian Empire.

Muḥammad Shaibānī's success in bringing Māwarānnahr under Uzbek rule was built on his grandfather Abu'l Khair's attempts to subjugate the Timurids in the first half of the 15th century. These attempts were, however, marred by opposition to Uzbek power from within. The clans which broke away from Abu'l Khair were called Kazakhs; when the Uzbeks under Muḥammad Shaibānī occupied Transoxiana, these Kazakh clans became the rulers of the steppes north of the Syr-Darya. They formed three hordes or khanates, the Great Horde (*Ulu žüz*), the Middle Horde (*Orta žüz*), and the Little Horde (*Kiši žüz*). In the beginning of the 17th century the Kazakhs were involved in a bitter and bloody war against the Mongolian Oirats or Kalmucks, who invaded their territory north of the Aral Sea and the Caspian Sea. The Mongolians were to continue to be a threat for the Kazakhs. The 17th and the first half of the 18th century are characterized by incessant fighting between the Kazakhs and their Mongolian aggressors, who had founded a powerful nomadic state in the Dzungarian steppe.[15] From the end of the 18th century onwards the Kazakhs increasingly came under Russian and Chinese rule. Today the Kazakhs live in a wide area from the Caspian Sea to the Tienshan Mountains. They are mostly found in Kazakhstan, but also in China, in Xinjiang, where they are the second-largest Turkic-speaking minority, with a large number of them still practicing a nomadic way of life.[16]

---

[15]For the history of Dzungaria see Zlatkin 1983: 59ff.

[16]On the history of the Kazakhs, especially their recent history, see Olcott 1987.

Like the Kazakhs, the Karakalpaks (Turkic *qara qalpaq* means "black hat") belonged to the Golden Horde. It is believed that the Karakalpaks originally descended from the *černye klobuki*, "black hats," first mentioned in Russian chronicles of the 12th century. These belonged to the group of Oghuz-Pecheneg Turks, but they were apparently later "Kipchakisized" by being incorporated into the Golden Horde.[17] From the 15th century onwards they migrated to the east; their presence in Central Asia is first attested for the 17th century. They have been living on the lower course of the Amu-Darya, south of the Aral Sea, since about the middle of the 18th century. First dependent on the khanate of Khiwa, they became part of the Russian Empire when Khiwa fell in 1873. Today the Karakalpaks live mostly in Kara-kalpakistan (in Uzbekistan). Although nomadism is on the decline, many traits of the nomadic world can still be found in Karakalpak society, one of them being their traditional tribal organization. The Karakalpaks divide into two *arïs* (literally "thills, shafts between which a horse is hitched to a wagon"), the Qoñïrat and the On Tört Urïw (the Fourteen Tribes). The former are further subdivided into the clans of the Šüllik and Žawïngïr, the latter into the clans of the Qïtay, Qïpšaq (Kipchak), Keneges, and Mangït.[18]

Best known among all Turkic peoples for their oral epics are probably the Kirghiz. They live mostly in the region of the Tienshan and Pamir Mountains, both on the Russian, Chinese, and Afghan sides.[19] Like the Kazakhs, the Kirghiz have clung to their nomadic way of life until the present day. Their epic poetry has been made famous through Radloff's translations and in particular by his discussion of the "Homeric question" with reference to the improvisational art of the Kirghiz epic singer. The history of the Kirghiz is complicated by the fact that a people bearing the name "Kirghiz" is found along the upper course of the Yenisei already in the 9th century. In A.D. 840 a Kirghiz federation defeated the Uighurs, who at that time were still settled in what is present-day Mongolia, thus causing the migration of the Uighurs into

---

[17]See Menges 1947: 5; Muminov et al. 1974: I, 89-101.

[18]See Ždanko 1950; Nasyrov 1983: 60f.

[19]As a result of the civil war in Afghanistan the Kirghiz have fled and are now settled in the vicinity of Lake Van in Turkey; on the Kirghiz of the Afghan Pamirs see Dor, Naumann 1978.

the Tarim basin. The relationship between the Kirghiz of the 9th century and the ancestors of the present-day Kirghiz is, however, far from clear, and it cannot be proved that today's Kirghiz descend from the Yenisei-Kirghiz. By the 13th century Kirghiz clans had moved into the Tienshan area and become part of Chaghatay's realm. During the Oirat raids of the 17th century some Kirghiz clans fled into Eastern Turkestan. In the 18th and 19th centuries the Kirghiz came successively under the rule of the Manchu, the khans of Kokand, and Imperial Russia. Today the majority of the Kirghiz live in Kirghizia; in Xinjiang there are about 100,000 Kirghiz, most of them living in the prefecture of Qïzïl-Su west of Kashgar.

Linguistically the Kirghiz are closely connected to the (Southern) Altaians of the Altai Mountains, from whom extensive recordings of epic poetry have also been made. The Altai is presumably the original home of the Turks, and it is perhaps no coincidence that some of the most archaic features of the Turkic peoples have been preserved among the Altaian Turks, in particular shamanistic beliefs and practices. This is also true of other Turkic tribes living in and around the Altai, such as the Tuvinians, the Khakas and the Karagas.

When discussing the traditions of what I have loosely termed here the central core of Turkic epic poetry, it will become clear that the edges of this central core are blurred, both towards the east when we move from the Islamized Turks to the shamanistic world of the Altaians and Tuvinians, and towards the southwest when we move from the nomadic milieu of Central Asia to the sedentary Turks of Transcaucasia and Anatolia. The Turks of the southwest of the Turkic linguistic area are descendants of the Oghuz, who migrated from their original home in Central Asia to the southwest from the 10th century onwards. In 1071 the Seljuks, an Oghuz tribe, defeated a Byzantine army near Malazgerd in eastern Anatolia, opening the way for the Turkish conquest of Asia Minor. While both the Turks of Anatolia and the Balkans and the Azerbaijanians of Transcaucasia and northwestern Iran have produced basically sedentary Near Eastern civilizations, the Turkmens of northeastern Iran and Turkmenistan, also descendants of the Oghuz, have preserved their nomadic way of life into the present century. Oral epic poetry flourishes among all of these Southwest-Turkic peoples; there is furthermore an important early Oghuz epic extant in two 16th-century manuscripts (but of considerably older date), the *Book of Dede Qorqut* (see Chapter Two).

Before concluding this necessarily brief and sketchy survey of the Turkic peoples, at least one more Turkic-speaking people should be mentioned, the Yakuts of northern Siberia. They must have originally lived in the area around Lake Baikal, from where they moved northwards, hence coming into close contact with peoples such as the Tungusic Evenki and Lamut and the Palaeo-Siberian Chukchi and Koryak. It is uncertain when this migration took place, as there are no historical records about Yakut history prior to the beginning of the Russian expansion into their territory in the first half of the 17th century. Owing to their remote and inhospitable habitat, the Yakuts have like the Altaians preserved a number of archaic customs and traditions, which are also reflected in their epic poetry. Although the framework of this book does not allow for an extensive discussion of Yakut epic poetry, reference to the Yakut *oloŋxo* (epic) will have to be made occasionally when it comes to discussing archaic layers in the Turkic oral epics of Central Asia.

The Turkic Languages

In a book on poetry and poetic texture some remarks on language and linguistic structure might not seem out of place. The typologically most characteristic feature of the Turkic languages is agglutination. Grammatical categories such as number, case, possession, tense, or mood are expressed by clearly distinguished affixes, "glued" to the stem of the word. Let us take the English expression *in my arms* as an example. In this English phrase plurality is encoded by a suffix (-*s*), while location and possession are expressed by free morphemes, the preposition *in* and the possessive pronoun *my*. In the Turkic languages all three grammatical categories are expressed by suffixes added to the stem of the word, i.e. to the lexeme translating English *arm*. Thus we have in Turkish:

kol —	lar —	ım —	da
arm —	PLURAL —	POSSESSIVE —	LOCATIVE
		1st PERSON	
		SINGULAR	

Compare Uzbek *qol-lar-ïm-da*, Kazakh *qol-lar-ïm-da*, or Yakut *xol-lar-ïm-ŋa*. To give just one more example: In the English sentence *I didn't come*, negation is expressed by a free morpheme (*not*), often contracted and used as a clitic (*n't*), tense by a suffix (-*d*), "amalgamated" with the stem of a free morpheme (*did* from *do*), and person by the personal pronoun *I*. In Turkish, as in other Turkic languages, the corresponding sentence consists of just one word, with clearly distinguishable affixes:

gel —	me —	di —	m
come —	NEGATION —	PAST —	1st PERSON SINGULAR

Compare once again Uzbek *kel-me-dim*, Kazakh *kel-me-dim*, or Yakut *käl-be-tim*.

In these forms a second trait of most Turkic languages is implicit, vowel-harmony. Vowel-harmony is basically a process of assimilation: the various affixes can assume different forms in order to match the quality of the stem-vowel. Thus the plural-suffix in Turkish is either *-lar* or *-ler*, depending on whether it is affixed to a stem with a velar or a palatal vowel: *kol-lar*, "arms," from *kol* with a "dark" vowel, but *it-ler*, "dogs," from *it* with a "light" vowel. Vowel-harmony is also found in other languages, such as Mongolian or Hungarian; it endows the language with a melodious flow and leaves a quite distinctive acoustic impression on the hearer.

Vowel-harmony is only one linguistic trait the Turkic and Mongolian languages (such as Khalkha Mongolian, Kalmuck, Buriat and others) have in common. The Turkic and Mongolian languages are also very similar in morphological and syntactic structure; furthermore, they share a number of lexical items, not all of which seem to have been borrowed from one language into the other. It is possible that the Turkic languages are genetically related to the Mongolian languages, and with them in turn also to the Manchu-Tungusic languages (such as Manchu, Nanay, Evenki, Lamut and others), spoken in the far eastern fringe of northern Asia. The Turkic languages would then like the other two language-families go back to a common Proto-Altaic language. Linguists are, however, divided on this issue, the critics of the "Altaic hypothesis" arguing that the similarities between these languages could very well have arisen through a long process of contact and intermingling, a process which seems to have been going on for a long time already when Turkic or presumably Turkic tribes are first mentioned in Chinese sources. Comparative philology, so successful in the reconstruction of Proto-Indo-European, yields far less reliable results in the case of the Altaic languages. The main reason for this is simply a matter of dates:

while Indo-European languages such as Greek or Hittite are attested as
early as the second millenium B.C., the earliest documents for an Altaic
language date from no earlier than around A.D. 700.[20]

Owing to these uncertainties, there is no universally accepted
classification. For our purposes it will be sufficent to give a rough and
simplified outline. Comparatively isolated from the other Turkic languages and counting as a branch of its own (often termed Bulgarian,
after the Turkic Volga-Bolgars of the 8th to the 14th centuries) is
Chuvash, spoken in the Chuvash Autonomous Region on the Volga, east
of Kazan. Another language which is often assumed to have separated
from the body of Turkic languages at an early date is Yakut, spoken in
a widely spread-out area in northern Siberia, in particular in the Yakut
Autonomous Republic. Apart from these two languages (and their
dialects) and some other languages whose affiliation is controversial (e.g.
Salar in China or Khalaj in Iran), the rest are commonly arranged into
four geographically contiguous groups: a Southwest group, a Northwest
group, a Central group, and an Eastern group. The SW-group comprises as main languages Ottoman Turkish (Turkish of Turkey), spoken
from Anatolia to the Balkans; Azeri or Azerbaijanian, spoken in
northwestern Iran and in Azerbaijan, Turkmen, spoken in northeastern
Iran, in northwestern Afghanistan; and in Turkmenistan; other SW-
Turkic languages are Gagauz, spoken in Moldavia; various Iranian
Turkic languages (or dialects) such as Aynallu or Qashqay; and originally probably also Salar, spoken in China (mostly in Gansu).

The NW-group of Turkic languages comprises Tatar and Bashkir,
spoken mostly in the Tatar and Bashkir Autonomous Republics on the
Volga, Krimtatar, Karaim, a number of smaller Turkic languages,
spoken in the Caucasus (Karachay-Balkar, Noghay and others), as well
as Kazakh, Karakalpak, and Kipchak-Uzbek. The Central group of

---

[20]For general information on the Turkic languages see inter alia the first volume
of Deny et al. 1959-64; Gabain et al. 1963: 1-204; Baskakov et al. 1966; Menges 1968;
Comrie 1981: 39ff. On the Turkic languages of China see Yolboldi, Qasim 1987. The
"Altaic hypothesis," postulating a common origin of the Turkic, Mongolian, and
Manchu-Tungusic languages, has been advocated by a number of linguists, but has not
yet found universal approval among Turkologists. N. Poppe ends his discussion of the
"Altaic Theory" (Poppe 1965: 125-156) with the words: "To conclude this section, one
may remark that the genetic affinity of the Altaic languages may not have been definitely proved, as some scholars believe, but no one has yet advanced reasons against
it which might be acceptable to a linguist." (Poppe 1965: 156). Other proposals, like
that of G. J. Ramstedt or R. A. Miller, to include Korean and Japanese, have met with
widespread scepticism; see Miller 1971.

Turkic languages comprises Uzbek and Modern Uighur (and their dialects). The Eastern group of Turkic languages, finally, comprises Kirghiz and the Turkic languages of and around the Altai Mountains. The subdivision of this group is controversial. Kirghiz is often separated from the other languages of the Eastern group; according to K. H. Menges Kirghiz belongs together with Kazakh, Karakalpak, Noghay, and Kipchak-Uzbek to an "Aralo-Caspian group" of Turkic languages. Altaian Turkic is a cover-term for two distinct groups of languages or dialects (the distinction between these two terms is a moot point), the Southern Altaian Turkic languages/dialects (Altaian proper, Telengit, Teleut) and the Northern Altaian Turkic languages/dialects (Lebed, Kumandin and others). Other Eastern Turkic languages are Khakas, Chulym, Karagas, Tuvinian, and Shor, to which the language of the Yellow Uighurs, spoken mostly in the province of Gansu in China, is sometimes added.[21]

It might be helpful to finish this section with a simplified grouping of the Turkic languages enumerated above (see following page):

---

[21]This classification is a gross simplification of a complex and disputed state-of-affairs. The genealogical classification of the Turkic languages has been discussed in great detail in Baskakov 1969: 210-354. In the influential survey of Turkic languages by Deny et al. (1959-64: I) a fivefold classification is proposed: Southern Turkic (= SW-Turkic), Western Turkic (= NW-Turkic without Kazakh, Karakalpak, Noghay, and Kipchak-Uzbek), Central Turkic (= Kazakh, Karakalpak, Noghay, Kipchak-Uzbek, and Kirghiz), Eastern Turkic (= Uzbek, Modern Uighur, Yellow Uighur, Salar), and Northern Turkic (Altai-Turkic, Khakas, Chulym, Shor, Tuvinian, Karagas, and Yakut); Chuvash is treated separately. Compare also Comrie 1981: 42-47.

I   Chuvash

II   SW-GROUP (Oghuz)   ┌─ Turkish
                            ├─ Azerbaijanian
                            ├─ Turkmen
                            └─ Gagauz

III   NW-GROUP (Kipchak) ┌─ Tatar
                            ├─ Bashkir
                            ├─ Karaim
                            ├─ Crimean Tatar
                            ├─ Karachay-Balkar
                            ├─ Noghay
                            ├─ Kipchak-Uzbek
                            ├─ Kazakh
                            └─ Karakalpak

IV   CENTRAL GROUP
        (Chaghatay)   ┌─ Uzbek
                            └─ Uighur

V   EASTERN GROUP   ┌─ Yakut
                            ├─ Altaian
                            ├─ Khakas
                            ├─ Shor
                            ├─ Chulym
                            ├─ Karagas
                            ├─ Tuvinian
                            ├─ Yellow Uighur
                            └─ Kirghiz

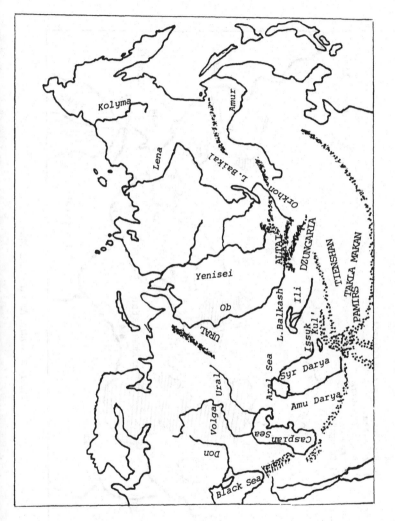

Figure 1: Central Asia and Siberia (Physical Map)

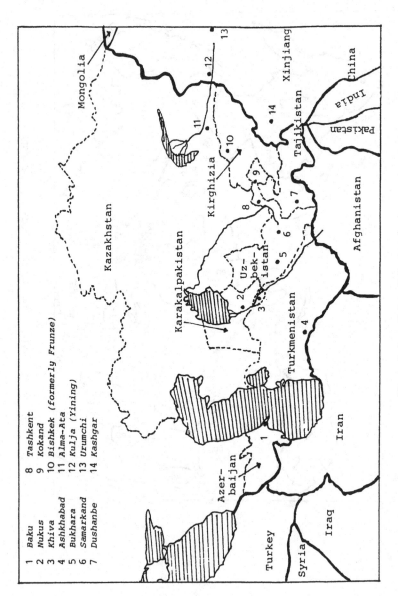

1 Baku
2 Nukus
3 Khiva
4 Ashkhabad
5 Bukhara
6 Samarkand
7 Dushanbe
8 Tashkent
9 Kokand
10 Bishkek (formerly Frunze)
11 Alma-Ata
12 Kulja (Yining)
13 Urumchi
14 Kashgar

Figure 2: Central Asia (Political Map)

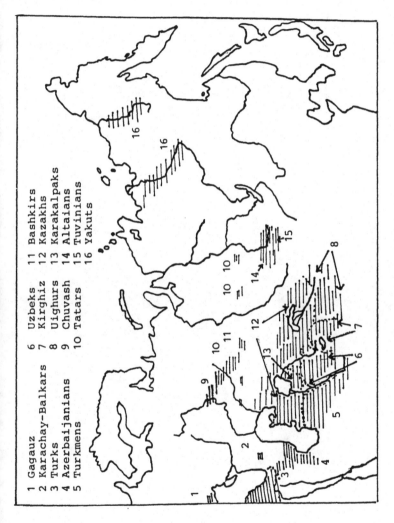

1 Gagauz   6 Uzbeks   11 Bashkirs
2 Karachay-Balkars 7 Kirghiz   12 Kazakhs
3 Turks   8 Uighurs   13 Karakalpaks
4 Azerbaijanians   9 Chuvash   14 Altaians
5 Turkmens   10 Tatars   15 Tuvinians
                                  16 Yakuts

Figure 3: The Turkic Peoples

Chapter Two

Turkic Epic Poetry:

The Earliest Documents

Oğuz Qağan

Kenä künlärdän bir kün Ay-qağannuŋ közü yarïp bodadï,
erkäk oğul toğurdï.
Ošul oğulnuŋ öŋlügi čïrağï kök erdi,
ağïzï ataš qïzïl erdi,
5   közläri al,
sačlarï, qašlarï qara erdilär erdi.
Yaqšï näpsikilärdän körüklügräk erdi.
Ošul oğul anasïnïŋ kögüzündün oğuznï ičip
mundun artïğraq ičmädi.
10 Yig et, aš sürmä tilädi.
Tili(gä) kelä bašlaďï.
Qïrïq kündün soŋ bedüklädi,
yürüdi,
oynadï.
15 Adağï ud adağï däg,
belläri böri belläri däg,
yağrï kiš yağrï däg,
kögüzi aduğ kögüzü däg erdi.
Bedäninüŋ qamağï tüg tülüklüg erdi.
20 Yïlqïlar kütäyä turur erdi,
atlarğa minä turur erdi,
kik aw awlaya turur erdi.
Künlärdän soŋ, kečälärdän soŋ y(i)git boldï.[1]

One day Ay Qağan's eyes began to shine
and she gave birth to a boy.

---

[1] I have basically followed Ščerbak 1959: 22-23, with minor changes in punctuation; see Bang, Rachmati 1932: 686.

33

This boy's face was blue,
his mouth was fiery red,
5   his eyes were brown,
his hair and his eyebrows were black.
He was more beautiful than the Good Spirits.
This boy drank the first milk from his mother's breast,
but wanted to drink no more.
10   He asked for raw meat, soup and wine.
He started to talk.
After forty days he became big,
ran around,
played.
15   His legs were like those of the bull,
his sides were like those of the wolf,
his shoulders were like those of the sable,
his chest was like that of the bear.
His whole body was covered in hair.
20   He tended the horse-herds,
mounted the steeds,
and hunted the deer.
After (but a few) days and nights he had become a young man.

This is the beginning of a text written in Old Uighur script and preserved in the Bibliothèque Nationale in Paris (MS Turc 1001). The text, called *The Legend of Oğuz Qağan* or *The Book of Oghuz* (*Oğuz-nāme*), is one of the earliest of a series of mostly historical texts on the origin of the Turkic tribes, and in particular the Oghuz. It is fraught with linguistic, philological, historical, and literary problems, some of which have been solved by a long line of editors, translators, and commentators.[2] Other problems, however, remain, such as the date of the text, its linguistic and tribal affiliation (does it belong to the Uighurs, the Kazakhs, the Southwest Turks, or to all of them?),[3] as well as its poetic form. According to A. M. Ščerbak the text in the Paris MS

---

[2]See Radloff 1891: x-xiii (translation), 232-244 (text); Pelliot 1930; Bang, Rachmati 1932; Ščerbak 1959; the Modern Uighur and Kazakh editions and translations are based on Ščerbak's edition; see Geng et al. 1980; Geng et al. 1986. The *Oğuz-nāme* by Rašīd ad-Dīn (d. A.D. 1318) has recently been studied and translated by Šukjurova 1987.

[3]This question is hotly debated; the titles/subtitles of the Modern Uighur and the Kazakh translations are an indication of this debate in China.

is a 15th-century copy of a text which goes back to the turn of the 13th to the 14th century and was probably written in Turfan.[4]

The legend narrates the birth, miraculous childhood, heroic deeds, and military exploits of Oğuz Qağan (or Khan), the *hḗrōs epṓnymos* of the Oghuz tribe.

One night, after a successful hunt, a beautiful maiden appears to Oğuz Qağan, who falls instantly in love with her. She bears him three sons, Kün (Sun), Ay (Moon), and Yultuz (Star). On another hunting expedition Oğuz Qağan encounters another beautiful maiden and is overcome by her charm. She too bears him three sons, Kök (Sky), Tağ (Mountain), and Täŋiz (Sea). At a feast, lasting for forty days and forty nights, Oğuz Qağan, proclaiming himself khan, determines to set out to conquer the world:

"Men senlärgä boldum qağan,
alalïŋ ya taqï qalqan,
tamğa bizgä bolsun buyan,
kök böri bolsungïl uran;
5 temür džïdalar bol orman;
aw yerdä yürüsün qulan,
taqï taluy taqï müran;
kün tuğ bolğïl kök qurïqan,"
deb dedi.[5]

"I am your khan;
let us take bow, arrow, and shield,
our motto shall be 'Luck,'
our war cry shall be 'Grey Wolf,'
5 let there be a wood of iron lances;
may the wild ass run about on the hunting ground,
may there (be) both sea and rivers;
may the sun be our standard, the sky our tent,"
he said.

Oğuz Qağan, together with his warriors, subdues the neighboring khans and subjects their people to his rule. On these expeditions, his army is preceded by a grey wolf who gives advice to Oğuz Qağan. In a series of adventures various nobles and warriors of Oğuz Qağan's retinue perform some feat or other which earns them a nickname. Thus when a beg (nobleman) brings back Oğuz Qağan's runaway horse from the icy mountains and is all covered in snow, he is named Qarluq (from *qar*, "snow") by Oğuz Qağan and instituted as local ruler. In a similar

---

[4]See Ščerbak 1959: 101-107. A. von Gabain discusses the text in the context of Old Uighur literature and stresses its archaic character; see Gabain 1964: 218ff; compare also Hatto 1965: 115f.

[5]Bang, Rachmati 1932: 708/709; Ščerbak 1959: 32-33.

way other men and peoples are named (e.g. Qïpčaq, Qalač). The legend
closes with Oǧuz Qaǧan's division of his realm among his sons. His
minister had a dream in which he saw a golden bow stretching from
sunrise to sunset and three silver arrows flying towards the north.
Oǧuz Qaǧan sends his three older sons to the east, where they find a
golden bow, and his three younger sons to the west, where they find
three silver arrows. At the "abdication feast" the elder brothers sit to
their father's right; they are called Buzuq, "broken," from the golden
bow which was divided among them. The three younger brothers sit at
their father's left; they are called Üč Oq, "three arrows," from the silver arrows they had brought back from their search.

This text is clearly an aetiological legend, attempting to explain the
origin of the Turkic tribes (Qarluq, Qïpčaq etc.), in particular that of the
Oghuz, their relationship to other Turkic tribes, and their subsequent
tribal partition. The Oghuz epic of *Dede Qorqut* shows a similar division
into Üč Oq and Boz Oq ("destroying arrows," instead of Buzuq).[6] The
legend of Oǧuz Qaǧan has also been incorporated into historical works
on the Oghuz, in particular the *Universal History* (*Džamiᶜ at-tawārīx*)
by the Persian historian Rašīd ad-Dīn (d. A.D. 1318) and the *Pedigree
of the Turkmens* (*Šedžere-i terakime*) by the khan of Khiva Abu'l Ġazi
(1603-1664), and Ottoman historiography later draws the direct descent
of the leading Turkish tribe from Kün, Oǧuz Qaǧan's eldest son.[7]

But although the text can be studied as a legendary history of the
Oghuz, it can also be studied as a work of narrative fiction. The legend
is written in prose, yet alliteration, syntactic parallelism resulting in
rhyme and assonance, as well as a strong rhythmic patterning of the
text are frequent features. Examples of parallelistic structures are
found, in the introductory passage quoted above, in the description of
the hero's face in lines 4 to 6, in the sequence of verbs in lines 12 to 14,
in the syntactic construction of lines 20 to 22, and in the doubling of the

---

[6]Instead of Üč Oq the *Book of Dede Qorqut* has also the name Ič Oǧuz (Inner
Oghuz), instead of Boz Oq also Taš Oǧuz (Outer Oghuz); see in particular the last story
in *Dede Qorqut*, "How the Inner Oghuz rebelled against the Outer Oghuz and how
Beyrek was killed"; see Lewis 1974: 210, note 134; Rossi 1952: 16ff.

[7]On the partition of the realm of the khan of the Oghuz among his sons in the
Universal History by Rašīd ad-Dīn see Šjukurova 1987: 61f.; Jahn 1969: 43; see also
illustration 17 in Jahn 1969; compare the corresponding passage in the *Pedigree of the
Turkmens*, Kononov 1958: 48. On Ottoman historiography in this context see Lewis
1974: 211, note 140.

adverbial phrase in line 23.[8] To these poetic means one might add the alliteration in e.g. lines 1 or 16 and the comparison of the hero's appearance and strength with that of wild animals in lines 15 to 18, once again clearly parallelistic:

> Adağï ud adağï däg,
> belläri böri belläri däg,
> yağrï kiš yağrï däg,
> kögüzi aduğ kögüzü däg erdi.

> His leg bull-leg-like,
> his sides wolf-sides-like,
> his shoulders sable-shoulders-like,
> his chest bear-chest-like was.

Parallelism leads to rhyme and assonance, as is shown even more clearly in the second passage quoted above, Oğuz Qağan's speech to his warriors. In fact, this passage is quite clearly metrical; each line has a regular number of eight syllables, thus conforming to a widespread metrical pattern of Turkic epic poetry. Without pursuing the stylistic analysis further, I will simply note that the *Oğuz-nāme* is, from a stylistic and metrical point of view, a highly patterned text, with subtle transitions from prose to rhythmical prose and to verse. Formally, there is a close link with Turkic oral epic poetry, as will be seen when questions relating to meter and rhythm will be discussed more fully in Chapter Seven.

As to content, the narrative is also closely connected to later Turkic oral epic poetry, for instance by the motif of the hero's precocious strength, represented in the opening passage.[9] This motif (together with related motifs) is so widely spread, from the Greek Heracles to the West African Ozidi, from the Irish Cúchulainn to the Central African Mwindo, that it is hardly surprising to find it also well-represented in Turkic epic poetry.[10] One example shall suffice; it comes from the

---

[8]See Gabain 1964: 219.

[9]See *Motif* F611.3.2; *Motif* refers to Stith Thompson's *Motif-Index of Folk Literature*; see Thompson 1955-58.

[10]See Bowra 1952: 94ff.; on this motif in Kazakh epic poetry see Winner 1958: 52; in Tatar epic poetry see Urmančeev 1980a: 45-57; in Turkic and Mongolian epic poetry in general see Lipec 1984: 41-52. Bowra (p. 96) quotes an example from Radloff's text of *Manas*. This motif is extensively discussed in the context of Turkic oral epic poetry in Žirmunskij 1960: 195-197.

Kirghiz epic *Er Töštük*, in the version recorded by W. Radloff:

	Baybičenin džaq džetkende,
40	bir erkek bala tuudu.
	Džaŋa tuuġan bu bala
	eki qonboy ene dedi,
	altï qonboy ata dedi.
	Iläman qoy džayġanda,
45	džaŋa tuuġan bu bala,
	džürmölöp turdu ordunan,
	atasïna keldi de:
	"E atam, atam," dedi,
	"üygö qaytïp džat," dedi,
50	"men bu qoydu qaytarayn."[11]

	When the time of the *baybiče* (the oldest wife) had
	come,
40	she gave birth to a boy.
	This newly-born child
	said "Mother" after two days,
	said "Father" after six days.
	While Iläman was looking after the sheep,
45	this newly-born child
	crawled away from his place,
	came to his father and said:
	"O my father, my father,
	turn back home, lie down,
50	I will herd these sheep."

There can be no doubt then that the legend of *Oġuz Qaġan*, though clearly not an epic but rather a mythical history of the Oghuz, is both as to its form and to its content cast in an epic garb and hence a precious document for the historical development of Turkic epic poetry. Whatever its precise date, the *Oġuz-nāme* is by no means the oldest surviving text testifying to the cultivation of epic poetry among the Turks of Central Asia. The runic inscriptions from the Orkhon and Yenisei valleys (8th c.) celebrate not only the heroic deeds of the rulers they commemorate but exhibit also a rudimentary kind of rhythmic prose which has led some scholars to see in them the beginning of Turkic poetry.[12] When reading these texts it is hard to believe that

---

[11]Radloff 1885: 527 (text volume); 531 (translation volume).

[12]This has been argued in particular by I. Stebleva; see Stebleva 1976: 8ff. Her view has, however, been criticized; see Žirmunskij 1974 [1968]: 675. — A. von Gabain has argued that one of the runic inscriptions (from Khoito Tamir; 8th c.) represents the oldest heroic poem in Turkic; the inscription is, however, so fragmentary and its

they could have been composed in the absence of a living tradition of
panegyric and epic poetry. The memorial stone for Kül Tigin records
the fights for predominance among the Turkic tribes and Prince Kül's
bravery and heroic deeds:

> Bir yïlqa biš yolï süŋüšdümüz.
> Aŋilk Toğu balïqda süŋüšdümüz.
> Kül tigin Azman aqïğ binip
> oplayu tägdi.
> 5   Altï ärig sančdï,
> sü tägišindä yitinč ärig qïličladï.
> Ikinti Qušlağaqda,
> Ädiz birlä süŋüšdümüz.
> Kül tigin az yağïzïn binip
> 10   oplayu tägip
> bir ärig sančdï.
> Toquz ärig ägirä toqïdï.
> Ädiz bodun anda ölti.[13]

> In one year we fought five times.
> First of all we fought at the town of Toğu.
> Prince Kül mounted his white horse Azman
> and charged in high spirits.
> 5   He cut down six men,
> in close combat he cut down with his sword the seventh man.
> The second time at Qušlağaq
> we fought with the Ädiz.
> Prince Kül mounted his brown horse,
> 10   charged in high spirits,
> and cut down a man.
> Pursuing nine men, he felled them.
> There the Ädiz army was destroyed.

The story continues in this manner; five times Kül Tigin is victorious,
each time mounting his horse and mowing down his enemies. The
language of these stone inscriptions is quite clearly repetitive, parallelistic, and formulaic. It is not just the "hieratic" language of official
proclamations chiseled into stone; the passage has, with its epithets for
horses and its verbal nuances for the description of fighting and doing
battle (*süŋüš-, täg-, sanč-, qïlïčla-, ägir-, toqï-*), a decidedly "epic" ring,
foreshadowing the language of later epic and panegyric poetry.

decipherment so problematic that such an interpretation must remain speculative. See
Gabain 1953: 550-553.

[13]I have taken the text from Gabain 1974: 279, but arranged it in the manner
of Stebleva 1976: 187; for the translation compare also Stebleva 1976: 78.

Dīvān luġāt at-Turk

The first unequivocal examples of poetry in a heroic vein are found in the *Dīvān luġāt at-Turk* of Maḥmūd of Kashgar, which was compiled in 1073. Maḥmūd drew up a dictionary of the Middle Turkic language and its dialects known to him, interspersing his lexicographic commentaries with quotations from popular poetry. These citations have been pieced together by a number of scholars, most notably by C. Brockelmann, who edited and translated the poems under the headings of "Dirges," "Heroic Songs," "Drinking- and Hunting Songs," "Complaints," "Praise-Songs," "Chiding Songs," "Love Songs," "Nature Poetry," "Debate between Summer and Winter," and "Gnomic Poetry."[14] The number of heroic songs is debatable, as several stanzas could be arranged in various ways, either forming independent poems or being part of other poems. In order to illustrate the type of heroic poetry current in Maḥmūd's time, I will quote one of the shortest heroic songs, entitled by Brockelmann *The Campaign against the Uighurs*, leaving aside the question of whether other stanzas found in the *Dīvān* should be incorporated into this poem:[15]

> Bäčkäm urub atlaqa
> Uyġur daqï Tatlaqa,
> oġrï, yawuz ïtlaqa,
> qušlar kibi učtïmïz.

> 5   Aġdï qïzïl bayraq,
> toġdï qara topraq,
> yätšü kälib Oġraq,
> toqšïb anïŋ käčtimiz.

> Qudruq qatïġ tügdümiz,
> 10   täŋrig ögüš ökdümiz,
> kämšib atïġ täkdimiz,
> aldab yana qačtïmïz.

[14]See Brockelmann 1923; 1924.

[15]See Brockelmann 1923: 10-11. Stebleva rearranges the stanzas of Brockelmann's text as 5-6-3-1-2-4; see Stebleva 1976: 206-207 (text) and 133-135 (discussion and translation). I am following Stebleva's arrangement, as well as her transcription, which I have, however, brought in line with the transliteration system adopted in this book and to which I have added punctuation marks.

15

Kimi ičrä oldurub
Ïla suwïn käčtimiz,
Uyġur taba bašlanïb
Mïŋlaq älin ačtïmïz.

20

Kälŋizläyü aqtïmïz,
kändlär üzä čïqtïmïz,
furxan äwin yïqtïmïz,
burxan üzä sïčtïmïz.

Tünlä bilä bastïmïz,
tägmä yaŋaq pustïmïz,
käsmälärin kästimiz,
Mïŋlaq ärän bïčtïmïz.

Fastening the war-emblem to the horses,
towards the Uighurs and the Tats,
the robbers, the nasty dogs,
we flew like birds.

5

The red banner was lifted up,
the black dust rose up,
the Oġraqs approached
and we tarried, fighting with them.

10

We bound the horses' tails up tightly,
gave praise to God,
spurred the horses on and reached them,
tricked them and fled anew.

15

We sat down in the boat
and crossed the river Ïla,
directing our course against the Uighurs
we invaded the land of Mïŋlaq.

20

We poured (on them) like a mountain-stream,
we rode out against the towns,
we destroyed the Buddhist temples,
and we defiled their gods.

At night we attacked,
we lay in ambush on all sides,
we cut off their locks,
and mowed down the men of Mïŋlaq.

These lines describe the fights between a non-Buddhist Turkic tribe
and the Buddhist Uighurs, the Oġraqs, and a people called "Tats,"

probably Persians.[16] The historical context of the poem is not entirely
clear. According to Maḥmūd its protagonists were Islamized Turks,
although it is noteworthy that the word for "God" is still the Old Turkic
word *täŋri* (1.10). It is possible, although Maḥmūd does not say so, that
the victorious Turks of the poem are Qarluqs, a Turkic tribe who fought
on the side of the Arabs when they defeated the Chinese on the river
Talas in 751.[17] In order to reach the land of the Uighurs the Moslem
Turks had to cross the river Ïla, most probably the present-day Ili. This
means that the Uighurs had already migrated southwest from the
Orkhon valley, after the destruction of their empire by the Kirghiz in
840. Little is known of the Oġraqs, who according to Maḥmūd lived in
the vicinity of the Ïla, and even less is known of the land of Mïŋlaq,
where, according to the poem, the Uighurs lived. As the Uighurs
became Islamized in the 10th century (not without desperate resistance
from the local Buddhists), it is unlikely that the poem dates from later
than the 10th century; it might very well come from the 9th century,
although in the absence of appropriate historical sources and in view of
the uncertainties regarding the poem's composition no definite date can
be given.

Looking at the structure of the poem, we note that it is basically a
praise-poem. The poet identifies with his own side and exalts the heroic
exploits of his compatriots. Yet the prevailing mode is nevertheless
descriptive: a sequence of events is narrated (it need not concern us here
whether the sequence is correct in the form the poem has been put
together by its editors) and the various elements of the sequence are
presented in explicit descriptions rather than implicit allusions as is
typical of praise-poetry. We are told that the war-emblems were
fastened to the horses, that the red banners were raised, that the horses'
tails were bound up tightly, and we are made into witnesses of the
military expeditions which are celebrated. As will be seen later, some
of the images encountered in this poem (the heroes raising their
banners, riding on their horses as swiftly as flying birds) belong to the

[16]The name "Tat" is normally used for non-Turks living among Turkic peoples,
in particular for Iranians (Persians, Tajiks and others). In the *Dīvān luġat at-Turk* it
usually denotes the Persians, but it can also refer to the Uighurs. See Minorsky 1936:
698; Mutallibov 1960: I, 490.

[17]On the Qarluqs and the Islamization of the Turks see Spuler 1966: 168-176; on
the Qarluqs in the *Dīvān* see Mutallibov 1960: I, 498.

common poetic stock of the Turkic oral epic. Metrically, the short line of seven or eight syllables is also typical of Central Asian Turkic oral epic poetry, while the arrangement of the lines in four-line stanzas is a later development and hardly represents the oldest stratum of epic verse (see also Chapter Seven). There is no doubt then that some of the verses interspersed in Maḥmūd's *Dīvān* come from heroic songs, which are in significant ways similar to the Turkic oral epics recorded many centuries later. They once again testify to the popularity of poetry in a heroic vein among the Turkic-speaking tribes of Central Asia at an early date.

The Book of Dede Qorqut

Turkic epic poetry is also attested, though unfortunately not preserved, in various historical writings.[18] The first fully fledged epic poetry in a Turkic language is found in two 16th-century manuscripts which transmit the *Kitab-i Dede Qorqut, The Book of Grandfather Qorqut*.[19] Like the *Oğuz-nāme* it is concerned with the early history of the Oghuz; but while the legend of Oğuz Qaġan is in prose, at times in a kind of rhythmic prose approaching metrical regularity, the tale-cycle of Dede Qorqut is in a mixture of verse and prose. This form is typical of a number of epic traditions among the Turkic peoples and will be discussed in detail later. At this stage it should simply be noted that my use of the term "epic poetry" covers both epics in verse and epics composed in a mixture of verse and prose. A finer distinction into various subgenres of epic poetry, taking account of both form and content, will be given in Chapter Five.

Although the manuscripts containing the *Book of Dede Qorqut* date from the 16th century, it can be shown that the epic tales themselves must go back to the time when the Oghuz were still to be found on the lower Syr-Darya, i.e. to the period between the 9th and the 11th

[18]See Gabain 1964: 216.

[19]For English translations see Sümer, Uysal, Walker 1972 and Lewis 1974; for an Italian translation see Rossi 1962. For studies of the *Book of Dede Qorqut* see especially Gökyay 1973, Žirmunskij 1974 [1962], and Korogly 1976; a useful comparative analysis of the motifs found in the tale-cycle is given by Ruben 1944: 193-283.

centuries.[20] As most of the twelve tales in the *Book of Dede Qorqut* exemplify in many ways typical traits of the epic poetry that we will be concerned with in this book, I wish to look at one of them in more detail in this chapter.

In the opening section of the tale-cycle the figure of Dede Qorqut or Qorqut Ata is introduced, a singer and soothsayer (*ozan, biliçi*) of the Oghuz, into whose mouth a number of wise sayings, proverbs, maxims and lore about women are put.[21] Dede Qorqut plays an active part in the various tales, as a wise man and counselor, but above all as the singer who composed the tales and handed them on to following generations:

Dedem Qorqut boy boyladï, soy soyladï, bu Oğuz-nāmeyi düzdi, qošdï, böyle didi.[22]

My Grandfather Qorqut told stories, told tales, composed this book of the Oghuz, put it together, spoke in this way.

This is the traditional formula, occurring at the end of many of the tales. It is first found at the end of the first tale, the *Tale of Buğač Khan, Son of Dirse Khan.* The contents of this tale can be summarized as follows:

Bayïndïr Khan, the overlord of the Oghuz, is one day giving a feast, for which he has three tents erected, a white tent for those of his guests who have a son, a red tent for those of his guests who have a daughter, and a black tent for those of his guests who have neither son nor daughter. While the Oghuz nobles with children are to be honored, those without children are to be humiliated: they are to sit in the black tent on black felt and they are to be given mutton-stew from black sheep. When Dirse Khan, who is without children, is subjected to this treatment, he leaves the feast and returns to his wife, on whom he vents his anger and grief. His wife proposes that he feed the hungry, clothe the naked, rescue debtors from their debts and give an enormous feast to the nobles of the Inner and Outer Oghuz.[23] In this way Dirse

[20] On the dating see Boratav 1982-83 [1958]; Rossi 1962: 27-54; Žirmunskij 1962; Žirmunskij 1974 [1962]: 523ff.; Korogly 1976: 157ff.

[21] On this figure and the legends about him see him see Žirmunskij 1974 [1962]: 532ff.; on the term *ozan* see below p. 64.

[22] Ergin 1958-63: I, 94; I have regularized Ergin's text to conform to the transcription system employed here.

[23] On this bipartition of the Oghuz clans in *Dede Qorqut* see footnote 6 above.

Khan would merit everybody's praises and God might fulfill their wish for a child. This is indeed what happens: God grants them a son, who grows up to become a strong youth.

When this boy is fifteen years of age he happens to play knuckle-bones with three other boys in an arena in which a ferocious bull is to fight with a camel. Instead of obeying the men's order to run away when the bull is let out, the boy faces the bull and kills the beast after a heroic fight. When Dede Qorqut is called on to give the boy a name, he praises him and bestows the name "Buġač" (a derivation from *buġa*, "bull") on him. He also suggests making the boy a prince and giving him a throne, which, when done, leads to jealousy among his father's forty companions. Plotting the boy's downfall, they slander him before his father, who is rather easily persuaded of his son's wickedness and is cunningly made to shoot an arrow between his son's shoulder blades on a hunting expedition.

Buġač is wounded to death, but still alive. After the departure of the hunting party, Hïzïr, an Islamic saint, appears, touches his wound three times and prophesies that he will recover through an ointment made of his mother's milk and the flowers of the mountains. Buġač's mother, highly suspicious when Dirse Khan and his hunting party return without her son, goes in search of Buġač together with her forty maidens. She finds him mortally wounded and proceeds to squeeze her breasts when she is told of the saving ointment. But no milk comes. Only when trying for the third time, this time striking her breasts, does milk come mixed with blood. The ointment is prepared and Buġač recovers. He leads henceforth a secret life, unknown to his father.

Dirse Khan's forty companions, however, hearing that Buġač is alive and well, plan to forestall the khan's punishment of their treachery when the truth comes to light. They secretly take Dirse Khan prisoner and lead him away to hand him over to the infidels. When Dirse Khan's wife learns of this, she urges her son to rescue his father. Buġač, obedient to his mother's command, pursues the traitors with his forty companions and catches up with them. Dirse Khan, seeing Buġač approach and not recognizing him, takes pity on the young man, asks for his lute and sings a song in which he entreats his rescuer to save his own life. Buġač, however, is not deflected from his mission; he gives a signal to his companions, who have been lying in hiding, attacks the scoundrels and frees his father. At the news of Buġač's heroic exploit, Bayïndïr Khan gives the boy a begdom and a throne.

The story ends with Dede Qorqut making a tale about the Oghuz out of these adventures, a lament for the departed heroes of yore, and a series of benedictions on "my khan" (*xanum*).

This story occupies about eighteen pages in Ergin's edition. It takes less than half an hour to read the story aloud, somewhat longer if the poems were sung rather than recited. As can be inferred from these remarks, the narrative proceeds at an even, comparatively swift pace, with little elaboration and digression. The prose is crisp and terse, limpid in its syntactical organization, without convolution and prolixity. The very beginning of this tale will illustrate this point:

> Bir gün Qam Ġan oġlï Xan Bayïndïr yirinden turmïš-idi. Šāmī günlügi yir yüzine dikdürmiš-idi. Ala sayvanï gök yüzine ašanmïš-idi. Biŋ yirde ipek xalïčasï döšenmiš-idi. Xanlar xanï Xan Bayïndïr yïlda bir kerre toy idüp Oġuz biglerin qonuqlar-idi. Gine toy idüp atdan ayġïr deveden buġra qoyundan qoč qïrdurmuš-idi.
>
> (Ergin 1958-63: I, 77-78)

> It is said that one day Bayïndïr Khan, son of Qam Ġan, rose up from his place. He had his sun-tent put up on the ground. His many-colored canopy rose high into the sky. In a thousand places small silk carpets were spread. Once a year the Khan of Khans, Bayïndïr Khan, used to make a feast and entertain the Oghuz begs (nobles). Once again he made a feast and ordered stallions to be slaughtered from the horses, bulls from the camels, and rams from the sheep.

It is instructive to look at this passage more closely. Word order in Turkish and the Turkic languages demands that the verb be put at the end of the sentence. As the morphological structure of the Turkic languages is agglutinative, this implies that in a descriptive passage like the one quoted the various sentences might end with the same morpheme. The roots of the finite verbs used in this introductory passage are *tur-*, "to stand up"; *dik-*, "to set up"; *aš-*, "to go beyond"; *döše-*, "to spread"; *qon-*, "to settle"; and *qïr-*, "to break, kill." Some of these are used in derived forms, as causatives (*dikdür-*, "to make set up"; *qïrdur-*, "to make kill"), as passives (*döšen-*, "to be spread"), intensives (*ašan-*, "to rise up"),[24] and more complex derivations (from *qon-*, "to settle", *qonuq*, "guest," is derived, and from *qonuq* the verb *qonuqla-*, "to treat as a guest, entertain"). These verbs are all put into the past tense (*-idi*) and for the most part also into the dubitative mood (*-miš*); a verb form like *turmïš-idi* is hence translated literally as "it is said that he rose up." The verb form *qonuqlar-idi*, on the other hand, uses the aorist morpheme *-r*, which expresses a habitual action, hence in the given case the translation: "he used to entertain." There are also two occurrences of a nonfinite verb form in this passage, the gerund with the suffix *-p* in *toy idüp*, "making a *toy* (a feast)."

I have dwelt on the linguistic analysis of these introductory sentences of the tale in order to emphasize what does not always come across in translation: the tendency of Turkic "epic prose" to be organized in

---

[24]On the function of the morpheme *-n-* as in *ašan-* see Ergin 1958-63: II, 443-4.

syntactically parallelistic stuctures. The rhythmic flow of this passage is marked by the sentence-final verbal suffixes, which by virtue of their phonetic similarity segment and punctuate the text into recognizable rhythmic units, producing an effect not unlike that of rhyme in a poem. Parallelism is indeed a pervasive trait not only of the passage quoted but of the whole text. Notice the parallel structure of the second and the third sentence:

Šāmī günlügi	yir yüzine	dikdürmiš-idi.
His sun-tent	on the earth's face	he had set up.

Ala sayvanï	gök yüzine	ašanmïš-idi.
His many-colored canopy	into the sky's face	it rose high.

Intimately linked to parallelism is "petrification." The expression *atdan aygïr, deveden bugra, qoyundan koč qïrdur-*, "to make slaughter the stallion from the horses, the bull from the camels, the ram from the sheep," in the last sentence quoted is found twice in the first tale and a further five times in the rest of the cycle. It is also found in the Kazakh tale of *Dudar Qïz*:[25]

> Üyünö keldi, šïlqïdan aygïr aldï, sirdan buqa aldï, qoydan qošqar aldï, esikden teke aldï.

> He came into the house; from the horses he took a stallion, from the cattle he took a bull, from the sheep he took a ram, from the goats he took a billy goat.

The story continues with Bayïndïr Khan's command to erect three tents and put his guests into them according to whether they have a son, a daughter, or no children. When the childless Dirse Khan is introduced, the narrative switches into verse:

> Meger Dirse Xan dirler-idi bir bigüŋ oğlï qïzï yoğ-idi. Soylamïš, görelüm xanum ne soylamïš:

> > Salqum salqum taŋ yilleri esdüginde,
> > saqallu bozač turğay sayraduqda,
> > saqalï uzun Tat eri baŋladuqda,
> > bidevi atlar issini görüp oqraduqda,
> > aqlu qaralu sečilen čağda,
> > göksi gözel qaba tağlara gün degende,
> > big yigitler džïlasunlar birbirine qoyulan čağda,

---

[25] As noted by Lewis 1974: 195. The Kazakh text is quoted from Radloff 1870: 310 (text volume).

alar sabah Dirse Xan qalqubanï yirinden örü turup qïrq yigidin boyïna
alup Bayïndïr Xanuŋ sohbetine gelür-idi.

(Ergin 1958-63: I, 18)

Now Dirse Khan, they say, had neither a heroic son nor a daughter.
He is said to have said, let us see, my khan, what he said:

> When the cool morning breeze blows,
> when the bearded grey lark sings,
> when the long-bearded Persian calls to prayer,
> when the Arab steeds, seeing their master, neigh,
> at the time when dark and light are separated,
> when the sun-rays touch the high mountains on their beautiful
> flanks,
> at the time when the noble warriors and heroes come together,

in the early morning Dirse Khan got up from his place, rose, gathered
his forty warriors and came to Bayïndïr Khan's feast.

The verse-passage is introduced as if it were a speech, which it is not,
as is clear from the prose-continuation.[26] This passage occurs again at
a later point in the story, when Dirse Khan sets out on a hunting
expedition with his son.[27] Quite clearly, these lines represent a kind of
dawn-song, a lyrical interlude evoking the time of early morning by a
series of poignant images (the singing of the lark, the neighing of the
horses, the prayer call, the light striking the mountain side). At each
occurrence the beauty of nature, the freshness of dawn, serves as a background to a sinister, if not tragic event: the humiliation of Dirse Khan
at Bayïndïr Khan's court and later the near-murder of Buġač. This
passage is unusual in not being (like most verse-passages) a "speech-
poem," a verse-passage spoken by one of the protagonists, but it is not
unusual in its lyrical tone. Other lyrical elements in this tale are verses
addressed by Dirse Khan to his wife, in which he describes her beauty

---

[26]Lewis has consequently omitted the introductory phrase in his translation,
while Sümer, Uysal, Walker make the last verb of the verse-passage finite and let
Dirse Khan address his companions; see Lewis 1974: 27; Sümer, Uysal, Walker 1972:
10. In view of the later occurrence of the same verse-passage, where it is not presented
as direct speech, Lewis' translation must be considered the more likely analysis. On
the meaning of *Tat* see above note 16.

[27]See Lewis 1974: 32-33.

in a "cataloguing" fashion familiar from both medieval European and Oriental love poetry:[28]

> Berü gelgil, bašum baxtï, ivüm taxtï,
> ivden čïqup yorïyanda selvi boylum,
> topuǧïnda sarmašanda qara sačlum,
> qurïlu yaya beŋzer čatma qašlum,
> 5   qoša bädem sïǧmayan tar aǧïzlum,
> güz almasïna beŋzer al yaŋaqlum,
> qavunum, viregüm, düvlegüm,
> görür misin neler oldï.[29]

> Come here, luck of my head, throne of my house,
> my wife with the body of a cypress when you leave the house,
> my wife with black hair, winding itself round your heels,
> my wife with joining eyebrows like a drawn bow,
> 5   my wife with a small mouth, in which two almonds would not fit,
> my wife with red cheeks, which are like autumn apples,
> my sugar melon, my honey melon, my green melon,
> do you see what happened?

Among the lyric genres represented in the tale of Buǧač are also a praise-poem, spoken by Dede Qorqut when he names Buǧač after his first heroic deed, and a lament, recited by Buǧač's mother when she sees her husband return from the hunt without her son.[30] The final poem, like the dawn-songs also not a "speech-poem," develops the *Ubi sunt* topos: "Where are the heroes of yore?", or in Villon's words, "Où est le neige d'antan?"[31]

There are eleven verse-passages in this first tale (according to Ergin's edition), ranging from 6 to 35 lines.[32] Metrically the verses are of irregular length, gravitating, however, towards lines of about 7 or 8 and 11 or 12 syllables. The meter is syllabic and not quantitative as in

---

[28]On the *blason* in medieval European and Oriental literature see Stemmler 1988.

[29]Ergin 1958-1963: I, 79; on the translation of *virek* as "honey melon" compare Lewis 1974: 28; Ergin 1958-1963: II, 314, glosses *virek* as "kavun ?".

[30]See Lewis 1974: 31; 34-35.

[31]See Lewis 1974: 40.

[32]The verse-nature of some passages is controversial; Lewis has 13 verse-passages. The manuscripts do not indicate verse-passages, with only one exception; see Rossi 1962: 88.

Classical Arabic, Persian, Turkish, and Chaghatay poetry.[33] Rhyme too
is irregular; the lines often have assonance rather than rhyme, and most
rhymes are grammatical rhymes, i.e. created by the identity of endings.
Apart from the few exceptions mentioned, all verse-passages are direct
speeches. These speeches are normally introduced by a verb of saying
(such as *soyla-*, "to say, recite") and were obviously meant to be sung.
This can be deduced not only from the descriptions of Dede Qorqut
singing to his *qopuz* (lute) in the epic tales themselves, but also from
later practice (see Chapter Four, pp. 100ff.).

The tale is told like an oral tale: with the persona of a narrator or
singer addressing an audience. The formula "Let us see, my khan,
what he said," as found at the beginning of the dawn-song quoted above,
serves as a standard introduction to the "speech-poems." It is a formula
which has survived into contemporary traditions of Turkic oral epic
poetry. I shall quote just one instance from a Turkish, a Turkmen, and
an Azerbaijanian version of *Köroğlu*:

> Köroğlu Ayvaza teselli etmek için aldı sazını, bakalım ne söyledi...
>
> Köroğlu took his *saz* (lute) in order to comfort Ayvaz. Let us see what
> he said...
>
> (Turkish; Radloff 1899: 5)

> ... bir bäš keleme söz aydar gerek, gör-baq, näme diyyär...
>
> ... it is necessary to say a few (lit. one, five) words. Let us see, what he
> said...
>
> (Turkmen; Karryev 1983: 42)

> Sonra lä'nät šeytana deyib, aldï sazï; göräk nä dedi...
>
> After having cursed the devil, he took his *saz*. Let us see what he
> said...
>
> (Azeri; Tähmasib 1959: 40)

---

[33]See Gandjeï 1957: 154f.; Rossi 1962: 87-91; Žirmunskij 1974 [1962]: 618; Korogly
1976: 189-198. On the metrics of Turkic oral epic poetry see Chapter Seven, pp. 172ff.

The verse-passages in the *Book of Dede Qorqut* are highly patterned,
both in wording and in their structure;[34] a noticeable trait is that two
or more verse-passages might correspond to one another. Thus when
Buğač's mother curses the flowing waters of the Kazilik Mountain, the
growing grass, the running stag, the lions and the tigers, as she suspects
them of their guilt in the near-murder of her son, Buğač's answer takes
up the suspects in the same sequence and vouches for their innocence;
or when Dirse Khan offers his son his pick of horses, sheep, camels,
tents, girls, and *aq saqals* (white-bearded men), Buğač refuses them in
that order.[35] In each reply Buğač's words culminate in naming his
father: first as the culprit, then as the person who despite all that has
happened will be saved by his son.

The relationship between father and son, in the form of paternal
treachery and filial altruism, is the main theme of the tale, a theme
embedded in a framework of traditional story-patterns.[36] It is through
the traditionality of its story-pattern, the motifs making up the
narrative, that the *Tale of Buğač Khan* is connected both with Turkic
epic poetry and with epic traditions lying outside the Turkic world. The
tale starts out with the motif of the childless couple and the subsequent
miraculous conception of the hero. The miraculous conception (and
birth) of the hero is one of the most widespread motifs in heroic
poetry.[37] Together with the motif of the childless couple it is also
extremely productive in Turkic epic poetry and forms the conventional
initial situation of the Turkish minstrel-tale.

Next in the tale comes the first heroic deed of the protagonist and the
subsequent naming-ceremony. Here too we are in the presence of one
of the most common narrative elements of Turkic epic poetry. The
name-giver, normally a dervish or an *aq saqal*, is a reminder of the
sacred nature of the ritual and recalls pre-Islamic beliefs. In the *Book
of Dede Qorqut* we find a parallel in the *Tale of Bamsï Beyrek*, where
the young hero is also given a name by Dede Qorqut in similar

[34]On the poetic form of the *Book of Dede Qorqut* see Žirmunskij [Zhirmunsky]
1985 [1965]: 333-340; Žirmunskij 1974 [1962]: 615-629; Korogly 1976: 187-204.

[35]See Lewis 1974: 36; 38-40.

[36]For a comparative analysis of the *Book of Dede Qorqut* see Korogly 1975.

[37]See *Motif* D1925.3 *Barrenness removed by prayer, Motif* T548.1 *Child born in
answer to prayer.* See further Chapter Six, pp. 164f.

circumstances, i.e. only after he has completed his first heroic deed.[38] In a comparative context, the Old Irish legend of Cúchulainn as told in the *Cattle-Raid of Cooley* comes to mind. As the army of the men of Ulster with Cúchulainn at its head approaches to meet the host of Connacht, Fergus explains to King Ailill and Queen Medb of Connacht who Cúchulainn is and how he came by his name. Culann, the smith, had a fierce dog, which he let loose one night without knowing that the boy Cúchulainn (at that time still called Setana) was due to visit him. When the boy approached Culann's hall:

> The hound sprang. Cúchulainn tossed the ball aside and the stick with it and tackled the hound with his two hands: he clutched the hound's throat-apple in one hand and grasped its back with the other. He smashed it against the nearest pillar and its limbs leaped from their sockets.
>
> (Kinsella 1970: 83)

Everyone rejoices at the boy's courage, and Cathbad, the druid, comes forward to give him his name:

> "Cúchulainn shall be your name, the Hound of Culann," Cathbad said. "I like that for a name!" Cúchulainn said.
>
> (Kinsella 1970: 84)

It is interesting to note that in the Celtic tradition also a priest-like figure performs the rite of name-giving.

The conflict in the story is brought about by envy and calumniation, but in the end it is resolved by heroism and love: the love of a mother for her son, who brings about his miraculous "resurrection" with the milk from her breasts, and the love of a son for his father. Here too we find some of the most common motifs of folktale, romance, and epic. Calumniation is a powerful device to initiate a story, as is witnessed by a number of folktale-types such as those subsumed under the heading of the "Calumniated Wife."[39] The resurrection of the dead hero (here only mortally wounded) points to shamanistic features in the Turkic

---

[38]See Lewis 1974: 62-63. Other parallels from Turkic and Mongolian epics have been compiled by V. Žirmunskij in his study of *Alpamïš*; Žirmunskij 1960: 183ff.

[39]See e.g. in Aarne's and Thompson's catalogue of folktale-types (abbreviated as AaTh) the numbers AaTh 887 (*Griselda*), AaTh 712 (*Crescentia*), AaTh 881 (*Oft-proved Fidelity*), AaTh 706 (*The Maiden Without Hands*), AaTh 894 (*The Stone of Pity*); compare *Motif* K2110.1 *Calumniated wife*. For an analysis of folktales and medieval romances compare Schlauch 1927; Frenzel 1980: 52-70.

epic, which will be discussed later. This motif is typically found in the Altaian epic tales, as well as in the Mongolian epics, epic traditions which are intimately connected with a shamanistic world.[40]

The plot of the tale is basically that of a rescue story: one of the protagonists of the story is imprisoned (or led into captivity) and is subsequently freed by the hero. This story-pattern occurs more than once in the *Dede Qorqut*-cycle (see tales No. 2, 3, 4, 7, 10, 11), also with variations on the theme of the relationship between father and son (Uruz and Qazan). The rescue-and-return story-pattern is widely spread in oral narrative and is not particular to Turkic epic poetry; I will come back to this story-pattern in connection with my discussion of the epic of *Alpamïš* and of the *Köroğlu/Göroğlï*-cycle (see Chapters Six and Ten).

Before leaving the *Book of Dede Qorqut*, another tale in the cycle should be mentioned, the *Tale of Basat and Tepe-Göz* (No. 8). It is this story which first brought the Oghuz epic to the attention of Western scholars, because it is — quite clearly and unequivocally — a version of the Odysseus-Polyphemus episode in Homer's *Odyssey* (Book 9). The Orientalist H. F. Diez was the first to see the parallel in 1815, followed in 1857 by a long essay from the pen of Wilhelm Grimm.[41] Grimm maintained that both Homer and the Oghuz singer drew on a common source, substantiating his claim by citing a number of additional folk-tale variants. The number of these variants can be increased today, but the problem of the precise relationship between Homer's version and the tale found in the *Book of Dede Qorqut* remains to be solved.[42] What matters in the present context is the fact that this episode is yet another element in the *Dede Qorqut*-cycle which establishes a connection, at least of a typological kind, between this earliest fully fledged Turkic epic cycle and epic traditions in other languages and cultures.

* * * * *

[40]Compare *Motif* E105 *Resuscitation by herbs*, *Motif* E113 *Resuscitation by blood*. On the motif of the mother's milk used in resurrecting the hero see the parallels from Kirghiz and Altaian epic poetry adduced by Žirmunskij 1974 [1962]: 604, note 21. On the motif of resurrecting the hero in Mongolian epic see Heissig 1981b.

[41]See Grimm 1857.

[42]See Mundy 1956; Korogly 1974; on Turkic parallels see also Žirmunskij 1960: 66, fn. 12; Tursunov 1975.

The *Book of Dede Qorqut* is the written record of an oral epic cycle which has undergone considerable transformations and adaptations to the Ottoman world of the 14th/15th century, but which nevertheless shows its roots in Central Asia. If we strip the tales of the trappings due to their late form of transmission, we move, so to speak, from eastern Anatolia to the lower reaches of the Syr-Darya and from the 14th/15th century back to the 9th/10th century. The next we hear of Turkic oral epic poetry from Central Asia is when oral epics were recorded in the 19th century. A big gap ensues in the chain of transmission, as far as the written evidence is concerned. There is, indeed, a flourishing written narrative poetry, from the 11th century *Qutadǧu Bilig* (The Wisdom of Happiness) by Yusuf of Bālāsāghun, a kind of Mirror of Princes in 11-syllable couplets, to the love-epics of Navā'ī (1441-1501) or Fuzuli (d. 1555), which have exerted a strong influence on the love-romances of Central Asia. But the oral epic of Central Asia only becomes tangible for us with the advent of ethnographers and linguists who take the trouble to write down what they hear. There is the occasional manuscript prior to the 19th century, such as a collection of songs from the epic cycle of *Köroǧlu/Göroǧli* (see p. 319). There is also a type of popular written literature devoted to the exploits of the *ǧāzīs*, the fighters for Islam, appropriately called *gazavat-name* in Turkish (from Arabic *ǧazawāt*, "raids, holy wars," and Persian *nāme*, "book"). These "popular novels," such as those devoted to the feats of Seyyid Baṭṭāl or of Melik Danišmend, were transmitted in writing but were destined for a popular audience. Not only are these narratives stylistically very close to oral epic and romance, but their performance too reflects a popular tradition: the *gazavat-name*s were often read to an audience by professional entertainers, the *meddah*s or *qïssa-xāns*.[43]

But the serious collecting of oral epic poetry only began in the 19th century, with scholars like the Hungarian Armin (Hermann) Vámbéry (1832-1913), who traveled to Central Asia in the guise of an Ottoman dervish; the Kazakh nobleman and ethnographer Čoqan Valixanov (1811-1865); the Orientalist Abubekir Axmeddžanovič Divaev (1855-1933), a Bashkir by origin; the Russian traveler and geographer Grigorij Nikolaevič Potanin (1835-1920); and most importantly the Turkologist

---

[43]On this genre see Fleischer 1888; Levend 1956; Mélikoff 1960: I, 41-52; Köksal 1984. On the *meddah*s and *qïssa-xāns* see Chapter Three (pp. 87ff.).

Wilhelm Radloff (or Vasilij Vasilevič Radlov) (1837-1918).[44] Their work has been complemented in this century by extensive collecting in the Central Asian and Siberian part of the former Soviet Union, and recently also in China. Indeed the material collected has taken on such gigantic proportions, particularly in traditions like the Kirghiz, that it has become almost unwieldy. Only a small portion has been edited, not all in scholarly editions. But despite the limitations of our present field of vision, it is incontestable that 19th-century and contemporary Turkic oral epic poetry has its roots in earlier forms of Turkic "epic" as reviewed in this chapter. This will become clear when we look at some of these epics and epic traditions in later chapters of this book.

[44]See Žirmunskij's short survey in Chadwick, Zhirmunsky 1969: 271ff.

Chapter Three

The Singer: Shaman, Minstrel, Poet

Epic Singer and Shaman

The yurt is full of people, the fire is burning. In the silence setting in someone says: "Šïyaan am." Starting with the invariable formula *šïyaan am* the narrator begins his tale. With his eyes closed and swaying in the rhythm of the tale's melody, he tells of the mighty heroes of old and their heroic deeds.[1]

(Grebnev 1960: 8)

This scene, evoking the setting for the performance of heroic epic poetry among the Tuvinians, is typical of other Turkic peoples as well: the people gather in a yurt, at night, with a singer in their midst; they have come to listen to his tale, to let themselves be entertained all night; as the silence sets in, the singer begins his epic tale, declaiming or chanting in a way peculiar to each tradition, captivating his listeners' attention and casting a spell on his audience. L. V. Grebnev continues his description by mentioning the belief among the Tuvinians that one had to listen attentively to the singer, because the life of a person who fell asleep during the performance of an epic tale was in danger of being curtailed. The singer is clearly more than an entertainer and his tale more than entertainment: the spell he casts on his audience is real enough, a spiritual force wielding power over the life of his listeners.

There is a close connection between singer and shaman, the master of verbal art and the wielder of healing power, in the archaic cultures of northeastern Asia, and traces of shamanism are found in all traditions of Turkic oral epic poetry. The relationship between shaman

---

[1]The expression *šïaan am* corresponds to Old English *hwæt* as it is found at the beginning of *Beowulf* and could be translated as "Lo and behold!"

and singer is most obvious among those Turkic tribes where shamanism
was practiced until recently, i.e. among the Yakuts and the various
Turkic tribes of the Altai. Singer and shaman are actually two distinct
figures in these traditions, but there are many indications that they
were originally one, as among some Tungus and Palaeo-Siberian
peoples. The performers of epic tales among the Nivkh, a Palaeo-
Siberian people formerly called "Gilyak," were mostly shamans or
descendants of shamans:

> The Gilyak narrator/singer is of an exceptional nature, he is truly the
> chosen one of the gods. It is not without reason that the singers/nar-
> rators are in most cases shamans or their descendants. We are told
> about famous Gilyak shamans that, besides performing all kinds of
> supernatural feats, they regularly spent whole days telling tales and
> singing improvised songs without interruption.
>
> (Šternberg 1908: xi)

The closeness between shaman and singer is underlined by the story of
the shaman Dupdullan Kamoski of the Ket (another Palaeo-Siberian
tribe, formerly called "Yenisei Ostyak"), who, when asked to perform a
heroic tale, started after a while to sway rhythmically with the upper
part of his body, working himself into a state of trance and singing
shamanistic hymns instead of heroic poetry.[2]

The shaman is an ambivalent figure, changing in appearance as well
as in the functions he performs from culture to culture. Although forms
of shamanism are found in many parts of the world, shamanism as a
religious phenomenon is most characteristic of northeastern Asia:

> Throughout the immense area comprising Central and North Asia,
> the magico-religious life of society centers on the shaman. This, of
> course, does not mean that he is the one and only manipulator of the
> sacred, nor that religious activity is completely usurped by him. In
> many tribes the sacrificing priest coexists with the shaman, not to
> mention the fact that every head of a family is also the head of the
> domestic cult. Nevertheless, the shaman remains the dominating
> figure; for through this whole region in which the ecstatic experience
> is considered the religious experience par excellence, the shaman, and
> he alone, is the great master of ecstasy. A first definition of this
> complex phenomenon, and perhaps the least hazardous, will be
> shamanism = *technique of ecstasy*.
>
> (Eliade 1964: 4)

[2]See Findeisen, Gehrts 1983: 145.

It is through this technique of ecstasy that the shaman performs his functions: he enters into communion with the gods, the dead, with spirits and other supernatural beings, and is thus capable of wielding power and performing superhuman feats. He has the power to cure, to prophesy, to ascend into heaven, to descend into the underworld, and to act as a psychopomp for the dead.[3] One of the most fascinating aspects of shamanism for the student of epic poetry is the initiation of the shaman through sickness and dreams. These visions are paralleled by the initiation which epic singers experience in many traditions.

The following account, collected from the Yakut Nikolaj Šadrin in 1925, is a typical example of shamanic illness:

> If someone is to become a shaman he suffers already in his adolescence from a mental disease for a period of two, three, sometimes up to six years.
>
> Before he becomes a shaman he sees in a dream how the souls of dead shamans gather "from above and below" and, becoming evil spirits (*üörder*), cut his body into pieces. They scatter his blood, black through the beating of the shamanic drum, "on all roots and sources of illness" ....
>
> It is said that the shaman then falls asleep and lies as if dead for three days and three nights. During all that time he neither eats nor drinks anything.
>
> (Ksenofontov 1928: 13)

Compare with this account the following vision recorded from the Kirghiz singer Džaníbay Kodžekov:

> One day I went to Qočqor and fell asleep on the way. Suddenly I saw in my dream three riders riding along with lances, on whose points fires were burning. One of them pierced me with a spear and carried me away on it. The lance went through me, but its point continued to have a burning fire as before. The riders told me that such a punishment was conferred on me, because I didn't continue the work of my fathers.
>
> Then the riders started to prepare food. I turned to them with the question: "You are supernatural, aren't you, and not real people?" To this one of them gave the answer: "I am Semetey, and these are Külčoro and Qančoro [heroes of the epic]." I would have liked to eat the food prepared by them, but Qančoro ate it all up; because of this there arose a fight between him and Külčoro. Finally Qančoro brought me fresh food; this was millet. He poured the grains into my mouth

---

[3]There is no room here to give a detailed account of shamanism. The relationship between shamanism and epic poetry among the Turkic and other peoples of northern Asia is discussed in Chadwick 1932-40: III, 192-218; Hatto 1980 [1970]. For Siberian shamanism see inter alia Radloff 1893: II, 1-67; Harva 1938: 449-569; Eliade 1964; Findeisen, Gehrts, 1983; Alekseev 1987.

and I swallowed them. The grains were *džomoq* (heroic tales). He poured a lot of them into me.

I regained consciousness in my own house, being ill. I was ill for a long time. After my recovery I went into the mountains and there I began to recite *Manas* to myself, but after some time I recited the epic also in front of a big crowd of people. This is how I became a *manasčï* [a singer of *Manas*].

(Kydyrbaeva 1984: 113-114)

What is interesting here is that the future epic singer sees the heroes of the epic he is to sing about just as the future shaman sees the souls of the dead shamans. In both cases the chosen one is to carry on the work of his predecessors, into which he is initiated through pain and illness. The torture and sickness described in Kodžekov's account are clearly of an initiatory nature, comparable to the shaman's experience:[4]

> ... all the ecstatic experiences that determine the future shaman's vocation involve the traditional schema of an initiation ceremony: suffering, death, resurrection. Viewed from this angle, any "sickness-vocation" fills the role of an initiation; for the sufferings that it brings on correspond to initiatory tortures, the psychic isolation of "the elected" is the counterpart to the isolation and ritual solitude of initiation ceremonies, and the imminence of death felt by the sick man (pain, unconsciousness, etc.) recalls the symbolic death represented in almost all initiation ceremonies.

(Eliade 1964: 33)

Illness and suffering are, however, a rare feature in the initiatory visions of epic singers. A more common feature of these dreams and visions is the appearance either of supernatural beings such as the *čiltan* (Forty Saints) or the heroes of the epics themselves. The Kirghiz singer Čoyuke remembers the following vision:

> One day in summer, when I was returning home from work, I hobbled my horse in the pass of Qïzïl-Qïy, lay down in the grass and fell asleep. In my dream it seemed to me that as I was riding along the pass of Qïzïl-Qïy, an old man came towards me and made me go with him. Finally, we found ourselves next to a herd of horses. Walking through the herd, we arrived at a big yurt, into which we entered. There a man of an exceedingly ferocious appearance was lying on a quilt; I greeted him, but he gave no answer. Not far from the bedding, folded away in layers, there was a vessel with *qïmïz* in it. The old man, who had led me into the yurt, went to the vessel and poured me some *qïmïz*. I

---

[4]On the initiatory illness and election of the Turkic shaman of Siberia see also Alekseev 1987: 137-162.

drank it in one gulp. "This man here is called Manas. Remember!" he said.

Then he led me out of the yurt and on to another one. There a handsome man with a white face and big eyes was sitting; he also had an exceedingly ferocious appearance. There also I drank some *qïmïz*, and the old man told me the name of this man, Almambet. In this manner the old man led me into forty yurts and I drank a bowl of *qïmïz* in each one. When I woke up, it was already evening. From this day on I have been reciting the epic.

(Kydyrbaeva 1984: 113)

The old man or *aq saqal* ("white-beard") here is clearly some kind of supernatural helper and guide, corresponding to similar figures in shamanistic initiation-dreams. In the tradition of Islamized Turkic peoples like the Kirghiz the *aq saqal* in dreams and visions is normally identified with the Islamic saint Hïzïr; he appears regularly in the folktale motif of the childless couple who are given an apple-pip or some other miraculous means for producing offspring.[5] Initiation-dreams and visions are also found among the Turks of Azerbaijan and Turkey:[6]

> ^cÂshiq Rasūl of Tabriz says he dreamt that a figure approached him bearing a small *sāz* [plucked instrument]. This person asked Rasūl if he could play the *sāz*. Rasūl immediately picked up the *sāz* and began to play. When he awoke, he found that he could indeed play the *sāz* the very first time he tried.

(Albright 1976: 221-222)

The most famous initiatory vision in Western medieval literature is Bede's story of the Northumbrian poet Cædmon. V. Žirmunskij has compared Bede's account to the initiatory visions of Turkic and Mongolian singers and has linked these visions to the initiation experiences of future shamans.[7]

But the initiatory vision is only one element connecting the shaman with the singer. As will be discussed later (see Chapter Four), the manner of performance of the epic poems or heroic tales also points to a shamanistic background. Some of the instruments used by the singers to accompany themselves are also related to shamanism. The *qobïz* of

---

[5] On Hïzïr see Wensinck 1978; on his role in the initiation-dreams of the Turkish *aşıks* see Boratav 1964: 34-35; Başgöz 1952: 332.

[6] On initiatory visions among the Turkish *aşıks* see Başgöz 1967; Moyle 1990: 55-69. On the *ašïq/aşık* see below.

[7] Compare Žirmunskij 1979 [1960]; Magoun 1955; Lester 1974.

the Karakalpaks or the *morin-xuur* of the Mongols is, with its horsehead instead of a scroll on top of the peg-box, a clear reminder of the shaman's ecstatic journey (see also the remarks on the Kazakh *baqsï* below).

The epic tales of the Turkic peoples, in particular of the Altai, also reveal numerous shamanistic traces; some of these will be discussed in connection with the actual narratives. At this point I would like to focus on one further indication of the close relationship between singer and shaman, the terminology employed in various Turkic languages for the singer and narrator of epics and epic tales.

Terms for Singers

In Yakut the singer of epic poetry is called *oloŋxohut*, "singer of the *oloŋxo*." This term is a *nomen agentis* derived from *oloŋxo*, "epic poem," a word most probably related to Turkmen and Kazakh *öleŋ*, "song."[8] The same pattern is found in other Turkic languages: the term for the singer is a noun derived from a word meaning "song," "poem," "tale" etc. Thus in Uighur the singer of *dastan*s is called *dastanči* or *qošaqči* (from *qošaq*, "song"); *dastanči* is one of the terms also found in Uzbek. The singer of the Kirghiz heroic epic *Manas* is called *manasčï*; this term has been used only since the Revolution, the earlier term for the singer of heroic poetry in general was *džomoqču*, from *džomoq*, "heroic epic." One type of Karakalpak singer is called *žïraw*, a derivation from *žïr*, "heroic epic," "song."[9] The term *žïraw* is also found in Kazakh, and a similar derivation from Old Turkic *yïr/ïr* is found in Kirghiz (*ïrčï*). The Altai singer of epic poems is called *qayčï*, from *qay*, "to sing (in a particular manner)" (see below).[10]

Two of these derivational bases call for further comment. Kirghiz *džomoq* has a number of Turkic parallels with meanings like "tale,"

---

[8]See Puxov 1962: 5, note 1; Räsänen 1969: 371.

[9]From Old Turkic *ïr/yïr*, "song"; see Räsänen 1969: 166, 201.

[10]Similar formations are found in neighboring languages. From Mongolian *tuul'*, "epic," the Tuvinian word for the heroic tale, *tool*, is borrowed, and both languages have corresponding derivations for the narrator of the heroic epic, Mongolian *tuul'č* and Tuvinian *toolču*. Compare Radloff 1893-1911: III, 1191 (s.v. ²*töl*).

"parable," "speech," and "riddle." There is good reason to postulate an etymological relationship with Mongolian *domog̃*, "legend," from *dom*, "magic"; the meaning of Mongolian *dom* is preserved in Ottoman Turkish *yum*, "bad omen."[11] A similar combination of meanings relating to the activity of the shaman and the narrator/singer is found in the Tungus word *nimŋa*, "to tell tales, to shamanize."[12] Traces of this combination are also found in the Chuvash term *yumax*, "tale, riddle," which, like Chuvash *yumăç*, "magician, quack," is derived from *yum*, "magic."[13] All this points to a close connection between shaman and singer at an earlier stage in the history of the Turkic (and more generally Altaic) peoples.

An interesting word, leading to the same conclusion, is also the Altaian term for singer, *qayči*. This word can be glossed as "the narrator of a heroic epic who performs in a peculiar guttural singing style, called *qay*, with the accompaniment of a two-stringed plucked instrument, the *topšuur*."[14] One of the characteristics of the singing of epic poetry among a number of Turkic peoples is the use of a guttural singing style and a strained voice. It is found among the Altaians, the Tuvinians, the Uzbeks, the Karakalpaks, the Turkmens and others, and it has often been connected with the shamanistic origins of epic song (see below pp. 112f.). The word *qay-* is interesting in this connection. In Yellow Uighur (a Turkic language spoken in Ganzu and Qinghai in China) *qay* means "bewitchment (causing illness); spirit of a shaman."[15] This must be an old meaning of the word as it can be connected to Chaghatay *qay*, "omen, fate" and *qay sal-*, "to cause someone to become ill."[16] It hardly seems speculative to posit a connec-

---

[11]The relationship between Kirghiz *džomoq* and Mongolian *domog̃* is fairly straightforward, at any rate within the framework of comparative Altaic linguistics; see Poppe 1960: 69. For the link between Mongolian *dom* and Ottoman Turkish *yum* see Poppe *ibid.*; Zenker 1866: II, 976 (s.v. *jum*).

[12]See Räsänen 1969: 206 (s.v. *jomak*); see also Cincius et al. 1975-77: I, 594. In Khakas an epic is called *nïmag̃*, a word clearly related to Tungus.

[13]See Salmin 1987.

[14]Surazakov 1961: 7, note 4; compare Radloff 1893-1911: II, 3 (s.v. [2]*kai*).

[15]See Malov 1957: 49; Räsänen 1969: 221.

[16]See Zenker 1866: II, 687 (s.v. *kaj* Sbst.); Malov 1957: 49.

tion here between the possession of the shaman by a spirit causing his illness and the utterance of a poet seized by divine inspiration; as we have seen, the initiatory visions also support this thesis.[17]

Not all words designating the singer of tales point, however, to shamanism. Some of these terms refer to the verbal and poetic skill of the narrator and singer and have no etymological connection with shamanism. The Kazakh singer of oral epic poetry is usually called *aqïn*, a Persian loan word (from *āxūn*, "orator; tutor; preacher").[18] This word is also found in Kirghiz, where it denotes both the improvising singer and the poet in general.[19] In Uzbek, famous "improvising singers" of *dastans* have received the honorary title *šāir*, the general term for poet in Uzbek (from Arabic *šāᶜir*).[20] The singer of epics is called *čäčän* in Tatar and *säsän* in Bashkir.[21] This word is also found in other Turkic languages; it basically means "eloquent" and, as a noun, "orator."[22] In the Oghuz epic of *Dede Qorqut* the singer of epic tales is called *ozan*, a word possibly derived from the same root as Turkmen *ūz*, "master."[23]

By far the most interesting term for the singer is Uzbek *baxši*. This word is already found in Old Turkic (Old Uighur); here *baxši* denotes a scholar and teacher, in particular a Buddhist teacher. The same meaning is assigned to Mongolian *bağši* and Tungus *paksi*, words which

---

[17]The same point is made by A. T. Hatto in a detailed commentary on the occurrence of the verb *qayla-* in Radloff's *Manas*; see Hatto 1990: 432.

[18]Other etymologies for *aqïn* have been proposed. According to Radloff the word is related to Kazakh *ağïl-*, "to pour out," an etymology also endorsed by Äwezov, while Judaxin proposes a connection to Uighur *axon*, "honored person"; see Ismailov 1957: 25-26.

[19]See Judaxin 1985 [1965]: I, 42 (s.v. *aqïn*).

[20]See Borovkov et al. 1959: 544; Žirmunskij, Zarifov 1947: 26.

[21]See Sägitov [Sagitov], Zaripov, Sulejmanov 1987: 30; Urmančeev 1984: 46ff.

[22]Thus in Kazakh, Uzbek, Kirghiz, Teleut etc.; see Räsänen 1969: 407a.

[23]See Sevortjan 1974ff.: I, 569; Doerfer 1963-75: II, 147. On the use and meaning of *ozan* in Ottoman Turkish see Köprülü 1966 [1934]: 131-144.

are clearly related.[24] The most likely etymology for this word is
Ancient Chinese *pâk-ši* (Modern Chinese *bo-shi*), "master, teacher."[25]
What is interesting about the word *baxši* is that it has two senses in
those modern Turkic languages that have preserved it. In Uzbek,
Turkmen, and Karakalpak the term *baxši* (and its phonetic variants)
denotes the singer of oral epic poetry, in Karakalpak more narrowly one
type of singer (see below). In Kirghiz and Kazakh, however, *baxšï/baq-
sï* means "shaman, sorcerer, quack." Once again singer and shaman
are associated in terminology. Although no known Uzbek *baxši* of this
century combined the art of singing with the art of healing, older
singers did in the 1940s still remember such a union of singer and
shaman in former times.[26] The Kazakh and Kirghiz *baxšïs*, on the
other hand, are shamans, or rather "Western" transformations of the
Siberian shaman, namely quacks and practitioners of popular medi-
cine.[27]

I will conclude this short survey with the word for the singer of epic
poetry in the Azerbaijanian and Turkish traditions, *ašïq* (Turkish *aşık*).
This word is derived from Arabic *ʿišq*, "love," and denotes the lover,
more specifically someone who has become a wandering minstrel
because of some unhappy love affair. The *ašïq* performs not only
narrative poetry, but also lyric poetry; in fact many *ašïq*s, such as the
blind Turkish singer Veysel of our own day, perform only lyric poetry.
The *ašïq* accompanies himself on a plucked instrument, generically
called the *saz* in Turkish; *saz şairi* is hence another designation for this

[24]*Baxši* is the most common term applied to the singer in Uzbek. Other terms
are, however, also found: the Khorezmian singer is called *dastanči* ("singer of
dastans") besides *baxši*; in the Surxandaryā region the singer is also called *yuzbāši*
(lit. "head of a hundred," an administrative post in the Central Asian khandoms); in
the districts of Leninabad and Osh the terms *sāqi* (Persian for "cupbearer") and
sāzanda (Persian for "musician") are used; in the Ferghana valley in addition to *baxši*
the term *sannāwči* (lit. "talker") is also employed. See Abdullaev 1989: 113.

[25]See Räsänen 1969: 59; Gabain 1974: 326; Köprülü 1966 [1942]: 145-156.

[26]See Žirmunskij 1979 [1960]: 403.

[27]N. Chadwick has given an extensive description of their practices on the basis
of an earlier work by J. Castagné. See Chadwick 1932-40: III, 210-213; Castagné 1930.
On the survival of shamanistic practices and ideas among the Kirghiz see Bajalieva
1972: 117-148.

singer.[28] With the *ašïq* we have left the archaic world of the Siberian
shaman and singer and entered a more modern world of popular
entertainment, a change not unlike the transition from the Anglo-Saxon
scop to the medieval minstrel. It is important to realize that when
talking about "the singer of Turkic oral epic poetry" many different
types of singers can be referred to. Some of these will be looked at in
more detail in the remainder of this chapter.[29]

The Karakalpak *Žïraw* and *Baqsï*

After this survey of some of the most common terms used for singers
of epic poetry in the Turkic languages let us now look at a few
individual singers and traditions. I will start with the Karakalpak
singers, as they stand in many ways at the crossroads of traditions and
styles. The Karakalpaks distinguish between two types of singers, the
žïraw and the *baqsï*. The differences consist on the one hand in the
instrument they use to accompany themselves, and on the other in the
types of epics they perform and in the manner of their performance.
The *žïraw* uses the *qobïz*, a horsehair fiddle, while the *baqsï* plays the
dutar, a two-stringed lute-type instrument. Broadly speaking, the
žïraw specializes in epic poetry of a heroic nature and the *baqsï* in
love-romance. The distinction between heroic epic and romance is,
however, not a fast one, and we hence find a certain overlap in the
repertory of the two types of singers.[30]

Žumabay-žïraw Bazarov, one of the *žïraw*s I have recorded, is from
the Šumanay district of Karakalpakistan. He was born in 1927 and
went to school for seven years. He wanted to become a *žïraw* when still
a boy and had the good fortune to have as his teacher a famous

---

[28]Another designation is *halk şairi*, "folk singer." See Boratav 1973: 21-22. On
the Turkish *aşık* and his repertory see especially Eberhard 1955; Moyle 1990 (with
particular emphasis on the life and work of Aşık Müdami). Müdami's life-story in his
own words is printed in Başgöz 1986b: 124-137.

[29]For a survey of singers and singer-types see also Chadwick, Zhirmunsky 1969:
322-334.

[30]For a discussion of genre see Chapter Five; on the repertory of some of the
singers mentioned see Chapter Four.

Karakalpak singer, Esemurat-žïraw Nurabullaev, with whom he studied for three years in Kungrad. In 1981 he had two pupils, aged 12 and 23, one being a son of his. His teacher, Esemurat-žïraw, was born in 1893; Esemurat is one of the major links between the contemporary *žïraws* and the singers of the 19th century and earlier.[31] Esemurat's father was himself a *žïraw*, named Nurabulla, from whom he learned the epic poems *Qoblan, Šaryar, Edige*, and *Šora*, at first in the family till his sixteenth year, then as his pupil for another sixteen years, accompanying his father on his travels. From 1933 to 1936 Esemurat-žïraw worked in a kolkhoz, from 1939 onwards in the Kungrad kolkhoz theater. In 1939 Esemurat first became known outside Karakalpakistan when he successfully took part in folk music festivals in Tashkent and Moscow. After the war he had several pupils, among them his son Äžimurat. Esemurat was well-known as an excellent *qobïz*-player. Several of his melodies have been recorded on tape. His version of *Qoblan* was taken down in 1939 and first appeared, with abridgements, in 1959. His version of *Alpamïs*, which was published in 1960, is the longest of all the known versions of the epic. While the largest Uzbek version comprises about 14,000 verse-lines, Esemurat's version is about 18,000 verse-lines long. His versions of other epics such as *Šora, Šaryar*, and *Edige* have been taken down from his pupils. Esemurat-žïraw died in 1979.

Esemurat's father Nurabulla lived from 1862 to 1927.[32] A number of *dastans* in the form they are known today stem from him. Nurabulla was a singer who was always eager to broaden his repertory. He learned the epic poems *Qoblan* and *Edige* first from Turïmbet-žïraw and later added to his knowledge of these epics by staying with Qazaqbay-žïraw in Bukhara. In Qazaqbay's repertory also were the epics *Alpamïs, Šaryar*, and *Šora*; Nurabulla had already learned *Alpamïs* from Paleke-žïraw and *Šaryar* from Erman-žïraw before he went to Bukhara. Nurabulla belongs to a "school" of *žïraws* which is said to go back to a singer of the time of the rule of Khan Tokhtamysh over the Noghay horde (14th c.), Soppaslï Sïpïra-žïraw.[33] No "genealogy" can, however, be constructed reaching back before the 18th century. What

---

[31]On Esemurat-žïraw see Maqsetov 1983: 77-92; Ayïmbetov 1988: 88f.

[32]On Nurabulla see Maqsetov 1983: 26-41; Ayïmbetov 1988: 83f.

[33]See Maqsetov 1983: 8-25; Davkaraev 1959: 25.

can be established is the fact that the Karakalpak *žïraw*s whose work has been recorded (either from the singers themselves or from their pupils) fall into two groups, the "school of Soppaslï Sïpïra-žïraw" and the "school of Žien Taġay-ulï." The former are mostly connected to the "lower" Karakalpaks (living in the southern part of Karakalpakistan on the lower reaches of the Amu Darya) and show a number of similarities to the epic traditions of the Khorezmian Uzbeks, the Turkmens, and the Kazakhs, in language, manner of performance, and repertory. The latter trace their ancestry back to a *žïraw* of the mid-18th century, Žien Taġay-ulï. They are found mostly among the "upper" Karakalpaks, i.e. the Karakalpaks living in the northern part of Karakalpakistan on the shores of the Aral Sea.[34]

Like the *žïraw*s, the Karakalpak *baqsï*s can be grouped into two "schools." The pupils of Muwsa-baqsï (1836-1907) sing the *dastan*s in Karakalpak, while the singers of the "school of Süyew-baqsï" use the Khorezmian dialect of Uzbek and are generally very close to the Khorezmian tradition of Uzbek epic poetry.[35] A number of famous Karakalpak *baqsï*s were women (e.g. Hürliman [1861-1906], Qanigül [1900-1928]). One of the best-known *baqsï*s of the former "school" is Genžebay-baqsï, from whom I was able to record various samples of his art in 1983 and 1990.[36] Genžebay was born in 1929; his principal teacher was his own father, Tilewmurat-baqsï Atamurat-ulï, a well-known singer (d. 1950). Tilewmurat-baqsï's teacher (*ustaz*) in turn was Arzï-baqsï, with whom Tilewmurat learned for eight years. During this time Tilewmurat-baqsï mastered the *dastan*s *Yusup and Axmet, Sayatxan and Hamra, Ġärib-ašïq, Hürliqa and Hamra*, as well as the branches *Bäzirgen* and *Qïrmandäli* from the *Köroġlu/Göroġlï*-cycle. Tilewmurat-baqsï also learned epic poems from Kazakh singers. These *dastan*s he passed on to his pupils and to his son. Genžebay started playing the *dutar* when he was seven or eight years old; at the age of twelve he had already learned the *dastan*s *Yusup and Axmet, Qïrmandäli*, and *Sayatxan and Hamra*. Genžebay's career is in many ways typical of the singer surviving as a professional into modern times. He

[34]On these two "schools" see Davkaraev 1959: 25-26.

[35]See Davkaraev 1959: 26; on the Karakalpak *baqsï*s see also Ayïmbetov 1988: 129-147.

[36]See Reichl 1985b; Maqsetov 1983: 188-196.

attended his village school up to the eighth class, finishing there in 1944. From 1950 until 1954 he studied at the Pedagogical Institute in Nukus. He worked intermittently as a teacher, from 1956 to 1960 at a Middle School. He also worked for various journals, for the theater, for the Karakalpak branch of the Uzbek Academy of Sciences and since 1977 for Nukus Television and Radio. He is therefore a familiar figure in contemporary Karakalpakistan.

The Uzbek *Baxši*

In my discussion of the Karakalpak *žïraw* and *baqsï* I have used the term "school." This term is not meant to suggest a school in the sense of an institution in which one can attend classes; it rather symbolizes the relationship between various singers as it can be traced through the chain of transmission from teacher to pupil. The idea of a "singer school" has been elaborated in particular by reference to the Uzbek tradition of oral epic poetry. The Uzbek *baxši* Bekmurād Džorabāy-oġli (1878-1956) gives a vivid picture of the "school" he belongs to at the end of his *dastan Awaznïŋ arazi* (Awaz Insulted) from the *Köroğlu/Gör-oğlï*-cycle:

> Bu yol bilan aytip otgan Awazni
> qāraqalpāqda Xālmurādday šāirdi.
> Xālmurād baxšidan bu yol qālgandi,
> Čankut baxši undan ta'lim ālgandi.
> 5   Goroġli, Awazxān aytib tayrifin
> dāim kopniŋ ortasiga sālgandi.
> Awazxānni bāšqalar ham aytadi,
> kopisiniŋ aytgan sozi yālġāndi.
> Sababi šul kopi ustād kormagan,
> 10 šuytib ayt deb, ustād ta'lim bermagan.
> Āti Awaz bolgan bilan soziniŋ
> kop sozlari mānandiga kelmagan.
> Čankutniŋ šāgirdi Qurbān šāirniŋ
> āwāzasi kop džāylarga yāyildi.
> 15 Qāzāq, qāraqalpāq, turkman, ozbek,
> yana tādžiklar ham unga qāyildi.
> Nurāta rayoni tuġilgan džāyim,
> šāirlikka boldi yāšlikdan ra'yim.
> Bāšqa išdan buni men kop suyardim,
> 20 šāirlikni korib ozimga qāyim.
> Ixlās qilib yurar edim yāšimdan,
> kambaġallik, mehnat ketmay bāšimdan,

Qurbān šāir aytganini korganda,
tāŋ ātganča ketmas edim qāšindan.
25   Bu dāstānlar neča aytib otilgan,
kop aytib ular mašqiga etilgan.
Tiŋlaganman Qurbān šāir sozini,
aytgan sozlari koŋlima bitilgan.

(Zarif 1965: 122)

In this manner *Awaz* was performed
in Karakalpak by Xālmurād-šāir.
This manner was bequeathed by Xālmurād-baxši;
Čankut-baxši learned it from him.
5   He narrated *Goroġli* and *Awazxān*
to a lot of people.
Others also narrate *Awazxān*,
but the words these many (singers) say are lies.
The reason for this is that these many (singers) have no teacher (*ustād*);
10   there is no teacher telling them: "Say it in this way!"
Although their words are about Awaz,
many of them do not correspond to the tale.
The voice of Čankut's pupil, Qurbān-šāir,
spread to many places.
15   The Kazakhs, the Karakalpaks, the Turkmens, the Uzbeks,
even the Tajiks were in ecstasies about him.
The district of Nurāta is the place where I was born;
to become a *šāir* has been my wish since my youth.
I have loved this profession more than anything else,
20   thinking the profession of a *šāir* fitting for me.
From my youth I have been devoted to it,
in poverty, without doing any work,
attending to what Qurbān-šāir was saying
I did not move from his side till morning dawned.
25   Those *dastan*s have been narrated many times;
having been narrated often, they have ripened to perfection.
I have listened to Qurbān-šāir's words;
the words he has spoken have been written in my heart.

Bekmurād Džorabāy-oġli, from the village of Qotir in the district of
Nurāta, belonged to the "school of Nurāta" in southern Uzbekistan (in
the province of Samarkand).[37] His teacher was Qurbān-šāir from Māzār
qišlāq (village), a singer who died in the 1930s. As Bekmurād points
out, Qurbān-šāir's teacher was Čankut-baxši, whose teacher in turn was
Xālmurād-baxši. Like Čankut-baxši, Xālmurād-baxši was a Karakalpak
žïraw. The close interconnection between various traditions is stressed

[37] For a discussion of this passage and of the school of Nurāta see Mirzaev 1979:
44-46.

by Bekmurād's statement that Qurbān-šāir sang to Kazakhs, Karakalpaks, Turkmens, Uzbeks, and Tajiks, and we know (among others from
one of his pupils, a Karakalpak singer) that Bekmurād himself was able
to sing his *dastan*s in Uzbek, Kazakh, and Karakalpak. He also sang
to the Tajiks; another of his pupils was a Tajik and sang his improvised
songs (*terma*) both in Uzbek and Tajik.[38] The Karakalpak influence on
this "school" seems to have been quite strong; we know that the
Karakalpak *žïraw* Nurabulla, who was mentioned earlier, also came to
Nurāta.[39]

Teaching and learning consist, first of all, in being together and, on
the part of the pupil, in listening attentively to the singer's words and
not moving from his side all night till the early morning (see ll. 23-24).
This being together was not just a matter of an occasional encounter but
had a formal character. A master-singer (*ustāz*) would take a pupil
(*šāgird*) into his household for two to three years, teaching him his
*dastan*s and the art of performing them, while the pupil was expected
to help the singer, normally by working as a farmhand. Gradually the
pupil would be allowed to perform improvised songs (*terma*) or parts of
*dastan*s together with the singer, to continue a *dastan* or to take his
turn in performing an epic. At the end of his apprenticeship the pupil
would perform to an audience of connoisseurs. If he was successful, the
teacher would present him with a set of clothes and a *xalat* (coat of
honor), sometimes also with a *dombira* or a *dutar* (lutes), and would
wish him luck in his future career.[40]

The repertory of an Uzbek *baxši* comprises on average about five to
ten *dastan*s, but a talented *baxši* was certainly in the past able to
perform about thirty to forty *dastan*s. Some singers did, however,
exceed this number noticeably. Among the Uzbeks of southern
Tajikistan (the Uzbek-Laqay) the *Köroğlu/Göroğlï*-cycle is said to consist
of 32, in some regions even of 64 branches; no singer is, however, known
to be able to perform the whole cycle.[41] Of exceptional size was the
repertory of the singer Polkan-šāir (1874-1941), who knew about seventy

[38]See Mirzaev 1979: 44.

[39]See Mirzaev 1979: 45.

[40]See Žirmunskij, Zarifov 1947: 35-37; Mirzaev 1979: 34-37.

[41]See Mirzaev 1979: 56.

*dastan*s, the longest among them (*Qirān-xān*) comprising no less than 20,000 verse-lines. Not all of these *dastan*s have, however, been written down; Zubaida Husainova lists only twenty-seven texts in her inventory of *dastan*s recorded from Polkan-šāir.[42]

Apart from the "school" of Nurāta several other "*baxši* schools" (*baxšilik maktabi, dāstānčilik maktabi*) have been distinguished. The most famous singer of the "school" of Bulunġur (in the province of Samarkand) was Fāzil Yoldāš-oġli (1872-1955), whose version of *Alpāmiš* is justly celebrated. Fāzil and the other singers of this "school" cultivated in particular the heroic style in Uzbek epic poetry. Fāzil was one of ten pupils of the singer Yoldāš Mulla Murād, who in turn was the pupil of a renowned singer of the latter half of the 18th century, Muhammad-šāir Yoldāšbulbul.[43] Another important "*baxši* school" was the "school" of Qorġān (in the province of Bukhara). In this small village there are said to have been seven families with over twenty singers in the middle of the 19th century. The most distinguished representatives of this "school" were the singers Ergaš Džumanbulbul-oġli (1868-1937) and Muhammadqul Džānmurād-oġli Polkan (1874-1941). Ergaš has left us a long poem, interspersed with prose, in which he describes his own life (*Tardžimai hāl* [Autobiography]). His father, Džumanbulbul, was also a well-known singer:

> Kičči uliniŋ Džumanbulbuldir āti.
> Oz waqtida šāirlarniŋ ustādi,
> har qanday toy bolsa, katta yiġinda,
> hamma elga pisand bolgan abyāti.

> (Zarif 1971: 8)

His (i.e. Mulla Xālmurād's, Ergaš's grandfather's) youngest son's name
is Džumanbulbul (the nightingale Džuman).
In his time he was a master of *šāir*s.
Whatever feast there was, in a big gathering,
his verses pleased everybody.

Ergaš continues to describe his father's mastery:

> Bir tāš yolga bārar edi dāwuši,
> āldida gapirālmasdi bir kiši,
> dāwuši sāz edi qulāqqa mayin,
> dāwušiga muwāfiq sāz čertiši.

---

[42]See Husainova 1976: 155-156.

[43]See Mirzaev 1979: 40-41; Zarif 1973: 8-12.

5   Yigirma xil āhaŋ bilan soz aytib,
     yigirma xil naġma, dombira čertib,
     xāh katta, xāh kičik ešitsa,
     har qanday ādamni balqitib, eritib.

     Šuytib otkan kozga dunyāni ilmay,
10   tāpkanin sarf qilgan, sira māl qilmay,
     šāirligin, čečanligin bildirib,
     bir damda yiġlatib, bir dam kuldirib,
     šuytib otgan u zamān Bulbulniŋ,
     hammani oziga qāyil qildirib.

                                        (Zarif 1971: 9)

     His voice carried the distance of a *tāš* (ca. 8 km);
     nobody was able to raise his voice in front of him.
     His voice was soft and harmonious to the ear;
     to his voice corresponded the playing of his instrument.

5   In twenty different melodies he sang,
     in twenty different tunes he played the *dombira*.
     Whether his listeners were big or small,
     he charmed and delighted every kind of person.

     Living in this way, paying no attention to the world,
10   he spent what he had gained, hoarded no possessions.
     He made known his *šāir*'s art, his mastery.
     At one moment he made people weep, at another he made them
         laugh.
     Living in this way in the time of Bulbul,
     he made everybody admire him.

Ergaš's father had three sons and two daughters, Ergaš being the
youngest child. The father was quite clear as to what he wanted his
children to do, or rather not to do:

     Bizga wasiyati: — Šāir bolma, deb,
     qoliŋga dombira, dutār ālma deb,
     men sendan rāziman, bālam, har waqtda,
     zinhār meniŋ kasbim sira qilma, — deb...

                                        (Zarif 1971: 11)

     His injunction to us was: "Don't become a *šāir*,
     don't take the *dombira*, the *dutar* into your hand!
     I shall be pleased with you, my child, at all times,
     if only you don't take up my profession!"

But despite these warnings Ergaš became a singer, and what is more,
one of the most accomplished Uzbek singers of this century. Ergaš was,

unlike most other singers of the past, literate; this explains why a
number of his *dastans* were written down by himself. As with other
singers, part of Ergaš's repertory consisted of *termas*; about twenty were
written down.[44] The narrative poetry recorded from Ergaš is of varying
length and character. In his œuvre there are eight traditional *dastans*.
Five of these belong to the *Köroğlu/Göroğli*-cycle,[45] one is a love-
dastan (*Kuntuğmiš*), and two are heroico-romantic *dastans* (*Alibek and
Balibek, Yakka Ahmad*).[46] In addition to these, fragments and abstracts
of *dastans* have been preserved, as well as his version of a Kazakh love-
romance, *Qïz Žibek* (written down by the singer himself). Ergaš also
composed the obligatory praise-poem on Lenin (*Ortāq Lenin*, "Comrade
Lenin").

The Uzbek folklorist Hādi Zarif has compiled an elaborate genealogy
of the "school" of Qorğān. According to his research, Džumanbulbul,
Ergaš's father, was the pupil of Borān-šāir (Kičik Borān, "Little Borān"),
who in turn was taught by a singer of the same name, Borān-baxši
(Katta Borān, "Big Borān"). These singers belong to a complicated
lineage, comprising over fifty names. They all ultimately go back to a
singer of the 17th/18th century, Yādgār-baxši.[47]   Looking at Zarif's
genealogy with its solid and dotted lines, and its single and multiple
branchings, one might wonder whether direct teacher-pupil relationships
and indirect influences are quite as clearly plottable as Zarif has
assumed. The idea of a "singer school" has in fact been criticized, in
particular on the basis of the many contacts singers had with other
singers of other "schools" and of other Turkic traditions. We have
already seen that Karakalpak singers had an influence on the "school"
of Nurāta; in a similar way Turkmen *baxšï*s have influenced the

[44]The Archives of the Folklore Institute of the Academy of Sciences in Tashkent
contain also a satirical poem (*hadžwiya*) and information given by the singer on the
"school" of Qorğān. See the list in Husainova 1971: 183-185.

[45]These are: *Dalli* (written down in 1926 by himself), *Qunduz and Yulduz* (written
down in 1926), *Xāldārxān* (written down in 1927 by himself), *Rawšan* (written down
in 1928), *Xuškeldi* (written down in 1936-1937, also by the singer himself).

[46]On the question of genre see Chapter Five. *Kuntuğmiš* was written down in
1926; *Alibek and Bālibek* was written down in 1925 by the singer himself; *Yakka
Ahmad* was written down in 1926. The latter is closely related to *Alpāmiš*; see
Mirzaev 1971.

[47]See Zarif 1970: 41.

"school" of Narpay, especially its most talented representative, Islām Nazar-oġli (1874-1953).[48] T. Mirzaev has, however, defended the notion of a "singer school," arguing that the art of the singers is traditional and is generally handed on from singer to singer in a teacher-pupil situation, notwithstanding the fact that multiple influences can complicate the picture and that with some singers or in some traditions manuscripts and printed editions also play a role in shaping a *baxši*'s repertory.[49]

The written transmission of texts is attested for the Khorezmian "school," which is known for its emphasis on the musical side of performance.[50] Other "schools" are the "school" of Qamay (in the province of Qašqadaryā); the "school" of Šerābād in the south of Uzbekistan, whose influence spread to southern Tajikistan; the "school" of Piskent with Berdi-baxši; and the epic tradition of the Uzbek-Laqay in southern Tajikistan.[51] I will return to some of these "schools" when discussing repertory, manner of performance, the question of "composition in performance," and the problem of written contamination in the tradition of Turkic epic poetry (see Chapter Eight). We will also meet one or the other of these singers again when looking at some of their poems in more detail.

The Kazakh *Aqïn*

The term *žïraw*, used for one type of Karakalpak singer, is also found among the Kazakhs. It is the term employed for some of the Kazakh singers of former times, such as Buqar-žïraw (1693-1789), who lived at the court of Khan Abïlay (1711-1781). Figures like Buqar-žïraw were not only poets but were also involved in politics as commentators on contemporary affairs and counselors of the khan. In more recent times the term *žïraw* denotes in particular the singer of heroic epic poetry and is of regionally restricted usage; it is found mainly in the Aktyu-

---

[48]See Mirzaev 1979: 49; Mirzaev 1978.

[49]See Mirzaev 1979: 42ff.

[50]See Mirzaev 1979: 56-59; Reichl 1985b: 625; see also Chapter Four, pp. 111f.

[51]On these "schools" see Mirzaev 1979: 50-56.

binsk, Kïzïl Orda, and West Kazakhstan provinces of Kazakhstan.[52]
The most widely employed term for the singer of epic poetry among the
Kazakhs is, however, the term *aqïn*.[53] Like other terms discussed so
far it is ambiguous. While *aqïn* denotes in its widest sense the poet in
general, and is hence the common word for "poet" in Kazakh, it has,
when applied to oral literature, the more restricted sense of an
improvising singer. "Improvisation" as encountered in the literature on
Turkic oral epic poetry from the time of Valikhanov and Radloff
onwards means various things. In regard to narrative poetry it
contrasts with "memorization" and stresses the fact that the singer has
not merely memorized a poem or a text. Put positively, the singer's
work and performance can be characterized by one or both of the
following: 1) he is capable of producing "new" epics (or branches of epic
cycles); 2) he is capable of what Parry and Lord call "composing in
performance," i.e. of creatively adapting a "text" to his audience.
Without wanting to anticipate my discussion of "improvisation" in
Chapter Eight, I will simply quote a short passage from E. Ismailov's
book on the Kazakh singers to illustrate the way the performance of the
Kazakh *aqïn* is dependent on his audience:

> In 1942 we had the good fortune to hear the epic of the Forty Heroes
> from the mouth of the well-known singer Murïn-žïraw (1860-1952), and
> to be present also at the performance of songs and poems on the theme
> of the Great Patriotic War [World War II] by Nurpeyis Bayǧanïn. It
> appeared that Murïn-žïraw could not always sing with the same
> enthusiasm. In the mornings and in day-time he sang very listlessly
> and unwillingly, leaving large gaps in the text. In the evenings, when
> a great number of epic fans gathered, who would not only listen but
> also accompany his performance with applauding shouts, Murïn-žïraw
> sang one and the same poem with pathos and with a great deal of
> beautiful and artistic detail. But when also in the evenings there was
> no such sympathetic atmosphere, he sang listlessly, pleading a headache
> and complaining about his bad memory, sometimes even refusing to
> sing. Asked why he could not sing the epic of the Forty Heroes in
> day-time as well as in the evenings, Murïn-žïraw answered that earlier
> on he performed the *batïrlar žïrï* (heroic epic) only in the evenings.
> This is completely normal, because only in the evenings and on holidays

---

[52]See Ismailov 1957: 47; Qarataev et al. 1972-78: IV, 552-553 (article "Žïraw");
Kunanbaeva 1987.

[53]See Ismailov 1957: 25-43; Qarataev et al. 1972-78: I, 239 (article "Aqïn").

could an *aqïn* count on a large audience, when everybody was free from his daily work.

(Ismailov 1957: 32)[54]

The picture of the *aqïn* as an "improvising" singer — in the senses loosely characterized above — is, however, more complicated. Leaving aside for the moment the question of what the composition of a new epic precisely means and also the problem of what "composition in performance" entails in the case of Turkic epic poetry, it must be understood that "improvisation" has yet another meaning when applied to a Kazakh singer, or for that matter also to singers of other Turkic traditions. The Uzbek *baxši* does not only perform *dastan*s, but also *terma*s, improvised songs. The same is true of the Karakalpak *baqsï* and *žïraw* as well as of the Kazakh *žïraw* and *aqïn*. Some of the genres associated with the performance of epic poetry will be looked at later. Here I will only single out the Kazakh genre *aytïs*. The *aytïs* (a derivation from *ayt-*, "to speak") is a song-contest, comparable to the Old Provençal *tenso*. There are many kinds of *aytïs*, such as the *qïz ben žigit aytïsï* (*aytïs* between a girl and a young man), *din aytïsï* (religious *aytïs*), *žumbaq aytïsï* (riddle *aytïs*), *aqïndar aytïsï* (*aytïs* between *aqïn*s).[55] It is probably fair to say that the *aytïs* is the favorite genre of Kazakh oral poetry.

My own experience with Kazakh oral poetry in the autumn of 1989 was mostly with *aytïs* poetry. The Xinjiang branch of the Chinese Academy of Social Sciences had, with the help of the Ili Province Writers' Union, invited four singers, two professional male singers and two women, to accompany me to Lake Sayram, where I was to stay in a Kazakh nomadic encampment.[56] The singers performed songs they had composed themselves, such as autobiographical poems; songs they had inherited from oral tradition, such as a long *aytïs* between two singers of the nineteenth century;[57] and also songs suited to the

---

[54]Ismailov continues by giving eight further examples of a singer's dependence on outside influences for his performance; see Ismailov 1957: 33-35.

[55]See Emsheimer 1956; Ġabdullin 1964: 297-316; Smirnova et al. 1968: I, 324-340.

[56]The singers were Božïqan Medelqan-ulï, Müslimbek Sarqïtbay-ulï, Qulan Quwanbek-qïzï, and Xayïpžamal Äbdilada-qïzï.

[57]These traditional, non-improvised *aytïs* are performed by one singer, taking the roles of both singers.

particular situation. It was the latter that would lead to singing contests, not only between the singers present but also with the audience. As soon as we arrived at our destination and were seated in the yurt, the professional singers unpacked their *dombiras* and started joking in song about the length of time it was taking our hosts to provide us with refreshments. These charges not only provoked laughter among those gathered in the yurt but also brought a sung reply from two women among the audience, who kept up a witty exchange with the professionals for quite a while. On other occasions, too, members of the audience would enter into a singing contest with the professionals although they knew they had little chance of winning. One man had high hopes that his son at least would one day get the better of the singers; his son was still an infant, for whom the father had already made a small *dombira*! These singing contests can last for days; on this occasion the singers kept up their singing, mostly in the *aytïs* manner, all night till about five o'clock in the morning.[58]

When characterizing an *aqïn* as an "improvising" singer one also has in mind his capability of performing improvised songs like the *termes*[59] and entering into singing contests in the *aytïs* manner. Ideally, "improvisation" would also comprise his ability to "compose in performance" and even to compose new epic poems. This ideal type is, however, not always met with in practice. Although one would like to differentiate the "improvising" *aqïn* from the merely reproductive *žïršï* or *öleŋši*,[60] both types can come together in one and the same singer:

> It must be emphasized that not everyone who performs with a *dombira* before an audience can be called an *aqïn*, a composer of new works. Among these performers there were also the *žïršï* and the *öleŋši*, i.e. the merely reproductive singer. However some *aqïns* combined in themselves both meanings, i.e. they were both improvising *aqïns* and reproductive *žïršïs*.
>
> (Ismailov 1957: 27)

---

[58]One of the *aytïs* in Müslimbek's repertory is published in *Mura*, 1983.2, 23-30 (see Sarqïtbay-ulï et al. 1983). — The texts of a three-day *aytïs* festival are published in Waxatov et al. 1963.

[59]The Uzbek word *terma* corresponds to Kazakh, Kirghiz, Karakalpak *terme*; the word is a derivation from the verb *ter-*, "to gather."

[60]The word *žïršï*, like *žïraw*, is a derivation from *žïr* [Old Turkic *yïr*]; *žïr* designates the heroic epic in Kazakh; *öleŋši* is a derivation from *öleŋ*, a type of lyrical song.

Ismailov goes on to list some of these singers, among them the celebrated singer and poet Džambul Džabaev (1846-1945).[61] Džambul has been accorded an exalted position in twentieth century Kazakh literature and he has exerted a profound influence on other Kazakh singers and poets. He was born in the Semireč'e (Kazakh: Žetisu, Seven Rivers) area of southern Kazakhstan near the Kirghiz border in 1846. Of a poor family of farm laborers, he became interested in singing very early on, an interest which was furthered when he was able to become the pupil of Süyinbay Aronov, a famous *aqïn* of his time (1827-1895). Džambul made his name by participating in public song-contests, where he was invariably victorious. After the Revolution, he was one of the most outspoken supporters of the Soviet regime. A great number of his poems celebrate the achievements of socialism, sing the praises of the leaders of the revolutionary movement, and take up topical themes of Soviet society. In 1938 Džambul was elected deputy to the Supreme Soviet of the Kazakh SSR. During the years of World War II, Džambul composed a number of poems on patriotic issues, such as his poetic tribute to the besieged people of Leningrad. He died on June 22, 1945, almost one hundred years old.

Among Džambul's works there are two long narrative poems, composed in the style of the heroic epic. *Ötegen-batïr* (Hero Ötegen) was written down in 1937.[62] The poem describes the exodus of the Kazakhs from the Žetisu region under Ötegen's leadership. Fleeing from an area of strife, warfare, and suppression, the Kazakhs, after a long and wearisome journey, in the course of which Ötegen defends them against several monsters barring their way, reach the land of Žideli Baysïn. There Ötegen dies. But his dream of finally finding freedom for the Kazakhs will only come true in the Soviet period, and Džambul ends his poem with a long eulogy of Stalin, "the hero of heroes"! Despite the political bias, the poem as such is traditional. Džambul learned it from Süyinbay, who in turn learned it from his grandfather Küsep, said to be the first composer of *Ötegen-batïr*. The plot of the poem is related to other Kazakh epic poems (such as *Oraqtï-batïr*); the point of reference

---

[61]This is the better-known Russian form of the name; the Kazakh form is Žambïl Žabaev. On Džambul see Ismailov 1957: 101-226, 320-323. His works are collected in Žabaev 1955; for a selection in Russian translation see Džambul 1949.

[62]The text is edited in Žabaev 1955: I, 133-161, and translated in Džambul 1949: 130-160. See Ismailov 1957: 136-150.

in history lies in the 18th century, when the historical Ötegen (born in 1699) lived.

Džambul's second narrative poem, *Suranšï-batïr* (Hero Suranšï), is even more clearly rooted in Kazakh history. Suranšï Akimbekov lived from 1816 to 1865 and took part in the campaign of the Russians against the khanate of Kokand. Süyinbay, Džambul's teacher, was Suranšï's contemporary and friend; he was among the first poets who celebrated Suranšï's heroic deeds after his death. There is no doubt that the inspiration for Džambul's poem, narrating Suranšï's fights against the khan of Kokand Qudiyar and extolling his brave opposition to feudal suppression, came from his teacher, although the precise relationship between what Süyinbay sang about Suranšï-batïr and Džambul's narrative is difficult to assess.[63]

It might be appropriate at this point to comment shortly on the uses of epic poetry to serve political purposes. Most of the Central Asian Turks have lived under Communist rule for over half a century. As, according to Marxism, all works of literature, whether written or oral, are part of a society's superstructure, there is a certain obligation for a poet to reflect his society's values in order to be heard. The Soviet Union has seen a certain amount of oral narrative poetry on contemporary themes, treated from a Marxist-Leninist point of view, such as Marfa Krjukova's *bylina* on Lenin or Fāzil Yoldāš-oǵli's *dastan Ā čildāw*, in which the fight of the Red Army against the *bāsmači*, anti-Communist partisans in Central Asia (1918-1923), is described from the Communist point of view.[64] Although the "actualization" of the tradition is itself traditional, heroic epics on the victorious path of Communism have not really become a vital part of the tradition. Indeed, Džambul's adulatory praise of Stalin is somewhat of an embarrassment today, despite the respect shown the Kazakh singer in contemporary Kazakhstan. When political themes are treated in poetry, it is not in the form of the epic or heroic song, but rather in the form of the shorter lyric, and it is among specimens of that genre that celebra-

---

[63]Džambul's text was written down in 1938; it is edited in Žabaev 1955: I, 162-196. See Ismailov 1957: 150-168; see also Ġumarova [Gumarova] 1956, who has studied the traditional diction of the poem.

[64]On Marfa Krjukova see Bowra 1952: 28, 116f., 339f. and passim. *Ā čildāw* has been recorded twice, each manuscript comprising about 900 pages, roughly the length of Fāzil's *Alpāmiš*. On topical themes in Uzbek epic poetry see Žirmunskij, Zarifov 1947: 458-496.

tions of the Communist Party or their leaders are to be found. We will not encounter the kind of political bias exemplified in Džambul's narrative poetry in the epics discussed in this book.

This is not to say that modern society does not make its demands on the contemporary singer. It is unusual today for Kazakh singers in Xinjiang to make a living from their art. One *aqïn* I was able to record in Xinjiang in 1989 worked as a manager of a fruit company in Urumchi. This singer, Šeriyazdan Soltanbay-ulï, was born on December 20, 1934, in Abitan Awïlï in the Altay District of Xinjiang; he belongs to the Törtuwïl clan of the Nayman tribe. He comes from a poor family and became interested in singing narrative poems at the age of seven. Šeriyazdan claims to know about fifteen *xïssas*,[65] many of which have been edited in the journal *Mura* and in the multivolume collection of Kazakh epic poetry.[66] He used to sing regularly, sometimes through the night, but his voice has unfortunately deteriorated. Šeriyazdan feels that today no one, at least in Urumchi, is interested any more in his singing.

Another *aqïn* I was able to record in Xinjiang in 1989 was exceptional in that he was still able to make a living from his art. Müslimbek Sarqïtbay-ulï is the manager of the Nïlqï District Cultural Hall, organizing folkloristic entertainment and responsible for the training of folk singers. Müslimbek was born in the autumn of 1946 (his exact date of birth is unknown). He comes from the *awïl* (village) Čoŋžï in the district of Nïlqï in the province of Ili. He belongs to the Džaŋbïršï clan of the Qarakerey tribe, which is in turn a tribe of the Nayman tribal group. Müslimbek began training as an *aqïn* in earnest when he was twelve years old. His primary teachers were his parents, who were both singers. His father, Sarqïtbay, was a famous *aqïn*, renowned in particular for his epic songs; he died in 1981 at the age of eighty-five.[67]

As I have said earlier in this chapter, the word *aqïn* is the general term for "poet" not only in Kazakh, but also in Kirghiz. As in Kazakh it also denotes the "improvising" singer, in particular the singer improvising *terme*s and similar lyrical genres. The singer of epic poetry is called *manasčï* or, if his repertory is focused on *Semetey*, a branch of

---

[65] On this term, often used to designate any epic poem, see Chapter Five, p. 125.

[66] On his singing-style and repertory see Chapter Four, pp. 107ff.

[67] On Müslimbek's singing-style and repertory see Chapter Four, p. 109.

the *Manas*-cycle, *semeteyči*. An earlier term is, as discussed above, *džomoqču*. The Kirghiz term *ïrčï* corresponds to the Kazakh term *žïršï*; as in Kazakh the term is applied to singers of narrative poetry who are "reproductive" rather than "creative." Judaxin glosses the term in his dictionary as "folk singer; rhapsode (performer of extracts of the heroic epic, normally memorized)."[68] What Ismailov said about the "purity" of singer-types in Kazakh in the quotation given above (p. 78), is also true of the Kirghiz singers. While some singers can be clearly classified as either "creative" or "reproductive," others can be less easily put in one or the other category.

The Kirghiz *Manasči*

Although the collection of Kirghiz epic poetry started in the 19th century, it is only in this century that the collecting of Kirghiz heroic poetry has been undertaken on a large scale. In Kirghizia an enormous text corpus has been recorded from Kirghiz singers, said to amount to over two million verse-lines.[69] Two singers are particularly famous for their versions of *Manas*, Saǧïmbay Orozbaqov (1867-1930) and Sayaqbay Qaralaev (1894-1971). Saǧïmbay's version comprises over 180,000 lines; it has been edited in four volumes; a bilingual edition with commentary in the series "Èpos narodov SSSR" is in progress.[70] Sayaqbay's version is by far the most voluminous of all Kirghiz versions. It comprises 500,553 verse-lines and treats of Manas, his son Semetey, and his grandson Seytek.[71] A full edition of Sayaqbay's version is also in progress.[72] Between 1958 and 1960 an edition of the *Manas*-trilogy in four volumes

[68] Judaxin 1985 [1965]: II, 439 (s.v. *ïrčï*).

[69] See Sadykov et al. 1984ff.: I, 443-491; Musaev 1979: 60-91. On *Manas* see also Hatto 1987a.

[70] For the edition of the Kirghiz text only see Orozbaqov 1978-82; for the bilingual edition see Sadykov et al. 1984ff.

[71] For a list of the texts recorded from Sayaqbay see Sadykov et al. 1984ff.: I, 458-460.

[72] See Džaynaqova, Qïdïrbaeva [Kydyrbaeva] 1984ff.; Qïrbašev, Sarïpbekov 1987ff.

appeared, a composite and adapted text made up from various versions, in particular Sayaqbay's and Saġïmbay's.[73]

A survey of Kirghiz singers from the 19th and 20th century distinguishes four groups, defined on a geographical basis: 1) the singers of the Čuy valley; 2) the singers of the Issyk-kul' region (Kirghiz *ïsïq köl*, "hot lake"); 3) the singers of the Tienshan area; and 4) the singers of southern Kirghizia.[74] These groups resemble the "schools of singers" discussed earlier in connection with Uzbek and Karakalpak oral poetry. According to this grouping, Sayaqbay Qaralaev belongs to the singers of Issyk-kul' region, while Saġïmbay Orozbaqov belongs to the singers of the Tienshan area.[75]

Saġïmbay, the older of these two singers, was born in 1867 in Qabïrġa on the northern shore of the Issyk-kul'.[76] His father was a famous musician, a *surnay*-player (the *surnay* is a kind of oboe). Saġïmbay started performing the epic *Manas* at the age of fifteen or sixteen. From the information we have, one of his teachers was Čoŋbaš Narmantay, another was Narmantay's pupil Tïnïbek (1846-1902). Saġïmbay was fifty-five years old when scholars started writing down his version of *Manas*:

> Qayum Mifatxov started writing down the texts of *Manas* from Saġïmbay in the summer months of 1922, with Ibray Abdïraxmanov continuing his work. The latter worked with the *manasčï* for about four years and completed the writing-down of the first part of the epic — *Manas* in the narrow sense — in August 1926. According to information given by people who knew about this and by I. Abdïraxmanov himself, but also according to Saġïmbay's personal "complaints," which were written down in verse-form at the end of almost every larger episode of the epic, the process of writing down the epic on paper did not always run evenly and under the same conditions. The work, begun

---

[73]See Yunusaliev [Junusaliev] 1958-60. This edition, often referred to in native criticism, has been justly criticized for its composite nature, as it does not allow us to assess any one version of a Kirghiz singer. Both Sayaqbay's and Saġïmbay's versions of the *Manas*-cycle have been criticized by A. T. Hatto for their length and innovations in style and content, in Hatto 1990: xivff.; for a discussion of traditional style and diction in *Manas* see Chapter Eight.

[74]See Kydyrbaeva 1984: 12-64.

[75]See Kydyrbaeva 1984: 26-30, 41-48; several traditions have, however, merged in Saġïmbay Orozbaqov (see Kydyrbaeva 1984: 48-50).

[76]On Saġïmbay see Äwezov [Auezov] 1961: 29-33; Musaev 1979: 51-55; Kydyrbaeva 1984: 41-48; Sadykov et al. 1984ff.: I, 444-445; Laude-Cirtautas 1987.

briskly and yielding fairly fruitful results in the first year (when the episodes from the initial events of the epic until the time of Manas' marriage were written down), started to drag more and more. The reason for this was in the first place Sagïmbay's difficult financial state; he had up to that time supported his family with his earnings from performing the epic by going round the auls. In addition to this, the singer's serious nervous illness could not have failed to influence the course of recording the texts, in particular the content and artistic level of the material dictated by him. This can be easily seen in the extant written records of the second part of the "Great Expedition," especially in the narrative of the events connected with Manas' death. Because of the deterioration of the *manasčï*'s health, the remaining parts of the epic, *Semetey* and *Seytek*, failed to be written down from him. Sagïmbay Orozbaqov died in 1930.

(Musaev 1979: 52-53)

Sayaqbay Qaralaev, the other great singer from Kirghizia, was born in 1894 in a place called Džeti-Oġuz in the province of Issyk-kul'.[77] He took part in the peasants' rising against the Tsar in 1916 and joined the Red Army in 1918. Having heard about Manas first from his grandmother, Sayaqbay learned the *Manas*-epic from the singer Čoyuke (1886-1928) of the "Issyk-kul' school." But, as a traditional singer, he also traced his talent back to supernatural inspiration:

> One day when I was riding in a place called Čïmïndï-say I started to feel unwell and, having become unconscious, fell off my horse. After some time I found myself in a yurt, where there was a young hostess who offered me meat in three bowls, one made of gold, one of silver, and one of copper. I ate some meat from these bowls and then went outside the yurt, where I was met by Almambet [one of Manas' companions] on his horse Sarala. He ordered me to perform the epic *Manas* and disappeared. When I woke up, I discovered that I was indeed able to sing about Manas without hesitation.

(Kydyrbaeva 1984: 29)

The *Manas*-trilogy was recorded from Sayaqbay in the 1930s and 1940s by various scholars; he also knew other epics, such as *Er Töštük*, as well as other genres of Kirghiz oral poetry.[78] In 1939 Sayaqbay was given the title of "Folk Artist of the Kirghiz SSR," and he has been awarded various orders and medals. Sayaqbay died in Frunze (Bishkek) in 1971.

---

[77]On Sayaqbay Qaralaev see Musaev 1979: 55-59; Kydyrbaeva 1984: 26-30; Sadykov et al. 1984: 457-458.

[78]See Kydyrbaeva 1984: 30.

One group of Kirghiz singers is not included in Kydyrbaeva's survey of "schools," namely that of Xinjiang. There are said to be over seventy *manasčï*s still alive in "Chinese Turkestan," some of them only in their thirties. The most famous of these is no doubt Džüsüp Mamay, whom I was able to meet twice in Urumchi, once in 1985, when he sang the opening section of his version of *Manas* to me, and again in the autumn of 1989. Džüsüp Mamay was born in April 1918 in Qoŋur-ölöŋ in the Qara-qulaq county of the district of Aqči in Qïzïl-su, the Kirghiz autonomous prefecture of Xinjiang. Mamay belongs to the Qïzïl-tuqum clan. His father Mamay was a herdsman and farmer (*dïyqan*); when Džüsüp was seven, his father sent him to a religious school, which he frequented all in all for only six months (going to school only in winter) and where he learned to read and write from the mulla; his father died when Džüsüp was sixteen. Džüsüp Mamay had no initiation dream and is sceptical about such visions. But he remembers that when his mother Burul was pregnant with his older brother Balbay, a soothsayer correctly predicted the sex of the child and announced what the boy's name would be. It is actually from this older brother that Mamay has learned his art. Balbay had traveled widely, even to distant Kashmir, and was an avid collector of Kirghiz epic poetry. He collected "branches" four to eight of the *Manas*-cycle for over ten years and wrote down what he collected.[79] Having become a revolutionary, Balbay was put in prison by the Kuomintang in the 1930s and died there. Mamay was also imprisoned at the age of seventeen. When he was released, his brother's material had unfortunately been lost.

Mamay tells how from the age of eight onwards he has been busy acquiring and enlarging his repertory. He can sing for twenty-four hours if need be, although nowadays he does not do so any more, as his voice has deteriorated. In 1961 he sang day and night for several months. At that time, scholars started to write down his version of

---

[79] I use the term "branch" as it is occasionally used for the individual members of tale-cycles or epic cycles such as the branches of the *Roman de Renart* or the branches (Turkish *kollar*, lit. "arms") of the *Köroğlu/Göroğlï*-cycle. While the *Manas*-cycle collected in Kirghizia consists of three epics, the cycle collected in Xinjiang consists of eight parts. "Branches" four to eight (*Kenenim, Seyt, Asïlbača-Bekbača, Sombilek,* and *Čigitey*) continue the trilogy into the following generations. According to my interlocutors in Urumchi, "branches" four to eight are only known in Xinjiang; they might very well be later additions. The edition of Mamay's version is in progress (see Mamay 1984ff.); its size is estimated at 24 volumes (see Hu 1982; Hu, Dor 1984).

Manas. Then came the Cultural Revolution and the recording of his poetry had to wait until a new start could be made in 1978. Mamay has a vast repertory of epic poetry at his disposal. Apart from the eight parts of the *Manas*-cycle, running to over 200,000 verse-lines, he knows a great number of *dastans*. When asked how many *dastans* he knew, Džüsüp Mamay gave the number twenty-five,[80] to which another eleven *dastans*, coming from non-Kirghiz traditions, have to be added; among the latter he mentioned the Kazakh epic cycle *Šayïmaran*. Besides epic poems, Mamay also knows songs and folktales. Like Ergaš, he is a literate singer who has written down some of his *dastans* himself, though helped by folklorists or relatives.

During my two stays in Xinjiang I was able to record epic poetry from two more Kirghiz singers. On October 19, 1985 I recorded the singer Abdurahman Düney, who at that time was fifty-eight years old, during a wedding-feast in the Kirghiz (winter-) village of Gäz in the Pamirs, about 120 km southwest of Kashgar. Düney sang an episode from *Semetey*, the second part of the *Manas*-cycle. He had not planned to sing at the wedding, but obliged me when pressed by the elders present at the feast. His version is quite poor as compared, for instance, to Mamay's printed version, but it is not without interest (see below pp. 229ff.). Unfortunately, I could not get any more information about this singer, who was possibly a *semeteyči* rather than a *manasčï*. A second extract from the *Manas*-cycle was sung to me in Artïš in the prefecture of Qïzïl-su by a man called Ärzi Turdï on September 23, 1989. The extract he sang is entitled *Almambetnin Armanï*, a complaint-mono-logue spoken by Almambet, Manas' milk-brother and companion. Ärzi Turdï is not a professional singer. He had worked as a telegrapher and knew some English; in 1989, aged forty-eight, he was editor of a Kirghiz-language journal. The poem he sang he simply remembered from his childhood, when an *aq saqal* had taught it to him.

At the same time, I was able to record the epic *Qurmanbek* from a Kirghiz singer who, although he did not make his living from singing, was certainly considered a professional by the local scholars and aficionados. Mämbet Sart belongs to the Čoŋ-baǧïš clan and was born

---

[80]Some of Mamay's versions of Kirghiz epics apart from *Manas* have been publish-ed: *Qurmanbek*, for instance, comprising 345 pages in print, or *Toltoy*, comprising 650 pages in print; see Mamay 1984; 1985. Among the list of unpublished epics are *Džurda*, *Qoyun Alïp*, *Batïr-bek*, *Kälde-bek*, *Tarlan*, and the *Köroǧlu/Göroǧlï*-cycle.

in Oytesken, Xinjiang, in 1942. He lives now in Uluĉat, ca. 100 km
northwest of Artïš, where he works as a forester and shepherd. He had
five years of elementary school and two years of lower middle school; he
can read and write. Mämbet started singing epic poetry at the age of
nine, in 1951. The epic *Qurmanbek* he learned as a nine-year-old from
his father-in-law Džamantay (who died in 1969 at the age of eighty).
Džamantay was, in Mämbet's words, an "improvising singer"; he had
learned the epic from his grandfather (*čoŋ ata*). Mämbet's version of
the epic is fairly conservative when compared with other versions
available in print. Mämbet has three pupils between the ages of twenty
and thirty; they learn the epic by writing it down or recording it on
tape. Apart from *Qurmanbek* Mämbet knows a number of lyrical songs
and can improvise songs (*terme*). He has also composed a narrative
poem about his life (*Ömür Dastan*). Mämbet sings the lyrical songs to
the accompaniment of the *qomuz* (a plucked instrument), but the epic is
always sung without musical accompaniment. He sings at wedding-
feasts and other feasts, but *Qurmanbek* meets only the interest of older
people.

Meddah and *Qïssa-xan*

Although various types of singers have been discussed in this chapter,
we have so far only considered singers who both transmit and perform
epic poetry orally. Written versions of epic poems can, however, also
play a role in the transmission of epic poetry. In some traditions, like
that of Khorezm, manuscripts or chapbooks are freely used by the
singers:

> It is well-known that in Khorezm the influence of the feudal urban
> centers, with which the life of the rural population of the small oasis
> was intimately connected, was particularly strong. Here singers who
> can read and write are not rare. They do not improvise the verse-parts
> of their *dastan*s, but learn them by heart, holding sometimes the
> manuscript of the poem in their hands as a help for their recitation.
> (Žirmunskij, Zarifov 1947: 55)

Written material is, however, also used by singers of other traditions.
A. Kunanbaeva quotes the Kazakh *žïršï* Alquwat as saying: "Normally three to four days suffice for me to learn any text. (Slyly:) But I also

make some notes, for myself."[81] There are also a number of popular
editions of Kazakh epics, which were prepared in Kazan in the 19th
century. These chapbook-like editions had some influence on the
transmission of epic poetry, just as modern, more scholarly editions have
sometimes influenced a singer.

But apart from singers using written material either in acquiring the
mastery of a poem or in actually performing epic poetry, there is also a
type of narrator to be found in the Turkic world who is often a reader
of texts rather than a "singer of tales." These narrators are called
meddah in Turkey, a word originally meaning "panegyrist, eulogist"
(from Arabic *maddah*, a derivation of *madaha*, "to praise"). The
Turkish *meddah*, although he often used manuscripts and printed
editions, was famous for his lively and often pantomimic style of
recitation:

> The meddâhs, professional narrators, are masters of oratory. They
> enact mostly comical situations from the everyday life of the lower
> strata of society, which on the basis of astute observation they copy and
> caricature. They represent these situations with humor and liveliness,
> favoring the form of the dialogue and imitating in it various dialects
> and voices. They emphasize their gestures through the use of a stick
> and a cloth.
>
> (Jacob 1904: 6)

G. Jacob adds in a footnote that "occasionally narrators degrade
themselves in front of a plain audience to become readers of chapbooks."[82] The *meddah* was also connected with the Turkish *orta oyunu*
(popular theater), from which he re-enacted scenes, and with the
Karagöz shadow play.[83] The tales he told were characterized by a
certain realism; they were in plain prose, without the adornment of
songs, and were hence quite different from the narratives in verse and
prose of the Turkish *aşıks*. The *meddah* was typically found in the
coffeehouses of larger towns. In modern Turkey this type of narrator

[81]Kunanbaeva 1987: 103.

[82]Jacob 1904: 6, fn. 2.

[83]See Uplegger 1964: 148-152.

has died out; the last *meddah* was *meddah* Sürûri, who could still be heard in the 1930s in the coffeehouses of Istanbul.[84]

Other Turkish terms for the type of narrator denoted by *meddah* are *kıssahân* or *şehnâmehân*. These narrators tell tales which are based on translations from Persian or Arabic, as is indicated by the word *şehnâmehân*, "narrator of the *Shah-nāme*," Ferdowsi's *Book of Kings*. Their repertory consisted also of the *gazavat-names* mentioned earlier (see above p. 54). The *kıssahân* or *qïssa-xan* (from Arabic *qiṣṣa*, "story," and Persian *xwān*, "reader") is, like the *meddah*, also found in Central Asia. H. Vámbéry, in his *Travels in Central Asia* (1865), describes the colorful life at the Labi Hāwuz in Bukhara, a famous square with an artificial pond in its middle, with its teahouses, shops, and its mosque of Diwan-begi, "where the dervishes and *meddahs* (narrators) tell the feats of famous warriors and prophets in verse and prose with strenuous gestures."[85] The activity of these *meddahs* and *qïssa-xans* was one of the main channels for the transmission of written poetry to a popular audience and hence also to oral singers:

> In the towns and the villages around towns there were also professional readers (the so-called *qïssa-xan*), who read popular books aloud to an illiterate audience, performing in the bazars or, by invitation, in private homes. On these occasions an experienced reader could re-tell a text from memory, with corresponding individual deviations. The folk singers (*ašulači*) had in their musical-poetic repertory works of Classical Uzbek poetry and music. Through these routes the influence of written literature has long since penetrated into Uzbek oral epic poetry.
>
> (Žirmunskij, Zarifov 1947: 28-29)

* * * * *

When the various terms for singers discussed earlier on in this chapter were exemplified by reference to specific singers in specific traditions, some characteristics have emerged which we can also find in other Turkic traditions, such as those of the Yakuts, Tuvinians, Altaians, Uighurs, Bashkirs, Turkmens, Azerbaijanians, and Anatolian Turks. There is no space here to treat all these traditions fully, and

---

[84]See Boratav 1973: 72-79; on the Turkish *meddah* see, apart from Jacob 1904 and Uplegger 1964, also Nutku 1976.

[85]Vámbéry 1865: 142; on the Karakalpak *qïssaxan* see Ayïmbetov 1988: 147ff.

even the four traditions we have looked at in more detail (Karakalpak, Uzbek, Kazakh, and Kirghiz) are in need of further elaboration. I will simply list the most salient of these characteristics, before taking up some of them again in subsequent chapters. In general, training for a singer starts early, often before the child (commonly a boy, but there are also female singers) has reached his tenth birthday. In some traditions the poetic gift of a singer is explained by an initiatory dream or vision (Kirghiz, Azerbaijanian, Turkish); in many traditions the singer's profession runs in the family, but there is no "singers' caste" among the Turkic-speaking peoples as in some societies. The apprentice singer has, as a rule, a teacher; this teacher-pupil relationship can become fairly formal, as in Uzbekistan. According to these relationships "schools" of singers can be distinguished in some traditions (Uzbek, Karakalpak, Kirghiz), although many cross-influences may make the construction of a "singer-genealogy" somewhat tenuous.

Despite the tremendous variety of singer-types, a certain dichotomy into "creative" and "reproductive" singers is discernible. The definition of what is to count as a "creative" singer varies from tradition to tradition, but it seems to imply in most cases that the singer is capable of composing a "new" song, such as adding a branch to a cycle of epics, and of varying his performance of an epic poem according to the demands of the audience. The "reproductive" singer is even more difficult to define. Some singers might be "reproductive" in the sense that they have learned an epic in a particular form and adhere to this form in the way one adheres to a memorized poem, while at the same time being capable of producing "improvised" shorter songs. In other cases "reproductive" might simply mean that the singer has a strong sense of textual stability, but does in actual fact vary his text from performance to performance, a variation made possible by his command of a particular technique. Many transitional forms and intermediate stages occur. In some of the epic tales in verse and prose — the Turkmen and Uzbek *dastan*, the Turkish *hikâye* and so on — some parts might be more variable than others. In the Khorezmian *dastan*s the verse-parts are fairly stable, while the prose, despite having its own formal constraints, is more flexible. Here, as in other cases, the factor of oral literature which has been written down is to be reckoned with. Many contemporary singers are able to read and write; they sometimes even contribute their own versions to the folklore archives or literary journals of their region.

The role of a singer in society also varies from tradition to tradition as well as from era to era. While the Oghuz *ozan* as represented in the figure of Dede Qorqut is, like the Kazakh *žïraw* of the 17th and 18th centuries, a respected member of the khan's retinue comparable to the Anglo-Saxon *scop*, singers like the Azerbaijanian and Turkish *ašïq* (*aşık*) have become popular entertainers in the coffeehouses, not unlike the minstrels of the Middle Ages. Professionalism has in many traditions become rare, although, as can be seen from the examples discussed, there are ways of surviving as a singer even in modern times. The archaic shamanistic nature of the singer has left its vestiges even in those traditions where Islam is the ruling religion (as in the initiatory visions, the manner of singing, and the use of particular musical instruments); it is more clearly visible in the Altaian, Tuvinian, and Yakut traditions. Some of these shamanistic features will be the subject of later chapters, as will questions of creativity, textual transmission, variation, performance, and repertory. I will conclude this chapter with a quotation from Radloff's introduction to his Kirghiz volume. Radloff cites a Kirghiz singer who answered the scholar when he asked him whether he could sing this or that poem: "I can in general sing every poem, because God has laid the gift for singing into my heart. He puts the words on my tongue, without my having to look for them. I have learned none of my poems: everything flows from my inner being, my inner self."[86]

---

[86]Radloff 1885: xvii.

Chapter Four

Performance

Ritualistic Aspects and Ceremonial Structure

At the beginning of the previous chapter I quoted a passage describing the quasi-ritualistic nature of the performance of Tuvinian epic poetry. What characterizes the performance of the Tuvinian heroic epic is also true of other Turkic traditions. Singer and listeners are united by a special bond, not just of physical togetherness, but more importantly of involvement in a ceremonial event. The parallel to drama comes to mind, in particular to Greek tragedy or medieval drama: the audience cannot sit back, following the unfolding action from the safe distance of a spectator or looker-on, but is drawn into the performance and takes part in it as in a rite or ritual. However controversial the origin of Greek tragedy might be, its close connection to the cult of Dionysos and hence its roots in rite are incontestable. As to medieval drama, we know that the great drama cycles of medieval England, for instance, though on the surface exemplifications of Biblical truths, are on a deeper level also re-enactments of divine mysteries, re-creating the history of salvation in a way not unlike that of the liturgy of the Church.

There are several aspects of the performance of Turkic epic poetry which underline this quasi-ritualistic side of it. One of them is time. A special time has been set aside for storytelling: the mood of the audience is festive, reflecting the outward circumstances prompting the performance, which are very often those of a feast or a celebration. The time of the performance is special in various ways. For one thing, a "subjective," "aesthetic" time is created in the act of performing and listening, which contrasts with the "objective" time-flow of everyday life.

93

The discrepancy between the experience of time in the course of watching a play, listening to a story or to a piece of music, and the "real" time of our clocks and watches is, of course, not peculiar to oral art. It is also characteristic of the reading process, as Proust has so well described in his *À la recherche du temps perdu*, when he lets his Marcel, immersed in a book in the garden of his aunt in Combray, wonder how quickly the hourly bell of Saint-Hilaire has rung once again, how even two hours have passed without his noticing it (*Du coté de chez Swann*). But unlike the reading of a book, which can be controlled by the reader, taken up and interrupted at his own pleasure, the performance of oral epic poetry is regulated far more strictly by social conventions. Only particular times are usual, even permissible in some traditions, for the telling and singing of epic poetry.

W. Radloff remarks about the performance of Abakan Tatar epic poetry that the heroic tales were normally recited in the evening, especially in the camps, where the men would spend the night during their hunting expeditions in autumn. He adds: "The reciting singer, illuminated by the fire and surrounded by the intently listening crowd, is a sight worthy to be portrayed by an artist."[1] The telling of tales, the singing of songs, and the performance of epic poetry during the hunting season is characteristic of a great number of Siberian peoples. This custom is found among the speakers of Uralic languages like the Mordvinians, of Tungusic languages like the Nanay or the Evenki, of Mongolian languages like the Buryats, and of Turkic languages like the Yakuts, the Khakas, the Shors, and other Turks of the Altai.[2] The telling of tales is here connected to the hunting-ritual: by singing and storytelling the tutelary spirits of the animals to be hunted are either soothed or even distracted so that they will no longer pay attention to their charges. The Yakut lord-spirit of the woods and animals, Baay Bayanay, was, according to Yakut belief, so fond of tales that the hunters would tell tales in the night before a hunt, and if Baay Bayanay was pleased, their success in hunting was assured.[3] In a similar way the Khakas would begin their storytelling by addressing the lord-spirit of the mountain with the words: "Listen and give us more animals, and

[1] Radloff 1893: I, 384.

[2] See Alekseev 1980: 244ff.; Trojakov 1969.

[3] See Alekseev 1980: 244.

we will tell you more tales." In order to ensure success in hunting, a singer would be taken on the hunting expeditions. There were special taboos connected to storytelling; thus it was forbidden to tell tales during day-time in the hunting season, also during the summer months.[4]

Although the performance of epic poetry is in some Siberian traditions linked to hunting and based on mythological ideas like that of a tutelary spirit of the animals or a lord-spirit of the woods, it is even in those traditions not necessarily confined to the hunting season. Among the Yakuts, for instance, a hunting (or rather fishing) expedition was only one of many occasions for the singing of epic poetry, the *oloŋxo*:

> Until the Revolution the *oloŋxo* was mostly performed in a family circle, which was furthered by the fact that the Yakuts lived in separate yurts, separated one from the other by great distances. In such yurts usually one or two (sometimes three or four) families lived.
>
> In the long winter evenings the heads of the families would invite a neighboring singer to come to supper and sing an *oloŋxo*. It used to be the case that the *oloŋxo* was performed by some traveling singer who had happened to come and stay the night.
>
> The *oloŋxo* was also performed at great gatherings and feasts: in the breaks during the time of fishing, horse-races, various meetings, but especially at the *ïhïax*-festival[5] and at weddings....
>
> The *oloŋxo* was performed in the evening and at night. The singers began to perform at about five or six o'clock in the evening and finished at midnight (and often also at daybreak). The performance lasted for eight to ten (and at times also twelve to thirteen) hours in succession, with short intervals. The sequel was performed the following night, and if that was for some reason impossible, the singer gave a short summary of the plot. In this manner they sang for one, two, three nights and more. From this stems the practice of how the people measure the *oloŋxo*: an epic which could be performed in one night was considered short, one which could be performed in two nights of middle size, and one which took three or more nights to perform long. The *oloŋxo* of the largest scale were sung in the course of seven nights.[6]

---

[4]Alekseev 1980: 260. By "tales" heroic tales are meant, i.e. narratives falling within the genre of "epic poetry" in its wider sense; see Chapter Five. Trojakov reports from one of his Khakas informants that ordinary tales could be told at any time, but the telling of heroic tales or of tales in which tutelary spirits were mentioned was restricted to special times; see Trojakov 1969: 32.

[5]A festival in spring when *qïmïz* is made.

[6]This short description of the performance of the *oloŋxo* is given by I. V. Puxov and G. U. Ėrgis, two well-known scholars in the field of Yakut oral poetry, in the afterword to the edition and translation of *Qulun Qullustuur*, one of the better-known

Several elements are noteworthy in this account. First, the singing of an epic poem is a communal event. There is either a feast of some kind, ensuring the presence of a group of people, or, if an *oloŋxohut*, a singer of *oloŋxos*, happens to visit someone, other people are invited to be present at his performance. Secondly, the epic poems are performed at night, sometimes lasting all night. Thirdly, the singing of an *oloŋxo* might last several nights, up to seven nights. All these elements are also typical of the performance of oral epic poetry among the Turks living further southwest, including those of the "central traditions." The occasion for the performance is usually a feast, often a wedding, but often also a religious festival. As the majority of the Turks we are concerned with here are Moslems, the most common religious context for storytelling is the month of Ramazan (*ramaḍān*), the ninth month of the Moslem year, in which the believers are required to fast from sunrise to sunset. After sunset, however, they are allowed to have a meal (*ifṭār*), and it is then that an assembly of people will spend the evening listening to the performance of a singer. In Turkey the singer is an *ašïq (aşık)*, a narrator of *hikâyes*,[7] and the place of assembly is the coffeehouse:

> The *hikâyes* are performed at wedding-feasts, during the long winter nights in the village rooms, near big and small towns also in coffeehouses during the Ramazan nights. Famous singers are persons whose art of storytelling has after the long time of apprenticeship become professional. In return for their art they receive their income in the form of a fee or also in the form of various presents. The *aşıks* who perform in the coffeehouses make a bargain with the owner of the coffeehouse and agree on a fee, in the Ramazan period often for the whole month.
>
> (Boratav 1973: 63)

This is precisely the situation which prevails also among the Moslems of Yugoslavia:

> Among the Moslems in Yugoslavia there is a special festival which has contributed to the fostering of songs of some length. This is the festival of Ramazan, when for a month the men fast from sunrise to sunset and gather in coffee houses all night long to talk and listen to epic. Here is a perfect circumstance for the singing of one song during

Yakut epics; Timofeev-Teplouxov et al. 1985: 553-554.

[7] Also called *hikâyeci*; on the *ašïq* see above p. 65f.; on the genre of the *hikâye* see below p. 127.

the entire night. Here also is an encouragement to the semiprofessional singer to attain a repertory of at least thirty songs. It was Parry's experience that such Moslem singers, when asked how many songs they knew, frequently replied that they knew thirty, one for every night of Ramazan. Most Moslem kafanas engage a singer several months in advance to entertain their guests, and if there is more than one such kafana in the town, there may be rivalry in obtaining the services of a well-known and popular singer who is likely to bring considerable business to the establishment.

(Lord 1960: 15)

The singing of epic poetry during the Moslem month of fasting is in the Central Asian republics a thing of the past; it was only as recently as 1990 that Moslems were officially allowed to observe Ramazan again. A thing of the past also is the singing of *dastans* at the courts of the Central Asian rulers in the 19th century. We have, however, accounts of such performances, like that of Ernazar-baxši at the court of emir Nasrullā of Bukhara (who died in 1860), of Rizā-baxši at the court of khan Muhammad-Rahim II of Khiva or of Suyar-baxši at the court of khan Khudāyar of Kokand. The *baxšis* of Khorezm are said to have taken seventeen nights to sing the *Köroğlu/Göroğlï*-cycle for the khan of Khiva, while Ernazar-baxši is, according to legend, said to have been able to sing for seventy nights in succession the epic *Alpāmiš*, inventing ever new obstacles to the hero's flight from the Kalmucks.[8]

The Uzbek *dāstān*, like the Yakut *oloŋxo*, is performed at night. This performance follows a fairly rigorous pattern:

When the singer (*baxši*) came to a village he stayed with his friends or with a person who had invited him specially and in whose house the performance was arranged. By the evening all neighbors had gathered in the house. The singer was put on the seat of honor. Around him, along the walls, but also in the middle of the room if there were many guests, the men would sit. In the old days women and children did not take part in these gatherings and would listen through the windows and the doors. The evening began with small refreshments. Then the singer sang the so-called *terma* (literally "selection") as a prelude to the performance of the main part of his repertory: short lyric pieces of his own composition, excerpts from *dastans*, sometimes songs from Classical literature — all of these songs works of small dimensions (approx-imately up to 150 lines), forming a unity by their function as a prelude, attuning the singer himself and his audience to the more serious epic theme. There are *termas* in which the singer enumerates the *dastans* of his repertory, turning to his audience with the question: "What shall

[8]See Žirmunskij, Zarifov 1947: 32f.; Mirzaev 1979: 19.

Performance

I sing?" ("*Nima aytay?*"). A special group in this genre is formed by
songs in which the singer addresses his *dombira*, the unfailing
companion of his poetic inspiration ("My dombira," "*Dombiram*"). Such
songs, which are interesting for their autobiographic elements, have
been written down from a number of singers (Fāzil Yoldāš-og̣li, Polkan,
Abdullā-šāir and others).

Then the performance of the *dastan* itself begins, which lasts from
sunset to sunrise, with an interval at midnight. Gradually the singer
enters into a state of inspiration; he "boils" (*qaynadi*); the word "boil"
(*qaynamāq*) is used in this context in the sense of "get excited, sing
with enthusiasm." The *baxši* himself uses at this point the expression:
"*Bedawni minib haydadim*" ("Mounting the steed I rode it hard"); his
dombira is the *bedaw*, the good steed galloping along. Physical signs
of the singer's inspired state are the sharp, rhythmic jerks of his head,
with which he accompanies the "throwing out" of each verse-line. He
is covered in perspiration and takes off one after the other of the *xalats*
(robes) he is wearing. Nonetheless, a good singer, a master of his art,
preserves the ability to listen attentively and sensitively during the
performance of a *dastan* to the reactions of the audience to his playing.
Depending on the degree of interest and participation shown by the
listeners, he enlarges or shortens the text of the poem. Even the choice
of the plot and the more detailed elaboration of single episodes take
their cue from the composition of the audience and its taste, as it is
known to the singer: among old people or elderly listeners he will sing
differently than among young people, etc.

At midnight there is an interval. The singer interrupts the
performance at a particularly interesting moment; on leaving the room
he leaves his top *xalat* and his belt-scarf, in which he puts his *dombira*
face down (*dombira tonkarmāq*), behind in his seat. During his absence
someone in the audience spreads his belt-scarf in the middle of the room
and everyone of those present puts whatever he has got ready as
payment into it, payment in kind or in money. This remuneration had
been prepared by the guests earlier, but depending on the quality of the
performance the size of the gifts gets larger or smaller. In addition to
these presents, which they brought along, in the old days the rich gave
the singer they had invited also more valuable gifts at his departure:
a new *xalat*, a horse, or livestock; among these gifts a horse was held
a particularly honorable present.

These performances of a singer continued for several nights, from
three or four nights to a whole week and longer, sometimes in different
houses in turn, by mutual agreement with the host at whose house the
singer was staying. At that time the singer performed one or several
*dastan*s, depending on the speed of the performance, which was in turn
determined by the interest of the listeners. An epic poem like *Alpāmiš*,
which in Fāzil's version runs to about 6,000 verse-lines in print,[9] with
a corresponding amount of prose, needed for its performance usually two

---

[9]The printed edition Žirmunskij and Zarifov refer to here is a shortened version;
on Fāzil's version of *Alpāmiš* see below Chapter Six, pp. 161ff.

nights (each part took up one sitting). If there was, however, a keen interest on the part of the audience, the singer was able to lengthen the performance by several times. The *baxši* left the selection of the *dastan* always to his audience, but the listeners themselves could ask him to sing according to his judgement.

(Žirmunskij, Zarifov 1947: 29-31)

It is usual with singers to introduce their performance of epic poetry with *termas* even in situations which do not conform to the one described by Žirmunskij and Zarifov. During my first field trip to Central Asia in 1981, the Uzbek singer Čāri-šāir (born in 1927), was given permission to stop work for the day and sing to me in the guest-house of the kolkhos in Buqa, where he worked. Typically he started off with a *terma* entitled "*Dombiram*," added another *terma*, in which he praised the Communist party, and finally moved on to epic poetry. Hādi Zarif, in his anthology of Uzbek popular poetry, has edited a number of introductory poems by various Uzbek singers. I will illustrate this genre by a poem entitled "*Dombiram*" from the singer Polkan (1874-1941):[10]

> Kārsāniŋ zardāli, qāpqāġiŋ tutdan,
> maqtaw bilan keldiŋ Qataġan yurtdan.
> Qutulmadim senday yāġāč naymitdan,
> tirnāqniŋ āfati bolgan dombiram.

> 5   Guyiŋ kelsa Polkan gapni oylamas,
> rayhān gulda bulbul senča soylamas.
> Gulduraw čiqasan fayzli keča,
> tāmāšālar qilar džem'i baybiča.
> Sen bolgansan menga adrasu-parča,
> 10 yalaŋġāčġa čāpān bolgan dombiram.

> Yaŋi tār tārtayin tāriŋni uzib,
> undan soŋ soylarsan suyagiŋ qizib,
> adamlar ketmasin madžlisni buzib.
> Maskaw, Nižniy, Qazan, Noġayni kezib
> 15 saharni qidirib yurgan dombiram.

> Your resonator is from the apricot tree, your soundboard from the
>   mulberry tree,
> you have come, full of praise, from the land of Qataġan.
> There was no hope that I could free myself from your wood,
> my *dombira*: you are a disaster for my fingernail!

[10]Zarif 1939: 50. I have somewhat regularized Zarif's text to bring it in line with the transcription system adopted for this book.

5   When your melody rises, Polkan cannot think of any words;
    not even the nightingale, sitting on the basilisk flower, can sing like
       you.
    Your voice resounds in the pleasant night,
    when all the women are filled with delight.
    You are my *adras* (half-silken cloth) and my brocade,
10   my *dombira*: you are a coat for the naked!

    When I mount a new string, pulling out the old one,
    you talk with fever in your bones,
    so that the people cannot leave and upset the gathering.
    You have roamed through Moscow, Nizhniy, Kazan, Noghay,
15   my *dombira*: you have gone for a stroll in many a town!

Introducing the performance of epic poetry by a recital of various songs and poems is a custom widespread among Turkic peoples. Turkish *aşıks* commence their telling of a *hikâye* by singing and reciting several lyrical poems, among them improvised poems addressing specific members of the audience.[11] Kazakh singers also perform a number of songs in a fixed order before they begin reciting an epic. The singer begins with a *bastaw*, an opening-song, in which he talks about himself, his teachers, and his repertory; he then sings one or more *termes*, songs devoted to topical or ethical issues; after an interval the singer resumes his performance, first singing one or more *tolğaws*, meditative poems on themes like the transience of life, before he begins the epic poem itself.[12] In a similar manner, the Karakalpak *žïraw* Žumabay, when I first recorded him in 1981, performed two *termes*, the first one on his *qobïz*, and a historical *tolğaw* (entitled *Ormanbet biy*) before starting the recitation of epic poetry.

Performance and Recitation: Musical Aspects

Turkic verse-epics are, as is the case with most oral epic traditions the world over, sung or chanted. Besides verse-epics, the mixture of verse and prose is, however, typical for many Turkic epic traditions, in particular the "central traditions." As the *Book of Dede Qorqut*, discussed in Chapter Two, shows, this form has a long history in Turkic

---

[11]See Başgöz 1975: 154.

[12]See Kunanbaeva 1987; on the genre of the *tolğaw* see Abylkasimov 1984.

literature. In contemporary oral traditions this form of narrative occurs mainly among the Turks of Anatolia and the Balkans, the Azerbaijanians, the Turkmens, the Uzbeks, the Uighurs, the Kazakhs, and the Karakalpaks, but it is also found in other Turkic traditions. In performance, the prose-parts of these epics are declaimed by the singer, usually in a loud and clear voice, with short pauses after each rhythmic-syntactic unit, while the verse-parts are sung or chanted. The discussion of the various types of epic singers in the previous chapter should have made it clear that, although there is some justification in talking about "Turkic epic poetry" and the "singer of Turkic epics" in general, distinctions must be made between different Turkic peoples and epic traditions. One of the distinguishing traits is the actual manner of performing epic poetry: while in most traditions the singer accompanies himself on a musical instrument, in others he uses no instrument at all. Among those singers who use a musical instrument some play a plucked instrument such as the *dutar* or the *dombira*, others a bowed instrument such as the *qobïz* or the *ğïdždžak*. Singing styles vary also from tradition to tradition, sometimes even from singer to singer. There is no space here to discuss more than three or four traditions and even here my discussion will have to be fairly general, leaving out musicological details and technicalities.

I will begin with the musical performance of Kirghiz epic poetry. The Kirghiz epic *Manas*, unlike most Turkic epic poetry illustrated below, is sung without the accompaniment of a musical instrument. If a Kirghiz epic (such as *Qurmanbek*) is in a mixture of verse and prose, the prose-parts are as in other traditions recited and only the verse-parts are sung. It has been noted that in the case of prosimetric *dastan*s, in particular love-romances, the *aqïn* plays a musical instrument to accompany himself, usually the *qomuz*, but sometimes also the *qïyaq*, a bowed instrument.[13] Although such *dastan*s in verse and prose are found among the Kirghiz, heroic poetry proper, and in particular the epic *Manas*, is generally in verse only.[14]

As to the musical performance of Kirghiz verse, the following points can be made. Kirghiz epic poetry of the heroic type (like *Manas*) is

[13]See Vinogradov 1958: 94, 112; Beliaev 1975: 18. The *qïyaq* is in appearance and playing technique similar to the Karakalpak and Kazakh *qobïz*.

[14]On the meter of Kirghiz and other Turkic oral epic poetry see Chapter Seven, pp. 172ff.

basically sung in a "stichic" mode. This is to say that despite melodic and rhythmic variation (which is normal) every line is sung to the same melody (or maybe better, the same melodic pattern). A singer might have more than one melody (or melodic pattern) in his repertory, which means that he changes from one melody to another in the course of his performance. Nevertheless, the verses are sung in a "stichic" mode, as these various melodies are not usually combined to form larger melodic patterns. A "stichic" mode is hence opposed to a "stanzaic" mode of melodic patterning. In the latter case regular metrical units like stanzas would be sung to a melody which is composed of several melodic phrases and which is repeated for every stanza. This is the usual way of singing Western songs. Kirghiz epic melodies are characterized by their regular rhythmic organization; from the standpoint of Western music the use of the terms "bar" or "measure" are appropriate.[15] While the meter might give the impression of irregularity (varying number of syllables), the rhythmic-melodic organization of the verse-lines is on the whole fairly regular, the music hence counterbalancing possible metrical "irregularities."

There is one particular melody or melodic pattern which is peculiar to the singing of *Manas*. About 60% of the epic is sung to this melody-type, called *džorğo söz*, literally "flowing speech," in Kirghiz.[16] Tonally, this melodic pattern is characterized by various features. The most distinctive feature of the "*Manas*-melody" is its final cadence, a descent from g or a to c, either in a succession of minor and major third (g − e − c) or major third and fourth (a − f − c). This melodic pattern is used by all singers; it is found in the *Manas*-extract recorded by R. Dor in the Afghan Pamirs and in the transcriptions of the melodies taken down from Toqtobek Bağïšev or Sayaqbay Qaralaev.[17] Among my own recordings the "*Manas*-melody" is prominent in the introduction to *Manas* performed by Džüsüp Mamay, as well as in an extract from

[15] A measure is defined as: "A group of beats (units of musical time), the first of which normally bears an accent. Such groups, in numbers of two, three, four, or, occasionally, five or more, recur consistently throughout a composition and are marked off from one another by bar lines." (Apel 1969: 513)

[16] For a musical analysis of the performance of Kirghiz epic poetry see Vinogradov 1958: 116-139; Vinogradov 1984.

[17] See Dor 1982: 4; Dor, Naumann 1978: side 1, band 1; Zataevič 1971: 189 [No. 130] (Toqtobek); Beliaev 1975: 17 (Sayaqbay).

Semetey of the *Manas*-cycle sung by Abdurahman Düney and in the episode from *Manas* entitled *Almanbetniŋ Armanï* contributed by Ärzi Turdï (see above p. 86). This melody-type can also be used for the singing of other Kirghiz epic poetry. It was used by the singer Sart Mämbet for his performance of the epic *Qurmanbek* (see above pp. 86f.).

The "*Manas*-melody" is, in virtue of its intervallic formation, to our ears both melodious and song-like, but other melodic patterns are more in the recitative style. V. S. Vinogradov, in his detailed analysis of the singing of *Manas*, distinguishes four melody-types. His fourth type is the "*Manas*-melody"; types 2 and 3 are far less melody-like. Type 1 is a kind of recitative which is equivalent to intoning, i.e. an essentially non-melodic utterance of verse-lines at the same pitch. The recitative-like chanting-style is found for instance at moments of climax in the story, such as battle scenes or emotional outbursts of the protagonists.[18]

While the performance of Kirghiz heroic epic poetry is monodic without the use of an accompanying instrument, the singer of lyrical songs and lyrical love-epics (the *aqïn*) plays the *qomuz*, an instrument also used for solo performances. The Kirghiz *qomuz* is a plucked lute-type instrument, with three strings and without frets;[19] the word is etymologically related to Turkish *qopuz*, the instrument employed by Qorqut and other characters in the *Book of Dede Qorqut*, as in the formula *Dedem Qorqut geldi, qopuz čaldï*, "My Grandfather Qorqut came and played the *qopuz*."[20] The instrument is associated with the professional singer, the *ozan*, as in one of the proverbs enumerated in the introductory chapter:

> Qolča qopuz götürüp ilden ile bigden bige ozan gezer. Er džömerdin er näkesin ozan bilür.
>
> (Ergin 1958-1963: I, 75)

> Carrying his *qolča qopuz* the *ozan* wanders from land to land, from beg to beg. The *ozan* knows the generous man and the stingy man.

---

[18]For melody-types 2 and 3 see Vinogradov's examples 7 and 8, respectively; Vinogradov 1984: 500; for melody-type 1 see Vingradov 1984: 493f.

[19]See Vinogradov 1958: 162-176.

[20]Ergin 1958-63: I, 243.

The *qopuz* (or *qolča qopuz*, "arm-*qopuz*") in *Dede Qorqut* is undoubted-
ly a plucked instrument like the *qomuz*.[21] This is borne out by early
loans of this word in non-Turkic languages, as in Middle High German
or Ukrainian, where the respective term also denotes a lute-type instrument.[22] Etymologically related to *qopuz* and *qomuz* is the term *qobïz*,
the name of the instrument used by the Karakalpak *žïraw*.

Among the Karakalpaks the *qobïz* does, however, designate a bowed
rather than a plucked instrument. The *qobïz* is an archaic fiddle comparable to the Yugoslav *gusle* and the Mongolian horse-headed *xuur*.
Many Karakalpak instruments have a horsehead like the Mongolian
xuur, and horse-symbolism, with the *qobïz* as a horse and the singer as
a rider, is widespread. This applies also to the *qomuz*, whose parts are
designated by such words as *teek*, "a small peg used to fasten the bridle
on the neck of a foal," for the bridge, and *qutqun*, "strings with which
the crupper is fastened to the saddle," for the tailpiece.[23] Once again
an intimate relationship between singer and shaman is implied. Among
the Kazakhs the *qobïz* used to be the instrument of the *baqsï*, the
shaman who had degenerated into a quack (see Chapter Three). Nora
Chadwick, in *The Growth of Literature*, has stressed the role of the
qobïz in the Kazakh *baqsï*'s exorcisms and magical cures:

> The *baksha* has no drum, but the articulate part of his performance,
> which forms the greater part of it, is chanted throughout in poetry, and
> is largely accompanied by the *kobuz*, and it appears to be exclusively,
> or almost exclusively, by the music of this instrument in the hands of
> the *baksha* himself that the latter brings himself into a state of ecstasy.
> (Chadwick 1932-40: III, 210)

With its horse-symbolism the *qobïz* carries the singer "away" just as the
ritual staff or the ritual drum are thought of as horses transporting the
shaman to the Other World:

[21]According to K. and U. Reinhard the *qolča qopuz* is a *qopuz* which has been
built with a long neck in order to facilitate using a bow; Reinhard 1984: II, 87. The
contexts in which the term *qolča qopuz* appear in *Dede Qorqut* do, however, not
suggest the use of a bowed instrument.

[22]See Sachs 1913: 221 (s.v. *Kobus, Kobza*); Sachs 1930: 216-217. On the Central
Asian *qobïz* see also Karomatov 1972: 107-110; Slobin 1976: 248-251.

[23]See Vinogradov 1958: 165. See also Radloff 1893: II, 59-60. In Mongolian
folktales the horsehead of the *morin-xuur* (lit. "horse-fiddle") is explained in a manner
similar to the European folktale of the singing bone (AaTh 780); compare Taube 1973.

The iconography of the drums is dominated by the symbolism of the ecstatic journey, that is, by journeys that imply a break-through in plane and hence a "Center of the World." The drumming at the beginning of the séance, intended to summon the spirits and "shut them up" in the shaman's drum, constitutes the preliminaries for the ecstatic journey. This is why the drum is called the "shaman's horse" (Yakut, Buryat). The Altaic [= Altaian] drum bears a representation of a horse; when the shaman drums, he is believed to go to the sky on his horse. Among the Buryat, too, the drum made with a horse's hide represents that animal. According to O. Mänchen-Helfen, the Soyot shaman's drum is regarded as a horse and is called *khamu-at*, literally "shaman-horse." ...

The Kirghiz [= Kazakh] *baqça* does not use the drum to prepare the trance, but the *kobuz*, which is a stringed instrument. And the trance, as among the Siberian shamans, is induced by dancing to the magical melody of the *kobuz*. The dance...reproduces the shaman's ecstatic journey to the sky. This is as much as to say that the magical music, like the symbolism of the shamanic drum and costume and the shaman's own dance, is one of many ways of undertaking the ecstatic journey or ensuring its success. The horse-headed sticks that the Buryat call "horses" attest the same symbolism.

(Eliade 1964: 173-174, 175)

Like the Kirghiz bard, the Karakalpak *žïraw* uses basically one melody, which is repeated with only small variations from line to line. The melodic pattern employed by Žumabay-žïraw is comparatively simple; it is characterized by a sort of recitation tone on f', a rising to g' or a' and a final drop to d'. As in Kirghiz epic poetry, there is no clear division into stanzas; there are, however, short solo melodies for the *qobïz*, breaking the verse-passages up into stanza-like units. The *qobïz* accompanies the singing by also playing the melody and varying it slightly. This kind of performance agrees closely with the musical style of the Serbo-Croatian singers.[24] The use of the instrument to give the singer a chance to pause in the recitation and to underline dramatic passages in the narrative corresponds also to the performance of Serbo-Croatian singers.

Entirely different from the performance style of the *žïraw* is the musical style of the Karakalpak *baqsï*. The *baqsï* typically performs love-romances; the verse-parts of these *dastans* in verse and prose are sung to the accompaniment of the *dutar* (Persian *dutār*, lit. "two

---

[24]On Žumabay's musical style see Reichl 1985b: 632ff.; on the Serbo-Croatian guslars see Wünsch 1934; Becking 1933; Herzog 1951.

strings"), a lute-type plucked, two-stringed instrument with frets.[25]
Among my recordings from Karakalpakistan are the performances of
two *baqsïs*, Ubayxan-baqsï and Genžebay-baqsï. Ubayxan Sadïqov's
(1931-1984) teachers were Eščan-baqsï and Žapaq-baqsï;[26] he himself
had three pupils in 1981. Ubayxan-baqsï performed a poem by the
Turkmen poet Maxtumquli (18th c.), excerpts from the romance *Ğarip-
ašïq* (*Ašïq Ğarib*), and a long excerpt from the *dastan Bahadïr*. This
dastan is the work of the popular poet Abbaz Dabïlov and treats in
idealized form episodes from the history of the Karakalpaks. *Bahadïr*
is interesting as an example of a literary work, written (in the 1940s) in
a popular style, which has found its way into oral tradition.[27] Genžebay-baqsï, whom I recorded in 1983 and 1990, sang poems by the
Karakalpak poets Berdax and Äžiniyaz, both of the 19th century,
excerpts from the romance *Ğarip-ašïq* and the *dastan Görug̣lï*, as well
as Karakalpak folk songs.

Musically the style of the *baqsï* can be characterized by a number of
traits. The melodic structure is more complicated than that of the
žïraw, one of the main differences being that it is stanzaic rather than
stichic, i.e. a poly-motif melody rather than a single-motif, repetitive
melodic pattern. This melody is song-like rather than recitative-like,
with an abundance of melismatic ornamentation. A good singer knows
a hundred and more melodies (*nama*). It is to be noted that the verse-
structure, too, is stanzaic; the love-romances are regularly interspersed
with poems in stanzas, often of four lines, the verse-lines being normally
of eleven or twelve (rather than seven or eight) syllables. In singing,
the *baqsï* prefers the higher ranges of the voice. Sustained notes recur
regularly; they are sung in a pulsating, vibrato manner with trill-like
ornamentation. When accompanying himself on the *dutar*, the *baqsï's*
playing is characterized by frequent modulations. This style is very
similar to that of the Turkmen *baxšï*, whose influence on the Karakalpak *baqsï* is also felt in the latter's repertory. The *baqsï* can also be
accompanied by further players, as Genžebay-baqsï by his pupil

---

[25]See Sachs 1913: 124 (s.v. *Dutâr*); Karomatov 1972: 123-134; Slobin 1976: 224-
235.

[26]On Eščan-baqsï see Maqsetov 1983: 140-159.

[27]See Maqsetov [Maksetov] et al. 1977: 214, 224ff.

Karimbay Tinibaev, who plays the *ğïdždžak* (a type of spike-fiddle).[28] This mode of performance calls for an attentive and sensitive collaboration between singer and accompanying player; the musical element in its rich texture tends to predominate over the textual aspect of the performance.

The Karakalpaks and the Kazakhs are linguistically and culturally closely related to one another, but this does not prevent their epic and musical traditions from exhibiting a number of differences. The Kazakh *žïršï* and *aqïn* accompany themselves on the *dombira*, a two-stringed, plucked lute-type instrument, without frets and somewhat shorter than the *dutar*.[29] Exceptions are, however, found. The Kazakh singer Šeriyazdan Soltanbay-ulï (see above p. 81), whom I recorded in Urumchi in 1989, contrary to tradition, did not use the *dombira*. He used to sing his poems to the accompaniment of the *dombira* but decided later to sing them solo, in order to give more prominence to the text of the epics, saying that in this way his listeners could understand the words more clearly. According to him, every poem has its own melody; without the right melody the epic poems would not be interesting to the audience.

This *aqïn*'s repertory is fairly wide. According to his information he knows about fifteen narrative poems (*xïssas*). Of these a number have been published: *Bögenbay, Qïz Žibek, Qalqaman Mamïr, Eŋlik-Kebek, Kešuwbay, Sätbek-batïr, Täwke-batïr, Abïlayxan*.[30] Some of these are historico-heroic epics (like *Bögenbay, Qalqaman Mamïr*), others love-romances (like *Qïz Žibek, Eŋlik-Kebek*), others historical songs (*Abïlayxan*). The singer also knows a number of historical *aytïs*, such as the *aytïs* between Axdanberdi and Kököyqïz or the *aytïs* between Biržan and Sara. In 1989, Šeriyazdan sang the third part of *Bögenbay*. In this excerpt he uses two melodies (or melody-types). The first is very close to a kind of psalmody chanting style, rhythmically fairly free, while the second is far more song-like and also far more rhythmically pronounced.

---

[28]On the *ğïdždžak* see Karomatov 1972: 110-116; Slobin 1976: 243-248.

[29]On the *dombira* (Kazakh *dombïra*) see Marcuse 1964: 295; Karomatov 1972: 116-123; Slobin 1976: 212-224; the word is etymologically related to *tanbur*, the "parent instrument" for this type of lute; see Sachs 1913: 375f. (s.v. *Tanbûr*).

[30]I have not been able to find the published versions of all the epic poems he said to have been published; for *Bögenbay* see Balïqšï-ulï et al. 1984: 74-287; for *Abïlay* see Egewbayew 1985: 1-84; for *Kešuwbay* see ibid.: 136-187; for *Sätbek* see ibid.: 188-208; for *Eŋlik-Kebek* see Egewbayew et al. 1988: 147-198.

Both melody-patterns are basically poly-motif melodies, corresponding
in each case to stanzas of four or more lines. When one looks for the
reason lying behind the alternation between the two melodic patterns,
it becomes evident that it is the metrical/formal organization of the text
which governs the change of melodies. The text is stanzaic, with stanzas
of four lines, rhyming a—a—b—a, but also with stanzas of more than
four lines. The verse-lines are of either 11/12 syllables or of 7/8
syllables. The first stanza reads:

> Ertede qalmaq xanï ölgen Šïnar,
> tuqïmï sol qalmaqtïŋ žawġa qumar.
> Žalġïz ul toġïz žasta qalġan eken,
> bul künde öz elinde xandïġï bar.

> In former times when the Kalmak khan Šïnar had died,
> the seed (descendants) of this Kalmak desired (to rush on) the enemy.
> His only son was in his ninth year;
> at that time he was khan over his own people.

As to the musical side of this stanza, the four lines of text have four
different melodic phrases, which are, however, fairly similar to one
another. The scale is clearly pentatonic, ranging over an octave. The
melody-type is both "concentric" in that it has clear "recitation tones"
as well as "tumbling" (in ethnomusicological terms) in that it "jumps"
up and down from the "structural tone" to the fifth and the octave.[31]

When the singer switches to his second melody he also changes the
meter. We now have stanzas of four and more lines with verse-lines of
7/8 syllables. The first stanza in the recorded extract where Šeriyazdan Soltanbay-ulï changes reads:

> Bügin žatïp kördim tüs,
> körgenim qattï qïyïn is.
> Elïŋnen saŋlaq žïyġïzïp,
> belïŋdi baylap, tüyinis.

> (Bögenbay is speaking:)
> Today when I was lying down I had a dream,
> what I dreamt was a very difficult affair.
> Gathering the best from your people,
> (Sarïbay) get ready, assemble!

As to form and range this melody is identical with the previous one.
The main difference is in style: there is both a clear rhythmic pattern

---

[31]For the description of musical styles in ethnomusicology see Nettl 1964: 145ff.

(a two-beat bar, so to speak) and a pronounced predilection for steps in seconds and their repetition.

The second narrative poem I was able to record from a Kazakh singer in 1989 is the heroic lay *Täwke-batïr*, sung by the singer Müslimbek Sarqïtbay-ulï (see above p. 81). Müslimbek learned this heroic song from his father at the age of twenty. His father's repertory consisted of more than ten narrative poems, among them *Qïz Žibek* and *Quralay Suluw*. According to Müslimbek's information, his father was illiterate, which was also true of himself at the time he learned *Täwke-batïr* from his father. Müslimbek's repertory comprises two narrative poems, *Qïz Žibek* and *Täwke-batïr*, as well as two long poems, song-contests between *aqïns* of the 19th century.[32] Müslimbek is a master of the improvised topical song and of the *aytïs*.

Müslimbek uses the *dombira* to accompany himself; his performance is generally more "song-like" than that of Šeriyazdan. His lay on a Kazakh *batïr* (hero) Täwke of the Nayman tribe is composed in four-line stanzas, rhyming a—a—b—a, with verse-lines of 11/12 syllables. Every stanza is sung to basically the same melody, which consists of four melodic phrases. The melody is clearly pentatonic, ranging over an octave; the singer does, however, exceed the octave occasionally, such as at the very beginning when he reaches up to a whole tone higher than the octave. His melody exhibits several structural tones (or mesa tones), the "base-tone," as well as the octave and the major third. We also get fifth-jumps and one-step patterns, thus combining some of the characteristics of the two melody-types used by Šeriyazdan Soltanbay-ulï.

Like the Kazakh *aqïn*, the Uzbek *baxši* plays the *dombira*. Other instruments are, however, also found; the Khorezmian *baxši*, for instance, accompanies himself on the *dutar* or the *tar* (Persian *tār*, "string"), a double-bellied plucked instrument of Persian provenience; some singers have also used the *qobïz*.[33] The prose-parts of the *dastan* are normally recited without accompaniment, but it is also possible that the singer performs them in a kind of recitative to the accompaniment

[32]His version of *Qïz Žibek* has been published in *Mura*; see Sarqïtbay-ulï 1982. The two long poems are "Tiržan — Sara aytïsï" and "Äset — Ïrïsžan aytïsï."

[33]See Mirzaev 1979: 11-12; on the *tar* see Sachs 1913: 377 (s.v. *Tār*); Zonis 1973: 156-159.

of the *dombira*.[34] There is some variety in the performance of Uzbek epic poetry depending on the region and the "schools" mentioned in Chapter Three. R. S. Abdullaev enumerates three geographical musical styles: the manner of performance typical of the Samarkand region, which is represented by the "schools" of Qorġān and Bulunġur; the performance style found in the provinces of Surxandaryā and Qašqadaryā; and finally the Khorezm style.[35] In view of the similarities between the first two styles and their common difference from the third, they can be grouped together somewhat summarily as the "Southern Uzbek style." A representative of this style is the *baxši* Čāri-šāir (born in 1927), whom I was able to record in Buqa, about 50 km south of Tashkent, in 1981. Without going into the details of musical analysis, I will merely make a few points briefly.[36] It is typical of this particular style of singing that the singer starts in a lower register, in a constricted, somewhat gutteral voice, and ascends into higher registers in the course of the song. At the climax the singer breaks into a kind of high recitative, called *qaynamāq*, literally "to boil," (compare p. 98 above). Although the melody is composed of only a few melodic formulas, it is by no means monotonous. The stichic basis of the music is recognizable, but it differs from truly stichic melodies in its greater variability. The melodic formulas are combined in various ways to build larger units, resulting in a more complex melodic patterning than in more archaic traditions as described below. The singer performs the song with great emphasis on his musical skill, in particular when singing sustained notes, which normally correspond to interjections such as *ey!* at the end of a line or a stanza. The *dombira* plays an active part, both as an accompanying instrument and as a solo instrument between stanzas.

There is some variety in the musical performance of the Uzbek *dastan* depending to a certain degree on the metrical and formal structure of the epic poem. Type-scenes like the hero's ride through the desert or battle-scenes, encountered above all in heroic *dastan*s like some of the

---

[34]See Abdullaev 1989: 114, who notes that some singers perform both prose and verse in the same recitative manner to the accompaniment of the *dombira*.

[35]See Abdullaev 1989: 114; he adds the Karakalpak style as a fourth style found in Uzbekistan.

[36]See also Reichl 1985b: 618-623.

branches of the *Köroğlu/Göroğli*-cycle, are typically in "laisse-type" verse-portions with lines of 7 or 8 syllables.[37]   The verse-parts of love-*dastans* are, on the other hand, usually stanzaic, often in 11/12-syllable lines. While the lyrical verse-interludes in the romances are musically closer to the folk song in their melodious composition, the laisse-type octosyllabic lines are often sung to a faster beat, in particular when they describe the hero's ride, with the *dombira* imitating the galloping of the horse.

The hallmark of the Khorezmian *baxši* is the preponderance of a melodious musical style, close to the folk song and far removed from the stichic melodies of singers like the Karakalpak *žïraw*. The sung parts of the *dastans* exhibit a rich musical texture, with a great deal of ornamentation and melodic elaboration and variety.[38] Another characteristic of this tradition is also indicative of the importance the musical side plays in the performance of epic poetry, namely the fact that the *baxši* does not only accompany himself on a lute-type instrument but is further accompanied by a small ensemble. The fiddle *ğïdždžak* and the flute *bulamān* are represented, as well as various other instruments.[39] A number of recordings of Khorezmian *dastans* have been issued on records from the singer Rozimbek Murādov, who is a professional musician and who graduated from the conservatory in Tashkent. He plays the *tar* and is accompanied by players of various string-instruments and drums, *dutar*-players, *ğïdždžak*-players, and players of the *dāira* (a kind of tambourine).[40]

The oasis of Khorezm has both through its historical importance and its geographical position served as a central point in the transmission of epic poetry and musical styles in Central Asia. The Karakalpak *baqsï*, the Khorezmian *baxši* and the Turkmen *baxšï* overlap not only in their repertory (see Chapter Eight, pp. 249ff.), but also show many similarities in the way they sing and play. The most salient features

---

[37]See Chapter Seven, pp. 172ff.

[38]See Mirzaev, 1979: 57; Abdullaev 1989: 115-116.

[39]On the *bulamān* see Vertkov, Blagodatov, Jazovickaja 1963: 118 (*balabán*).

[40]On the record *Goroğli wa Bāzirgān* (Melodija), for instance, he is accompanied by a *dutar*-player and two *dāira*-players; on the *dāira* see Sachs 1913: 104 (s.v. *Dâire*); Slobin 1976: 264-269. For further details on this singer's performance, see Reichl 1985b: 625-628.

are vocal and instrumental virtuosity, melodic variety, and strophic, song-like melodies. Such a characterization is, of course, a gross oversimplification and does not take into account the idiosyncrasies found in the various traditions and among the different singers. But it does set these styles off from the performance manner of, for instance, the Kirghiz *manasčï* or the Karakalpak *žïraw*. Viewed from a wider perspective, this group of styles accords in many respects with the way Azerbaijanian *ašïq*s and Turkish *aşık*s perform the *dastan* and the *hikâye*. In both traditions the singer sings the verse-parts to the accompaniment of a plucked instrument, the *dutar* in Azerbaijan and the *saz* or *bağlama* in Turkey.[41]

I have mentioned that some singing-styles like that of the "southern Uzbek" *baxši* are characterized by a constricted voice, a tense, "laryngeal" articulation. R. S. Abdullaev calls this singing-style "*gortannaja pevčeskaja manera*," "guttural" or "laryngeal singing-style," "throat-singing."[42] This manner of singing brings us once again back to the shamanistic aspects of Turkic epic poetry. Just as some of the instruments of the singers, like the *qobïz*, remind us of the close connection between singer and shaman, so does this particular manner of singing. Singing with a "pressed," tense voice is attested for the performance of the Central Asian shaman (or his successor the quack) just as a peculiar type of "throat-singing" characterizes both the shaman and the epic singer in several Altaian traditions. A. Kunanbaeva quotes one of the singers she worked with as saying: "The voice of Žienbay was the voice of a real *žïraw*, close to the voice of a *baqsï* [shaman]..."[43] This closeness between singer and shaman is particularly noticeable in the Altai. As we have seen earlier, the Altaian term for singer, *qayčï*, is derived from the verb *qay-*, "to sing (in a particular manner)" (see p. 63). This particular "manner" is closely related to the famous "throat-sing-

[41]The term *saz* denotes the family of instruments in question (lute-type instruments with frets); the *bağlama* is a large *saz*; see Sachs 1913: 335 (s.v. *Sâz*); Reinhard 1984: II, 90-93. — For musical transcriptions of the various verse-parts in a Turkish version of *Köroğlu* see Arsunar 1963; for the performance of the *dastan Köroğlu* by the Azerbaijanian *ašïq*, also in comparison with the art of the Turkish minstrel, see Mamedov 1984. Transcriptions of melodies of the Turkish *aşık* are also found in Başgöz 1975; on the performance of the *aşık* see also Reinhard 1984: II, 104-120.

[42]Abdullaev 1989: 115.

[43]Kunanbaeva 1987: 108.

ing" of the Tuvinians and Altaians. In my short survey of the terms for "singer" in the Turkic languages, I commented on the etymological connection between the verb *qay-* and words denoting "the spirit of a shaman" or "illness" in other Turkic languages, underlining the shamanistic background to epic singing and epic performance. There is no space here to pursue this question and to give a detailed description of the performance of the Altaian *qayčï*, the Khakas *xaydžï*, the Tuvinian *toolču*, or the Yakut *oloŋxohut*, as these traditions lie outside the scope of this book. It should be borne in mind, however, that an older shamanistic world lies at the basis also of the "central traditions" of Turkic oral epic poetry, a world which would need closer scrutiny if the most archaic layers of Turkic epic poetry were to be uncovered.[44]

Singer and Audience

The close bond knitting singer and audience together and the dependence of the singer on his audience have been repeatedly remarked not only in reference to Turkic epic poetry, but also in reference to other traditions of the oral epic. Maximilian Braun specifies three functions of the audience for the Serbo-Croatian singer: the listeners form a kind of "resonator" for the singer's performance and influence by their behavior the quality of the recitation; they are also the "real" carriers of the tradition insofar as their taste determines the choice of poems and thereby acts as a selective mechanism for the survival of particular songs; and the audience can finally participate actively in the performance, not only by choosing particular songs but also by eliciting particular versions, in which for instance their own families and clans are duly considered.[45]

Although the importance of the singer-audience relationship has been understood since the early 19th century, there are almost no studies devoted to this aspect of performance. The main reason for this dearth of material is doubtless the fact that the major part of epic poetry has been recorded under studio conditions. Most scholars in the former

[44]For a description of the musical performance of the Altaian *qayčï* see Šul'gin 1973; of the Khakas *xaydžï* see Stojanov 1988; for a discussion of the performance of the Yakut *oloŋxohut* see Illarionov 1982: 96-115.

[45]Braun 1961: 84-85.

Soviet Union and in China write the texts down from dictation; the
tape recorder is only occasionally used. As to Western scholars working
in this area, they are handicapped by the severe limitations imposed on
their movement and are hence obliged to record wherever they are able
to get in contact with a singer. This applies also to my recordings.
Although I have recorded oral poetry in yurts and during *toy*s and
although a number of my recordings were made in private homes or
guesthouses with an appreciative audience present, many were also
made in the rooms of the Academy of Sciences or the University in
Nukus or in hotel rooms in various Chinese towns. Even then, however,
the presence of an audience and in particular their reaction to the
singer were important. Exclamations of wonder or of applause had
always to punctuate a singer's performance, otherwise his interest in
singing and in giving his best would have slackened. These exclamations and mutterings of the audience are in large part formulaic. "At
certain moments the singer stands in need of the support of the
audience, which expresses itself in exclamation-formulas and increases
his strength by its approval."[46]

A good singer transports his audience, and a good audience influences
and furthers the singer's performance. The effect of a passionate
performance on an impressionable audience has been vividly described
by the Hungarian Turkologist H. Vámbéry, who in 1863 traveled to
Central Asia in the disguise of an Ottoman dervish. He writes in the
preface to his edition and translation of the Uzbek *dastan Yusuf and
Ahmad*:

> I think back with fondness to those moments of my life in disguise
> on the Lower Oxus, when I listened, in the heat of summer, lying in the
> company of Uzbek men in the shade of the enormous *qāra-yāġāč* ..., to
> the reading of the popular epic here edited. Among the listeners some
> were staring, brooding gloomily, others were jerking their limbs and
> letting their flaming eyes rove in the distance, while the younger
> members of the company were groaning, sighing and shouting: "Ya
> Allah, ya Allah!" They were seized by martial fervor and could hardly
> restrain their impatience to go to war.[47]

[46]Kunanbaeva 1987: 108.

[47]Vámbéry 1911: 6-7. The *qāra-yāġāč*, lit. "black tree," is a kind of elm. Vámbéry
does not explain who the reader was, a professional storyteller (*qïssa-xān*), a singer
using a text, or simply someone who could read and write.

But the audience can also be critical. Fāzil Yoldāš-oġli is said to have been criticized by a villager when singing the love-epic *Sanābar-xān* on the grounds that he should stop all these sighing and complaining songs of the unhappy lovers and rather "sing from heroic *dāstāns*, which strengthen our spirit" ("...*bizga ruhimizni kotaradigan qahramānlik dāstānlaridan kuyla*").[48] This brings to mind the appeal to a Serbo-Croatian singer shouted by one of his listeners, which was reported by M. Murko: "Decorate the man and the horse properly, you don't have to pay for it!"[49] The influence of the audience on the singer has also been noted by W. Radloff. One of the poems of *Manas* recorded by him, the third in his edition, shows some idiosyncracies of plot which Radloff attributes to his presence:[50]

> Talking about this [third] episode I would like to draw attention to the fact that during his whole performance the singer represents Manas as a friend of the White Tsar (the Russian emperor) and of the Russian people. The Tsar intervenes everywhere in the course of the narrative as an active protagonist. This involvement of the Tsar has been motivated by my presence alone; the singer thought that the Russian civil servant could take it amiss that Manas had defeated also the Russians; he provided hence a change which would please me. This occurrence shows us clearly how the singer pays heed to his listeners in the course of his performance.
>
> (Radloff 1885: xiv)

The most detailed description of the interaction between singer and audience in the Turkic world has been given by İ. Başgöz. Başgöz reports on two performances of the same *hikâye* by the Anatolian *aşık* Müdami.[51] Müdami performed his *Öksüz Vezir* (The Orphan Vezir) first before a traditional audience in the coffeehouse of Poshof in eastern Anatolia, then before a select audience of teachers and local dignitaries in the teachers' union hall. Although the two versions of the *hikâye*, both in their prose- and in their verse-parts, are basically identical,

[48]Mirzaev 1979: 23; see also Žirmunskij, Zarifov 1947: 35.

[49]*Nakiti momka i konja, nećeš mu za svoje pare kupovati.* See Braun 1961: 62.

[50]As A. T. Hatto points out in his critical re-edition of Radloff's version of *Manas*, "we have no means of knowing whether Radloff was right in surmising that this general background of Russian overlordship was due entirely to his own presence, since unfortunately we are not told whether the recording of the poem was tête-à-tête or before a group of Kirghiz listeners." Hatto 1990: 73.

[51]See Başgöz 1975 and 1986b.

there are numerous deviations in the second version. The audience Müdami had in the teachers' union was clearly unappreciative (some members of the audience left in the course of the performance), which caused the singer to leave out most of his personal asides and digressions, as well as several introductory songs. His story becomes far less lively and witty, and his involvement is quite clearly minimal.

One sign of the singer's involvement with his tale is when he starts to cry at specific points in the story, obviously identifying with the misfortune of his protagonists.[52] The identification of the narrator with his protagonists has been aptly termed "breakthrough into performance" by Dell Hymes in his studies of American Indian narrators, who at particular points in the telling of a story switch from the language of the story into the language of the character.[53] In Turkic oral epic poetry this "breakthrough into performance" is also accomplished by the musical and mimic execution of an epic. In Uzbek the singing-style changes from singing to recitative at what is graphically called the "boiling point" of an episode (*qaynamāq*). Similar observations have been made among Kirghiz singers:

> Qaralaev repeats in "Qanïkey's *arman*"[54] one and the same recitative-like melody up to ten times, but endows it each time with new expressive nuances: now an exclamation, now a simple cry, now a loud sigh, here he uses strong accents, there soft, smooth transitions etc. In quick succession major and minor thirds alternate. At times the number of syllables per line increases, then the musical rhythm becomes fragmented, the sentence longer. But the descending cadence leaves the strongest impression: fifth, fourth, tonic. Tensing his vocal chords, Qaralaev accentuated these notes normally by a guttural timbre, singing the last note crescendo to *ff* and cutting it off suddenly. Sometimes he changed this recitative-like melody for another, a rhythmically and metrically more pronounced melody. The whole *arman* was structured by their alternation, adapted to the two-line stanza, the *beyt*.
>
> (Vinogradov 1984: 494)

It is interesting to note that the tensing of the voice, discussed above, is here interpreted as a dramatic effect. The dramatic component in

---

[52]See Başgöz 1975: 196, 197.

[53]See Hymes 1981: 79ff.

[54]Qanïkey is Manas' favorite wife. The *arman* (from Persian *ārmān*, "unfulfilled desire, regret") is a melancholy-meditative type of song.

Qaralaev's — as in any other good singer's — performance is also enhanced by the singer's gestures. Unfortunately, Qaralaev, as many other great singers of Central Asia, lived before the age of video-recording so that photographs are all we possess.[55] Although for an adequate interpretation of oral epic poetry the live performance under traditional, "natural" circumstances must be the object of inquiry,[56] our fragmentary knowledge of actual performances imposes severe limitations on our interpretations of Turkic epic poetry, limitations which can only be partially overcome by piecing together what ethnographic scraps chance has left us.

[55]Some of Qaralaev's gestures are illustrated by the photographs in Kydyrbaeva 1984: plates 1-4.

[56]This has been emphatically stressed in Hatto 1989b and 1991.

Chapter Five

Genre

However, the origin of the words drama, epic, and lyric suggests that the central principle of genre is simple enough. The basis of generic distinction in literature appears to be the radical of presentation. Words may be acted in front of a spectator; they may be spoken in front of a listener; they may be sung or chanted; or they may be written for a reader.... The basis of generic criticism in any case is rhetorical, in the sense that the genre is determined by the conditions established between the poet and his public.

Northrop Frye, *An Anatomy of Criticism*[1]

Epic

Turkic epic poetry is, as we have seen, often performed at specific times, in some traditions even at particular seasons like the hunting and fishing season. Setting aside a special time for the telling of tales is not confined to the Turks and other peoples of Siberia; it is of widespread, if not universal occurrence. The British anthropologist B. Malinowski gives a vivid account of the Trobriand islanders' special time for storytelling, which is in many ways comparable to the descriptions given of the Khakas or Yakuts:

> Late in November the wet weather is setting in. There is little to do in the gardens, the fishing season is not in full swing as yet, overseas sailing looms ahead in the future, while the festive mood still lingers after the harvest dancing and feasting. Sociability is in the air, time lies on their hands, while bad weather keeps them often at home. Let us step through the twilight of the approaching evening into one of their villages and sit at the fireside, where the flickering light draws

[1]Frye 1957: 246-247.

119

more and more people as the evening falls and the conversation brightens. Sooner or later a man will be asked to tell a story, for this is the season of *fairy tales.* If he is a good reciter, he will soon provoke laughter, rejoinders, and interruptions, and his tale will develop into a regular performance.

At this time of the year folk-tales of a special type called *kukwanebu* are habitually recited in the villages. There is a vague belief, not very seriously taken, that their recital has a beneficial influence on the new crops recently planted in the gardens. In order to produce this effect, a short ditty in which an allusion is made to some very fertile wild plants, the *kasiyena*, must always be recited at the end.

(Malinowski 1926: 20-21)

The Trobrianders also have two other types of story. The second type of story has no magical effects and its telling is tied neither to a special season nor to a particular manner of performance. These stories are, in distinction to the *kukwanebu*, stories which are believed to be true. Although, as Malinowski explains, one might be inclined to differentiate various subtypes of these "true stories" — such as historical accounts, legends, and hearsay tales — the Trobrianders designate them all by the same term, *libwogwo.* There is finally a third type, stories which are regarded as sacred, i.e. sacred tales and myths, called *liliu* by the islanders.[2] One of the reasons why Malinowski reproduces the native taxonomy of stories rather than imposing his own is that in his opinion a classification and typology of narrative entirely based on the text is inadequate for a full understanding of these types. In adopting a native classification one takes into account that a story is not just a text but also a social and cultural event. The "essence" of a particular type of story "is not to be found in a mere perusal of the story, but in the combined study of the narrative and its context in the social and cultural life of the natives."[3]

Malinowski's approach is favored by anthropologists, ethnographers, folklorists, and sociolinguists. Much attention has been paid to genre in the analysis of communicative events, and folklore genres have been studied intensively by folklorists and anthropologists.[4] It is generally

[2]Malinowski 1926: 20-28.

[3]Malinowski 1926: 27-28.

[4]See the examples in Saville-Troike 1989: 30ff.; for various approaches in folklore studies see the collections of articles by Ben-Amos 1976 and Oring 1989; on the importance of performance factors see also Abrahams 1976.

recognized that the native taxonomy should serve as basis for genre distinctions and that both textual and extratextual factors must enter into the definition of narrative genres. For V. Propp, for instance, a folklore genre "is defined by its poetics, by its use in life, by the form of its performance, and by its relationship to music."[5] These classification principles can — and should — also be applied to Turkic oral epic poetry. There is a close connection between manner of performance and type of narrative, between text and occasion, between a particular type of singer and his repertory in Turkic oral narrative. In order to arrive at a better understanding of the generic nature of Turkic epic poetry one has to look both at the textual side of the narratives (loosely, form and content) and at the performance side of the "epics," ranging from the manner of recitation to their place within the value system of a society. This is not to say that when talking of Turkic epic poetry the Aristotelian notions of genre have to be abandoned. Much of what Aristotle and the Western literary tradition have to say about epic poetry is indeed helpful and valuable also for an understanding of Turkic oral epic poetry, but the literary scholar's theorizing must be supplemented by the account of the ethnographer (and musicologist) to be fully appropriate to the subject of our study.

The theoretical literature on genre in general and on the epic in particular is so vast that there can be no question of reviewing it in the present context.[6] Some distinctions will nevertheless have to be made in order to avoid misunderstandings in my discussion of Turkic oral epic poetry. The Aristotelian definition of epic — or as he calls it, *epopoiía*, epopee — is a convenient starting-point. According to Aristotle the epic is representational (*mimētikḗ*) and narrative (*diēgēmatikḗ*), in meter (*en métrō*), and of a certain length (*mēkos*); like tragedy it is a metrical representation of heroic action (*mímēsis spoudaíōn*), but its meter is different in being the heroic hexameter.[7] This definition is so much

---

[5]Propp 1964: 149.

[6]For a comprehensive treatment of genre, from a linguistic perspective, see Fowler 1982; for a short summary of the literature on "epic" see Merchant 1971. For a short discussion of the oral epic as a genre see Bynum 1976; for an analysis of the various factors entering into the definition of heroic/epic poetry see Hatto 1989b: 147ff., 290ff. and *passim*.

[7]*Poetics*, 1449b, 1459b.

taken for granted in literary scholarship that M. Bowra can write in his study of the literary epic from Virgil to Milton:

> In the disputable and usually futile task of classifying the forms of poetry there is no great quarrel about the epic. An epic poem is by common consent a narrative of some length and deals with events which have a certain grandeur and importance and come from a life of action, expecially of violent action such as war. It gives a special pleasure because its events and persons enhance our belief in the worth of human achievement and in the dignity and nobility of man.
>
> (Bowra 1945: 1)

Furthermore, epic poetry is said to reflect a totality which, by hindsight, is seen to contrast sharply with the private world of the novel. Taking the *Māhābhārata*, the *Rāmāyaṇa*, the *Iliad*, and the *Odyssey* as his models, G. W. F. Hegel stresses the all-comprehensive and objective nature of epic poetry:

> The entire world-view and objectivity of a nation, represented in its objectivizing form as something that has really happened, constitute therefore the content and the form of the epic in its proper sense.
>
> (Hegel 1955 [1842]: II, 406)

In his *Vorlesungen über die Ästhetik* Hegel sees the epic as a reflection of the naive collective consciousness of a nation at an early, though not the most primitive, stage of its development, as the poetic product of a heroic age, with heroism and wars against foreign peoples for its main themes.[8] Hegel does not overtly differentiate between oral epics and literary epics, although some such distinction is implicit in his historicism. It is only later writers who have set the oral epic apart from the literary epic, terming the former "primary" and the latter "secondary."

Western ideas on the epic have been elaborated from Aristotle onwards with the Homeric poems as norm.[9] The *Iliad* and the *Odyssey*, with all the differences between them, are the models against which other candidates for the inclusion in the genre of epic are generally measured. It follows from this that the epic is conceived as a heroic epic, a narrative which represents heroic action (Aristotle's *mimēsis spoudaiōn*). This implies the central role of man as hero, of man

[8]Hegel 1955 [1842]: II, 407ff., 413ff.

[9]For a recent study of the "idea of epic" in classical literature and its effect on the Western tradition see Hainsworth 1991.

endowed with unusual strength and power, greater than human but not
supernatural in a magical sense. The emphasis of heroic poetry on
human prowess and honor leads to the exclusion of a vast amount of
narrative poetry in which the hero possesses shamanistic or
supernatural powers:

> In certain parts of the world there is still a flourishing art of telling
> tales in verse, often at considerable length, about the marvellous doings
> of men. What counts in them is precisely this element of the marvel-
> lous. It is far more important than any heroic or even human qualities
> which may have an incidental part. This art embodies not a heroic
> outlook, which admires man for doing his utmost with his actual,
> human gifts, but a more primitive outlook which admires any attempt
> to pass beyond man's proper state by magical, non-human means. In
> different ways this poetry exists among the Finns, the Altai and
> Abakan Tatars, the Khalka Mongols, the Tibetans, and the Sea Dyaks
> of Borneo. It presupposes a view of the world in which man is not the
> centre of creation but caught between many unseen powers and
> influences, and his special interest lies in his supposed ability to master
> these and then to do what cannot be done by the exercise of specifically
> human gifts.
>
> (Bowra 1952: 5)

Bowra realizes, however, that it is difficult to draw a watertight line
between heroic and non-heroic epic poetry, and he concedes that "even
the most obviously heroic heroes in Homer and *Beowulf*, still more in
the less sophisticated poetry of the Kara-Kirghiz or the Uzbeks or the
Ossetes or the Kalmucks or the Yakuts," may occasionally resort to
supernatural means.[10]

If one wants to study that oral poetry which the "singer of tales" of
the various Turkic traditions discussed here cultivates, a limitation to
the epic in Aristotle's understanding of the genre or to the heroic epic
in Bowra's sense would leave us with a truncated and hardly representative body of texts. From the repertory of one and the same singer some
narrative poems might be selected, but others would have to be
excluded. Žumabay-žïraw's *Qoblandï*, for instance, qualifies as a heroic
epic, but his *Šaryar* — whose plot is closely related to the folktale of
the Calumniated Wife, in particular in the form the folktale has in
Pushkin's *Tsar Saltan* — does not. One would also have to distinguish
between different singers' versions of an epic poem. Few would hesitate
to consider Fāzil Yoldāš-oġli's version of *Alpāmiš* with its 14,000 verse-

[10]Bowra 1952: 5.

lines an epic on a par with poetry like *Beowulf* or Avdo Međedović's *Wedding of Smailagić Meho*, but one might entertain doubts about Saidmurād Panāh-oġli's version of *Alpāmiš*, for instance, which is much reduced in size and comprises only about 1,600 verse-lines. In the same epic cycle some branches will be called "epics" — in Aristotle's and Hegel's meaning — by rights, while others will not. The 19th-century poems of the *Manas*-trilogy, as recorded by Radloff and Valikhanov, bear comparison with the Homeric epics, at least in "grandeur," while later parts of some 20th-century versions belong more properly to the world of romance. For the Karakalpaks both *Qoblandï* and *Šaryar* are representatives of the same genre, for the Uzbeks *Alpāmiš* in Fāzil's as well as in Saidmurād's version belong together, and for the Kirghiz there is no generic distinction between the different parts of the *Manas*-cycle. The general term used by the Karakalpaks, the Uzbeks, and the Kirghiz, as well as by a number of other Turkic peoples, for this type of poetry is *dastan*.

The word *dastan* is a Persian loanword, where it has a number of meanings, such as "story," "epic poem," or "verse-narrative." In Classical Persian *dāstān* is, for instance, used by Ferdowsi in his *Shahnāme* for the various sections of his work. As a term specifically denoting oral epic poetry it is found in Uzbek, Uighur, Azerbaijanian, Turkmen, Karakalpak, Kazakh, and Kirghiz.[11] In these languages this term is defined both by formal criteria and by criteria relating to the communicative event. Formally, a *dastan* is a narrative in verse or in a mixture of verse and prose; it is of sufficient length to comprise more than one episode and to allow for the elaboration of individual scenes (with monologues and dialogues). More important than these formal criteria (of which those concerning narrative structure and length are, of course, relative rather than absolute terms) is the definition of a *dastan* with reference to the communicative event. A *dastan* is a narrative which is performed in a ceremonial setting (as described in Chapter Four) by a professional singer (and only derivatively by an amateur) in a particular singing and reciting style and, as a rule, to the accompaniment of an instrument. There is never any doubt in the mind of a listener whether he or she is listening to a *dastan* or not. As in

---

[11]The form of the word is *dastan* in Kirghiz, Kazakh, Azerbaijanian; *dāstān* in Uzbek; *dästan* in Uighur and Karakalpak; *dessān* in Turkmen; and *destan* in Turkish and Crimean Tatar.

some traditions *dastans* are predominantly love-romances, this term is often taken to mean "romance"; but this does not conform to the usage prevalent among singers and their audiences. There are, however, deviant uses of this term in some traditions. Turkish minstrels call their tales *hikâyes*, but some scholars designate the heroic epic by the word *destan* (contrasting the *destan* with the *hikâye*, the love-romance), while others reserve this term for historical poems.[12]

Besides *dastan* other words are used in the various traditions, often denoting specific subgenres of the oral epic. In Kirghiz, the word *džomoq* is glossed as "heroic epic" in Judaxin's dictionary; but Judaxin then goes on to give a quotation from the Ayčürök-episode in *Semetey*, the most romance-like part of the *Manas*-cycle, at least in the 20th-century versions.[13] In Kazakh, the word *qïssa* (or *xïssa*, from Arabic *qiṣṣa*) is in its narrow sense used for (generally stanzaic) narrative poetry whose plots are derived from Persian or Arabic stories such as *1001 Nights* or *The Forty Viziers*; the term is, however, often employed synonymously with *dastan*, especially among the Kazakhs of Xinjiang.[14] In some traditions, like that of the Karakalpaks, *dastan* is used both for the epic repertory of the *žïraw* and of the *baqsï*, but there is a keen awareness of the difference in subgenre in the repertory of these two singer-types. A difference between heroic epic and romance is in many traditions also implied by the values attached to these forms. Epics like *Alpamïš* or *Manas* are regarded as a national heritage, and in popular thinking such epics are seen as true accounts of past history. For the *aq saqals* in a Kirghiz village with whom I had to negotiate my recordings in 1985 "something true" meant epic poetry, "lies" folktales. This is not to say that the fictional element is not understood by the audience; the singers themselves warn that only half of what they are telling is the truth:

> Köbü tögün, köbü čïn,
> köpčülüktün köönü üčün.
> Körüp turġan kiši džoq,

---

[12]See Elçin 1967; Boratav 1973: 37ff.

[13]See Judaxin 1985 [1965]: I, 259 (s.v. *džomoq*). For the Ayčürök-episode see below pp. 224ff.

[14]In the Arabic script of Xinjiang this word is spelled *xïsa*. On this epic subgenre see Smirnova 1968: 102f.

köböytkön menen iši džoq.
5   Küpüldötüp ïrdasaq,
köpčülüktün köönü toq.
Ataŋardïn džomoġu
aytbay qoysoq bolobu?
Atadan mïras ïr bolup,
10   aytïp qaldïq ošonu.
                    (Mamay 1984ff: 1(I), 1f.)[15]

Much (of my story) is lies, much of it is the truth,
(told to delight) the hearts of many.
There is no one who has seen (what has happened);
no one needs to worry about exaggerations.
5   When I sing with a loud, thundering voice,
the hearts of many will be delighted.
Should I not tell
your forefathers' heroic tale (*džomoq*)?
The song (*ïr*) is the forefathers' heritage:
10   I have been left to sing it.

Fāzil šāir aytar bilganlarini.
Bu sozlarniŋ biri yālġān, biri čin,
waqti xušlik bilan otsin korgan kun,
eblab-seblab aytgan sozim boldi šul.
5   Hāy desaŋ keladi sozniŋ ma'quli,
šāir bolar biliŋ ādam faqiri,
šuytib adā boldi gapniŋ āxiri.
                    (Zarif, Mirzaev 1979: 395)[16]

Fāzil-šāir speaks all that he knows.
Some of these words are lies, some are the truth.
May the days of our life pass in joy!
These have been the words I have spoken with difficulty.
5   If you give a shout, you show your approval of my words;
the singer is a poor man, you know.
This then brings my story to an end.

Verse and Prose

A *dastan* can be both in verse and in a mixture of verse and prose.
As the Oghuz *Book of Dede Qorqut* shows, the mixture of verse and

---

[15]This is the beginning of Mamay's version of *Manas*; compare also Hu, Dor 1984:
31. Note that the terms *ïr* ("song") and *džomoq* occur in this passage.

[16]These are the last lines of Fāzil Yoldāš-oġli's variant of *Alpāmiš*.

prose has a long history in Turkic literature. There is no convenient word in English for this form, which is by no means unique to the Turkic traditions. In Sanskrit the term *champū* is used for narratives in which a highly artistic prose alternates with verse. This term is sometimes also employed for non-Indian narratives of a similar form.[17] Prose interspersed with verse-passages is also the form of the Old Irish "sagas." This formal trait is, according to Myles Dillon, one of several that link Old Irish literature to that of India:

> The oldest narrative form known to Indo-Europeans seems to have been a prose tale with verse dialogue, the verse being fixed and unchanging, the prose left to the creative memory of the story-teller. This was the old Indian form. It is the Irish form. The sagas are in prose. But when the champions are claiming the hero's portion in *The Story of Mac Da Thó's Pig*, they salute each other in verse; when the child Deirdre is born, the druid prophesies in verse; when Deirdre bids farewell to Scotland, and when she laments the death of her lover, she speaks in verse.
>
> (Dillon 1968: 13-14)

The Turkic texts in verse and prose are in many ways similar to the Sanskrit *champū*s on the one hand and to the Old Irish sagas on the other. Yet this flavor of the archaic, which Dillon stresses for the Old Irish sagas,[18] is not true of the Turkic epic in verse and prose in general. The term "saga," favored by the Chadwicks, suggesting an archaic form and at the same time the preponderance of prose and the fixity of the verse-parts, does therefore not adequately capture the mixture of verse and prose in Turkic *dastan*s. Similar reservations apply to the Old French word *chantefable* (or *cantefable*), which denotes the genre of *Aucassin et Nicolette*, a 13th-century love-story in verse and prose. Shorter love-tales like the Turkish *hikâye*s, in which the prose-narrative alternates with songs, fit the genre of the *chantefable* remarkably well; but for longer *dastan*s, in particular of a heroic nature, the term *chantefable*, as it is generally understood, would be misleading. I will therefore use what seems to me a more neutral term, "prosimetrum." This term does not so much designate a genre as a form. It is only occasionally used in English, mostly by classicists and medievalists to describe works like the Menippean satire or Boethius' *Consola-*

---

[17]See Mylius 1983: 228f. On the mixture of verse and prose in contemporary Indian oral epics see Smith 1987: 596ff.

[18]See also Thurneysen 1921: 53-57.

tion of Philosophy. However, verse and prose stand in a particular relationship to one another in Turkic epic poetry and constitute a form *sui generis*, in their total effect quite unlike the prosimetric forms of other literatures, even if similarities are discernible.

The mixture of verse and prose is, as in the Old French *chantefable*, closely linked to the alternation between declaiming and singing (see Chapter Four). As to content, the prose-passages are characteristically narrative, in the sense that the course of events is related in prose, while the verse-passages are more "static," reserved for speeches, lyrical monologues, and dialogues. There are, however, also narrative verse-passages, often type-scenes such as battle-scenes or journeys, while the prose-portions can also contain "static," descriptive passages. The interrelationship between verse and prose can be quite intricate and far from a mechanical switch between prose-narrative in which the emphasis is on action and plot development and static verse-lyricism. The prose itself can be highly patterned and rhythmical, with imperceptible transitions into verse.

The beginning of one of the Uzbek *Köroğlu/Göroğlï*-epics can serve as an example for the gradual change from prose to verse:

> Burungi otgan zamāninda, eli ozbak āmāninda, qibladan tumanin-da, Taka-Yāwmitniŋ elinda, Čambilbelniŋ belinda dawrānni surib, qirq yigitni yiġib, āltin piyālaga maylar quyib, kunda ertan čulāninga qoy-soqimlar soyib, yurtni yiġdirib, āčni toydirib, qirq yigitga silāwsin ton kiydirib Goroğlibek otdi.
>
> (Zarif 1981: 5)

> In the days of yore, when the Uzbek people were flourishing, there lived in the direction of Mekka (southwest), in the tribe of the Taka-Yāwmit, on the hill of Čambilbel, Goroğli-bek, ruling in glory, with his forty companions, filling the wine in golden goblets, slaughtering every morning fattened sheep for a public feast, calling the people together, feeding the hungry and clothing the forty yigits in lynx robes.

There is a close connection between prose and verse in the Uzbek text quoted, insofar as the various syntactic units of the opening passage exhibit syntactic parallelism and are linked by rhyme or assonance:

> Burungi otgan zamāninda,
> eli ozbak āmāninda,
> qibladan tumaninda,
> Taka-Yāwmitniŋ elinda,
> 5   Čambilbelniŋ belinda
> dawrānni surib,

```
     qirq yigitni yiġib,
     altin piyālaga maylar quyib,
     kunda ertan čulāninga qoy-soqimlar soyib,
10   yurtni yiġdirib,
     āčni toydirib,
     qirq yigitga silāwsin ton kiydirib
     Goroġli-bek otdi.
```

It is only a short step from prose of the illustrated type to verse. The agglutinative structure of the Turkic languages makes it almost inevitable that syntactically parallelistic segments should be linked by rhyme or at least assonance (see Chapter Seven, pp. 172ff.).

Apart from passages like the one quoted, which seem to hover between prose and verse, Uzbek *dastans* also contain passages which are very much like the passages in rhymed prose in the *Arabian Nights*. The main function of these passages in rhymed prose (termed *sadžᶜ*, from Arabic) is descriptive, of place, situation, and character.[19] A particularly ornate use of this stylistic trait is found in the description of the slave-girl Āqqiz in Ergaš Džumanbulbul-oġli's *dastan Rawšan*:

Āqqiz šunday qiz edi: āti Āqqiz, Zulxumārga *naq qiz*. Āqqiz ozi *āq qiz*, ozi tolgan *sāġ qiz*, orta boyli *čāġ qiz*, oynagani *bāġ qiz*, uyqiči emas *sāġ qiz*, eri yoq — ozi *tāq qiz*, kop kalāndimāġ qiz, yaxši tekis boz bālani korsa esi yoq — *ahmāq qiz*, qāra koz, bādām *qāwāq qiz*, sinli-*siyāq qiz*, ozi semiz — turiši *yāġ qiz*; oyinga *qulayrāq qiz*, toġri išga *bolayrāq qiz*, ozi anqāw *ālayrāq qiz*, tanasi toš qoygan *keŋ qiz*, saġrisi *doŋ qiz*, urušqāq emas — *džon qiz*, a'zāsi bari *teŋ qiz*; yaxšilardan *soŋ qiz*, et kotargan *gošdār qiz*. Biqini tār, *tošdār qiz*, aqli kam *xušdār qiz*. Āq yuzin korsaŋ, *āyday*, hurkak-asāw *tāyday*, ālġir-*qarčiġayday qiz*. Yuwāšligi *qoyday*, semiz emasmi, yāysaŋ eriydi sariġ *māyday*.

(Zarif 1971: 126-127)

Āqqiz was such a girl: her name was Āqqiz (White-Girl), she was Zulxumār's maid. Āqqiz was a girl of light complexion, she was a girl of exuberant health, of middle size, a girl like a pleasure-garden. She was fresh and not sleepy; she did not have a husband; she was unmarried; she was a girl who was always merry and who lost her mind when she set eyes on a well-built young man — a silly girl. She was a girl with black eyes and almond-shaped eyelids, a girl of stately build, plump and round, playful, and lethargic when it came to doing work, standing about idly. She was a girl with a full bosom and round shoulders. She was not at all quarrelsome; she was a simple, even-tempered girl. She was a girl who came after the best. She was a well-fed girl, with a small waist and full breasts, and with certain limits

[19]The role of rhymed prose in the Uzbek *dastans* is discussed by Sarimsāqov 1978: 63-84.

to her intelligence. When you look at her white face, it is like the moon. She was a girl fearful and stubborn like a foal, like a falcon with sharp claws. She was as good as a lamb — was she not fat? If you spread her out she melts like butter.

Other passages in *sadž*[c] are the descriptions of the *locus amoenus*, the pleasance where the beloved girl promenades and enjoys herself with her slave-girls, set pieces in the Uzbek love-*dastans*, which have been stylistically influenced by similar scenes in Classical Persian verse-epics like Nizāmī's *Khosrou and Shirin* or *Leila and Majnun* (12th c.).[20] Although the verse-portions of Turkic *dastans* are both from the point of view of performance and of poetics the dominant element, the art of telling in prose is also an important part of a singer's skills.

Romance

The mixture of verse and prose is found both in heroic epics and in love-epics; but it is more often linked to the latter than to the former. In those traditions which have pure verse-epics, the prosimetric form is generally characteristic of love-epics. This is particularly true of the Kazakhs, whose heroic epics like *Alpamïs* or *Qoblandï* are predominantly in verse and whose love-epics like *Qïz Žibek* are typically in verse and prose. Other traditions which only have the prosimetric epic, such as those of the Turks, Azerbaijanians, Turkmens, Uzbeks, and Uighurs, show a marked predilection for romance in their epic poetry. "Romance" is a useful, but also a controversial term to denote love-*dastans* and related non-heroic epic poetry. According to the *Princeton Encyclopedia of Poetry and Poetics* "the meaning of the term 'romance' is obscured by the fact that both in medieval and modern times it has been used so loosely."[21] Its very looseness does, however, recommend the term "romance" as a general label for a wide variety of epic subgenres in which the heroic mode is not the dominant mode. The contrast between epic in the restricted sense of heroic epic and romance has been most convincingly stated for medieval literature:

[20]See Mirbadaleva 1975: 116; Reichl 1985a: 28-30.

[21]Preminger et al. 1974: 486.

Whatever Epic may mean, it implies some weight and solidity; Romance means nothing, if it does not convey some notion of mystery and fantasy. A general distinction of this kind, whatever names may be used to render it, can be shown, in medieval literature, to hold good of the two large groups of narrative belonging to the earlier and the later Middle Ages respectively. Beowulf might stand for the one side, Lancelot or Gawain for the other. ...

The two great kinds of narrative literature in the Middle Ages might be distinguished by their favourite incidents and commonplaces of adventure. No kind of adventure is so common or better told in the earlier heroic manner than the defence of a narrow place against odds. ...

The favourite adventure of medieval romance is something different, — a knight riding alone through a forest; another knight; a shock of lances; a fight on foot with swords, "racing, tracing, and foining like two wild boars"; then, perhaps, recognition — the two knights belong to the same household and are engaged in the same quest.

(Ker 1908: 4-6)

Ker is thinking here of chivalric romance, the Arthurian *roman courtois* and related forms of medieval narrative. But romance as a mode of literature is neither confined to the Middle Ages nor to European literature. Parallels to the medieval *roman* can also be found in the Persian and Georgian verse-epics of the 11th and 12th centuries,[22] and romance as a form of popular narrative poetry can be found in a great variety of literary traditions, from some of the tales in the *1001 Nights* to the Urdu love-*dastans* or the oral narratives from the Minangkabau of West Sumatra.[23] What is typical of all of these narratives is the "romantic experience" which lies at the basis of romance as a genre:

Romance as a genre, a series of related genres, is characterized by conventions, motifs, archetypes, which have been created in order to express the experiences in their essential nature. Amongst these motifs are, for instance: the mysterious challenge or call; the first sight of the beloved; the lonely journey through a hostile land; the fight with the enemy, often a monstrous creature. It is the experience which *creates* these conventions, because it cannot be described so well in any other way.

(Stevens 1973: 16)

---

[22]See Meletinskij 1983; compare also Meletinskij 1986: 140-167.

[23]See Heath 1987-88 (*Arabian Nights*); Dextjar' 1979 (Urdu); Phillips 1981 (Minangkabau).

Turkic romance has been subclassified in many different ways by native and Russian scholars.[24] All these various subgenres have a number of features — relating to narrative structure, style, and performance — in common. The theme of romance is love and adventure rather than prowess and heroism as expressions of a heroic ethos. The narrative structure is episodic, often resulting in a fairly loose concatenation of adventures. The lovers are led through a series of calamities, obstacles, and separations to their final reunion; the hero engages in a series of fights, valorous deeds, horse-stealing and bride-winning exploits, often gratuitously and as an expression of his unbridled recklessness and daring:

> In love-romance motifs and subject-matter of an adventurous and chivalric kind are generally developed. Thus the hero, in order to find his beloved, sets out on a dangerous journey, performs heroic feats on the way, fights against monsters and demons, and rescues his beauty from evils spirits and dragons.
>
> (Mirbadaleva 1975: 113)

Love is not always a happy love; a number of love-epics have a tragic ending. In the Kazakh love-epic *Qïz Žibek* (Silk Girl), for instance, Tölegen wins Qïz Žibek, but is murdered on his way home with her by a rival, and Qïz Žibek ends up being married to Tölegen's younger brother.[25] Other well-known romances of unhappy love are *Tahir and Zühre*, found from Anatolia to Chinese Turkestan, and the Kazakh love-epic *Qozï Körpeš and Bayan Suluw*, also found among the neighboring peoples.[26] Stylistically, lyrical elements predominate in romance. In imagery, phraseology, and composition these verse-passages are greatly influenced by the popular love-lyric, but also by love-poetry in Classical

[24]For various classifications see Žirmunskij, Zarifov 1947 (Uzbek); Maqsetov et al. 1977: 9ff. (Karakalpak); Smirnova et al. 1968: 236ff. (Kazakh).

[25]*Qïz Žibek* is widely spread among the Kazakhs both in Kazakhstan and in Xinjiang; see Smirnova et al. 1968: 278-285; for a critical edition see Äwezov [Auezov], Smirnova 1963.

[26]On *Tahir and Zühre* see Boratav 1964: 33f.; Žirmunskij, Zarifov 1947: 294-301; Raquette 1930; Urmančeev 1984: 187-195. *Qozï Körpeš and Bayan Suluw* is also known outside the Kazakh people; versions of the romance have been recorded also from the Bashkirs and the Uighurs; see Urmančeev 1984: 170-187; on the Kazakh versions see Smirnova et al. 1968: 274-278; for a critical edition see Düysenbaev 1959. Some variants of this romance have a happy end. On Turkish *hikâyes* of unhappy love see also Spies 1929: 25-27.

Persian, Arabic, and Chaghatay. A great number of the verse-passages are devoted to the theme of love; they are lyrical monologues and dialogues, expressing the speakers' feelings of love, yearning, and sorrow. In performance, the musical skills of the *baxši*, *aqïn*, or *ašïq* as a singer and player are at least as important as his skill as a narrator.

The most widely represented types of Turkic romance are romance in a heroic mode (in Uzbek *qahramānlik-romanik dāstān*) and love-romance (*išqiy dāstān*).[27] "Heroic romance" is not to be confused with the heroic epic; it is romance-like in its plot-structure and in its style, even if the heroic qualities of the protagonists are emphasized. It is here that the more heroic and warlike of the *Köroğlu/Göroğli-dastan*s belong. Uzbek scholars generally distinguish the *dzaŋnama* (lit. "war-book") from heroic romance. In the *dzaŋnama* warlike deeds are extolled, especially the fight of the Moslems against non-Moslems or of the Sunnites (to which division most Turks belong) against the Shiites (generally the Persians). In this the *dzaŋnama* is strikingly similar to the Old French *chanson de geste*. A number of *dastan*s have their plots in common with folktales and give prominence to the marvelous and the fantastic; here a term like "fairy-tale romance" might be appropriate. In a group of romances (particularly cultivated by the Turks, Azerbaijanians, and Turkmens) the hero and lover is a minstrel, who expresses his passion and his feelings in the poems (or songs) he composes; *Ašïq Ğarib* is the best-known representative of this sub-genre.[28]

Heroic Lay and Heroic Tale

Apart from differentiating between heroic epic and romance, with their various subtypes, two other distinctions have to be made, one concerning length and scale, the other form. In his book *Epic and Romance*, from which I have quoted already, W. P. Ker draws attention

[27]See Mirzaev, Sarimsāqov 1981: 21ff.

[28]On the Turkish minstrel romance see Başgöz 1952; Eberhard 1955; on the Turkic love-epic see also Boratav 1964: 30ff.; on the Azerbaijanian love-romance see Tähmasib 1972: 177ff.

to the problematic nature of the noun "epic" in the expression "heroic epic":

> It must be confessed that there is an easily detected ambiguity in the use of the term epic in application to the poems, whether German, English, or Northern, here reviewed. That they are heroic poems cannot be questioned, but that they are epic in any save the most general sense of the term is not quite clear. They may be epic in character, in a general way, but how many of them have a claim to the title in its eminent and special sense? Most of them are short poems; most of them seem to be wanting in the breadth of treatment, in the amplitude of substance, that are proper to epic poetry.
>
> (Ker 1908: 116)

Following Ker's exploration of the scale and development of Germanic epic poetry, A. Heusler has systematized the distinction between long epic and short epic, or rather epic (*Epos*) and lay (*Lied*), stressing that the difference between the two is not merely a quantitative one, but concerns also narrative technique and style. The lay is generally restricted to one episode or focused on one dramatic situation, with little space given to elaboration and embroidering:

> Where then does the basic difference between a lay and an epic lie? In the first place, without doubt, in narrative technique. On the one side we have a compact, allusive, leaping style, what we call "lay-like conciseness." On the other side we have a leisurely, lingering, amplifying style, what we call "epic breadth." However far removed the Eddic *Lay of Attli* might be from the Old High German *Lay of Hildebrand* or the English ballad *The Battle of Otterburn*, however great the distance between the epics *Beowulf*, *King Rother*, and *The Nibelungenlied* might be, the general characteristics of the former are typical of the lay, while those of the latter belong to the epic.
>
> (Heusler 1905: 21-22)

The problem of distinguishing between longer and shorter forms of epic poetry is present in a great number of epic traditions. The Serbo-Croatian *junačke pjesme* are generally heroic songs or lays; it is only in the Moslem tradition of Yugoslavia that poetry on the scale of the epic has arisen.[29] Heroic songs rather than epics are also found in the neighboring traditions in the Balkans, the epic poetry of Albania, Greece, Bulgaria, and Romania, poetry for which various terms have been used (short epic, ballad, heroic song, even folk song), all of them

[29]M. Schmaus has studied this process of "epicization," of which the best-known product is *The Wedding of Smailagić Meho* by Avdo Međedović. See Braun 1961: 257ff.; Schmaus 1953; Lord, 1974.

stressing their essential difference from the fully developed epic poem.[30]
The lay is amply represented in Turkic epic poetry. There is actually
a difference between the lay as a subgenre of epic poetry and what one
might call "reduced epic poetry." Very often singers are not able to give
an epic poem in its entirety or to perform a complete version of an epic
or romance. From the Crimean Tatars both heroic *dastans* and
romances have been collected, among them versions of *Köroğlu*,
Qoblandï, and *Ašïq Ġarib*.[31] These *dastans*, however, have been
reduced in length to such an extent that most of the texts are no more
than short tales with interspersed verses. Through the loss of a living
tradition and the disappearance of the professional singer, epic poetry
has here been transformed to survive (barely) as a new genre, the
prosimetric tale, halfway between *hikâye* and folktale. Similar
transformations can be observed in other traditions. In some traditions
"epic poetry on a reduced scale" has given rise to lay-like and ballad-
like poetry, while in others the lay is cultivated side by side with heroic
epic and romance. The lay and its ballad-like variants deserve a more
detailed study than can be given in this survey.

Before leaving genre, one more form of Turkic epic poetry has to be
looked at briefly, the heroic tale. To call the heroic tale a form of poetry
seems to be a contradiction in terms. "Poetry" is here, of course,
intended in its broader meaning (equivalent to German *Dichtung*) and
not in its more narrow sense of verse-poetry. But "verse-poetry" and
"prose" are also relative terms. The demarcation line between the two
is not always easy to draw in the case of Turkic epic poetry, as the
analysis of formulaic-parallelistic passages like the opening of an Uzbek
Köroğlu/Göroğlï-dastan quoted above has shown. This applies also to
the heroic tale in some Turkic traditions. There are basically two types
of the heroic tale (*bogatyrskaja skazka* in Russian) found among Turkic
peoples. One type of tale is similar to the Russian folktales on heroes
of the *byliny*. Here epic poetry has in the course of time been recast as
prose tales, which have become part of the Russian folktale tradition,
although they betray by their subject matter and various stylistic traits

[30]The genre of the Romanian heroic songs, also in relationship to Serbo-Croatian
heroic poetry, is discussed by Gacak 1975b; for a characterization of the Albanian short
epic poem see Lambertz 1958: 95ff.; for Modern Greek oral epic poetry see Beaton
1980.

[31]See Radloff 1896; Bekirov 1980.

their origin in the *byliny*.[32]   To this type of tale belong the Tatar, Kirghiz, and Kazakh folktales of Er Töštük.

Er Töštük is a Kirghiz epic, of which various versions have been recorded.[33]   Its plot is related to the folktale of the Bear's Son (*AaTh* 301), a type which, it has been argued, also underlies the *Odyssey* and the Anglo-Saxon *Beowulf*; epic and folktale may both go back to some kind of archetypal story-pattern.[34]   While the Tatar, Kirghiz and Kazakh folktales of the Bear's Son can be called primary folktales, the folktales of Er Töštük are clearly secondary, i.e. derivations of epic poetry. This can be demonstrated by the verse-passages occurring in some of the Kirghiz and Kazakh folktales of Er Töštük. Thinking that his horse Čalquyruq (Kazakh Šalquyrïq) has died, Er Töštük (Kazakh Er Töstük) laments its death in a passage of forty-five verse-lines (in a Kazakh folktale):[35]

> Žüretuǧïn žolïmda,
> qulan ötpes šöl boldï,
> asqar-asqar taw menen
> šeksiz darya, köl boldï.
>
> ...
>
> Žayawïmda qanat bolǧan, Šalquyrïq,
> žalǧïzïmda žoldas bolǧan, Šalquyrïq,
> sasqanïmda aqïlïm bolǧan, Šalquyrïq.

> On the way that I have gone
> there was a desert, which no *qulan* (wild ass) had crossed,
> there were mountains, covered by eternal snow,
> there were endless rivers and lakes.
>
> ...
>
> When I could only walk, you were my wings, Šalquyrïq,
> when I was alone, you were my companion, Šalquyrïq,
> when I was confused, you were my mind, Šalquyrïq.

---

[32]See Astaxova 1962.

[33]For the Kirghiz version recorded by Radloff see Radloff 1885: 526-589 (text volume), 530-593 (translation volume); for Qaralaev's version see Qaralaev 1956. Both versions have been translated as a composite version by Boratav 1965.

[34]For a discussion of the relationship between AaTh 301, *Er Töštük*, and *Beowulf* see Reichl 1987; for a study of the difference between epic and tale in Turkic oral literature see Kidajš-Pokrovskaja 1975.

[35]Asïlxan 1983: 45; instead of *šöl* Asïlxan has *žol*, but compare Qasqabasov [Kaskabasov] 1972: 210; for a similar passage in a Kirghiz folktale version of *Er Töštük* see Kebekova, Toqombaeva 1975: 13-14.

This episode is missing in the Kirghiz version of the epic edited by Radloff, but a comparable passage, in which Er Töstük grieves over his horse's mortal wounds, occurs in Qaralaev's version:[36]

> Ay Čalquyruq buudanïm,
> sen ölgöndö, men öldüm,
> adam džürbös ač belde,
> quzġun učpas quu čöldö,
> sen ekööbüz teŋ öldük.

> O Čalquyruq, my courser,
> if you die, I die.
> On the lonely mountain pass, which no man has crossed,
> in the dry desert, over which no raven has flown,
> we have as equals exposed ourselves to death.

As shall be seen in Chapter Seven, this passage is a realization of the theme of the hero crossing the wilderness, a theme typical of Turkic epic poetry. The metrical form of the verses in the Kazakh folktale also points to the epic; the passage is in the epic meter *par excellence*. There can be little doubt that the Kazakh heroic folktale (*batïrlïq ertegi*) of Er Töstük is a derived form, which is not to say that Kazakh folklore might not also know the heroic tale as a primary form.[37] Similar derived forms of the epic are also found elsewhere: during my stay in Qïzïl-su in 1989 I was told of the existence of sizable prose retellings of the *Manas*-cycle among the Kazakhs in Xinjiang; these prose-versions were said to have developed into a separate story-cycle.

The second type of the heroic tale to be distinguished, the heroic tale as a primary form, is very difficult to discuss without entering into the complex and controversial question of origins. The heroic tale is often thought to constitute the most archaic layer of Turkic (and more generally Altaic and Siberian) epic "poetry," from which the verse-epics of the Kirghiz, Kazakhs, and other Turkic peoples have developed at a

---

[36] Qaralaev 1956: 256; compare Boratav 1965: 204. On the relationship between the Kirghiz and Kazakh versions of *Er Töstük* see Kebekova 1985: 116ff.

[37] Qasqabasov 1984: 204-219 distinguishes two types of the Kazakh *batïrlïq ertegi*, an archaic type and a type which was derived from the heroic epic in the 18th and 19th centuries; *Er Töstük* is clearly a representative of the latter type. According to Qoŋïratbaev 1987: 121-128 *Er Töstük* belongs to the group of Kazakh "folktale epics" (*ertegilik eposï*).

later stage.[38] I will not go into the problem of origins here but will simply list a few characteristics of the Tuvinian heroic tale. Like Altaian *čörčök*, Tuvinian *tool* denotes all types of narratives, whether fairy-tales, heroic tales, or heroic epics. In Altaian the difference between the meanings "folktale" and "heroic tale"/"heroic epic," can easily be established with reference to performance; a "heroic tale"/ "heroic epic" is a "narrative told in the manner of *qay*-singing."[39] In form, the *čörčök* is generally in verse, sometimes comprising thousands of lines, so that the term "epic" seems more justified than "tale." It has to be noted, however, that the epithet "heroic" is in need of qualification, as shamanistic traits are prominent in Altaian epic poetry. The distinction between folktale and heroic tale rests on similar criteria in the case of the Tuvinian *tool*. Among the Tuvinians heroic tales are basically performed in a chanting or singing style; a mere reciting is a recent development:

> Even today many narrators have not yet lost the old manner of performing epic poetry. To a melody, sung in one tempo or another, with a low or a high voice, the narrator performs the heroic tale in a recitative style. When one hears such a sung performance (*ïrlap ïdar* or *alǧanïp ïdar* in Tuvinian), it is possible to make out elements of verse-structure and a regular rhythmic patterning of the epic.
> (Grebnev 1960: 38)[40]

These verse-lines vacillate between 7/8 syllables and 10/11 or more syllables; there is no rhyme, unless caused by syntactic parallelism; there are no regular stanzas, but alliteration links individual lines together in irregular groups.[41] Radloff, who collected two heroic tales, printed them in lines of varying length, with a certain tendency to a

[38]This is for instance E. M. Meletinskij's thesis, which in the seventies was hotly disputed in a series of contributions to the journal *Sovetskaja Ètnografija*; see Meletinskij 1963: 247ff.

[39]In Altaian, *qaylap aydar čörčök*; see Surazakov, Puxov, Baskakov 1973: 22; compare also Hatto 1989b: 293; see also above p. 112f. On the *čörčök* as a heroic tale see Chadwick 1932-40: III, 101f.

[40]E. Taube notes, however, that this performance style is typical of both the heroic tales and folktales among the Tuvinians of western Mongolia; see Taube 1978: 349.

[41]Grebnev 1960: 38f.

verse-line of six, seven, or eight syllables.[42] The texts of Tuvinian heroic tales/epics which were published in this century have been edited as prose. They have often undergone literary adaptation so that they do not always provide reliable evidence of their metrical structure. Even so, the rhythmic patterning of the prose, in particular in the introductory passages and in set scenes, can be observed.

There are other traits of this type of narrative which bring the Tuvinian heroic tale near to the heroic epic. Apart from the manner of its performance and its rhythmically patterned form, the heroic tale shows a certain tendency to scenic elaboration and even cyclic development. The hero and his horse perform a number of feats, among which contests and combats play an important role. These are very often narrated in the fashion of a type-scene with a fixed series of motifs (the mutual insults of the combatants, the exaggerated duration of the fight, the sweat dripping down on the ground etc.) and in a formulaic style. Some of these heroic tales are of "epic length," such as *Boqtu-Kiriš and Bora-Šeeley*.[43] This text is also an example for the beginning of a cyclic development: it tells not only the adventures of the father but also of the son. E. Taube translated a variant which runs even to three generations; she remarks that the narrator had, in his own words, "matter for three winter nights."[44]

* * * * *

In conclusion, it has to be stressed that the epic poetry of the Turkic peoples encompasses a great variety of subgenres, modes, and forms. It should never be forgotten that "Turkic oral epic poetry" is a convenient abstraction which enables us to look for similarities between various Turkic traditions, but which should not make us blind to the differences between them. While some of the features which the various traditions

---

[42]See Radloff 1866b: 399-400 (text volume), 424 (translation volume). In his *Aus Sibirien* he called them *Märchen*; see Radloff 1893: II, 179; see also the quotation on p. 305.

[43]See Grebnev 1969.

[44]Taube 1978: 376.

discussed in this book have in common might be due to a shared heritage, others might be best explained as the result of cultural contact. Although a number of traditions, in particular the "central traditions," have poetry which conforms in conception, form, narrative technique, and scale to the Aristotelian notion of the epic or to Bowra's view of the heroic epic, this type of poetry cannot be considered wholly representative of the narrative repertory of the "singer of tales" among many Turkic peoples. The term *dastan* covers this general and all-inclusive concept of oral epic poetry. While content and form are important criteria for the definition of what is to count as epic poetry, various aspects of the speech event — setting, singer, and audience — are equally crucial for the delimitation of the epic. Sociological factors play an important role as well. By looking at the texts alone, one might be able to distinguish the heroic epic from other forms of epic poetry; but the essential qualitity of the heroic epic, the heroic ethos, can only be captured when the epic is related to the society in which it is performed and valued.[45] Various subgenres of oral epic poetry must be distinguished. According to subject matter and narrative structure the heroic epic can be set off from romance as well as from epic poetry with predominantly shamanistic traits. Romance comprises many varieties, among them love-romance, chivalresque adventure-romance, romance in a heroic mode, minstrel romance, and "fairy-tale romance." These subgenres and types are not mutually exclusive categories, nor is it always easy to categorize a narrative adequately. The generic distinctions discussed in this chapter can be no more than rough guidelines for the characterization of the repertory of a singer.

As to meter and style, prosimetric *dastans* are found side by side with epics in verse. The borderline between verse and prose is often blurred, especially in the narrative traditions of some of the Altaian peoples. Length and scope are decisive criteria in distinguishing shorter forms of epic poetry from longer forms, reduced epics from the fully fledged epic, the lay from the *dastan*, the branch from the cycle, but also epic poetry of clearly circumscribed proportions from "large-scale amorphous compilations of heroic and sub-heroic narrative material" like some of

---

[45]Compare Hatto 1989b: 147ff., 223ff.

the longer contemporary versions of the *Manas*-cycle.[46] These distinctions have been based mostly on inner and outer form; this is, however, not to say that quality is a "negligible quantity." The position that the Homeric epics have in the tradition of Western literature as models and paragons reminds us that *epos* is not only a genre label but also an evaluative term. Literary criticism, when applied to Turkic oral epic poetry, must also address the question of quality; but this can only be done when a frame of reference has been established. The foregoing discussion of genre with its descriptive rather than interpretative orientation was only concerned with providing at least some elements of such a frame of reference; other elements are, however, still needed before questions of poetics can be broached.

---

[46] Hatto (forthcoming): 1; I am quoting from the manuscript circulated at the conference. A. T. Hatto proposes the term "epopee" for this type of epic poetry.

Chapter Six

Story-Patterns

> The chartless seas of storiology are
> attractive but dangerous.
> Gordon Hall Gerould[1]

In my account of the earliest documents of epic poetry transmitted in a Turkic language in Chapter Two a summary of some of these texts was given. The story-patterns encountered then are by no means restricted to these early texts; they are typical of a large part of 19th-c. and 20th-c. Turkic oral epic poetry as well. For an understanding of the narrative structure of these epic poems a basic knowledge of their contents is a prerequisite. As, in view of the scarcity of translations of Turkic epic poetry into Western languages, the nonspecialist reader cannot be expected to be familiar with the poetry under discussion, I will illustrate some of the most common story-patterns found in Turkic oral epic poetry in this chapter. My analysis is focused on the Kazakh epic *Qambar-batïr*, some branches of the *Köroğlu/Göroğlï*-cycle, and the epic of *Alpamïš*, in particular the Uzbek version of *Alpāmiš* in Fāzil Yoldāš-oğli's variant. I have chosen these epics because they illustrate a variety of traditions (Kazakh, Uzbek, Karakalpak, Azerbaijanian, Turkmen, Turkish), of forms (verse-epic and prosimetric *dastan*), of subgenres (heroic epic and romance), and of story-patterns. This is not to say, however, that this choice is representative. The great number of Turkic epic traditions, the sheer mass of narrative material, and, despite their basic similarity, the heterogeneity of these epic traditions

---

[1]Gerould 1904: 339.

forbids a more than sketchy sampling of the Turkic "ocean of story-streams."

Qambar and The Making of a Hero

My first example comes from Kazakh epic poetry. The Kazakh epic poem *Qambar-batïr* (The Hero Qambar) is one of the best-known Kazakh epics. It has been transmitted in various versions and redactions. These versions and variants are closely related, with hardly any significant variations in their plot. The following summary is based on the text taken down by A. A. Divaev in 1920, which can be considered a representative and well-balanced variant of *Qambar-batïr*.[2]

> Äzimbay, a rich man of the Noghays, has six sons and a daughter. When his daughter, the beautiful Nazïm, comes of age, she is allowed to choose a husband from the men who have flocked to Äzimbay's encampment (*awïl*) as prospective husbands. But none of the suitors passing in review finds favor with Nazïm. One young man had, however, not been invited to this gathering, Qambar of the im-

---

[2]The earliest text of the epic poem is a printed edition which came out in Kazan in 1888 under the title *Qïssa-i Qambar* ("The Tale of Qambar"; in Arabic script). A second redaction of this *qïssa* appeared in 1903, also in Kazan, under the title *Toqsan üyli Tobïr* ("The Tobïr of the Ninety Yurts"; in Arabic script). The version of *Qambar* represented by these two editions is also found in manuscript form; the Kazakh Academy of Sciences in Alma-Ata contains four manuscripts, of which the earliest dates from 1895 and is a copy of the edition of 1888. Of the remaining three manuscript versions, two are also copies of written material, while the third was taken down from a singer. On these six texts see Äwezov [Auezov], Smirnova 1959: 345-346. The 1903 edition of *Qambar* is edited and translated (into Russian) *ibid.*: 9-35 (text), 129-156 (translation).

Two further texts are ultimately based on the 1903 redaction of *Qambar*, a text recorded in the twenties from the singer Barmaq Muqambaev and a text recorded in 1958 from the singer Raxmet Mäzxožaev. Muqambaev's version is edited and translated (into Russian) in Äwezov [Auezov], Smirnova 1959: 79-124 (text), 202-250 (translation); for the text of Mäzxožaev's version see *ibid.*: 403-425.

A further version came out in Tashkent in 1922 under the title *Qambar-batïr* (in Arabic script). This version was edited by A. A. Divaev, who had taken down the text from an unnamed singer, possibly Mayköt Sandïbaev, around 1920. His text has been edited several times; the authoritative edition, comprising 1851 lines, is that by Äwezov [Auezov], Smirnova 1959: 36-78 (text), 157-201 (translation).

Three further texts, preserved in the Kazakh Academy of Sciences, are based on this version. They have been recorded from various singers in the 1950s (see Äwezov [Auezov], Smirnova 1959: 370). *Qambar* is also available on record; the Tashkent branch of "Melodija" has issued two records which contain the epic, sung by Žumabay Medetbaev (Melodija C30-13449-52). This text agrees fairly closely with the text edited by Divaev.

poverished clan of the Tobïr of the ninety yurts, and it is precisely with
this young man that Nazïm falls in love when she first hears of him.
She meets Qambar when he is on his return from a hunting expedition
and invites him to take a rest in her yurt. Qambar, however, spurns
the girl's hospitality, feeling that he is not an acceptable match for the
rich bay's daughter. Nazïm's oldest brother Qabïršaq sees the young
man talking to his sister and calls to the other brothers to fall on the
have-not Qambar. Alšïoraz, the youngest of the six, admonishes his
brothers not to set too high a value on possessions and warns them
against a rash deed of anger. Qambar is allowed to depart in peace.

The khan of the Kalmucks, Qaraman of giant stature, has also heard
of Nazïm's beauty and wishes to marry her. He sends a delegation of
twenty men with Kelmembet as their leader to Äzimbay to ask for the
girl's hand. When they arrive at Äzimbay's encampment, Alšïoraz
mutilates Kelmembet — he cuts off his nose and ears — and his
companions are shamefully killed. Outraged by this, Qaraman marches
with an army of 5,000 men to Äzimbay's *awïl*. Kelmembet is once
again sent to Äzimbay, who now agrees to his daughter marrying the
khan of the Kalmucks, while hoping, however, that a way out of his
predicament may be found. On Alšïoraz's advice Äzimbay sends nine
men under Žädiger to Qambar with presents to entreat him to come to
their rescue. Žädiger's embassy is received favorably by Qambar and
he promises to help.

Qaraman is curious to see Qambar, of whose valor he had been told,
and sends Kelmembet to summon his vassal to his presence. Qambar
rides up to Qaraman and challenges him. In fierce combat he kills
Qaraman and overcomes the Kalmucks with the help of the Noghays.
Finally, Qambar and Nazïm are married, at a *toy* (feast) organized by
Äzimbay, which lasts for forty days.

The plot of this epic poem is fairly straightforward: a young woman
and a young man fall in love with each another but are prevented from
marrying by an obstacle, in our case the poverty of the young man. A
new suitor appears, who is welcome to neither the girl nor her relatives.
He is furthermore a threat to the girl's kin, being the khan of the
infidel Kalmucks, the traditional enemies and oppressors of the Central
Asian Turks. The young hero rushes to the wedding-feast of his
beloved, arrives there just in time, proves his worth by heroic deeds, and
marries the girl. Although the outline of the story might lead one to
classify *Qambar* as a love-story and hence the epic poem as a romance,
the epic is generally interpreted in the context of Kazakh heroic poetry.
There are good reasons for this, and a closer look at the story-pattern
and the main motifs of which the epic is composed make this clear.

The poem begins in a somewhat light-hearted vein. Äzimbay allows
his daughter to choose a bridegroom for herself, installing her in a
tower, from which she can view the assembled suitors. Their passing by

in file is described not without humor. Among the suitors there are also
old men, who have come in the hope of exchanging their old wives for
a beautiful young bride:

> Bir töbeniŋ üstinen
> Qïz Nazïm šïqtï basïna
> saldïrïp biyik munara.
> 90 Nazïmdï malsïz almaqqa
> šaldar da žaman želikken,
> qartayġan adam köp eken
> kempirden köŋil zerikken.
> Žarastï dep kiyedi
> 95 eltiri qara börikten.
> Qatïndarï üyinde
> qayġïlanïp žïlaydï,
> "Suluwdï alsa bayïmïz
> ayrïldïq, dep, serikten."
> 100 Ümitker bolïp barša tur
> "Sabaġïnan üzip ap
> žesem," dep, "pisken örikten."
>
> (Äwezov [Auezov], Smirnova 1959: 38)

> On a hill
> a high tower had been built,
> to whose top the girl Nazïm climbed.
> 90 Hoping to have Nazïm without payment,
> the old men got greatly excited.
> There were a lot of old men,
> who had become tired of their old wives.
> Thinking that it suited them, they put on
> 95 hats made of black lambskin.
> Their wives at home
> cried sorrowfully:
> "If our lord marries the beautiful girl,
> we will be separated from our companion."
> 100 The men were all full of hope,
> saying: "If only I could eat the ripe apricot,
> after plucking it from its bough!"

The motif of the princess choosing herself a husband from the suitors
gathered before her is widely spread in folk literature, often connected
to the motif of the princess throwing an object like an apple to the man
of her choice, normally a young man of unpromising outward appearance. It is found in many variants of the folktale types AaTh 314 *The
Youth Transformed to a Horse* and 502 *The Wild Man*, thus for instance
in the fairy-tale *Der Eisenhans* (The Iron Man) collected by the Brothers

Grimm (No. 136).[3] But it is also found in other folktales and folktale
types, as for instance in the Uzbek folktale *Zār Kākilli Yigit* (The Youth
with Golden Curls) or in the Uighur folktale *Padiša Bolǧan Padiči*
(The Shepherd as Padishah).[4] In *Qambar* this motif is not part of the
sequence characteristic of these folktales; the bridegroom chosen is
neither disguised as a scabby-headed youth nor does he have to perform
a particular suitor task. Indeed, Qambar is not even present at the
election, nor does he show any interest in wooing Nazïm. There is a
contrast, as in the folktale, between the richness of the girl and the
poverty of the hero; heroic exploits of the protagonist are also found in
the folktale, as for instance in the Grimms' fairy-tale of the *Eisenhans*,
where, however, their motivation and execution are different.

Qambar and Nazïm are destined for each other. This emerges from
their first meeting, when not only Nazïm shows her love for the hero,
but Qambar is equally drawn towards the girl; indeed, this attraction
is the reason why he wants to avoid her, wanting to spare himself the
shame of the poor man for whom the rich girl is unattainable. Once it
has become clear that the two love each other, the general course of the
narrative is set: Qambar will overcome the obstacle and the lovers will
be united in the end. A happy ending is of course not inevitable; a
number of Turkic, also Kazakh, love-romances sing of unhappy love
and have a tragic ending (see p. 132). What Qambar has to do to win
his bride honorably is to prove his worth, to show that his poverty does
not in any way impinge on his value as a desirable husband. This he
shows not by successfully completing some suitor task imposed by the
bride, but by actually defeating his rival, the khan of the Kalmucks.
Although Qambar's fight against Qaraman could be interpreted as a
suitor contest, in particular in view of Qaraman's giant stature (he is
called a *diw*, an ogre, in the poem),[5] the choice of the Kalmuck khan as

[3]On the Grimm tales see Scherf 1982: 91-97; see also *Motif* H311 *Inspection test
for suitors*, T55.7 *Princess elects herself husband from the young men present.* For
further occurrences of this motif see Geißler 1955: 183-184.

[4]For the Uzbek folktale see Sa'dulla et al. 1955: 199-205 and the translations in
Jungbauer 1923: 74-83 and Laude-Cirtautas 1984: 76-84; for the Uighur folktale see
Zunun, Momin 1982: 126-134 and the translation in Reichl 1986: 33-42.

[5]Compare e.g. *Motif* H335.4.4 *Suitor task: to kill (defeat) unwelcome suitor.*
Kazakh, Uzbek, Turkish *diw, div*, Kirghiz *döö* etc. are Persian loan words; Persian *diw*
(from Avestan *daēva-*, "daemon") is etymologically related to Latin *deus, divus* etc.

Qambar's rival brings the epic poem into line with other heroic epics of the Turks of Central Asia, in which the Kalmucks are the Turks' enemies *par excellence*. Besides, the contest between Qaraman and Qambar does not take place as a contest between suitors. Qambar appears rather as a liberator from Kalmuck oppression: he kills Qaraman both as Nazïm's forced bridegroom and as the embodiment of evil.

Qambar's fight against the Kalmucks and the Kalmuck khan is presented in the epic in a fairly specific form, that of the motif of the bridegroom or the husband returning home just in time before his fiancée or wife is (re-)married. This motif is found in many variations in world literature, often combined with the motif of the husband returning in humble disguise, such as that of a beggar, a pilgrim, or a minstrel. The best-known example is of course the return of Odysseus in the *Odyssey*; other well-known examples are the romance of *King Horn*, the *bylina* of *Dobrynja and Aljoša*, and the various versions of the epic of *Alpamïš* (see below). When compared to these tales, Qambar's arrival at Nazïm's wedding in the nick of time differs in various ways. Qambar is neither disguised nor does he have to prove his right to the girl's hand like the heroes in folktales such as that of the Dragon Slayer or the Bear's Son, who have been tricked by their companions and produce their evidence just before their rightful prize is wed to a deceiver.[6] Although Qambar rescues the girl from an unwanted alliance and will himself marry Nazïm, his motivation to fight the Kalmucks is not that of a suitor, but rather that of the hero who alone can save his people from destruction. This is brought out by the way Qambar is introduced in the epic: he is presented as a hunter, whose concern is the well-being of his tribe. There is possibly even a touch of the culture-hero in Qambar, when his role as a provider of food for the Argïn and Tobïr is underlined:

> Alpïs üyli arïǵïnïŋ
> toqsan üyli tobïrdïŋ
> ašïqqanïn toyǵïzdï.
> Batïr tuwǵan Qambardïŋ
> 250   tiymedi žoqqa zïyanï.
> Šekesinde Qambardïŋ
> bar eken altïn tulïmï,

---

[6] See AaTh 300 *The Dragon-Slayer*, part VII; AaTh 301 *The Three Stolen Princesses*, part VI.

surap alǵan qudaydan
Älimbay xannïŋ qulïnï,
255   eškimge aza bermedi,
qïzdan da zïyat qïlïǵï.
Aw qïlïp šïǵïp žönedi,
üyinde bolmay tïnïmï,
dalada žatqan žayïlïp,
260   buǵï, kiyik qurïdï.

(Äwezov [Auezov], Smirnova 1959: 41-42)

He fed the hungry
among the Arǵïn of the sixty yurts
and among the Tobïr of the ninety yurts.
Qambar, born as a hero,
250   did no harm to the destitute.
On Qambar's head
there was a golden forelock.
He possessed a one-year-old foal,
which Älimbay had received from God for his prayers.
255   He inflicted no pain on anyone
and his character was more tender than a girl's.
He went out hunting
and could not sit still at home.
The deer and gazelles
260   grazing on the steppe became his prey.

Qambar's pre-eminence as a valiant warrior is also emphasized by the embassies that are sent to Qambar, the Noghays' entreaty to come to their help, and the Kalmucks' command to assist at the *toy*.

The discussion so far has revealed a striking similarity between the central plot elements of the epic and corresponding motifs in folktales. But when comparing *Qambar* with the folktales in question, it also becomes evident that the basic narrative structure of the epic cannot be subsumed under a particular folktale type. This is also true when we move from the atomism of the Finnish school in folktale studies to functional analysis like that proposed by V. Propp. The higher level of abstraction that characterizes Propp's folktale morphology allows us to see the narrative pattern of the epic as basically that of redressing some act of aggression or villainy. Nazïm's forced engagement to Qaraman clearly matches Propp's function "A[16] *The threat of forced matrimony*," the embassy of the Nogays to Qambar to solicit his help corresponds to "B[1] *Call for help*," Qambar's departure is equivalent to Propp's functions "C *Consent to counteraction*" and " ↑ *Departure of the hero from home*," and the dénouement of the story can be captured by his functions "H *The hero struggles with the villain*" (more specifically

"H¹"), "I *Victory over the villain*" (more specifically "I¹"), and "W*
Wedding."[7] Although the narrative pattern of *Qambar* can (at least in
part) be written as a functional formula, this formula is so fragmentary
that one might question the relevance of folktale morphology here.
Most noticeable is the absence of the donor and the various functions
connected to this important *dramatis persona*. There is hence no search
and in a way, one might argue, no task in the sense of the folktale:
although it turns out that Nazïm is given to the person who rescues her
from Qaraman, this is not the task originally imposed on the suitors.

This is not to say that motif analysis, folktale typology, and folktale
morphology cannot be applied to the narrative patterns of Turkic epic
poetry. A number of *dastans* are so closely connected to particular
folktale types that their narrative structure can certainly be captured
by a motif sequence in the spirit of A. Aarne and S. Thompson or a
functional formula à la Propp. It has also been shown that the plots of
a number of Turkish love-*hikâye*s conform so rigorously to a general
pattern of motifs and plot elements that they can be described as
variations and realizations of an abstract structural pattern. We are
reminded here of Propp's view of the Russian fairy-tales as realizations
of one narrative archetype.[8] But in the case of *Qambar* the motifs of
the folktale are embedded in a tale that stresses the hero's proof of
worth in society. He is suitor and champion of the Noghays, and he
lives both in a timeless fairy-tale world, where he fights against
Qaraman the *diw*, and in a historically specified world, where he fights
for the Noghays against Qaraman the Kalmuck. A historical frame of
reference is given — the Noghays, it is to be remembered, formed part
of the Golden Horde under Batu (13th c.) — which connects the
narrative with the "time of the Noghays."[9] The motifs of the folktale

---

[7]See Propp 1968: 25ff.

[8]See Spies 1929: 28ff.; Başgöz 1976.

[9]The tribal name of the Noghays is of Mongolian origin (from Mongolian *noxoy*,
"dog"), which is not surprising in view of the mixed Turkic-Mongolian composition of
the Golden Horde (the Kazakh tribal name "Nayman," for instance, is also found
among Mongolians). Despite some research on the Noghays, much remains dark in
their history. In the 15th and 16th centuries, after the break-up of the Golden Horde,
one group of Noghays is found in the area of Lake Aral and the lower reaches of the
Syr-Darya. There they are closely associated with the Kazakhs, Karakalpaks, and
Kirghiz, which explains why the "time of the Noghays" is the time of the heroic past
in a number of Kazakh, Karakalpak, and Kirghiz epics. On the Noghays and their

are present, but they are reinterpreted in a tale that focuses on the hero, on his deeds of prowess and valor, which prove his right to Nazïm's hand even to those who looked down on him at the beginning of the tale.

Köroğlu/Göroğlï and The Winning of a Bride

Qambar might also be viewed as a story in which the theme of winning a bride plays an important role. This theme is widely represented in epic poetry. Probably the most famous bride-winning expedition in medieval literature is the story of how Brunhild was sought after by Gunther and won by Siegfried in his stead, the topic of the seventh *aventiure* of the Middle High German *Nibelungenlied*. Here we have one important type of a bride-winning narrative, the type where the hero has to perform a series of tasks and contests — he might even have to overcome the warlike maiden herself — before he can win the girl's hand. In a second type of what Germanists call *Braut-werbungsepen* the hero has to overcome a number of obstacles, generally of a martial kind, before he can marry the girl of his choice. The best-known examples of this type in Middle High German literature are the epic of *Kudrun* as well as the so-called *Spielmannsepen* (minstrel epics).[10] These types are also found in Turkic epic poetry. In the *Tale of Qan Turalï* in the *Book of Dede Qorqut*[11] the hero has to overcome a bull, a camel, and a lion before he can marry Seldžen Xatun, the daughter of the Christian king of Trebizond. On the way home, Qan Turalï falls asleep, but his bride is ready to defend him and herself against all assailants. Her father, having meanwhile regretted that he gave his daughter to a Moslem, pursues the couple with an army. Seldžen rouses her husband and herself fights victoriously against the attackers. She even rescues Qan Turalï from the enemy, a deed which

---

role in Kazakh epic poetry see Žirmunskij 1974b; Qoŋïratbaev 1987: 347-352.

[10]In particular the minstrel epics *König Rother, St. Oswald, Orendel*; see Frings 1939-40; Frings, Braun 1947; Geißler 1955; Žirmunskij [Schirmunski] 1961: 38-53; Schröder 1967.

[11]Ergin 1958-63: I, 184-198 (text); Sümer, Uysal, Walker 1972: 98-114 (translation); Lewis 1974: 117-132 (translation); see also Ruben 1944: 238-242.

causes Qan Turalï to fear that his bride's bravery might make him
appear a weakling. He decides to fight with her, but when he sees her
courage and love he is reconciled with his bride. This story combines
the motif of the suitor contests with that of the warlike bride, a
combination which is also found in the *Tale of Bamsï Beyrek* in the
Book of Dede Qorqut.[12]

Bride-winning epics are so widespread in Turkic epic poetry that their
proper treatment demands a separate book. I will have to restrict
myself to a few examples.[13] The theme of *Brautwerbung* occurs
frequently in the *Köroǧlu/Göroǧlï*-cycle. *Dastan*s and *hikâye*s on
Köroǧlu/Göroǧlï are popular among many Turkic peoples, from the
Turks of the Balkans to the Kazakhs, Uighurs and Tobol Tatars in
Central Asia and Siberia, as well as among speakers of non-Turkic
languages. As this cycle will be the topic of a later section (see Chapter
Ten), I will only comment on the name of the main protagonist at this
point. "Köroǧlu/Köroǧlu" is the Azerbaijanian and Turkish form of the
name and means "son of the blind man." It is found in those traditions
in which the hero's father is an equerry who is blinded by his cruel
master. "Göroǧlï" is the Turkmen form of the name (corresponding to
Uzbek "Goroǧli" or Uighur "Göroǧli"), which means "son of the grave."
This is the name of the hero in those traditions in which he is born in
a grave. In the following outlines I shall use the name-forms which are
found in the texts summarized.

The theme of winning a bride occurs in manifold variations in almost
all the versions and variants of the *Köroǧlu/Göroǧlï*-cycle (unless they
are fragmentary). One treatment of this theme is found in *medžlis*
("sitting") IV and V of Chodzko's translation of an Azerbaijanian version
of *Köroǧlu*, in the story of how Köroǧlu won the hand of Princess
Nighara.[14] This story has the following outline:

---

[12]Cf. *Motif* H331 *Suitor contests: bride offered as prize* ff.; *Motif* H332.1 *Suitor in
contest with bride*, H345 *Suitor test: overcoming princess in strength* and others. — For
the relationship of the story of Bamsï Beyrek to the epic of *Alpamïš* see Chapter Ten.

[13]For an extensive comparative treatment of the theme of winning a bride in
Turkic oral epic poetry see Žirmunskij's chapter "Geroičeskoe svatovstvo" in
Žirmunskij 1960: 218-273; compare also the discussion of this theme in Tatar epic
poetry in Urmančeev 1980a: 58-78.

[14]See Chodzko 1842: 91-154. Meeting IV in Chodzko's text is introduced by the
story of how Demirdži-Oǧlu became Köroǧlu's companion (*ibid*: 88-91). The Nighara-
branch has the number XIX A in Boratav's survey; see Boratav 1967. I leave

Princess Nighara is Sultan Murad's daughter. Every Friday when she goes to the mosque, the inhabitants of Istanbul are bidden to stay in their houses, while the shops should nevertheless stay open. Belly-Ahmed, on his visit to Istanbul, is curious to see Nighara and hides behind some boards in a greengrocer's shop. When he is discovered by Nighara and interrogated by her, he pretends to be one of Köroğlu's men. Nighara bids Belly-Ahmed to transmit a letter to Köroğlu, in which she confesses her love for Köroğlu and commands him to take her away with him. When Belly-Ahmed reaches Köroğlu's stronghold, he produces the letter as well as a miniature of the princess, whereupon Köroğlu has his horse Qïrat saddled and sets off for Istanbul.

In Istanbul Köroğlu stays with an old woman, buys himself a *saz*, white clothes like those of a mullah and a seal with the sultan's name. He has a *faqqï* (learned man) write a letter which identifies him as a messenger from Sultan Murad, at the time absent from Istanbul on a pilgrimage to Mecca. Köroğlu manages to gain admittance to Nighara's quarters, where he transforms himself into a minstrel and sings of his love for the princess. Although he is at first badly mistreated by Nighara's servant-girls, the princess finally relents and, having recognized Köroğlu in the *ašïq*, consents to elope with him the next morning. The next day, while Nighara is leaving town with her train of ladies in waiting, Köroğlu snatches her from her entourage, places her behind him on Qïrat and rides away with her.

Nighara's brother Burji Sultan is informed of the deed and gathers an army to pursue the fugitives. Meanwhile, Köroğlu decides to rest, informing Nighara that his sleep will last for either three or seven days. When Nighara notices the restlessness of Köroğlu's horse, she wakes him and urges him to continue their journey. Köroğlu, however, awaits Burji Sultan's arrival, defeats him, but spares his life for Nighara's sake.

Before Nighara and Köroğlu reach Čamlïbel, Köroğlu's fortress, they encounter two more obstacles. First their way is barred by the encampment of a European nobleman, who has come to Turkey to seek Nighara's hand. Köroğlu defeats the European and his retinue, but lets the young man flee at Nighara's request. They then come across a caravan led by a rich merchant, who on seeing Nighara desires to marry her. When the merchants realize who Nighara's companion is, they entreat the master of the caravan to make good his faux pas with a generous present. Nighara pleads for the culprit, and Köroğlu is satisfied to accept 1,500 tumans as recompense for the insult. The couple finally reach Köroğlu's fortress, where they are greeted by his valiant companions.

As can be seen from this summary, the winning of a bride is here of the type where the bride consents to an elopement, is even herself the

Chodzko's spelling of the various names, except that of the hero (spelled Kurroglou by Chodzko) and his horse (spelled Kyrat by Chodzko). On the Azerbaijanian text of the 19th-c. Tbilisi manuscript of the cycle see Korogly 1983: 212-216 (on this manuscript see p. 319).

instigator of her abduction.[15] The impediments to the lovers' union are
at first overcome by ruse and only later, on their flight, by heroism.
Köroğlu's feats of valor in Istanbul are of a somewhat uncouth and even
burlesque kind. He eats huge portions of pilaw to the horror of the old
woman, who had hoped to feast on the leftovers; he chops off the head
of the treacherous *faqqï* and kicks down a wall to cover the corpse; he
takes delight in frightening the *saz*-maker, who does not recognize his
customer at first; and he humbly endures whippings and beatings from
Nighara's ladies-in-waiting, finding ever new strength to sing a song of
love. On his return to Čamlïbel, Köroğlu falls like Qan Turalï in the
Book of Dede Qorqut into a heroic sleep;[16] but this does not lead to
warlike activity on the bride's part as in the story of Qan Turalï.
Köroğlu overcomes the pursuers and the fellow-suitor single-handed,
and his very appearance is enough to strike the merchants with terror.

There are several variants of this branch. The Azerbaijanian text
edited in 1941 ("Köroğlu's Journey to Istanbul") is simpler in narrative
structure: Köroğlu has heard of the beauty of Nigar-xanïm, the
daughter of the *xodkar*[17] of Istanbul, and decides to marry her. In
Istanbul, where he stays with a miller, he persuades the gardener of
Nigar's garden to let him enter. Nigar falls in love with Köroğlu and
flees with him. When Nigar's forty servant-girls tell the *xodkar* what
has happened, he rushes to their pursuit with a host of soldiers.
Köroğlu engages in battle and defeats the *xodkar* and his army with
the help of his companions, who have come to his aid.[18]

---

[15]See Geißler 1955: 35-43.

[16]In the Uzbek *dastan Yusuf and Ahmad* Yusuf has the custom of sleeping for
three days and of remaining awake for thirty days; see Vámbéry 1911: 26. On the
motif of the hero's sleep in Turkic and Mongolian epic poetry see Lipec 1984: 37f.;
compare also *Motif* F564.3.2 *Person sleeps for three days and nights*, F564.3.4 *Person
sleeps for nine months*.

[17]The word *xodkar* (in the 1941 edition in Arabic script) or *xotkar* (in later editions
in Cyrillic script) means, according to Orudžov et al. 1966-87: IV, 334, "ruler, chief."

[18]Alizade 1941: 13-26; the editor gives no source for this text. — This and
Chodzko's variant as well as a third variant, recorded in 1933, form the basis for the
text found in M. H. Tähmasib's edition of the Azerbaijanian *Köroğlu*-cycle. See
Tähmasib 1959: 45-71 (text), 403-406 (notes on the variants). Tähmasib's text follows
basically Chodzko's text with the following most important deviations: Nigar is the
daughter of the *xotkar* of Istanbul; Köroğlu stays with an old woman, whose son is
gardener in Nigar's pomegranate garden and helps at the elopement; the episodes with

Among the Turkish variants of the *Köroğlu/Göroğli*-cycle the fullest variant is the text recorded from Behçet Mahir.[19] His story of Köroğlu and Han Nigâr belongs, however, to a different branch. Han Nigâr is here a beauty from Dagestan in the Caucasus, who has refused all suitors ever since her lover died in Aleppo. When a dervish shows Köroğlu her portrait he falls in love with her and decides to marry her. Köroğlu pretends that he has a letter from her lover, proving that he is still alive, and thus manages to get into her presence. In their tête-à-tête Han Nigâr falls in love with Köroğlu and does not rebuff his embraces. Her three brothers agree to the marriage but stipulate that Köroğlu return to marry their sister when more of his companions have brought wives to Çamlıbel. Köroğlu bids farewell to Han Nigâr, leaving his sword with her and admonishing her to call the son she might give birth to "Hasan-bey." He also leaves her instructions to call any foal her mare might have from Kırat "Kamar-tay." Han Nigâr does indeed have a son (and her mare a foal), who in due course of time departs to find his father.[20] This branch is also found in the Azerbaijanian version of the cycle, where it usually goes under the name of "Köroğlu's Journey to Derbent."[21] It is just one of various stories on the theme of *Brautwerbung* in the Azerbaijanian version of *Köroğlu*, represented, for instance, also by the branches entitled "Köroğlu's Journey to Erzurum" and "The Coming of Mähbub-xanïm to Čänlibel (Çamlıbel)."[22]

Another variant of Köroğlu's wooing of Princess Nighara comes from much further afield, from a tale written down by W. Radloff among the Tobol Tatars, who live east of the Urals on the river Tobol. This tale,

the European suitor and the merchant caravan are missing.

[19]See Kaplan, Akalın, Bali 1973; on the Turkish variants see also Boratav 1984; Eberhard 1955: 30-49; Karryev 1968: 77-99.

[20]Kaplan, Akalın, Bali 1973: 77-104: for the continuation see *ibid.*: 105-130 ("Köroğlu — Han Nigâr — Hasan Bey — Telli Nigâr"); this branch has the number XIII in Boratav's survey; see Boratav 1967. For the contemporaneous birth of Hasan-bey and Kamar-tay see *Motif* B311 *Congenital helpful animal.*

[21]See Karryev 1968: 62; Alizade 1941: 128-148; Tähmasib 1959: 336-359 (text), 461-465 (on the variants). It is, however, not found in Chodzko's variant.

[22]See Karryev 1968: 60. A Russian translation of "Köroğlu's Journey to Erzurum" is included in Petrosjan 1975: II, 199-229.

entitled "Kür's Son,"[23] tells how Köroǧlu (Kürulï) hears about Nikar Xanïm's beauty from an old man and decides to marry her. When Köroǧlu reaches Istanbul he falls asleep and is made prisoner by Bul Bäk Xan. Nikar Xanïm comes to the prison, finds Köroǧlu playing the cither and releases him; but Köroǧlu returns to Istanbul, takes back his horse and defeats Bul Bäk Xan together with his companions, who had meanwhile reached Istanbul.[24]

Although these two stories, "Köroǧlu's Journey to Istanbul" and "Köroǧlu's Journey to Derbent," are not found in the eastern versions of the *Köroǧlu/Göroǧlï*-cycle (Turkmen, Uzbek, Karakalpak, Kazakh, Uighur), a number of eastern branches also treat of the theme of the hero's winning a bride. In the Turkmen and Uzbek versions of the cycle Göroǧlï is married to Āǧa Yunus Peri (among others). As her name indicates, Āǧa Yunus Peri is a fairy (*peri*), who lives in the fabulous country Bāǧi-Eram, from where she is abducted by Göroǧlï.[25] I will illustrate the various bride-winning expeditions of the eastern versions of the cycle by one branch only, the story of Göroǧlï's wooing of a heroic maiden. It is found in the Turkmen, the Uzbek, and the Karakalpak versions, where the branch is called "Harman Däli" (Turkmen); "Xirman-Dali," "Xarman-Dala" (Uzbek); or "Qïrmandäli" (Karakalpak). The word *däli/dali* (Turkish *deli*) means both "valiant" and "crazy," suggesting valor of a daring, if not foolhardy kind. As an epithet it is already found in the *Book of Dede Qorqut*; from Turkish the word has been borrowed into Serbo-Croatian, where in the heroic songs *delija* generally denotes a valiant man.[26]

The story of Harman Däli originated apparently in Khorezm. It is only found among Uzbek singers who belong to the "Khorezmian school"

---

[23]In the Tatar language Common Turkic /ö/ is represented as /ü/, thus *kür* corresponds to Turkish *kör*, "blind," although the word itself does not exist in Tatar; "blind" in Tatar is *suqïr*.

[24]See Radloff 1872: 258-261 (text volume); 323-328 (translation volume). The story is somewhat garbled and obviously only badly remembered by the narrator. On this version see also Karryev 1968: 250-254.

[25]On the Uzbek version see Žirmunskij, Zarifov 1947: 202-210; on the Turkmen version see Karryev 1968: 150-151.

[26]On *däli* etc. in the Turkic languages see Sevortjan 1974ff.: III (1980), 214-217. For the various meanings of *delija* in the Serbo-Croatian heroic songs compare Lord 1974: 250-251.

(see Chapter Four); furthermore, a number of Turkmen variants come from singers who lived in the province of Tašauz, i.e. a region in northeastern Turkmenistan which borders on the province of Khorezm of Uzbekistan and on Karakalpakistan; the Karakalpak variants, finally, come from *baqs*ïs whose repertory and language are closely linked to Turkmenistan. Four variants have been recorded from Karakalpak *baqs*ïs.[27] The following is a short summary of Mädireyim Mätžanov's variant:

> In Rum (Istanbul) there lived a rich man, Arïslanbay, who only in old age had a child, a girl, who becomes a beautiful woman. When his daughter Qïrmandäli comes of age, she promises her hand to a suitor who will defeat her in song and *saz*-playing as well as in wrestling. Whoever fails to defeat her will lose his life. She is sought after by many suitors, but none is able to defeat her. When she has had 360 suitors decapitated, an old woman promises to bring a worthy suitor, Göruǧlï, from Šämbilbel. The old woman challenges Göruǧlï, but his wife Aǧayunis, who, due to her magical powers, foresees his defeat, warns him of this expedition and advises him to seek the help of the *pir*[28] Ašïq Aydïn in Bostan. But Göruǧlï follows the old woman and reaches Rum, where he meets Qïrmandäli and her servant-girls beside a pond. In poetical dialogue he asks for water but must leave the last word to Qïrmandäli. When he tries to grab her, she wrestles with him and gets the better of him. Göruǧli's life is spared when he promises to bring his two pupils Miyrimžan and Qambaržan to enter into a singing contest with the beautiful woman.
>
> On his return, Göruǧlï boasts of his prowess but is put in his place by his wife, who by magic has knowledge of his shameful defeat. When Göruǧlï produces his two pupils for Qïrmandäli, they have no success either but are saved by the servant-girls, who take pity on them. Göruǧlï now decides finally to become a disciple of Ašïq Aydïn. He is, however, banished from the *pir*'s presence when in a fit of rage he kills his fellow sufis, one of whom had dared to criticize and hit him for his foolish behavior (Göruǧlï had managed to flood the mosque when he was meant just to pour water round its walls).

[27]Variants: (1) from Mädireyim Nämetullaev (1941); (2) from Ämet Tariyxov (1959); (3) from Mädireyim Mätžanov (1960); (4) from Bekmurat Žumaniyazov (1961). Of these, two variants have been edited, that by Mädireyim Mätžanov and that by Bekmurat Žumaniyazov. All four texts are preserved in the Karakalpak Branch of the Uzbek Academy of Sciences in Nukus; on these variants see Maqsetov [Maksetov] et al. 1977: 51-52, 53-55; Maqsetov, Täžimuratov 1979: 256-258. Mätžanov's variant is edited in Maqsetov, Karimov 1986: 156-181; Žumaniyazov's variant is edited in Maqsetov, Mämbetnazarov, Erpolatov 1963: 29-76.

[28]A *pir* (from Persian *pir*, "old") is a patron saint or, in Sufism, the leader of a religious order.

In a dream, Ašïq Aydïn sees Qïrmandäli, and he sets off together
with his new pupil, Qaramžan, to enter into a singing contest with her.
In this the *pir* is successful but, as he is 115 years old, he asks
Qïrmandäli to marry his young disciple instead of him. After the
unwillingness of Qïrmandäli's father has been overcome, the girl and
the young man are finally married in Bostan, where Qaramžan's father,
Master Badam, gives a sumptuous feast.

When Göruġlï hears what has happened, he travels to Bostan and
finds entrance into Master Badam's house under the pretext that his
dutar needs mending. Göruġlï even manages to have a tête-à-tête with
Qïrmandäli and to abduct one of Badam's daughters to give as wife to
one of his companions, Sapar. The *dastan* ends with the *toy* Göruġlï
gives in honor of Sapar's marriage.

The second Karakalpak variant which has been published agrees fairly
closely with this text. This is also true of the Turkmen and Uzbek
versions.[29]

While the story of Köroğlu's wooing of Princess Nighara (Nigar)
conforms to the pattern of a traditional *Brautwerbung*, the story of
Göroġlï's/Göruġlï's attempt to win Qïrmandäli's hand exposes the hero's
weaknesses. The first story unfolds in a predictable manner from the
hero's falling in love with the princess when he sees her miniature[30] to
his successful elopement and victorious elimination of all opposition to
his marriage. The plot is clear and straightforward; there is no subplot or second plot; elaborations are confined to the introduction of comic
scenes or the tripling of effects, as when Köroğlu overcomes Burji Khan,
the European suitor, and the merchant on his way back to Čamlïbel.
The second story starts equally traditionally, with the motif of the cruel
princess who kills her suitors if they are unable to fulfill the tasks
imposed on them.[31] But instead of the hero winning the bride, possibly
with the help of extraordinary companions, as in the folktale, the hero
fails in the end. Göroġlï omits procuring the help of the *pir*, and he

---

[29]Two of the Uzbek variants are known from Khorezmian singers, one from
Qurbānnazar Abdullaev (Bāla-baxši) and one from Xodžiyaz-baxši. B. A. Karryev
mentions five Turkmen variants, of which the text recorded from Pelwan-baxšï in 1937
is the fullest. Pelwan-baxšï lived also in the Tašauz region; it is noteworthy that the
verses in his variant agree closely with the verses in the Karakalpak variants; for
examples see Chapter Eight, pp. 249ff.

[30]See *Motif* T11.1 *Love through sight of picture*; compare also Geißler 1955: 24ff.

[31]Compare *Motif* T58 *Wooing the strong and beautiful bride*; AaTh 519 *The Strong
Woman as Bride (Brunhilde)*; Eberhard, Boratav 1953: 248-249 (No. 212 *Die
Männermordende)*; Geißler 1955: 55-63.

must consequently accept that the helper will win the prize for himself
and will dispose of it to Göroğli's disadvantage. There is a sequel to the
story to vindicate the hero's honor, bringing the story in a somewhat
strained manner back to Göroğli and his companions.

Compared to the story of Princess Nighara, the plot of the *Qïrmandäli*-branch is more involved. From Göroğli's various attempts to fulfill
the beauty's tasks the scene shifts to the *pir*, then to his disciple and
the latter's marriage and finally back to Göroğli. The various episodes
of the *dastan* are fairly loosely strung together; the story could have
ended with the marriage of Qaramžan, who remains, however, a
completely undeveloped character. The narrative nucleus of this branch
is the suitor test and hence the making and singing of songs. As in the
Turkish *hikâye Asuman ile Zeyçan* (Asuman and Zeydžan) the singing
contest between hero and heroine occupies a central position in the
plot.[32] It is here, in the lyrics, that the interest of the *dastan* lies, in
particular in the *aytïs*-like dialogues between Qïrmandäli and Göroğli
and between Qïrmandäli and the *pir*.[33] One could argue that the bride-
winning plot of the romance provides, as it were, no more than a
narrative frame for the various lyrical dialogues between the main
protagonists.

In *Qambar* the dominant mode is heroic. Despite his love for Nazïm,
Qambar is primarily represented as a warrior, not as a lover. Heroic
action secures private interests, but furthers also tribal concerns. The
obstacles in the hero's way are not insurmountable, and the conflict
between love and honor, honor and duty, in which he finds himself, can
be resolved without great effort on the hero's part. Qambar's heroism
is straightforward, without any psychological complexity or, as so often
in Germanic heroic poetry, any tragic involvement. In view of the
dastan's narrative simplicity and its comparative shortness (it comprises
less than 2,000 lines), we might hesitate to call it a heroic epic. When
Qambar is, however, compared to the branches of the *Köroğlu/Göroğli*-

---

[32]See Spies 1929: 98-103.

[33]In the Karakalpak variant recorded from B. Žumaniyazov there are three *aytïs*-
like dialogues, between Görugli and Qïrmandäli, between Görugli and the *pir*, and
between Qïrmandäli and the *pir*; see Maqsetov, Mämbetnazarov, Erpolatov 1963: 38-
40, 59-61, 68-69. In the Karakalpak variant recorded from M. Mätžanov there are also
three contest-dialogues, between Görugli and Qïrmandäli, between Qïrmandäli and
the *pir*, and again between Görugli and Qïrmandäli; see Maqsetov, Karimov 1986:
160-162, 171-173, 178-179.

cycle summarized in this section, its closeness to the heroic epic — and hence the appropriateness of calling the *dastan* a heroic poem — become immediately evident. In the *Köroğlu/Göroğlï-dastan*s discussed, the hero is never in any situation of serious conflict, nor have his deeds of valor any other legitimation than that of adventure. There is a certain swaggering bearing about Köroğlu and his companions, a reckless delight in showing off their muscles, which characterizes these tales as adventure-romances, in which the heroic elements are no more than colorful trimmings. Love is also subordinated to adventure. The theme of winning a bride provides the framework for the hero's exploits, but the bride could be — and is in other branches — replaced by a horse, a handsome youth, or simply the possessions of a rich merchant. Adventure is here not the *aventure* of the Arthurian knight, but rather the merry deeds of Robin Hood and his men, with sometimes a similar concern for social justice. With the *Köroğlu/Göroğlï*-cycle we are clearly in the world of romance, more specifically in that of the popular adventure-romance with its delight in stunts and amazing feats.

Alpamïš and The Return of the Hero

In *Qambar* the timely arrival of the hero at the wedding-feast of his beloved plays a decisive role in the dénouement of the story. This is basically a realization of the motif of the hero's return, although, as pointed out earlier, the form this motif has in *Qambar* is not that of the *Odyssey* or other return stories.[34] In Turkic oral epic poetry the finest parallel to the return of Odysseus is found in the story of Alpamïš.[35] This story is known to a great number of Turkic peoples, from the Aegean to the Altai, and it has been transmitted in many different

---

[34]*Motif* N681 *Husband (lover) arrives home just as wife (mistress) is to marry another*; it is usually combined with *Motif* K1815.1 *Return home in humble disguise* or some variants like *Motif* K1817.1 *Disguise as beggar* and K1817.1.1 ff. A detailed analysis of this motif in connection to the Alpamïš-story is found in Žirmunskij 1960: 274-312; see also Geißler 1955: 86-88; Holzapfel 1990.

[35]The name of this hero has different forms in different Turkic languages; it is "Alpāmiš" ("Alpāmïš") in Uzbek and "Alpamïs" in Kazakh and Karakalpak. I will in general use the form "Alpamïš," and the form "Alpāmïš" only when referring specifically to an Uzbek variant, "Alpamïs" when specifically referring to a Kazakh or Karakalpak variant.

forms, as prose folktale, heroic tale, prosimetric *dastan*, and verse-epic.
I will start my discussion with the summary of an Uzbek variant, that
of Fāzil Yoldāš-oġli's *Alpāmiš*.[36]

> Among the Qonġirāt of the sixteen clans (*uruġ*) there lived a rich
> man by the name of Dābānbiy. He had a son by the name of Alpinbiy,
> who in turn had two sons, Bāybori and Bāysari. Bāysari was a *bāy*, a
> rich man, Bāybori was a *šāh* (ruler). As they are both without children,
> they decide to spend forty nights in prayer at the tomb of the *pir*
> Šāhimardān,[37] where a voice prophesies that Bāybori will have twins,
> a boy and a girl, and Bāysari a daughter, and foretells the marriage of
> Bāybori's son to Bāysari's daughter. The prophecy comes true; Bāybori
> has a son by the name of Hakimbek and a daughter by the name of
> Qaldirġāč, Bāysari a daughter by the name of Barčin. Their names are
> given them by Šāhimardān, who appears in the guise of a dervish at
> their name-giving feast. When Hakimbek is only seven years old he is
> already able to lift his grandfather Alpinbiy's bow, weighing fourteen
> *bātmān* (a unit of weight ranging from 30 to 200 kg, depending on the
> region), and shoot arrows into the far distance. For this reason the
> people called him Alpāmiš, the last of the ninety heroes of the world.[38]

[36]This variant has been transmitted in two texts. The first text was written down
in 1922 by Ġāzi Ālim Yunusov, but the manuscript has disappeared; only a fragment
of this text has been preserved as an extract published in an Uzbek journal in 1923
(*Bilim očāġi* 1923.2-3: 45-59). The second text is extant in manuscript form (No. 18 in
the Archives of the Folklore Department of the Pushkin Institute of the Uzbek
Academy of Sciences in Tashkent). This manuscript comprises 933 pages, the main
bulk of which was written down by Mahmud Zarifov in the singer's house in the
village of Lāyqa (in the Samarkand region) in 1928. The first fifteen pages of this
manuscript were written down in the June of 1927; the rest was written down by M.
Zarifov in the course of two months in 1928. See Zarif, Mirzaev 1979: 396. Mirzaev
gives 946 pages as the total number of pages of the manuscript; according to my notes
from my stays in the Folklore Department in Tashkent the manuscript consists of 15
plus 918 pages. There have been many editions of this manuscript, none of them,
however, representing a critical edition of the complete manuscript. The fullest and
most reliable edition available to date is that prepared by H. Zarif and T. Mirzaev for
the series "Ozbek xalq idžādi." My references are to this edition (Zarif, Mirzaev 1979);
the text of this edition has been reprinted. According to information I was given by
T. Mirzaev and his collaborators in December 1990, the edition and Russian
translation of the full manuscript are ready for publication.

[37]Šāhimardān, "the shah of men," is the name of the caliph Ali (656-661) in
Moslem legend. According to Central Asian popular tradition he has seven tombs,
because when he was buried, the camel carrying his body miraculously became seven
camels running in different directions. Two of these tombs are believed to be in
Uzbekistan (Nurāta and Hamzaābād). See Tokarev et al. 1980-82: II, 186 (article
"Musul'manskaja mifologija").

[38]"Then all people came together and said: 'In the world 89 heroes (*alp*) have
lived; their head was Rustami Dāstān; may this Alpāmiš-alp be their last one.'
Alpāmišbek-alp becoming their last one, becoming one of the ninety heroes, becoming

When Alpāmiš one day explains to his father the meaning of the words "generous" and "stingy" as giving or withholding alms, he puts into Bāybori's head the idea of testing his brother's generosity by imposing a *zakāt* (alms-tax) on him. This leads to a quarrel between the brothers, and Bāysari decides to migrate to the land of the Kalmucks, together with a large part of the Qoṅǧirāt. On the way to the Kalmucks, Bāysari and his people lay waste to the cultivated fields of the Kalmuck khan's subjects, unaware of the ways of a sedentary population. The khan of the Kalmucks accepts Bāysari's protestations of innocence and lets him and his people settle on the shores of Lake Āyna near the Čilbir desert.

In their new home Barčin is courted by Qāradžān, Kokaman, and Kokaldāš, the sons of Surxayil, an old Kalmuck witch-like woman. The suitors are at first rebuffed, and one of them even knocked down by the maiden. But Barčin has to agree in the end to marry one of the brothers, being, however, allowed to get a respite of six months. She sends ten messengers with a letter to Alpāmiš to inform him of her predicament. Bāybori tries to intercept the message, but Qaldirǧāč, Alpāmiš's sister, shows the letter to her brother and incites him to come to Barčin's rescue. Qultāy, Bāybori's guardian of horses, attempts to prevent Alpāmiš from choosing a good horse on Bāybori's command but fails. Alpāmiš departs on Bāy-Čibār, a true *tulpār* (winged horse).

On his way Alpāmiš has a series of adventures. While he is sleeping in a graveyard, the Forty Saints (*čiltān*)[39] unite the souls of the two lovers in a dream. Later, in Kalmuck territory, he stays with the shepherd Kayqubād, where he again has a dream; at the same time Barčin and Qāradžān also have dreams. The latter is informed of Alpāmiš's arrival in his dream, and he goes out to meet him. In the course of their encounter, Qāradžān is converted to Islam and the two heroes become blood brothers. Qāradžān, acting as suitor for Alpāmiš, arrives at Barčin's tent two hours before the expiration of the six months' period. Barčin, however, asks for a further delay and sets four suitor tests: a horse-race, an archery contest, a shot-putting contest and a wrestling match. Qāradžān rides for Alpāmiš on Bāy-Čibār and wins the horse-race despite his brother Kokaldāš's treacherous behavior. Alpāmiš emerges as victor in the archery and shot-putting contests and kills the other contestants in the wrestling match. He finally wins Barčin's hand. But before Alpāmiš can return to his father's country, he has to fight together with his blood brother Qāradžān against the Kalmucks, who have been sent against them by Tāyči-xān, their khan,

---

one of their number, acquiring the name of a hero, received the name 'Alpāmiš' at the age of seven. Because he was able to lift the bow and shoot with it at the age of seven he was named 'Alpāmiš-alp'." Zarif, Mirzaev 1979: 9. — The singer is clearly trying to give an explanation for the name, but only succeeds in explaining the first part of his name (*alp*).

[39] The Forty Saints (*qïrqlar*, *čiltan*) are generally believed to be invisible saints who help those who by their piety deserve their assistance; see Tokarev et al.: II, 629 (article "Čil'tán").

at the instigation of Surxayil, the Kalmuck hag who had lost all her sons in the contests except the apostate Qāradžān. Having overcome their enemies, Alpāmiš and Barčin can move back to the old Qoṅġirāt country of Bāysin, but Bāysari prefers to stay behind in the land of the Kalmucks.

Meanwhile, old Surxayil succeeds in arousing the Kalmuck khan's anger against Bāysari. He is made destitute and has to make a living by guarding a herd of camels. When Alpāmiš is informed of his father-in-law's misfortune, he departs with forty companions and his sister's husband Bektemir, to come to his rescue. Surxayil has a palace built on Murādtepa, on their road to Bāysari's abode, where forty slave-girls try to turn the young men's heads. Despite these distractions, Alpāmiš and his companions defeat an approaching Kalmuck host. The heroes are then made drunk and the palace in which they are asleep is set on fire. All forty companions perish, but Alpāmiš is invulnerable. While still in his sleep, he is thrown into a subterranean dungeon (*zindān*).

When the news of the young heroes' death spreads to Qoṅġirāt, Ultāntāz, Bāybori's son by the slave-woman Bādām, usurps the position of ruler. He forces Alpāmiš's family to live in destitution and banishes Qaldirġāč to Lake Bābir. Barčin's son Yādgār, born after his father's departure, is living with Qaldirġāč.

One day, while Alpāmiš is languishing in his dungeon, he catches a wild goose, which has been injured. When the wild goose can fly again, he sends the bird with a letter to Lake Bābir. The letter falls into Yādgār's hands, and he asks Qāradžān to rescue his father. Qāradžān is, however, unable to pull Alpāmiš from his dungeon, as the rope is not strong enough, and he has to return home without having achieved his objective.

The Kalmuck khan's daughter Tāwka asks the shepherd Kayqubād to look after a he-goat she has bought at the bazar. When one day the goat falls into Alpāmiš's dungeon, the shepherd, who has earlier been Alpāmiš's host, recognizes the hero and provides him with food. Alpāmiš makes a *čaṇāwuz* (a kind of Jew's harp) from bone and gives it to Kayqubād. Kayqubād's playing attracts Tāwka's attention and she subsequently finds out about Alpāmiš. It is through Tāwka that Alpāmiš eventually regains his liberty. His horse is brought to the underground prison, and with the help of the saints, Bāy-Čibār pulls Alpāmiš from his dungeon with his tail. When the Kalmucks rush on Alpāmiš, he defeats their army, kills their khan and old Surxayil, puts Kayqubād on the throne, and marries Tāwka to the new khan of the Kalmucks.

After seven years in the *zindān* Alpāmiš arrives back home just before Barčin is to be married to Ultāntāz. On his way he hears what has happened in his absence. Alpāmiš meets his father's mother, Tarlān, who recognizes her grandson, and his sister Qaldirġāč, who only recognizes the horse and is uncertain about the rider. Qultāy, whom Alpāmiš meets next, is unwilling to believe his good fortune in seeing his lord again and asks for Alpāmiš's mark of recognition, the five fingers of Šāhimardān imprinted on his right shoulder. When he is satisfied as to Alpāmiš's identity, he agrees to exchange clothes with him. Alpāmiš wants to join the marriage-feast in disguise in order to put his wife's and friends' loyalty to the test. Here he encounters his son Yādgār, who is maltreated at the *toy*, his mother, who recognizes her son immediately, and his father, who has to serve as cupbearer at Ultāntāz's table. At Alpāmiš's request, Alpinbiy's bow is brought for him at the archery contest, a bow which he alone is capable of handling. When the singing of improvised marriage-songs (*yār-yār*) starts, Alpāmiš first exchanges humorous-satirical verses with Bādām, Ultāntāz's mother, and then tender love-songs with Barčin, whose verses attest to her faithfulness and love for her husband. Then the real Qultāy arrives on Bāy-Čibār and reveals the identity of the false Qultāy to the gathering. Alpāmiš has the usurper Ultāntāz executed and resumes the rule of the Qoṅġirāt. He is finally reunited with his wife, as well as with his friends and relatives, especially with Qāradžān, who had fled from Ultāntāz to Ālatāġ. Barčin's father, Bāysari, is asked to forget his old quarrel with his brother and invited to return to his former home. The Qoṅġirāt are once again united and live in happiness and prosperity.

I have provided a somewhat fuller summary of this *dastan* to give an idea not only of the main outline of the story but also of the intricate woof of the narrative thread. Fāzil's variant is particularly rich in details and a good example for the structure of the longer Uzbek *dastan*. As his variant is both a complete and representative version of the Alpamïš-story (see Chapter Ten) it can serve as a basis for analysis. The plot of *Alpāmiš* has two parts, the winning of a bride and the return of the hero. The first part, ending with Alpāmiš's marriage to Barčin, forms a unity and could stand by itself. But as other versions of the Alpamïš-story, among them the earliest variant, the *Tale of Bamsï Beyrek* in the *Book of Dede Qorqut*, show, the second part of the epic is an integral part of the Alpamïš-story, and the epic must be viewed as a whole.[40] The motif sequence of the first part of *Alpāmiš* is traditional, as typical of the Turkish *hikâyes* as of a great number of Central Asian *dastans*. I will single out only the most important ones. The hero's parents are at first without child and beget a child only through divine intervention (*Motif* D1925.3 *Barrenness removed by prayer*), a situation which also holds for the heroine's parents. In Turkish *hikâyes* conception is often brought about by eating an apple offered by a dervish, who later reappears like Šāhimardān in *Alpāmiš* when the child is to be

---

[40] A variant of the *dastan*, originally published in 1901 by A. Divaev, stops at the end of the first part. This variant has recently been reprinted and translated into English; see Paksoy 1989. On pp. 119ff. Paksoy gives a polemic comparison of several variants of the Alpamïš-story, voicing his criticism of Russian scholarship in general and Žirmunskij's work in particular.

named.[41]   When Bāybori and Bāysari promise to marry their as yet
unborn children to one another (compare *Motif* T65.5 *Children born on
same night betrothed*), the stage is already set for conflict, although the
quarrel between the brothers does not arise as quickly as in the "Tale
of the Viziers Nûr ad-Dîn and Shams ad-Dîn" in the *Arabian Nights*,
who start quarreling about the payments necessary for their children's
marriage when they have not even found a wife for themselves as yet.[42]
Alpāmiš performs, of course, the usual feats of a hero, proving in
particular his strength and skill in archery.[43] He also chooses himself
a horse worthy of his stature, a motif widely encountered in heroic
poetry.[44] As in other Turkic epics, Alpāmiš's horse is not only the
hero's faithful companion, but is eventually the means of his rescue.

An important role in the *dastan* is played by Alpāmiš's companion
Qāradžān. The friendship between two heroes belongs to the basic
inventory of heroic epic poetry.[45] As M. Bowra has observed, the hero
"cannot live entirely for himself, and needs a companion to whom he
can unburden his heart and whom he can make the partner of his
ambitions. That is why heroic poetry has its great pairs of gifted
friends, like Achilles and Patroclus, Roland and Oliver, Gilgamesh and
Enkidu, the Uzbek Alpamys and Karadzhan, the Armenian brothers
Sanasar and Bagdasar."[46] The friendship between Alpāmiš and Qāradžān is, however, of a special kind, unlike that of the other pairs

---

[41]For the Turkish *hikâyes* see Spies 1929: 19-21; for a detailed analysis of the
motif of the hero's miraculous birth to a childless couple see Žirmunskij 1960: 163-
175; the motif of the miraculous birth of the hero has been extensively studied by
Propp 1976 [1941]. Žirmunskij also discusses and analyses the role of saints etc. in
the name-giving ceremony in Turkic folk narrative; see Žirmunskij 1960: 175-188.

[42]This is the story of the twentieth to the twenty-fourth night; on this motif in the
Turkish *hikâyes* see Spies 1929: 21-22.

[43]Compare the birth and childhood of Oğuz Qağan; see Chapter Two, pp. 37f. On
the role of the hero's weapons, in particular his bow and arrows, in Turkic and
Mongolian epic poetry see Lipec 1984: 69ff.

[44]On this motif see Žirmunskij 1960: 199-208; Lipec 1984: 202ff.

[45]On the friendship between Alpāmiš and Qāradžān see Sulejmanov 1959. On the
role of friendship in Turkic and Mongolian epic poetry in general see Lipec 1984: 96-
99; compare also *Motif* P311 *Sworn brethren*, P312 *Blood-brotherhood*, P313 *Milk-
brotherhood*.

[46]Bowra 1952: 65.

enumerated by Bowra. Qāradžān is a Kalmuck, a Lamaistic Buddhist and hence an unbeliever in the eyes of the Moslems, and his becoming a friend presupposes his conversion to Islam. The most famous parallel in Turkic epic poetry is Manas' friendship with the Kalmuck Almambet. In Radloff's version of the *Manas*-trilogy, Almambet, the son of the Oirot (Kalmuck) khan, converts to Islam when, in an encounter with the Kirghiz Kökčö, the latter shows him the Koran. As Almambet's family turn a deaf ear to their son's proselytizing efforts, he moves to Kökčö's tribe. His stay with Kökčö is, however, not of a long duration. Almambet is slandered as having had an illicit relationship with Kökčö's wife Aq-erkeč and leaves Kökčö to join Manas. The two heroes have been destined for one another, and thus, when they meet, they hardly need to exchange greetings before embracing as friends. They return together to Manas' encampment, where his mother's breasts immediately fill with milk at the sight of Almambet:

Andan Almambet batïr ayttï deyt:
1850 "Enäkäŋnin aq emčäk
      aġïp turat, Manas-qan!
      Bir emčägin sen emgin,
      bir emčägin men emäyn!
      Belimdi qïndai buulayn!
1855 Džaqïp-baydan tuuayn!
      Seni-minän bir tuuġan adam bolayn!
      Bir emčägin Almambet emdi deyt,
      bir emčägin Manas emdi deyt!
      Emi üyünö bardï deyt,
1860 džïrġap-qulap džattï deyt —
      Manas-minän Almambet
      ököö bir tuuġan adam boldu deyt!

The warrior Almambet said: "Your mother's white breasts are flowing, Manas-khan! You suck the one, and I will suck the other! I shall bind my waist tight as a sword-sheath, I shall be born of Jakıpbay! I wish to be your Brother!" And Almambet sucked one breast, while Manas sucked the other. Then they went to their home rejoicing and frolicking. Those Two, Manas and Almambet, became Brothers![47]

[47]Hatto 1990: 70/71 (text and English translation). For consistency's sake I have adapted the Kirghiz text to the transcription system used here. On "Almambet, Er Kökčö and Ak-erkeč [Aq-erkeč]" see Hatto 1990: 13-47 (text and translation); see also the discussion of this branch of the *Manas*-cycle in comparison with the *Nibelungenlied* in Hatto 1987b; on "How Almambet came to Manas" see Hatto 1990: 49-71 (text and translation).

As in *Qambar*, the heroine in *Alpāmiš* is sought after by unwelcome suitors and manages to get a reprieve (compare *Motif* T151.1 *Six months' respite from unwelcome marriage*). The climax of the first part of *Alpāmiš* are then the suitor contests, in which both Alpāmiš and Qāradžān distinguish themselves.[48] They form with Alpāmiš's marriage to Barčin the "logical" conclusion to this part of the *dastan*, which, as even this sketchy analysis of its narrative structure makes clear, is a typical *Brautwerbungsepos*.

The second part of *Alpāmiš* is equally made up of motifs which are widely circulated in Turkic epic poetry and oral narrative. Figures like the *kampir* (old woman) Surxayil, plotting the hero's destruction, the helpful shepherd Kayqubād, the usurping bastard son or the infidel princess Tāwka belong to the stock-in-trade of the Uzbek and other Turkic epic traditions. Tāwka can be compared for instance to Khan Köbikti's daughter Qarlïġa in the Kazakh epic *Qoblandï*, who also falls in love with the imprisoned hero and helps to free him and his companion Qaraman. Unlike Tāwka, however, Qarlïġa is a heroic maiden, who successfully fights for and against the hero, becoming in the end his second wife.[49] The motif of the princess becoming enamored of the warriors locked up by her father appears also in the Old French *chanson de geste*, where in *La Prise d'Orange* Orable falls in love with Guillaume and in *Fierabras* Floripas falls in love with Gui de Bourgogne; the Saracen maidens help free the imprisoned heroes and finally become Christians. The deception of Alpāmiš and his retinue by Surxayil, their inebriation, the burning of their dwelling place, the invulnerability of the hero, the horse as helper, the bird as messenger with a letter etc. are all motifs for which parallels can be found both within and outside Turkic epic and narrative. Many of these have been brought together in V. Žirmunskij's study of the Alpamïš-story, to whose list a good number could be added.[50] I will, however, refrain from further

[48]See Žirmunskij 1960: 242 ff.; compare also *Motif* H331.4 *Suitor contest: shooting*, H331.5 *Suitor contest: race*, H331.6 *Suitor contest: wrestling*.

[49]For an edition and Russian translation of Qalmaġanbetov's variant see Kidajš-Pokrovskaja, Nurmagambetova 1975; on the Kazakh version of this epic see also Nurmagambetova 1988.

[50]Žirmunskij's parallels in the second part of his book (1960) come mostly from Altaian heroic tales, but are not restricted to these; see also Žirmunskij, Zarifov 1947: 79ff.

comment on these motifs and turn to the concluding part of the *dastan*, the return of the hero.

Here, too, my discussion will have to be fairly sketchy.   Return stories are known from many narrative traditions, and I will be able to mention only a few parallels to the Alpamïš-story. The return of the hero is a particularly popular narrative pattern in Serbo-Croatian heroic song.[51] The best-known instance of the motif of the husband returning in disguise to his wife's wedding in the Karadžić corpus of Serbo-Croatian heroic poetry is the song of Marko Kraljević and Mina of Kostur (*Marko Kraljević i Mina od Kostura*), in which Marko disguises himself as a black monk.[52]

In Russian epic poetry, the *bylina* of *Dobrynja and Aljoša* is the best-known example of the motif of the husband returning in disguise, in this case in the guise of a minstrel (*Motif* K1817.3 *Disguise as harper*). Dobrynja bids his young wife Natasja to wait six years for him to return from his expedition, before she gets married again, forbidding her, however, explicitly to marry Aljoša Popovič. Aljoša treacherously reports Dobrynja dead and woos Natasja. When Natasja and Aljoša are to be married, Dobrynja's horse stumbles and a voice from heaven tells him what is happening at home. Dobrynja returns, disguises himself as a *skomorox* (minstrel) and plays to the assembled company on his *gusli*. When he is allowed to drink to the bride's health, Dobrynja throws his golden ring into the cup and is recognized by his wife when she empties the cup.[53] The disguise of the returning husband or lover as a minstrel and his recognition by the ring he puts into the bride's cup is also found in the medieval romance of *King Horn* (see *Motif* H94.4 *Identification by ring dropped in glass (cup) of wine*). In one of the Middle English

[51]A. B. Lord has given a detailed synopsis of twelve texts in the Parry collection, which underlines the closely knit motif-sequence of this story-type; see Lord 1960: 242-259. For a book-length study of Serbo-Croatian return songs in comparison with the *Odyssey* and *Beowulf* see Foley 1990; on the narrative structure of Serbo-Croatian return songs see *ibid*.: 359ff.

[52]See Đurić 1977: 298-306 (originally published by Vuk Karadžić in 1845); for an English prose-translations see Ćurčija-Prodanović 1963: 80-86.

[53]This is the story according to Hilferding's variant, recorded 1871 on Lake Onega; it is re-edited in Balandin 1983: 113-122; for a partial list of variants see *ibid*.: 322; for an English translation see Chadwick 1932: 80ff. For a discussion of this *bylina* see Propp 1955: 265-274; on Dobrynja's disguise as a *skomorox* and the role of the *skomoroxi* in the transmission of the *byliny* see Zguta 1978: 82f.

versions of this story, Horn returns first disguised as a pilgrim, then disguised as a minstrel; it is at his first home-coming that he makes himself known through the ring he throws into the drinking horn.[54] The English traditional ballad of Hind Horn has radically reduced the story to the disguise and ring-motif. Hind Horn exchanges his clothes with an "auld beggar" and asks the bride for a drink for Horn's sake:

> The bride came down with a glass of wine,
> When he drank out the glass, and dropt in the ring.
>
> "O got ye this by sea or land?
> Or got ye it off a dead man's hand?"
>
> "I got not it by sea, I got it by land,
> And I got it, madam, out of your own hand."[55]

In the Turkic romance *Ašïq Ġarib*, popular from Turkey to Xinjiang, the lover becomes a master *saz*-player and singer and he arrives, dressed like Dobrynja and Horn in the guise of minstrel, just in time before his beloved is married to a rival.[56]

There is, as these few examples demonstrate, no dearth of material for a comparative study of Alpamïš's return. The fullest study of parallels to the return of Alpamïš to date is V. Žirmunskij's classic book on the Alpamïš-story. Žirmunskij explores the relationship of Alpamïš's return to Turkic oral narrative in general and to Homer's *Odyssey* in particular.[57] The similarity between the Turkic variants of the Alpamïš-

---

[54]The romance of *King Horn* is extant in an Anglo-Norman version and two Middle English versions, *King Horn* and *Horn Childe*. For a short characterization of the Middle English versions see Mehl 1968: 48-56; for the ring-motif in the Anglo-Norman and Middle English versions see Arens 1973: 228-237.

[55]The ring in the ballad of Hind Horn is also a life token (*Motif* E761.4.4 *Life token: ring rusts*), just as the ring in the romance of King Horn is a magic ring. The ballad is No. 17 in Child's collection, here quoted from variant A (Child 1882-98: I, 202); Child gives an extensive analysis of parallels, among them the *bylina* mentioned above; see *ibid.*: 187-201.

[56]The Turkish *hikâye* is available in a number of editions, many of which go back to Ottoman chapbooks; for a comparatively full variant see Güney 1964. For a Karakalpak variant see Maqsetov, Karimov 1985; for an Azerbaijanian variant see Tähmasib et al. 1979: 167-202; for an Uighur version see Raxman et al. 1981: 237-297.

[57]Žirmunskij 1960; a somewhat shortened version of this book is included in Žirmunskij 1974a: 117-348; my references are to the 1960 text. See also Žirmunskij [Zhirmunsky] 1967.

story and the return of Odysseus is so striking that some scholars have postulated a genetic link. Just looking at Fāzil's *Alpāmiš*, it can easily be seen that the final part of the *dastan* consists as in the Homeric poem of a series of meetings and recognitions (Alpāmiš the father with his son, Alpāmiš the son with his parents, Alpāmiš the brother with his sister, Alpāmiš the master with his servants, Alpāmiš the friend with his milk brother, Alpāmiš the avenger with the usurper, Alpāmiš the husband with his wife), a series of encounters, in which the faithful and the faithless are put to the test. We also recognize the familiar figures from Odysseus' household in the Uzbek *dastan*, in particular Eumaios the swineherd and Eurykleia the housekeeper, conflated into the figure of Qultāy, the faithful servant who recognizes Alpāmiš by his "scar," the imprint of Šāhimardān's hand on Alpāmiš's right shoulder.[58] And as if this were not enough to point our attention to Homer, Alpāmiš finally reveals his identity like Odysseus by bending his mighty bow. In view of these resemblances the idea certainly suggests itself that there is more than a typological link between the *Odyssey* and *Alpāmiš*, more than just the occasional migrating motif of oral literature having found its way into the Greek and the Uzbek tale. Although the problem of origin is beyond the scope of this study, the question of the dissemination and transformation of the Alpamïš-story among the Turkic peoples will be further examined in Chapter Ten.

Virtually nothing has been said in this chapter on the structure of the stories from a literary point of view. The story-patterns illustrated here certainly invite comment. I will, however, defer these comments to a later chapter, when narrative technique rather than narrative structure is in the foreground (see Chapter Nine). The main emphasis of this chapter was on familiarizing the reader with some of the material of the following chapters, by providing summaries, analyzing the most common motifs, and drawing attention to notable parallels to some of the better-known epics of the Central Asian Turks.

---

[58]For the Uzbek text see Zarif, Mirzaev 1979: 329-231. For the motif see *Motif* H51 *Recognition by scar* and ff. For a perceptive interpretation of the recognition scene in the *Odyssey* see Köhnken 1976.

Chapter Seven

The Varieties of Formulaic Diction

> The singer is able to improvise because he has learnt the
> epic technique or, to quote Goethe: *eine Sprache, die für
> dich dichtet und denkt.*
>
> Martin P. Nilsson, *Homer and Mycenae*[1]

Formula, Meter, Parallelism

The main reason why the language of oral poetry can be described as
"eine Sprache, die für dich dichtet und denkt," is doubtless its formulaic
nature. There is, however, no agreement in the many studies devoted
to formulaic style and diction on what is to count as a formula. A case
in point is Old English. Serious scholarship on the formulaic nature of
Old Germanic poetry began in 1889 with the publication by R. M. Meyer
of a collection of "formelhafte Elemente" in Old Norse, Old English, and
Old High German poetry, running to over 500 pages.[2] Today, one
hundred years later, our notion of the formula has been sharpened and
Meyer's all-inclusive use of the concept has been discarded. But even
so, the work of the various scholars who have done research on the
formulaic character of Old English poetry embodies widely diverging
and sometimes mutually contradictory views.[3] Despite disagreement
and controversy, most scholars today will concede, however, that their

---

[1]Nilsson 1933: 202.

[2]Meyer 1889. Heusler criticized Meyer for having "extended the notion of the
formula into the infinite" (Heusler 1943: 174).

[3]For a short summary and discussion see Foley 1988: 65-74; Reichl 1989a.

point of departure is Milman Parry's definition of the formula with
regard to the Homeric epics, and that this definition should indeed be
the basis for any definition of the formula, however much a particular
tradition might call for adjustment and refinement. According to Parry,
a formula is defined as "a group of words which is regularly employed
under the same metrical conditions to express a given essential idea."[4]
For Parry the metrical conditions governing the "group of words" were
those of the Greek hexameter, just as they are those of the South Slavic
deseterac for Lord or those of the alliterative line for scholars in the field
of Old Germanic poetry.[5]

When we look at the formulaic character of Turkic oral epic poetry,
we find a close relationship between meter and syntactic structure on
the one hand, and between syntactic patterning and parallelism on the
other. Metrical theory is a philological discipline fraught with terminological difficulties and dispute over principles. Turkic metrics is no
exception to this. It will not be possible to enter into the intricacies of
Turkic metrical theory here; some general remarks on the structure of
Turkic verse must suffice.[6] The verse of Turkic oral poetry is syllabic
and not quantitative as in Classical Turkish or Chaghatay poetry, which
is modelled on Classical Arabic and Persian poetry. The latter is called
ʿarūż (from Arabic), the former, in some traditions, *barmaq wazni*
("finger meter") or *hedža wazni* ("syllable meter").[7] Two types of verse-

---

[4]Parry 1971: 272.

[5]J. Foley has repeatedly argued that a discussion of formulaic style must pay
attention to the metrical conditions of the tradition under investigation and definitions
of the formula can therefore not mechanically be transferred from one tradition to
another; see Foley 1981; 1987. — The literature on formulaic diction is so vast that
I can only give summary references here. Parry's work on the Homeric formula is
collected in Parry 1971; for a discussion of formulaic diction in Serbo-Croatian oral epic
poetry see esp. Lord 1960: 30-67. For a general discussion of formulaic diction in
heroic epic poetry see also Bowra 1952: 222ff. For a short survey of the "oral-
formulaic theory" associated with Milman Parry and Albert B. Lord see Holbeck 1984;
for a recent history and methodology of the theory see Foley 1988. J. Foley has also
compiled an extensive bibliography of work related to the topics and concerns of oral-
formulaic theory; see Foley 1985.

[6]There is a sizable literature on Turkic metrics. An influential study has been
that by Kowalski 1921; compare Žirmunskij 1974 [1968], Žirmunskij 1985 [1965]. For
general surveys see Gandjeï 1957; Bombaci 1964; Xamraev 1969; compare also Boratav
1964: 11ff.

[7]On ʿarūż and *barmaq* see Xamraev 1969: 5ff., 64ff.

line are most widespread in the epics, a line of 7 or 8 syllables, and a
line of 11 or 12 syllables. The former is generally employed in passages
of indeterminate length, while the latter is predominantly used in
regular stanzas, most commonly of four lines. The hendecasyllabic (or
dodecasyllabic) line is probably the younger of the two; it is found
mostly in romance and among those Turkic peoples where the influence
of Classical literature has been strongest. But even here, as among the
Uzbeks, the heptasyllabic (or octosyllabic) line has survived in their
dastans, where often particular type-scenes and descriptive passages are
composed in the shorter verse-line.

The shorter verse-line can have seven or eight syllables, but sometimes less or more. Despite this fluidity in the number of syllables the
rhythmic patterns of Turkic verse in oral poetry are fairly regular. An
example will illustrate this. The following are the first four lines of an
extract from the *dastan Kuntuğmiš* recorded from the Uzbek singer
Čāri-šāir in 1981.[8]

> Arzim ešit xalāyiqlar!
> Uzaqtan keläyātibman,
> ġamli kunlarga bātibman.
> Bir güzeldi yoqātibman.

> Hear my wish, o people!
> I have come from afar,
> I have entered a sorrowful time (lit. I have sunk into sorrowful
> days).
> I am looking for a beautiful girl (lit. I have lost a beauty).

All four lines have eight syllables, but, when segmented into words,
each line has a different pattern of syllable groups:

> 2 + 2 + 4
> 3 + 5
> 2 + 3 + 3
> 1 + 3 + 4

If we want to find the rhythmic groups ("feet") of Turkic verse, not only
this segmentation has to be taken into account, but also stress and
pause patterns. In Uzbek, as in other Turkic languages, the main stress
falls as a rule on the final syllable of a word; exceptions are for instance

---

[8]See Reichl 1985b: 618ff.

imperatives, as *ešit* in line 1 above.[9] As to the segmentation of the line into two "breath-groups," there is a caesura after the third (l. 2), fourth (ll. 1 and 4), and fifth syllable (l. 3).[10] This results in the following patterns (disregarding secondary stress):

  oó + óo " oooó
  ooó " ooooó
  oó + ooó " ooó
  o + ooó " oooó

These patterns suggest a certain variability, which is, however, deceptive. When performed, the metrical structure is embedded in a musical structure. The syllables are sung to notes of fairly even duration, which are organized into groups of four, the first of each group bearing an accent. In other words, each line consists of two measures in quadruple meter.[11] The varying metrical patterns of the words are hence overlaid by a more rigid musical pattern, which creates an impression of regularity and uniformity:

  oó óo " o o o ó
4/4 ♩ ♩ ♩ ♩ | ♩ ♩ ♩ ♩

  o o ó " o o o o ó
4/4 ♩ ♩ ♩ ♩ | ♩ ♩ ♩ ♩

  oó o o ó " o o ó
4/4 ♩ ♩ ♩ ♩ | ♩ ♩ ♩ ♩

  o o o ó " o o o ó
4/4 ♩ ♩ ♩ ♩ | ♩ ♩ ♩ ♩

The musical meter need not be a quadruple meter. The "*Manas*-melody," for instance, is typically a triple meter. In its simplest form the musical pattern is the following:

[9]See Kononov 1960: 52-56; Tenišev et al. 1984: 403-421.

[10]"Caesura" is here to be understood as for instance in French syllabic verse, not as in Classical Latin or Greek quantitative verse; see Preminger et al. 1974: 95-97 (s.v. "Caesura").

[11]See Apel 1969: 513 (s.v. "Measure"), 523 (s.v. "Meter").

Heptasyllabic line:

```
    1  2   3  4   5  6   7
3/4 ♩ ♩ | ♩ ♩ | ♩ ♩ | ♩ 𝄾 |
```

Octosyllabic line:

```
    1  2   3  4   5  6   7  8
3/4 ♩ ♩ | ♩ ♩ | ♩ ♩ | ♩ ♩ |
```

Further complications are possible. Despite the regularity of the musical meter, the rhythmical pattern of the notes can be more varied. Instead of 8 notes of equal duration arranged in two 4-beat measures, we might have the following patterns:[12]

```
    1 2 3 4 5   | 6 7 8 (9)
4/4 ♩ ♩ ♩ ♩ ♩ | ♩ ♩ ♩ ♩
```

```
4/4 ♩ ♩ ♩ ♩ ♩ | ♩ ♩ ♩
```

```
4/4 ♩ ♩ ♩ ♩ ♩ | ♩ ♩ ♩. ♩
```

Hypermetrical lines can generally be accommodated in the musical meter: the same applies to lines with too few syllables. There might also be upbeats and extra bars, in particular for exclamatory particles ("oh," "ah") or melismatic passages on nonsense syllables. Verse-lines of 11 or 12 syllables are equally organized into metrical groups of generally three or four syllables, which correspond musically to patterns like the following:[13]

```
3/8 ♪ ♪ ♪ | ♪ ♪ ♪ | ♪ ♪ ♪ | ♪ ♪ ♪ |
```

```
3/8 ♪ ♪ ♪ | ♩ ♪ | ♪ ♪ ♪ | ♪ ♪ ♪ |
```

```
4/8 ♪ ♪ ♪ ♪ | ♪ ♪ ♩ | ♪ ♪ ♪ ♪ |
```

---

[12]These patterns are found at the beginning of *Qïz Žibek* as performed by Raxmet Mäzxožaev; see Äwezov [Auezov], Smirnova 1963: 331-32; Reichl 1989c: 362-63. See also the patterns discussed in Bajgaskina 1973.

[13]Reichl 1989b: 99; compare the transcriptions of Islām-šāir's formulas in Beliaev 1975: 289.

The regularity of the musical side of performance need not always be as clear as in the examples given. I have mentioned earlier that the Kazakh *aqïn* Šeriyazdan Soltanbay-ulï sang the 11/12-syllable lines in *Bögenbay* in a chanting style with a "flowing" rhythm, while the 7/8-syllable passages were sung to a clearly marked 3/4-meter (see Chapter Four, pp. 107ff.). The musical side of meter is doubtless important for a fuller understanding of Turkic metrics, but demands a more technical discussion than can be given here.

"Rhythmic speech" as it finds its expression in meter is the prerequisite of poetry. Radloff, in an article on the meter of the Altaians, which appeared in 1866, lists two types of procedures that lead to rhythmic speech among "primitive peoples" like the "Altaian Tatars":

> 1) The division of speech into verse-lines, with the purpose of investing these verse-lines with a certain melody by alliteration, harmony of the vowels, syllable counting, and intonation.
> 2) The combination of these verse-lines into stanzas, i.e. linking them closer to one another by means of verse-initial rhyme or end-rhyme.
>
> (Radloff 1866a: 87)[14]

Radloff continues by illustrating alliteration with an Altaian proverb:

> Yaqš-aa yanaš-qan yaqšï-zï yux-ar,
> yaman-xa yanaš-qan yaman-ï yux-ar.[15]
>
> If you are next to someone good, something of his goodness will rub off,
> if you are next to someone bad, something of his badness will
> rub off.

These lines illustrate two kinds of alliteration: horizontal alliteration, i.e. alliteration within the line as in Old Germanic poetry, and vertical alliteration, i.e. alliteration between the lines or, as the alliterating consonant is followed by the same vowel, verse-initial rhyme (*yaqš-aa — yaman-xa*). Alliteration as a line-binding principle is commonly found in Altaian, Yakut, and Kirghiz oral epic poetry, but is only rarely found in the other traditions. Radloff mentions, however, another principle of grouping lines into stanzas, namely end-rhyme. This is by far the more usual means of stanza-building in the "central traditions." Two types

---

[14]For a more detailed analysis of Altaian metrics see Katašev 1979.

[15]*Ibid.* The separation into morphemes follows that given by Radloff, who provides the lines also with a literal translation, morpheme by morpheme.

of stanzas have to be differentiated. One type is a stanza defined by a regularly recurring rhyming pattern. Fairly widespread is the *murabba* stanza (from Arabic *murabba*ᶜ, "square"), a four-line stanza, generally rhyming a—a—x—a. The phrase "regularly recurring" needs some qualification; in Uzbek *dastan* poetry, for instance, it can be observed that a singer finds a regular pattern only in the course of performing a verse-passage.[16] The second type of stanza is comparable to the Old French laisse. That is to say that the verses are linked together by end-rhyme or assonance into groups of varying length.[17] These "tirades" can be interrupted by nonrhyming lines or shorter line-groups not conforming to the rhyme or assonance.[18]

But these lines also exemplify another trait of Turkic oral poetry (both epic and lyric), namely syntactic parallelism. The two lines are both lexically and morphologically identical, the only variation consisting in the replacement of *yaqšï*, "good," in line 1 by *yaman*, "bad," in line 2. Literally the two lines read:

> To-the-good having-been-next-to his-good will-stick,
> to-the-bad having-been-next-to his-bad will-stick.

As has been argued convincingly by V. Žirmunskij, the rise of end-rhyme and assonance, Radloff's second principle of verse-grouping, in Turkic oral epic poetry, particularly in the "tirade"-type stanza, is intimately linked to parallelism.[19] Strict grammatical parallelism in an agglutinative language naturally leads to rhyme or assonance: if line A ends with a particular grammatical morpheme and line B is syntactically parallel to line A, it will also end with the same grammatical morpheme. The two morphemes will have the same consonants, but might differ in the quality of the vowels, as the Turkic languages have vowel-harmony. The assonance is automatically extended when the last word of a line has two or more grammatical morphemes. With these

---

[16]For a survey of rhyme-patterns in the Uzbek *dastan Rawšan* see Reichl 1985a: 38f.; for a discussion of rhyme and meter in the Uzbek *dastan Nurali*, like *Rawšan* a branch of the *Köroğlu/Göroğlï*-cycle, see Dor 1991: 164ff.

[17]See Preminger et al. 1974: 436 (s.v. "Laisse").

[18]The word *tirade* in English is generally synonymous with *harangue*. I am using the word here in the French sense, which is also occasionally found in English.

[19]See Žirmunskij 1985 [1965]. For an earlier analysis of the correlation between alliteration and rhyme in Turkic poetry see Ščerbak 1961.

sound-patterns arising from grammar, it is only a comparatively small step further to enrich the assonance or rhyme by choosing lexemes with the same stem-vowels (see the examples below).

Although we can expect rigorous syntactic patterning and parallelism of this kind in proverbs, it is not restricted to this folklore genre. Nor is parallelism restricted to languages of the agglutinative type, although the Turkic languages with their agglutinative morphology and concomitant syntactic structure favor grammatical or syntactic parallelism. Parallelism is probably one of the most widespread means of poetic patterning, ranging from the *parallelismus membrorum* of the psalms and the highly sophisticated use of parallelism in Classical Chinese lyric poetry to the multifarious parallelistic forms in oral poetry and folk lyric all over the world.[20]   As Roman Jakobson writes in his study of parallelism in Russian oral poetry, "Grammatical parallelism belongs to the poetic canon of numerous folk patterns."[21]

Parallelistic structures in Turkic are first found in the runic inscriptions of the 8th century (see Chapter Two); the earliest records of parallelistic lines in Turkic oral poetry occur in the 11th century *Dīvān luġāt at-Turk* by Maḥmūd of Kashgar. One of the battle poems has the following description of the hero's fight on his horse:

> Ïqïlačïm ärik boldï
> ärik bolġu yärü kördi,
> bulït örüb kök örtüldi,
> tuman törüb tolï yaġdï.
> (Stebleva 1976: 205)

> My courser became lively,
> he saw the place to be lively in;
> a cloud rose up, the sky became dark,
> a mist arose, a hailstorm broke out.

---

[20]The following is based partly on a paper read at a symposium on "The Study of Oral Tradition and the South-Slavs" at the School of Slavonic and East European Studies, University of London, July 6-9, 1987; for a Chinese translation of a revised form of my paper see Reichl 1990.

[21]Jakobson 1966: 403. On parallelism in oral poetry compare also Finnegan 1977: 98-102. Veselovskij's fundamental study of psychological parallelism is still worth reading; Veselovskij 1940 [1898]. For a classification of parallelistic structures in Mongolian oral poetry see Poppe 1958; Poppe's taxonomy is taken over from Steinitz's detailed study of parallelism in Finnish-Karelian folk poetry; Steinitz 1934.

The parallelism of lines 3 and 4 is one of content as well as expression. Syntactically each line consists of a gerundival construction (suffix -(ü)b) and a construction with a finite verb in the past (suffix -di), resulting in the sequence noun + verb (gerund) + noun + verb (past):

bulït	ör-üb	kök	ört-ül-di
cloud	having-risen	sky	was-cover-ed

tuman	törüb	tolï	yaǧ-dï
mist	having-risen	hail	rain-ed

Phonologically *örüb* is echoed by *törüb*, while semantically all four phrases are related, the closest semantic parallel existing, of course, between the rising cloud and the rising mist.

Parallelism in Turkic oral poetry is found both in epic and lyric. It is very common in the four-line popular poems called *mâni* in Turkish, *bayatï* in Azerbaijanian, *qošaq* in Uighur etc. Consider the following Uighur poem:

> Hawadiki lačinni
> qil bilän tutay däymän.
> Köŋlümdiki yarimni
> čay bilän žutay däymän.[22]

> I would like to catch with a horsehair string
> the falcon in the air.
> I would like to swallow with tea
> my beloved in my heart.

> Lit.: In-the-air-being the-falcon (direct object)
> horsehair-with may-I-hold I-say.
> In-my-heart-being my-beloved (direct object)
> tea-with may-I-swallow I-say.

Here the first two lines are mirrored in the third and fourth line. The syntactic construction of these two couplets is once again identical, and this results in a nearly identical sequence of grammatical morphemes, postpositions, and "construction words."

In epic poetry, the formulaic beginning is frequently in the form of parallelistic locative constructions (suffix -da), as for instance in the Karakalpak epic *Qïrïq Qïz* (Forty Maidens):

---

[22]Geng, Reichl 1989: 58; for a short survey of parallelism in Turkic folk poetry see Martyncev 1976.

Burïngï ötken zamanda,
sol zamannïŋ qädiminde,
qaraqalpaq xalqïnda,
ata žurtï Turkstanda,
Sarkop degen qalada,
az noǧaylï elatïnda...

(Maqsetov, Žapaqov, Niyemullaev 1980: 42)

In the days of old,
in the days of yore,
among the Karakalpaks,
in the homeland of Turkestan,
in a town called Sarkop,
in the small Noghay tribe...

Even more rigorously patterned are the beginnings of Altaian epics, as is illustrated by the opening lines of *Kögütöy*:

D'üs učarlu qara tayǧanïŋ,
d'üs qooldu kök talaydïŋ,
ayaŋ bolǧon d'aqazïnda,
ardžan suunïŋ d'aradïnda
kök buqanï minip d'ortqon
Kögütey öbögön d'urtap d'attï.

(Surazakov et al. 1958: 86)

In the black taiga (mountains) with the hundred waterfalls,
on the blue sea with the hundred cliffs,
on the mountain pasture,
at the back of a mineral spring,
riding on a blue buffalo,
lived old Kögütey.

The syntactic parallelism of the first two lines can be captured in the following morpheme-by-morpheme translation:

| hundred | waterfall-having | black | of-the-taiga |
| hundred | cliff-having | blue | of-the-sea |

Syntactic identity is enhanced by semantic similarity and contrast. *Qara*, "black," and *kök*, "blue," are similar in denoting colors, but different as to the colors they denote; *učar*, "waterfall," and *qool*, "cliff, steep coast," are similar in being both connected to steepness and, in the given context, to water, while *tayǧa*, "mountains," and *talay*, "sea," are the two opposites and complementaries of our world, land and water.

The similarities and contrasts built up in the first two lines are carried over into the following lines. In lines 3 and 4 we find again morphosyntactic identity, as well as semantic similarity. *D'aqa* and

d'arat, both having the basic meaning "rim," occur in identical constructions: they are nouns used as postpositions in the locative case (*-da*),
with a connecting possessive suffix (*-ï(n)-*). On the semantic level *ayaŋ*,
"mountain pasture," and *ardžan suu*, "mineral spring," take up the
land/water-contrast of the first two lines.

A Turkic epic might also begin with some maxim or gnomic verses,
arranged in parallelistic fashion, such as in the Kirghiz *Kökötöydün ašï*
(*The Memorial Feast of Kökötöy-Khan*) from the *Manas*-cycle:

> Altïn iyerniŋ kašï eken:
> ata yurtnuŋ bašï eken.
> Kümüš iyerniŋ kašï eken:
> tün tüškön kalïŋ köp Noġay yurtnuŋ bašï eken.
>
> A golden saddle has its pommel:
> a people has its chieftain.
> A silver saddle has its pommel:
> the Nogay teeming as shadows at nightfall have their chieftain.[23]

Gnomic verses often introduce verse-passages or individual stanzas (in
the case of stanzaic verse-passages), particularly in the epics of those
traditions in which the lyrical element is prominent, such as in the
Uzbek *dastans*:

> Kuygan alwān-alwān sozlar,
> ayrilgan bir-birin izlar... (*Rawšan*)
> (Zarif 1971; 106)
>
> Those burning with love speak many words,
> those separated seek one another...

In many cases such verse-lines are only loosely (if at all) connected to
the context in which they occur. They frequently contain a nature
image and are evocative rather than descriptive. Verse-lines of this kind
are a typical stylistic trait of Turkic epic poetry, which will be further
looked at in the following section.

---

[23]Text and translation from Hatto 1977: 2/3. — On parallelism in maxims and
proverbs see also Harvilahti 1987.

Formula and Formulaic System

In Chapter Six a short extract from the Kazakh heroic poem *Qambar* was given, describing the hopes of the old men to be Nazïm's choice (see p. 146). The passage quoted there continues:

     Altïn tuğïr üstinde
     Nazïm otïr qonaqtap
105 aq tuyğïnday erikken.
     Qara men töre talasïp,
     forïmïna qarasïp,
     aldïnan ötti körikten.
     Qïz Nazïmnïŋ maydanï
110 är toptïŋ boldï bazarï,
     tüsedi köpke säwlesi
     qağazday kirsiz ažarï.
     Osïnša žurttïŋ artïnan
     awmadï žanğa nazarï.
115 Žerdiŋ žüzin šaŋdattï
     žïyïlğan qoršap adamï.

(Äwezov [Auezov], Smirnova 1959: 38)

     On a golden perch,
     Nazïm was sitting
105 in boredom like a white hawk.
     Ordinary people and noblemen argued with one another,
     looked at her stature,
     and passed in front of the beauty.
     The *maydan*[24] where Qïz Nazïm was sitting
110 turned into a bazar, teeming with people of all kinds.
     Her brightness (lit. flame) shone on the many people.
     Her complexion was spotless like paper.
     Among so many peoples
     her gaze did not settle on a single person.
115 The people who had gathered and surrounded her
     raised the dust from the earth.

Before looking at the formulaic diction of this passage, a short comment on metrics might be in place. About half of the fourteen lines are heptasyllabic, half octosyllabic. As can be seen from the published musical transcription of *Qambar*, the two types of lines conform basically to the following patterns:[25]

---

[24]The word *maydan* (from Persian) means both "square" and "battlefield."

[25]See Äwezov [Auezov], Smirnova 1959: 396-403; this is also true of the performance on the record mentioned earlier (see p. 144).

Heptasyllabic line:

4/4   ♩ ♩ ♩ ♩ | ♩ ♩ ♩

Octosyllabic line:

4/4   ♩ ♩ ♩ ♩ | ♩ ♩ ♩ ♩

As to the "stanzaic" organization of these lines, we notice that all lines end in a three-syllable word. These "clausulae" can be arranged into four groups:[26]

(1)   Postpositions:
    a) 103 *üstinde* (rhymes with earlier 96 *üyinde*);
    b) 113 *artïnan* (rhymes with no other word).

(2)   Gerundival forms in *-p*:
    a) 104 *qonaqtap* (rhymes with earlier 101 *ap*);
    b) 106, 107 *talasïp : qarasïp*.

(3)   *-ken* (participle)/ *-ten* (ablative):
    a) 105 *erikken* (rhymes with earlier 91 *želiken*, 92 *köp eken*, 93 *zerikken*);
    b) 108 *körikten* (rhymes with earlier 95 *börikten*, 99 *serikten*, 102 *örikten*).

4)   Noun + possessive suffix (*-(s)i/ï*):
    a) with "dark" vowels:
    109 *maydanï : 110 bazarï*, 112 *ažarï*, 114 *nazarï*, 116 *adamï*;
    b) with "light" vowels:
    111 *säwlesi*.
    c) The form 115 *saŋdattï* (3rd person singular preterite) also conforms to this vowel-pattern.

This arrangement is quite typical of laisse-type passages in the epic poetry of the "central traditions": an indeterminate group of verse-lines connected by rhyme or assonance is interwoven with nonrhyming lines or a second and possibly also a third rhyming pattern. In our example there are two main assonance-groups, a (*qonaqtap, talasïp, qarasïp*) and b (*maydanï, bazarï, säwlesi, ažarï, nazarï, saŋdattï, adamï*). These groups are "interlaced" by a third assonance-group c (*erikken, körikten*) as well as a nonrhyming line x (*artïnan*). Leaving out the first line of

---

[26]On "clausulae" and rhyming patterns see also Žirmunskij 1974 [1968]: 647.

the extract, which is connected to a previous line, we have the following
pattern:

..... qonaqtap	a
..... erikken	c
..... talasïp	a'
..... qarasïp	a'
..... körikten	c'
..... maydanï	b
..... bazarï	b
..... säwlesi	b'
..... ažarï	b
..... artïnan	x
..... nazarï	b
..... šaŋdattï	b"
..... adamï	b

This particular passage describes a fairly individual scene. The
passage is certainly not a theme in the sense of oral formulaic theory;
this explains the low "formulaic density" of these lines as compared to
that of a type-scene or a "run" (see below). The formulaic density of a
particular passage is not only relative to the degree it is a typical scene
or part of one, but also to its length and to the size of the referent
corpus. The longer an extract is and the more numerous the random
passages selected for formulaic analysis are, the greater is the likelihood
that the analysis will be representative; and the larger the referent
corpus is, the more clearly the formulaic nature of a passage can be
shown.[27] The following formulaic analysis is based on a concordance of
somewhat over 8,000 lines of Kazakh epic poetry, the epic *Qambar* in
Divaev's version, and the epic *Qoblandï* in Šapay Qalmaġanbetov's
version.[28] Hence it must be stressed that a larger referent corpus may
substantially change the percentage of formulaic lines, although it
would not, I believe, give a radically different picture of the nature of
Kazakh formulaic diction.

Looking at the referent, we find that parallels can be cited for only
seven out of the fourteen lines quoted. I am deliberately using the
vague term "parallel" in order not to predetermine what is to count as

---

[27]For a discussion of the parameters to be taken into account in the computation
of formulaic density see Duggan 1973: 16ff.

[28]The concordance comprises 1851 + 6490 lines. The text of *Qoblandï-batïr* is
based on the edition by Kidajš-Pokrovskaja, Nurmagambetova 1975; compare also
Reichl 1989c.

a formula. As will be seen, the various types of formulaic diction can best be defined in the course of textual analysis. The first line in our sample having a parallel in the referent is line 105:

aq	tuyğïnday	erikken 105
white	hawk-like	being-bored

aq	tuyğïnday	quntïydï 1726
white	hawk-like	he-hunched-up-his-shoulders

Aq, "white," is one of the most common epithets in Turkic epic poetry. In *Qambar* not only the hawk *(tuygïn)*[29] is white (105, 1726), but also Nazïm's face *(žüz* 81) and bosom *(tös* 539), the various types of yurt *(üy* 416, 799; *orda* 1774),[30] the antelope *(böken* 228), the caftan *(ton* 1317), and the lumps of gold given as bride-price *(žambï* 1819). More important for formulaic diction is the use of *aq* as an epithet for arms. The sword, *semser*, has the epithet *aq* (665), and five out of six occurrences of *nayza*, "spear," are modified by *aq*, either as *aq nayza*, "white spear" (1007, 1574, 1735) or in the collocation *aq saptï bolat nayza*, "white-shafted steel spear" (836, 1680; compare 1123 *aq bolat*, "white steel"). The latter is formulaic in the strict sense that the same metrical unit is repeated with identical words, differing only in grammatical morphemes such as case endings, postpositions, or possessive suffixes:

aq saptï bolat nayza-men 826 ("with...")
aq saptï bolat nayza-ŋ-dï 1672 ("your [accusative] ...")

The epithet *aq* has in these lines three ranges of meaning.[31] In collocations like *aq tuyğin* the adjective denotes a physical quality, the actual color of a material object. When modifying parts of the body, as in *aq žüz*, "white face," or *aq tös*, "white bosom," the adjective not only denotes a color, but is also used evaluatively. "White" suggests here purity and beauty; this is brought out by line 112 quoted above, *Qağazday kirsiz ažarï*, "her complexion was spotless like paper." We might compare to this the use of the adjectival epithet λευκώλενος,

---

[29]Kazakh *tuyğïn* denotes a kind of hawk; compare Kirghiz *tuyğun* (Judaxin 1985 [1965]: II, 264, s.v. *tuyğun* I); see also Räsänen 1969: 497 (s.v. *tujkar*).

[30]The word *üy* denotes the normal yurt, while *orda* denotes a big yurt. See also below.

[31]On the word *aq* and its meanings in the Turkic languages see Laude-Cirtautas 1961: 38-50.

"white-armed," in the Homeric epics, the epithet of Hera and women in general. When *aq* is, however, used as an attribute of weapons, it denotes brightness and radiance. Here, too, we find parallels in other epic traditions. Beowulf's helmet, which he dons before descending into Grendel's underwater den, is described as *hwīt*, "white-shining" (*se hwīta helm*, l. 1448), an epithet which takes up the earlier mention of the shining boar-crests on the Geatish warriors' helmets (*Eoforlīc scionon*, l. 303). Shining armor and weapons are, of course, a common motif of heroic poetry. Hector is described in the *Iliad* as with a shining helmet (κορυθαίολος), and the various epithets used for weapons in the Homeric poems include a fair number of adjectives denoting a bright and radiant quality.[32]

The use of *aq* in *Qoblandï* presents a similar picture. Instead of the white hawk, we find the white gerfalcon (*suŋqar* 1114, 1462, 1882, 2479, 3649, 4079, 4099, 4189, 4780, 5681, 5770). As in *Qambar* the antelope (*böken* 4049, 4579, 4646, 5692), various parts of the body (*bet*, "face," 3930, 6340, 6431; *maŋday*, "forehead," 1142; *bilek*, "forearm," 2097, 2435; *tamaq*, "throat," 739), and the different types of yurts are white (*otaw*, "yurt for a newly wed couple," 255, 703, 5246; *orda* 1076, 5247; *šatïr*, "tent," 5264, 5724, 6385).[33] Finally, weapons and armor are also qualified by *aq*:

> *sawït*, "coat of mail," 1091, 2182, 2265, 2344, 2353, 2379, 2651,
>   3088, 3096, 3170, 3271, 4659;
> *semser*, "sword, saber," 3089, 5986, 6009;
> *nayza*, "spear," 2467, 5357;
> *almas*, "blade, sword" (lit. "diamond") 848;
> *süŋgi*, "spear," 2359, 2365, 6117;
> *beren*, "steel," 2372.

A number of these collocations occur in lines which are in a similar way formulaic as line 826 *Aq saptï bolat nayzamen* in *Qambar* discussed above. The phrase *aq bet* is twice linked with *tulïm*, "plait":

aq	bet-im-de	tulïm-ïm	6340
white	in-my-face	my-plait	

---

[32]See Chart III: "Epithets for Greek Swords and Spears" appended to Watts 1969; on Homeric κορυθαίολος see Whallon 1969: 54-57.

[33]In Karakalpak an *aq otaw* is a richly decorated white yurt.

```
aq      bet-iŋ-de      tulïm-ïŋ   6431
white   in-your-face   your-plait
```

These two lines occur, however, in a dialogue, in which the second speaker takes up the words of the first speaker. This technique of echoing the speech of one protagonist in that of another is fairly common in Turkic oral epic poetry; an example from an Uzbek variant of *Alpamïš* will be given below. Formulas in the strict sense are lines 4049, 4579, 5692, in which the speed of the rider is compared to that of the white antelope:

```
aq      bökendey        žosïldï
white   antelope-like   he/they-raced-along
```

Similarly the white spear (*aq süŋgi*) is always characterized as having notches in its shaft (in order to be easier to hold):

tolġamalï aq süŋgi 2359, 2365, 6117.[34]

Among the lines containing the epithet *aq* we have so far encountered four types: (1) lines which share only the same epithet + noun combination but are otherwise different; for example:

dem alïp <u>aq orda</u>da otïr edi   *Qambar* 1774
he was sitting in the white yurt resting

<u>aq orda</u>nïŋ aldïnan   *Qoblandï* 1076
in front of the white yurt

Qurtqaġa tikken <u>aq orda</u>   *Qoblandï* 5247
putting up a white yurt for Qurtġa

(2) Lines which share besides the same epithet + noun combination a common syntactic structure; for example:

```
aq      tuyġïn-day   erikken      Qambar 105
adj     noun-LIKE    verb
being bored like a white hawk
```

```
aq      tuyġïn-day   quntïydï     Qambar 1726
he hunched up his shoulders like a white hawk
```

(3) Pairs of lines of which the second is an echo of the first in the course of a dialogue; as in:

---

[34]For Kazakh *tolġamalï* compare also Kirghiz *tolġomoluu*; see Judaxin 1985 [1965] s.v. *tolġomo, tolgomoluu*.

aq betimde tulïmïm   *Qoblandï* 6340
my plait in my white face

aq betiŋde tulïmïŋ   *Qoblandï* 6431
your plait in your white face

(4) Lines which are formulas in the strict sense; for example:

aq saptï bolat nayzamen   *Qambar* 826
with the white-shafted steel spear

aq saptï bolat nayzaŋdï   *Qambar* 1672
your white-shafted steel spear

There is, however, also a further type of repeated line among the sample with the adjective *aq*. In *Qoblandï* the word *mata*, "cloth, material," is also qualified by *aq*. This collocation invariably occurs in the following two lines:

Bazarda bar aq mata,
oynaqtaydï žas bota   485-86, 693-94, 2583-84

At the bazar there is white material;
the young camel foal is frolicking.

Lines like these punctuate the epic at irregular intervals. They often contain nature images, but also proverbial and gnomic lore. Another instance of this type of lines in *Qoblandï* are lines 2087-89:

Arqada bar böriköz,
žaqsïda ǵoy täwir söz,
nege umïtsïn körgen köz?

In the steppe the *böriköz* ("wolf's eye," a medicinal herb) grows,
in a good man speech is found;
why should the eye which has seen forget?

These lines are repeated as lines 597-99, the first and second line as lines 2154-55, and the first and third line as lines 5317-18.[35] The practice of interspersing the poem with such lines, often of an "imagistic" kind, is also found in other Turkic traditions; further examples from Uzbek will be given below. These cliché-like lines are similar to the repeated couplets in Serbo-Croatian heroic poetry as described by A. B. Lord:

---

[35]See Kidajš-Pokrovskaja, Nurmagambetova 1975: 52f.; Reichl 1989c: 369f. See below pp. 203f. and Chapter Nine, pp. 276ff.

Just as formulaic lines with internal rhyme or with a striking chiastic arrangement have a long life, so couplets with clearly marked patterns persist with little if any change. For example:

Bez edelja nema umiranja, Without the fated hour there is no dying,
Od edelja nema zaviranja. From the fated hour there is no escape.
(II, No.24: 631-632)

or:

A zečki je polje pregazio,   Like a rabbit he crossed the plain,
A vučki se maši planinama.   Like a wolf he ranged over the
                                    mountains.
(II, No. 24:41-42)

It seems preferable to keep such couplets in a class by themselves and not to call them formulas, reserving that term for the components of a single verse.

(Lord 1960: 57)

The next line of the passage quoted above (p. 182) for which a parallel can be found in the referent corpus is l. 106:

qara men töre talasïp   *Qambar* 106
common folk and noblemen arguing with one another

qara men töre qaygïrdï   *Qambar* 32
ordinary people and noblemen grieved

The formulaic nature of these lines consists in having a fixed phrase, on the pattern of "rich and poor," "old and young," "high and low," which leaves three syllables of the line to be filled by a "clausula," for instance a verb as in our example. Line 117 conforms to the same pattern:

qasqa men žaysaŋ, bekterdiŋ   *Qambar* 117
of poor people and princes, begs ...

In *Qoblandï* similar phrases are *kempir men šal* ("old woman and old man," 1296), *küŋ men qul/qul men küŋ* ("slave girl and slave man," 259, 4229, 4238, 4239, 4244, 4245, 4247, 4506), *žal men žaya* ("mane and rump," 3316, 3715, 5232) and others.

While the formulaic nature of these lines consists in having a fixed phrase which leaves a slot of three or more syllables in the line to be filled, with purely metrical, but no grammatical or semantic restrictions on the words completing the line, the next line to be discussed adds a grammatical constraint to the metrical one:

forïm-ï-na qarasïp   *Qambar* 107
on-her-form looking

forïm-ï-na qarasaŋ   *Qambar* 46
on-her-form if-you-look

Here the verb *qara-*, "to look at," demands a noun in the dative case; furthermore, if the verb is used in any other form than the short imperative or the gerund in *-p*, it will have at least three syllables. This yields the following pattern (for a heptasyllabic line):

x x x (x)-x   qara-x
noun   -DATIVE   qara-ENDING

Examples (of repeated lines only):

töŋirek-ke qarasa   *Qambar* 289
to-the-environment if-he-looks

töŋirek-ke qarasqan   *Qambar* 1298
to-the-environment having-looked

aldï-art-ï-na qaradï   *Qoblandï* 4524, 5099
to-his-front-and-back he-looked

aldï-art-ï-na qaramay   *Qoblandï* 6237
to-his-front-and-back not-looking

žan-žaǧ-ï-na qaradï   *Qoblandï* 3277
to-his-side he-looked

žan-žaǧ-ï-na qarasa   *Qoblandï* 3689
to-his-side if-he-looks

Of a similar make-up are lines 108 and 109. For line 108 there are among others the following parallels in the referent:

aldïnan ötti körikten   *Qambar* 108
from-her-front they-passed by-the-beauty

basïnan ötti düniye boq   *Qoblandï* 2707
from-his-head it-passed the world-dirt

aldïnan kelip žïrlaydï   *Qoblandï* 5084
from-their-front coming she-cries

aldïnan šïǧïp Qarlïǧa   *Qoblandï* 5323
from-their-front coming-out Qarlïǧa

aldïnan šïǧïp söyledi   *Qoblandï* 5937
from-their-front coming-out she-says

The first part of these lines consists of a verb of movement, which is construed with a preceding ablative. This leaves a slot of three (or possibly four) syllables at the end, the conventional clausula. The same observation can be made for line 109, where the line begins with a genitive and continues with a noun ending in a possessiv affix:

Qïz Nazïm-nïŋ	maydan-ï	*Qambar* 109
Qïz Nazïm-of	place-her	
Qïz Nazïm-nïŋ	zaman-ï	*Qambar* 125
	time-her	
Qïz Nazïm-nïŋ	awïl-ï-nïŋ	*Qambar* 412
	village-her-of	
Qïz Nazïm-nïŋ	iš-i-ne	*Qambar* 445
	work-her-to	

A distinction must be made, however, between a case where the constraint on the slot to be filled is grammatical and metric and a case where the constraint is also lexical/semantic. If we take the name *Qarlïga* from *Qoblandï* we find on the one hand patterns like those above (with grammatical/metric constraints):

Qarlïga-nïŋ	ana-sï-n	*Qoblandï* 2817
Qarlïga-of	mother-her (direct object)	
Qarlïga-nïŋ	ald-ï-nan	*Qoblandï* 4709
	front-her-from	
Qarlïga-nïŋ	form-ï-na	*Qoblandï* 5125
	shape-her-to	
Qarlïga-nïŋ	iz-i-nen	*Qoblandï* 6064
	trace-her-from	

On the other hand, we find also formulas in the strict sense, i.e. lines composed of the same lexemes, with only minor variations as to grammatical morphology etc.:

Qarlïga-day	suluw-ïŋ	*Qoblandï* 2812, 2833, 2850, 2994,
Qarlïga-like	beauty-your	3023, 5098, 5270, 5384, 6463
Qarlïga-day	suluw-ǧa	*Qoblandï* 3035, 3580, 6031
	beauty-to	

Qarlïġa-day	suluw-dï	*Qoblandï* 3360, 4046, 6126, 6195
	beauty (dir. obj.)	

Qarlïġa-day	suluw-dïŋ	*Qoblandï* 5345, 5378, 6192, 6459
	beauty-of	

Qarlïġa-day	suluw da	*Qoblandï* 6077, 6211
	beauty also	

Finally, for the last line with parallels in our example (l. 115), there are metric, grammatical, and semantic constraints:

žer-dïŋ	žüz-i-n	šaŋda-t-tï
earth-of	surface-its (dir. obj.)	he-caused-to-be-dusty

To capture the parallels to this line, we must have recourse to the notion of a formulaic system. Parry had defined a formulaic system as "a group of phrases which have the same metrical value and which are enough alike in thought and words to leave no doubt that the poet who used them knew them not only as single formulas, but also as formulas of a certain type."[36] This somewhat loose definition has not remained unchallenged, and various competing definitions have attempted to make the notion of a formulaic system more precise. In relationship to Old English A. Riedinger has proposed a threefold distinction between system, set, and formula, which is also helpful for Turkic oral poetry.[37] According to Riedinger, a particular formula belongs with other formulas to the same set, if they all share at least one constant word and if the relationship of their variable elements can be semantically specified, i.e. if the variable elements are synonyms or belong to the same semantic field. From the examples given above we can classify the following lines as formulas:

töŋirek-ke	qarasa	*Qambar* 289; 1289
	qarasqan	

aldï-art-ï-na	qaradï	*Qoblandï* 4524, 5099; 6237
	qaramay	

žan-žaġ-ï-na	qaradï	*Qoblandï* 3277; 3689
	qarasa	

---

[36]Parry 1971 [1930]: 275. Compare also Lord 1960: 47ff.

[37]See Riedinger 1985.

These three formulas belong to a Set 1 with the pattern:

(1)   (Place-direction noun)-DATIVE + *qara*-ENDING

A second group of lines might be grouped together as belonging to a Set 2 with the pattern:

(2)   ("Body noun")-DATIVE + *qara*-ENDING

Examples:

forïm-ï-na	qarasaŋ qarasïp	*Qambar* 46, 107
awïz-ï-na to-their-mouth let-us-look	qarayïq	*Qambar* 1137
bet-iŋ-e birew qarasa to-your-face someone if-he-looks		*Qambar* 1238

These two sets of formulas, in which the nouns stand in a semantically specifiable relationship to one another, (partially) represent the formulaic system:

(A)   x x x (x)-DATIVE   *qara*-ENDING

While the notion of the formula allows only minor variation, generally limited to grammatical morphology, and the notion of the set puts a semantic constraint on lexical variation, the notion of the formulaic system is far more abstract. In the examples discussed here, one might argue that the second group of lines is not properly formulaic; there is too little repetition and the semantic relationship between "shape," "face," and "mouth" is far less stringent than that between the directional phrases in the first group. It is therefore doubtful whether (A) is a formulaic system; in this particular case it might be more correct to see Set 1 as a formulaic system, i.e. to equate the notion of a set with that of a formulaic system.

A proper formulaic analysis of line 115 does, however, demand a distinction between set and system. The line consists of two phrases and hence two ideas: (1) "surface of the earth" and (2) "raised the dust." If we take the first phrase as the constant element, we get the following parallels:

žerdiŋ	žüsin	šaŋdattï	*Qambar* 115
of-the-earth	its-surface	he-caused-to-be-dusty	

žerdïŋ	žüsin	sel aldï	*Qambar* 1359
of-the-earth	its-surface	the-torrent took-away	

žerdïŋ	žüsin	küŋrentip	*Qoblandï* 1926
of-the-earth	its-surface	causing-to-stir	

If we take the second phrase as the constant element, we get the following parallels:

awïldïŋ	üstin	šaŋdatïp	*Qambar* 1158
of-the-village	its-top	causing-to-be-dusty	

köšeniŋ	awzïn	šaŋdatïp	*Qoblandï* 1926
of-the-street	its-mouth	causing-to-be-dusty	

There is strict parallelism in all variants of the first phrase; furthermore, all three phrases are semantically related in as far as they are all geographical terms of some kind (earth, village, street) and specify a location (surface, top, mouth). The semantic affinity between the three variants of the second phrase is less tight, although it is arguable to see *küŋrentip*, "causing to stir," as semantically related to *šaŋdatïp*, "causing to be dusty."[38] We have hence a formulaic system:

žerdïŋ žüsin	šaŋdattï
awïldïŋ üstin	šaŋdatïp
köšeniŋ awzïn	sel aldï
	küŋrentip

represented by the sets:

(1)		
	žerdïŋ žüsin	šaŋdattï
	awïldïŋ üstin	šaŋdatïp
	köšeniŋ awzïn	küŋrentip

(2)   žerdïŋ žüsin   sel aldï

This discussion of a sample passage from *Qambar* has led to a distinction between four types of formulaic line. In the course of my analysis I termed one type of formulaic line "formula in the strict sense." This type of formula comprises lines which are repeated in the referent corpus without changes that affect its lexical composition. An example of this type of formula is *aq saptï bolat nayzamen* (*Qambar* 826). A

---

[38]On the meanings of Kazakh *küŋrent-* see Keŋesbaev et al. 1959-61 s.v. *küŋirent-*.

second type of formula is more variable than the first insofar as variation within the line is not restricted to grammatical morphemes or minor parts of speech. I have termed this type of formula a formulaic system, stipulating that the lexemes which can be substituted for one another stand in a specifiable semantic relationship to one another or can be classified into groups or sets of lexical units which stand in a specifiable semantic relationship to one another. An example of this type of formulaic line is *žerdiŋ žüsin šaŋdattï* (*Qambar* 115). In a third type of formulaic line the semantic constraint on the variable elements of the line is dropped. It consists of a fixed phrasal unit in the first part of the line and a slot, with metrical and possibly also grammatical constraints on the lexical units filling the slot. An example of this type of formulaic line is *Qïz Nazïmnïŋ maydanï* (*Qambar* 109). In a subtype of this kind of formulaic line the "fixed phrasal unit" is itself variable, but according to specifiable semantic and grammatical rules. An example of this subtype is *aldïnan ötti körikten* (*Qambar* 108). There is finally a fourth type of formulaic line, exemplified in the couplet *Bazarda bar aq mata/ oynaqtaydï žas bota* (*Qoblandï* 485-86). I shall call this type "cliché-line" or "cliché-couplet" (or "triplet"), stressing, with A. B. Lord, that repeated lines, couplets, or triplets of this kind should be set apart from the formula proper.[39]

So far I have talked of formulaic diction mainly on a quantitative basis and have hence classified formulaic lines according to the extent and degree to which they are invariant and variable. Other classifications are, however, also possible. C. M. Bowra divides formulas into two groups, noun-adjective combinations and repeated phrases. He considers the former as being mainly of poetic value with no narrative function and the latter as "being strictly functional and necessary to the narrative" somewhat in the sense Parry and Lord understand formulaic diction.[40] A. T. Hatto has studied the epithets in older Kirghiz epic poetry under thirteen headings, including quantitative ("shorter/longer"), functional ("laudatory/defamatory"), semantic ("king-epithets," "specific/generic"), and genetic criteria ("traditional/trans-

[39]For similar lines in the *Manas*-trilogy recorded by Radloff see Hatto 1980-82: II, 17ff.

[40]Bowra 1952: 222; for Lord's criticism of Bowra see Lord 1960: 284 (note 19).

ferred/reinterpreted/disintegrated").[41] K. N. Veliev has proposed a threefold classification of Turkic formulas on the lines of "syntagmatic," semantic, and "linguistic" principles.[42] Without going into a typology of formulaic diction, I will add to the quantitative discussion above a qualitative dimension by selecting from these various types of formulas the semantically most prominent one, the "noun-epithet combination," more precisely, the formulaic description of the hero by a "fixed epithet."

The main protagonist of *Qambar* is called "Qambar," "Er Qambar" (the hero Qambar), "Qambar bek" (the beg Qambar) or "Qambaržan" (dear Qambar) in the epic poem, i.e. he is referred to by either a two-syllable word or a three-syllable expression. Furthermore, in a number of lines the name "Qambar" is qualified by an attribute. Semantically, two types of epithet are found, an "animal-epithet" and a "horse-epithet." In line 1744 Qambar is compared to a lion:

> Arïstan tuwġan Qambar bek
> Lion-born   Qambar-bek

A look at the referent corpus shows that this line is formulaic:

Arïstan tuwġan	Qoblandï	*Qoblandï* 2090, 2092, 2096, 2311, 3403, 4782, 5603
	Qoblan	*Qoblandï* 47
Arïstan tuwġan	Bökenbay	*Qoblandï* 5772
	batïrdï (hero)	*Qoblandï* 4176
	batïrïŋ	*Qoblandï* 5556
	qurdas žan (dear companion)	*Qoblandï* 836

[41]See Hatto 1989a: 74f.

[42]"Syntagmatic" in Veliev's terminology refers to narrative syntax, by "linguistic" he means both linguistic form and stylistics/rhetoric. He brings examples only for his first group.   Veliev's term "formula" covers both formulas and formulaic passages/type-scenes. "Syntagmatically" defined formulas are initial, transitional, and final formulas; semantically defined formulas are formulas connected to various units of content (feasts, combats, journeys etc.) as well as gnomic formulas; linguistically defined formulas are formulaic metaphors, comparisons, phrases, syntactic units etc. See Veliev 1987: 90.

In Kirghiz epic poetry the corresponding formula is "tiger-born (Name)."
Compare:[43]

qabïlan tuuġan	Er Manas	*Manas (BM)* 350
	Manasqa	484
	Košoyġo	496
	Er Košoy	1148
	Alman Bet	*Manas (AK)* 77
	Almambet	*Manas (KK)* 316

The comparison of a heroic figure with an animal endowed with physical
strength and power is also found in the Uzbek *dastans*.[44] Heroes like
Alpāmiš or Goroġli and their companions are compared to the lion
(*arslan, šer*), the tiger (*yolbars*), the leopard (*qāplān*), the (ger)falcon
(*šunqār, lāčin*), the hawk (*qarčiġay*), the Arabian dromedary (*nār*), and
the dragon (*aždarhā*). Young heroes, on the other hand, are compared
to the young camel (*bota*) or the foal of the fallow deer (*quralay*).
Compare this passage from *Alpāmiš*:

> Bu sozni aytadi šunqār,
> šerday boldi mard yigitlar,
> āt qoydi, āblāhu akbar.
> Har qaysisi erday bolib,
> har yaġrini qirday bolib,
> tāġda aqirgan šerday bolib....
> (Zarif, Mirzaev 1979: 213-214)

> The gerfalcon (*šunqār*) (Alpāmiš) spoke this word
> and the heroic young warriors (*mard yigit*) became like lions (*šer*);
> they urged their horses on, shouting: "God is most great!"
> Everyone of them became a hero (*er*),
> every shoulder towered like a hill,
> they became like lions (*šer*), roaring on the mountain....

The second formula in *Qambar* to be discussed here contains a "horse-
epithet":

[43]These examples are taken from Hatto 1989a; see *ibid*.: 75, 88, 90, 91. The
abbreviations and titles for the various parts of Radloff's *Manas* are Hatto's; *AK* =
"Almambet, Er Kökčö and Ak-Erkeč [Aq-erkeč]" (Hatto 1990: 13-47), *BM* = "Bok-
murun" (Hatto 1990: 159-225), *KK* = "Közkaman" (Hatto 1990: 227-303).

[44]See Reichl 1989b: 102; on the comparison of the hero with wild animals in heroic
poetry see also Bowra 1952: 97.

Qara qasqa	attï	Qambar bek	*Qambar* 146
Black spotted.	with-the-horse	Qambar-bek	

Qambar with the black horse with the white mark[45]

Compare:

Qara attï	Qambar	qaramay	*Qambar* 424
black-horsed	Qambar	without-looking	

žalǧïz	attï	kedeyge	*Qambar* 624, 705, 1523
		kedeyniŋ	
only-one	with-the-horse	to/of-the-poor-man	

the poor man with only one horse

The pattern of this formulaic system can be described as "name (or characterization) of horse" + *attï* (horse-having) + "name of rider(s)." In *Qoblandï* we find the following realizations:[46]

qïrïq mïŋ	attï	Qïzïlbaš	2094, 2291, 2296, 2313, 2409, 2443

the Qïzïlbaš with the forty thousand horses

Tarlan attï	Köbikti	2640

Köbikti with the horse Tarlan

Taybuwrïl	attï	Qoblandï	3729

Qoblandï with the horse Taybuwrïl

This pattern is already found in the *Book of Dede Qorqut*, where the prophet Hïzïr is characterized as *boz atlu Hïzïr*, "Hïzïr with the grey horse"; Salur Qazan as *qoŋur atlu Qazan*, "Qazan with the chestnut-colored horse"; and the Christian king Šökli as *alaca atlu Šökli Melik*, "King Šökli with the piebald horse," or *alaca atlu kâfir*, "the pagan with the piebald horse."[47] It is also found in other Turkic traditions. In the Tuvinian heroic tale the hero is generally identified by his horse, for instance *Xan-Šilgi a'ttïg Xan-Xülük*, "Xan-Xülük with the horse Xan-Šilgi," or *Arzïlaŋ-Qara a'ttïg Xunan-Qara möge*, "the hero Xunan-Qara

---

[45] A *qara qasqa at* is a black horse with a bald spot or white mark (*qasqa*) on its forehead.

[46] See Reichl 1989c: 371.

[47] See Ergin 1958-63: I, 88, 90 (Hïzïr); 96, 168 (Qazan); 220, 96 (Šökli). On epithets in the *Book of Dede Qorqut* see also Başgöz 1978b.

with the horse Arzïlan-Qara."[48] In the Altaian version of *Alpamïš* (to be discussed in Chapter Ten), for instance, we find, as in other Altaian epic poems, whole-line "horse-epithets." Alïp-Manaš is *Aq-boro atqa mingen/ Alïp-Manaš*, "Alïp-Manaš, mounted on his horse Aq-boro," or the enemy khan *Aq-buwrïl atqa mingen/ Aq-qaan*, "Aq-khan, mounted on his horse Aq-buwrïl."[49] An elaborate "horse-epithet" is found at the beginning of the Yakut *olonxo Quruubay Xaannaax Qulun Qullustuur* (Qulun Qullustuur of Rough Character), possibly unsurpassed for length in Turkic epic poetry:[50]

```
     Bïlïrgï d'ïl bïdan mïndaatïgar,
     uruqqu d'ïl qulan uorġatïgar,
     tüört saxa törüü iligine,
     üs saxa üösküü iligine,
 5   ikki saxa iitille iligine,
     qulgaaġar quraġaččï qïïllaax,
     keteġer keġe qïïllaax,
     sannïgar sar qïïllaax,
     köxsüger köġön qïïllaax,
10   öttüger ötön qïïllaax,
     borbuyugar borčuq quobaxtaax,
     Üöhe Sibiirge aattammït aata
     töbötünen oonnyuur
     čimeči qugas attaax,
15   allaraa doyduga aattammït aata
     ataġïnan oonnyuur
     aydaar qugas attaax,
     orto doyduga aattammït aata
     quturugunan oonnyuur
20   [qunnyalïq] quyaar qugas attaax
     quruubay xaannaax
     Qulun Qullustuur dien
     buxatïïr üöskeebite ebite ühü.
```

[48]See Quular, Sarïg-ool 1963: 3ff., 193ff. The names have a meaning; *arzïlaŋ* means "lion," *xunan* "foal in its third year," *šilgi* "sorrel," *qara* "black," and *qan* "blood." *Külüg* is an archaic word for hero, derived from Old Turkic *kü*, "fame"; see Radloff 1893-1911: II, cols. 1471f. On the epithets for horses in Tuvinian heroic narrative see also Grebnev 1960: 33.

[49]Surazakov et al. 1959: 29 and *passim. Aq-boro* means "light-grey," *aq-buwrïl* "white-dapple."

[50]Timofeev-Teplouxov et al. 1985: 8. For help with the translation of this passage I am grateful to Professor A. T. Hatto. — On "king-epithets" in Kirghiz epic poetry see Hatto 1989a: 80ff.

> On the faraway height of past years,
> on the distant mountain ridge of by-gone years,
> when the four Yakuts had not yet been born,
> when the three Yakuts had not yet come into being,
> 5   when the two Yakuts had not yet been raised —
> with a horse on whose ear there were curlews,
> on whose neck there were cuckoos,
> on whose shoulder blade there were buzzards,
> on whose back there were mallards,
> 10   on whose thigh there were Siberian turtledoves,
> on whose (hollow of the) knee there were grey leverets,
> called in the Upper World
> the shining sorrel horse
> jerking its head,
> 15   called in the Underworld
> the clamoring sorrel horse
> kicking with its legs,
> called in the Middle World
> the wild sorrel horse
> 20   twitching its tail —
> there lived a hero
> with the name of Qulun Qullustuur
> of rough character.

Yakut *attaax* (lines 14, 17, 20) corresponds to Kazakh *attï*, Tuvinian *a'ttïg*, Turkish *atlı (atlu)*, "having a horse." This means that the whole passage (1-23) is one long sentence, in which *buxatïïr*, "hero," in the last line is modified by an extended epithet consisting of a number of participle phrases (*attaax*, "horse-having"; *dien*, "called, named"). The sentence is hence paraphrasable as "The ... horse-having, of-rough-character-Qulun Qullustuur-named hero lived." These lines are, incidentally, a good example for parallelistic structuring and horizontal alliteration. They are also an instance of formulaic patterning over a sequence of lines, intermediary between formula and theme. This type of passage, the formulaic beginning of an epic, will be looked at more closely in Chapter Nine; the typical scene, or theme in the terminology of "oral-formulaic theory," will be the subject of the next section.

Thematic Patterning

According to Parry and Lord a theme is a "group of ideas regularly used in telling a tale in the formulaic style of traditional song."[51] This term corresponds basically to what German scholars call *typische Szene* (type-scene) or *Erzählschablone* (narrative template), although the emphasis is somewhat different within different scholarly traditions.[52] Lord begins his discussion of themes in Serbo-Croatian epic poetry with the opening scene in the *Song of Bagdad*, a council at the sultan's court in Istanbul, and draws attention to the similar council scene at the beginning of the *Chanson de Roland*.[53] The Uzbek version of *Alpāmiš* in Fāzil Yoldāš-oġli's variant also begins with this theme. When Bāysari is told that he has to pay an alms-tax (*zakāt*) to his brother, he summons his tribesmen to a *madžlis* (council) to deliberate what to do (see p. 162). Bāysari opens the council with the following words:

> Āh urganda kozdan āqar selāb yāš,
> maslahat ber, on miṇ uyli qarindāš,
> Barčināyim boy yetgandir qalamqāš,
> zālim bilan hargiz bolmaṇlar yoldāš.
> 5 Qoṇġirāt eldan mālga zakāt kelibdi,
> maslahat ber, on miṇ uyli qarindāš!
> Qursin Hakimbegi, mulla bolibdi,
> bezakāt māllarni harām bilibdi,
> Qoṇġirāt eldan mālga zakāt kelibdi,
> 10 maslahat ber, on miṇ uyli qarindāš.
> Dardli qul dardimni kimga yāraman,
> ayriliq otiga baġri pāraman,
> muna elda siġindi bop turaman,
> oz akamga qanday zakāt beraman?!
> 15 Maslahat ber, on miṇ uyli qarindāš!
> Xazān bolib bāġda gullar solibdi,
> šum falak bāšimga sawdā sālibdi,

---

[51]Lord 1960: 68.

[52]The phrase *typische Szene* is associated in particular with W. Arend's study of typical scenes in Homer (1933); compare Parry's review, reprinted in Parry 1971: 404-407. The term "template" (*Schablone*) was used by older scholars like A. Heusler and has been revived as *Erzählschablone* for the translation of *theme*; see Voorwinden, de Haan 1979: 8 and *passim*.

[53]Lord 1960: 68; the *Song of Bagdad* is No. 1 in Parry, Lord 1953-54: I, 68ff. (translation), II, 8ff. (text).

Bāyboridan mālga zakāt kelibdi,
maslahat ber, on miŋ uyli qarindāš!
(Zarif, Mirzaev 1979: 11)

Amid sighs, tears flow from (my) eyes like a stream,
give advice, tribal companions (relations) of the ten thousand yurts!
My Barčin-āy with black eyebrows has come of age.
Don't ever associate with a tyrant!
5   From Qoṅġirāt came (a demand for) tax on (our) cattle (property).
Give advice, tribal companions of the ten thousand yurts!
May Hakimbeg (Alpāmiš) be cursed!   He has become a mullah.[54]
According to his knowledge cattle without tax is against the law;
from Qoṅġirāt came a demand for tax on our cattle.
10 Give advice, tribal companions of the ten thousand yurts!
As a sorrowful slave (of God), to whom can I tell my grief?
My heart is burning in the fire of separation,
among this people I have become a stranger (poor relation).
How should I pay tax to my older brother?
15 Give advice, tribal companions of the ten thousand yurts!
When autumn comes, the roses wither in the garden.
Cruel destiny has brought woe upon my head.
From Bāybori came a demand for tax on our cattle:
Give advice, tribal companions of the ten thousand yurts!

The passage continues for another 29 lines in the edited text. It is in
lines of 11 syllables with a fairly loose sequence of rhymes. The lines
quoted have the following rhyme-pattern:

a–A–a–a–B–A–b–b–B–A–c–c–c–C–A–b*–b–b–A

In this extract we have basically three rhymes, a (*āš*), b (*ibdi*), and c
(*aman*); we have furthermore three lines which occur again and again
in this verse-passage, refrain-like lines symbolized by capital letters (A,
B, C). The repeated lines function as the semantic focus of the passage:
A "Give advice!," B (and C) "We have to pay tax, should we give it?"
Often these key-lines are taken up in the following speech, as is also the
case here.[55]   A wise old man (*āq sāqāl*), called Yartibāy, replies to
Bāysari (in a passage comprising 49 lines in the printed edition),
repeating twice the couplet:

---

[54] I.e. "he has become proficient in reading and writing." This is an allusion to
the cause of the tax.

[55] On this type of line, termed "motif-line" by W. Feldman, see Feldman 1983.

Maslahat bermaymiz Bāysaribiyga,
āsilmaymiz Bāyboriniŋ dāriga...
(Zarif, Mirzaev 1979: 12-13)

We will not give advice to Bāysari-biy,
we will not hang on Bāybori's gallows...

and adding the four times repeated line:

Maslahatni, šāhim, oziŋ bilasan.
You yourself, my shah, know the advice.

Bāysari then suggests (in a passage of 59 lines) that they migrate to the land of Kalmucks, to which proposal Yartibāy (in a passage of 50 lines) agrees, repeating four times:

Qayda kočsaŋ, bizlar birga bāramiz...
(Zarif, Mirzaef 1979: 15-16)
Wherever you migrate to, we will go together...

and closing the *madžlis* (council) with the lines:

Birga kočsak, birga-birga bāramiz,
sen qayerda bolsaŋ, šunda bolamiz.
(Zarif, Mirzaev 1979: 16)

If we migrate together, we go together;
wherever you are, we will be.

There is a second type of repeated line in this passage, marked by an asterisk (b*):

Xazān bolib bāġda gullar solibdi
When autumn comes, the roses wither in the garden.

This line is repeated in the other speeches, with slight variations such as:

Xazān bolsa bāġda gullar solmaymi
When autumn comes, do not then the roses wither in the garden?

Such stock lines are very common in Uzbek *dastan*-poetry; they are of the same type as the cliché-couplets discussed above in relation to Kazakh epic poetry. These cliché-lines emphasize a certain tone and, by evoking natural phenomena, underline the mood of a passage. This particular verse is often used in contexts that suggest distress, unhappiness, or grief, just as the corresponding line occurs in situations of joy and happiness:

Yana bahār bolsa āčilar gullar
(Zarif, Mirzaev 1979: 18 and *passim*)

When spring comes again, the roses open up.

Line b* occurs over 30 times in Fāzil's variant of *Alpāmiš*. Some variants are:[56]

Xazān bolsa zāġlar qonar gulšanga
When autumn comes, crows settle on the rose-beds.

Xazān bolmay bāġda gullar solmasin
May autumn not come and the roses in the garden not wither!

These lines occur also in pairs:

Yana bahār bolsa āčilar gullar,
gulni korsa mast bop sayrar bulbullar

When spring comes again, the roses open up;
when the nightingales see the rose, they become intoxicated and burst
out singing.

Xazān bolmay bāġniŋ guli solmaydi,
solgan gulga sira bulbul qonmaydi

If autumn does not come, the rose in the garden does not wither,
and the nightingale will not perch on the withered rose.

The council scene consists of four verse-passages, distributed over two speakers and connected by prose-passages. It is highly patterned, but it is not stereotyped to the same degree as the council scene in the Serbo-Croatian *Song of Bagdad*. The receiving and sending of letters as in the *Song of Bagdad* is one of the most common ways of beginning a heroic song; about 30% of the songs collected by Vuk Karadžić begin with this theme.[57] In Turkic epic poetry, on the other hand, council scenes like the one opening Fāzil's variant of *Alpāmiš* occur with far lower frequency and are furthermore, despite their patterning, far more closely linked to the matter of deliberation. There are, however, typical

[56]See Mirzaev 1979: 70, where he lists 13 variants of this formula in Fāzil's *Alpāmiš*. For the occurrence of this formula in other variants of *Alpāmiš* see also Mirzaev 1968: 141; for this formula in Fāzil's *Rustamxān* see Kidajš-Pokrovskaja, Mirbadaleva 1972: 71. Compare also Kidajš-Pokrovskaja, Mirbadaleva 1971: 77ff.

[57]See Kravcov 1985: 260ff.

scenes in Turkic oral epic poetry which show a high degree of formulaic patterning both on the level of expression and that of content.

Such a theme is the arming of the hero before he sets out on a war-like expedition or a journey. This theme is one of the invariant elements of Turkic heroic epic poetry, in the epics of the "central traditions" as well as in the Yakut *oloŋxo* or the Turkish *destan*. A very short version of this theme, combined with the theme of the hero's ride, is found in one of the Kazakh variants of the Alpamïš-story:[58]

725	Saymandarïn saylanïp,
	altïnnan kemer baylanïp,
	abžïlanday tolġanïp,
	qïzïl nayza qolġa alïp
	Šubarġa qarġïp minedi,
730	qudaydan medet tiledi
	qarġïp minip žas bala
	ašuwï kernep žönedi.
	Läšker tartïp keledi,
	awïzdïqpen alïšïp,
735	ušqan quspen žarïsïp,
	key žerde bala šoqïtïp,
	key žerde basïn tögedi.
	Bir kün šapsa Šubar at
	aylïq žer alïp beredi.

725	He prepared his gear,
	bound his golden belt round his waist,
	turned about like a water snake,
	took his red spear into his hand,
	jumped onto Šubar,
730	asked God for his help;
	the young man jumped up,
	rode along, filled with wrath.
	He went to war,
	pulling his reins tight,
735	racing with the flying birds,
	where the young man was galloping,
	where he was heading for.
	When the horse Šubar had galloped for one day,
	he had covered the distance of a monthly journey.

In lines 725-729 (-732) the preparation of the hero for his journey is briefly described, while the journey itself is the subject of the following

---

[58] Äwezov [Auezov], Smirnova 1961: 23; see Reichl 1989c: 376f. This extract comes from Mayköt Sandïbaev's and Sultanqul Aqqožaev's variant.

lines. Just two or three strokes suffice to paint the hero's arming: he
fastens his golden belt round his waist (726), speedily swings himself
round (727), and takes his red spear into his hand (728). His psychological state is no more than alluded to when his anger is mentioned in line
732. The hero asks God for his help (730), swings himself on his horse
(731), rides along as fast (or faster) than a bird (735), and covers the
space of a monthly journey in one day (739). All these motifs and
images belong to the inventory of the theme of the hero's arming and
ride. In Divaev's variant of *Qambar* the hero's preparation-and-parting
is slightly more elaborate, consisting of the same basic motifs: the
donning of his armor, the invocation of God's help, the hero's anger, and
his ride on his horse, galloping as fast as a flying bird:

> Badana köz berik sawït
> basa üstine kiyedi,
> 1550 žaw žaraǧïn asïnïp
> žürmekke dayar boladï.
> Qurama bolat duwlïǧa
> šekesine qoyadï.
> Ordasïnda otïrïp
> 1555 šarapqa äbden toyadï.
> Awmin dep qol žayïp,
> bir qudayǧa tapsïrïp
> žurtïnan žawap suradï.
> Qoš aytïsïp Qambarǧa
> 1560 toqsan üyli tobïr me
> alpïs üyli arïgï
> amandasïp žïladï.
> Arïstan aman kelgey dep
> bäri de duǧa qïladï.
> 1565 Bastïrïp qattï qadamïn
> qara qasqa tulpardï
> qaharlanïp uradï;
> qustay ušïp asuwmen
> tezde žetip baradï.

> > (Äwezov [Auezov], Smirnova 1959: 71)

> He pulled the strong coat of mail with its fine mesh[59]
> over his head,
> 1550 took his deadly weapons
> and was ready to depart.

[59]Professor A. T. Hatto draws my attention to a similar formula in Kirghiz,
discussed in Hatto 1977: 197. With reference to the line *Badana közdi aq sawït* from
Qoblandï Hatto notes that this line "seems to show reinterpetation of *badana* 1. 'mail-
shirt' as *badana* 2. 'lentil', thus 'lentil-eyed' (mesh)." (*Ibid.*)

He put the helmet of wrought steel
over his temples.
Sitting in his *orda* (yurt),
1555 he had drunk a lot of wine.
Saying: "Amen!" he extended his arms,
commended himself to the One God
and took leave of his people.
Saying: "Farewell!" to Qambar,
1560 the Tobïr of the ninety yurts and
the Arġïn of the sixty yurts
cried when they said good-bye.
Saying: "May the lion come back safely!"
they all fell down in prayer.
1565 Urging on its vigorous steps,
he whipped the black horse with the white mark
angrily.
Flying like a bird, full of wrath,
he arrived in no time.

In another Kazakh variant of *Qambar*, that by Barmaq Muqambaev,
the account of the hero's armor is somewhat more circumstantial:

Qaruw-žaraq asïnïp,
moynïna ildi er Qambar
atasïnan qalġan mïltïqtï.
1360 Atasïnan qalġan bul mïltïq
talaydï žoq qïp qurtïptï.
Saramtal etti žumïstï,
saylanïp saluw urïstï,
aš beline bayladï
1365 baldaġï altïn qïlïštï.
Kiydi qïmqap mawïttï,
sïyïnġan piri Däwitti.
Kiyip aldï er Qambar,
aynalasï bes qabat
1370 atasïnan qalġan sawïtï.
Atadan qalġan mïyrasqor
talaydï burïn šawïpti.
(Äwezov [Auezov], Smirnova 1959: 110)

When putting on his weapons and armor,
Er Qambar hung round his shoulder (lit. neck)
the flintlock inherited from his father.
1360 This flintlock inherited from his father
destroyed and annihilated many.
He put his armor on in good order,
preparing himself for combat.
He bound round his slender waist
1365 the sword with the golden hilt.
He put on his coat of brocade,

putting his trust in the prophet David.
Er Qambar put on
the five-layered coat of mail
1370   inherited from his father.
His father's heirloom
had in former days wrought destruction.

The theme of the hero's putting on his armor and in particular of his saddling his horse is also characteristic of the composition of the Uzbek *dastan*. A detailed description of the hero's preparation for a journey is found in Ergaš Džumanbulbul-oġli's version of *Rawšan*.[60] After having curried his horse, the hero puts a sweat-cloth (*terlik*) of silk and a saddlecloth (*čirgi*) of velvet on his horse Džiyrānquš, puts the saddle-girth (*bellik*) round, a further saddlecloth (*džahaldirik*) of beaver-hide on, then a silver saddle (*egar*) with a golden pommel (*qāš*) and two golden stirrups (*uzangi*); he fastens a girth (*ayil*) of silk and throws a rug (*dawir*) with golden fringes over the horse, ties a crupper (*quyušqān*) of rhinoceros leather round the horse's tail, adorns the horse with a golden breastplate (*omuldirik*), puts a Chaghatay bridle (*yugan*) with forty decorative medallions (*qubba*) on and finally a bit (*suwluq*) of steel. The hero girds himself with his snake-tongued, lightning-like *xandžar* (dagger) (*ilān tilli, yašin turli xandžar*). He has also firestone and tinder (*čaqmāq, quw*), and a whip (*qamči*) with a golden pommel. He wears velvet trousers (*čalwar*) and a gold-embroidered coat (*xālāt*).

The scene in *Rawšan* can be matched with a similar passage in *Alpāmiš*, agreeing with it in almost every detail. After Alpāmiš has received word from Bārčin to come to her rescue, his sister Qaldirġač helps him to get ready for his journey:

Āša elga āšgan tārtar xorlikni,
Bek Alpāmiš qilar bukun erlikni,
Bismillā, deb sāldi ātniŋ ustiga
kimxābi mayindan bolgan terlikni.
5   Mard bolganlar qaraydakan durbini,
ustalar išlatar polat qirġini,
šul zamānda sāldi ātniŋ ustiga
zarligu zarbābdan bolgan čirgini.
Čirginiŋ ustidan qoydi bellikni,
10   bāz ustidan sāldi džahaldirikni.

[60]For the text see Zarif 1971: 62-65; it is translated in Reichl 1985a: 56-59 (verse-passage V). On this type-scene see also Žirmunskij, Zarifov 1947: 367f.; Bowra 1952: 394; Mirzaev 1968: 134-137. This passage in *Rawšan* is compared with similar type-scenes in the Serbo-Croatian epic by Lord 1987a: 302ff. (reprinted in Lord 1991: 211ff.).

Mullalar oqiydi zeru zabarni,
ustalar čāpadi teša-tabarni,
Bismillā, deb sāldi ātniŋ ustiga
tilla kārsān, qāši āltin egarni.
15 El kočirib Ālatāġdan āširdi,
sirin aytmay dušmanlardan yaširdi,
ikkāwi ham tilladandir uzangi,
yarqillatib ikki yāqqa tuširidi.
Qišman yāz ortasi hiššay sawrdi(r),
20 yāmān ādam mudām qilar ġāwurdi,
lāf aytganga bātmāndan ham āwurdi(r),
Bismillā, deb sāldi ātniŋ ustiga
čāčāġi zumratdan zarli dawurdi.
Gana-gana bandalarniŋ džāyildi(r),
25 xudā qilgan išga banda qāyildi(r),
Āy Qaldirġāč tārtdi ātniŋ belidan
sirti ipak, iči mayin ayildi.
Čuw, desaŋ, ozadi āsmānda qušdan,
heč kamlik bolmasa yorġa yurišdan,
30 Bismillā, deb tārtdi ātniŋ belidan
on sakkiz qubbali čaġatāy puštan.
Abzaliniŋ bari āla qayišdan,
saġrisiġa tašlab karki quyušqān.
Har qubbasi kelgan katta tardašdan.
35 Ātlantirmāq boldi šundayin bekni,
gardaniga tašlab omuldirikni.
Abzallagan ātni korib quwāndi,
āt bāšiga sāldi tilla yugandi.
(Zarif, Mirzaev 1979: 78-79)

Those who go away to a distant people suffer humiliation.
Beg Alpāmiš does manly deeds today.
Saying: "In the name of God!" she put over the horse
the sweat-cloth (*terlik*) of fine brocade.
5 The heroes look through the telescope,
the masters forge the steel for combat.
At this time she put over the horse
the saddlecloth (*čirgi*) of material interwoven with gold threads.
On the saddlecloth she put the saddle-girth (*bellik*),
10 and over that the top saddlecloth (*džahaldirik*).
The mullahs can read the *zer* and *zabar*,[61]
the masters hew with axe and hatchet.
Saying: "In the name of God!" she put over the horse
a golden saddle (*egar*) with a golden seat (*kārsān*) and pommel (*qāš*).
15 — He (Alpāmiš) had led the people to their pastures across the Ālatāġ;

---

[61]The *zer* and *zabar* are vowel-signs of the Arabic alphabet, standing for the /i/ and the /a/, respectively.

     he had hid from the enemies without revealing his secret. —
     Both stirrups (*uzangi*) are also made of gold;
     having polished them, she put them down on both sides.
     — In the middle of winter and summer lies the month of *sawr*.[62]
20   A bad man always makes a noise.
     Empty bragging is heavier than a *batman* (weight). —
     Saying: "In the name of God!" she put over the horse
     the golden rug (*dawur*) with emerald fringes.
     — Some people are ignorant.
25   Man is enraptured by God's work. —
     The beautiful Qaldirğăč put round the horse's flanks
     a soft girth (*ayil*), covered in silk.
     If you say "Hoy!" it will outrace the birds in the sky,
     with an ambling pace without flaw.
30   Saying: "In the name of God!" she put round the horse's flanks
     a Chaghatay saddle-girth (*puštan*) with eighteen decorative medallions.
     Its harness (*abzal*) was made of straps of different colors.
     She threw over the horse's rump a crupper (*quyušqān*) of rhinoceros
       hide.
     Each decorative medallion was bigger than a *tarkaš*.[63]
35   She prepared such a beg for the journey,
     putting the breastplate (*omuldirik*) over his horse's neck;
     she rejoiced in the looks of the harnessed horse,
     and put over the horse's head the golden bridle (*yugan*).

    The type-scene of the hero's preparation for combat and his departure
is clearly one of the universals of heroic poetry. It is not only found in
the different traditions of Turkic oral epic poetry, but also in a wide
variety of poetic traditions.[64] A. B. Lord compares this theme as it is
represented in Serbo-Croatian heroic song to the arming of Basil in
Digenis Akritas and that of Achilles and Patroclus in the *Iliad*.[65] A
number of medieval parallels could be cited here, in particular from the
Old French *chanson de geste*.[66] This is not the place to embark on a
comparative analysis of this theme; I will, however, quote just two

[62]*Sawr* is the second month of the Moslem lunar year (April 22nd — May 21st;
Arabic *ṣafar*).

[63]A case made out of wood or leather to store glasses or cups.

[64]For Tatar epic poetry see Urmančeev 1980a: 56f.; for the Tuvinian heroic tale
see Grebnev 1960: 118-127.

[65]See Lord 1960: 89ff.

[66]On the theme of the hero's putting on his armor in the *chanson de geste* see
Rychner 1955: 128 and 132ff.; on the arming scene in *Sir Gawain and Green Knight*
see Burrow 1965: 37ff.

geographically and culturally fairly remote examples, which help put the Turkic variations on this theme into a broader perspective. When in the Ainu *Song of Aeoina-kamui* the culture hero Aeoina-kamui (speaking, as is usual in Ainu heroic and mythic songs, in the first person) puts on his armor and departs to do battle against the Earth Crone, we encounter basically the same catalogue of arms and clothing as in the Turkic epics:

> Jumping up,
> I attired myself
> in a magnificent robe.
> I went inside
> my suit of metal armor.
> In a single wrapping
> I wrapped around myself
> my metal buckled belt.
> Under my belt I thrust
> my god-given sword.
> Over this I put on
> my elm-bark fiber coat with its hem in flames.
> Grasping in my hand
> my short-hilted spear,
> I went outside.[67]

Similarly, the ornate execution of the theme of the hero saddling his horse in the Uzbek *dastans* can be matched by a formulaic passage in the Fulani heroic song-cycle of *Ham-Bodêdio*. In one of the episodes of this cycle, Hammadi saddles his horse Bone-Yubaade (Crin-Fou, Crazy-Mane) in a fixed sequence of movements before he sets off on an expedition:

> Hammadi secoua selle
> et sangle
> et bricole et tapis de selle
> et, avec cela, tous les tissus: Hammadi les ajusta sur Crin-Fou.
> Hammadi foula le forgeron et le sellier s'étira; il se rassit sur un sellier,
> il prit en main un bourrelier,
> il empoigna une cordonnière; le forgeron dit qu'il était là, à la ganache de Crin-Fou.
> Hammadi ramena les six [pointes de ses éperons] sur les flancs de Crin-Fou. Crin-Fou s'enleva comme un nuage de saison chaude,

---

[67]Philippi 1979: 197. On this theme compare Bowra 1952: 191ff.; Bowra gives a similar quote from the Ainu epic *Kutune Shirka* (*ibid.*: 193). On the first person in the Ainu mythological and heroic epics, possibly connected with shamanism, see Dunn 1980: 331; Hatto 1989b: 153f.

> avança à pas légers comme un faon de gazelle,
> sauta un galet blanc,
> un œuf,
> une souche,
> une noix de doum,
> un trou.[68]

Parallels like these underline the typical, but they also emphasize the particular. In the Uzbek version of this theme, the hero does not set off on his journey before a relative, normally his father, gives him a piece of advice (often a series of gnomic sayings) and his parting blessing. The motifs employed in this part of the type-scene are again conventional, comprising formulas expressing parental love, the hope for a safe return, the grief of parting etc.[69]

Intimately linked to the theme of the hero preparing himself for an expedition is the theme of the heroic ride. In the Kazakh extracts quoted above, this theme comprised motifs like the hero angrily whipping his horse (*Qambar* [Divaev] 1566-67), the comparison of his ride with the flight of birds (*Alpamïs* 735; *Qambar* [Divaev] 1568) and the covering of great distances in little time (*Alpamïs* 738-39; *Qambar* [Divaev] 1569). These motifs appear also in other parts of these epic poems as well as in other Kazakh epics.[70] When Qambar is first introduced (in Divaev's variant), his ride on his horse is described as:

> Astïndaǧï bedewi
> suwïtuwï tüsken soŋ
> ušqan quspen žarïstï.
> 205　Quyïnday šaŋï burqïrap,
> atqan oqtay zïrqïrap,
> qïladï žaqïn alïstï.
>
> 　　　　　　　　(Äwezov [Auezov], Smirnova 1959: 40-41)

> After the racehorse under him
> had cooled off,

---

[68]Seydou 1976: 49, 51; compare *ibid.* 61 and 33f. Hammadi is identical with Ham-Bodêdio or Hama the Red; Crin-Fou (Crazy-Mane) is his horse. As the editor and translator of the cycle explains in a footnote, the various craftsmen stand for the objects they made.

[69]For details see Reichl 1989b: 103-105.

[70]For the occurrence of this type-scene in *Qoblandï* see Kidajš-Pokrovskaja, Nurmagambetova 1975: 108ff. [ll. 1786ff.], 209f. [ll. 6065ff.]. The comparison of the hero's ride with the flight of birds is already found in the *Dīvān luǧāt at-Turk*, in line 4 of the passage quoted in Chapter Two (p. 40f.).

it competed against the birds.
205 Like a storm raising the dust,
racing along like a flying arrow,
it shortened the long distance.

What is interesting in this passage are the verb-forms *burqïrap* and *zïrqïrap*. They are indicative of a further motif belonging to the hero's ride, that of the clangor of his arms and armor and of the horse's trappings. This motif is familiar from the First Book of the *Iliad*, where Apollo descends in anger from Mount Olympus:

τόξ' ὤμοισιν ἔχων ἀμφηρεφέα τε φαρέτρην.
ἔκλαγξαν δ' ἄρ' ὀιστοὶ ἐπ' ὤμων χωομένοιο,
αὐτοῦ κινηθέντος...
(*Iliad*, I.45-47)
... having the bow and the quiver, covered at both ends, on his shoulders.
The arrows clanged on the shoulders of the angry god,
while he was moving....

In the Uzbek *dastan*s this motif is expressed by a "run" with onomatopoetic verbs like the two Kazakh verbs (*qarqilla-, širqilla-, dirkilla-, čarqilla-* etc.). I will illustrate the theme of the hero's ride in Uzbek epic poetry by an extract from Fāzil's variant of *Alpāmiš*, with a few parallels from other Uzbek and Uighur *dastan*s:[71]

Dubulġa bāšda duŋullab,
kark qubba qalqān qarqillab,
tilla pāyanak urilgan,
uzangilarga širqillab,
5 Bedāw ātlari dirkillab,
ālġir qušdayin čarqillab,
qolda nayzasi solqillab.
Yurmāqči uzāq yoliga,
qaramay oŋu soliga,
10 Yetsam deb yārniŋ eliga.
Siltab yuradi Bāyčibār,
yaqin bolar uzāq yollar,
yol yurar dawlatli šunqār,
Qalmāq yurtini axtarar,
15 yālġiz ketdi bundan šunqār.
Hakimbek qildi ġayratdi,
qiladi ātga šiddatdi,

[71]The following examples are also quoted and discussed in Reichl 1989b: 106ff. For the motif of the horse jumping over rivers and ravines also present in this passage see *ibid*.

č“u-ha, dedi, qamči čātdi,
izǧār čolni tozān tutdi,
20   yolniŋ tanābini tārtdi.
Qir kelsa qilpillatdi,
arna kelsa irǧitdi,
or kelsa omganlatdi,
šuytip Hakim yol tārtdi.
                    (Zarif, Mirzaev 1979: 82-83)

The helmet on his head is ringing,
the bulging shield, made of rhinoceros hide, is resounding,
the tip of the golden scabbard is beating
against the stirrups and rattling.
5   The courser is racing forward,
flying like a bird of prey,
the spear in his hand is shaking.
He is intent on a long journey,
looking neither right nor left,
10   saying: "If only I could reach the country of my beloved!"
Bāyčibār is galloping forward,
the long way becomes shorter,
the mighty falcon is on his way,
seeking the land of the Kalmucks,
15   alone the falcon is riding along.
Beg Hakim (Alpāmiš) exerted himself,
urged his horse on,
said: "Hoy!" and swung the whip,
raised the dust in the cold desert,
20   rode on his way.
When he came to a mountain, he made his horse jump over,
when he came to a river, he made him jump across,
when he came to a slope, he made him gallop.
In this manner Hakim went his way.[72]

In Ergaš Džumanbulbul-oǧli's variant of *Rawšan* there are two
passages one might quote as parallels, Rawšan's ride to Širwān (left
column) and Hasan's ride to Širwān (right column):

Āt bāradi arillab,   Āt bāradi arillab,
ātgan oqday šarillab,   ātgan oqday šarillab,
āt alqimi, tāŋ šamāl   āt alqimi-tāŋ šamāl
mis karnayday zarillab.   mis karnayday zarillab,
...   5   suwsiz čolda Ǧirkok āt
...   bārayātir parillab.
Āt bāradi arqirab,   Āt bāradi asirlab,

[72]See also Zarif, Mirzaev 1979: 89-90. This passage is also translated in
Žirmunskij 1985 [1965]: 327f. For this theme see Žirmunskij, Zarifov 1947: 369-372;
compare also Bowra 1952: 164.

dawirlari yarqirab,
Bek Rawšanday pālwānniŋ
kākillari tirqirab.   10
Suwsiz čolda Džiyrānquš,
āqqan suwday širqirab,
šamālday bop bāradi,
suwsiz čolda pirqirab...

ātgan oqday tasirlab,
tilla uzangi, mahsi-kawš
tepsinganda qasirlab.

The horse is running snorting,
whizzing like a flying arrow.
The wind caused by the horse is
   like the morning wind,
ringing like a copper *karnay* (trumpet).
...   5

...
The horse is running snorting,
the saddlecloth shining.
The plaits of Beg Rawšan, the hero,
are swinging back and forth.   10
In the waterless desert, Džiyrānquš
is rushing ahead like flowing water,
racing like the wind,
snorting in the waterless desert... [73]

The horse is running snorting,
whizzing like a flying arrow.
The wind caused by the horse is
   like the morning wind,
ringing like a copper *karnay*.
In the waterless desert, the horse
   Ġirkok
is racing along.
The horse is running intoxicated,
whizzing like a flying arrow.
The golden stirrups, the boots
are banging together and ringing.

The "-*illab*-run" is also found in Islām-šāir's variant of *Ārzigul* (1) and in Umir Safar-oġli's variant of *Āyparča* (2):

(1)   Qirq azamatlar džonadi.
       Ātlar džonadi arillab,
       tilla qalqānlar šarillab,
       qār badan gulday pirillab,
       čollarda beklar džonadi.
                    (Mominov et al. 1975: 298)

       The forty heroes are riding.
       The horses are running snorting,
       the golden shields ringing,
       the snow-white bodies swaying like roses,
       the begs are riding in the desert.

(2)   Tebargisi tirqillab,
       āt bāradi pirqillab,
       abzal sālgan ātlarniŋ,

---

[73]Zarif 1971: 76-79 (XII = Reichl 1985a: 70-73), 181-194 (LI = Reichl 1985a: 178-190).

abrešim kākili yaltillab.
(Šādieva 1965: 19)

Their battle-axes are swinging back and forth,
the horses are running snorting,
the harness, put on the horses,
its silk tassels are shining.

This theme is normally expressed in "tirades" of hepta- or octosyllabic lines; in Fāzil's variant of *Alpāmiš*, however, there is also an instance of this "run" in endecasyllabic lines:

Bāyčibār bāradi šunday arqirab,
tuyāġida tort sixi bār yarqirab,
irġiganda qumlar ketdi tirqirab,
bārayātir čolda šunday širqirab.
(Zarif, Mirzaev 1979: 137)

Bāyčibār is running snorting thus,
the four points on his hooves shining.
When he jumped the dust flew in all directions;
in this manner he raced along in the desert.

This "run" is also represented in Uighur. In a passage in which Göroġli urges his companions on to come to Hawaz's rescue he says:

Arġimaq atlar ġirillap,
tilla qalqan dirillap.
Yolwaslardäk širillap
dondur Hawazxan üstigä.
(Tatliq et al. 1986: 252)

The thoroughbred horses are snorting,
the golden shield is shaking.
Roaring like tigers,
all rush together towards Hawazxan.

The three themes discussed here (council, arming, ride) represent actually three types of theme. A typical scene like the council scene at the beginning of Fāzil's variant of *Alpāmiš* is highly patterned, with refrain-like lines, lines taken up and varied in the dialogue, cliché-couplets etc., but yet devoid of a fixed sequence of motifs. The type-scene of the hero putting on his armor, saddling his horse and preparing for a warlike expedition is characterized by definite motifs, a particular sequence of events and a certain amount of formulaic phrasing. When we compare this theme with that of the hero's ride, however, we observe that formulaic patterning can extend even further to the coupling of the motifs with specific expressions, leading to a "run"-like fixity in the rhyme-words. This distinction also tells us something about the various narrative units available to the singer and the various techniques of composition used by him. Formulaic diction and thematic patterning are part of his art, of performing, transmitting, and composing. It is to the uses of formulaic diction in the composition and transmission of Turkic oral epic poetry that I wish to turn in the next chapter.

Chapter Eight

Composition in Performance and the Art of Memory

"Improvisation" and Composition in Performance

Wilhelm Radloff was probably the earliest scholar studying Turkic oral epic poetry who noticed the highly patterned, formulaic character of this type of poetry. In his famous introduction to the Kirghiz volume of his *Proben*, he enumerates a number of narrative units (*Vortragsteile*), which occur again and again in the epics, as so to speak prefabricated building blocks from which the singer can construct his epics: "The art of the singer consists only in stringing all these ready-made narrative units in such a way together as the course of the narrative demands and to link them with newly composed verse-lines."[1] Radloff's description, however valuable, has led to misconceptions about Turkic, and in particular Kirghiz oral epic poetry. The mechanical aspect of "composition in performance," to use A. B. Lord's term, is emphasized by the adverb "only" in the quotation above. Andreas Heusler, one of the leading scholars in the field of Old Germanic poetry in the first half of this century, based his view of Turkic oral epic poetry on Radloff's description, maintaining that the Germanic alliterative lay could never have been "formulaic and full of clichés" like Kirghiz epic poetry.[2]

Despite his emphasis on technique, Radloff calls the Kirghiz singer an improvising singer. The term "improvisation" is ambiguous. We talk of improvisation in music, in Oriental classical music, in European classical music as well as in forms of music like jazz or aleatory music, meaning somewhat different techniques of musical creation and

---

[1]Radloff 1885: xvii (translation volume). The English translation in Radloff 1990: 84 is somewhat shortened.

[2]Heusler 1943: 174.

219

performance in each case. We talk of improvisation in connection with dramatic genres like the *commedia dell'arte* of the Baroque era, meaning an again different kind of artistic spontaneity. When using the term "improvisation" in reference to oral epic poetry, the use of this term for other forms of oral verbal art comes to mind; we think of shorter improvised lyrics like the South German and Austrian *Schnada-hüpfel*, vendors' street rhymes, or Afro-American rap poetry, poetry created for an *ad hoc* circumstance. Although all these forms of improvisation are different, even a cursory glance at the examples alluded to shows some common ground for an understanding of "improvisation" also in epic poetry.

Improvisation and extemporization in classical music can be of very different kinds, ranging from fully fledged original compositions performed *ex tempore* on the harpsichord or the organ by such composers as Dietrich Buxtehude or Johann Sebastian Bach to improvised ornamentation or extensions of otherwise fixed music, such as the "divisions" in viol music or the cadenzas in the solo concertos. "Bach would improvise for two hours without stopping, and all upon one hymn-tune theme, working up out of it first a prelude and fugue, then a movement in thinner harmonies such as a trio, then a chorale prelude, and finally another fugue — of course combining with the original theme such new themes as occurred to him."[3] Bach was a musical genius whose art lies outside explanation in terms of technique and acquired skills. But generally speaking, extemporization in Baroque (as well as earlier and later) music is possible only because of fairly rigorous conventions governing the various "codes" of music; an improvised Baroque fugue might start off with a comparatively spontaneous melodic line, but this melodic line will soon be developed according to the clearly prescribed rules of the polyphonic structure of this particular musical form and within the framework of 17th or 18th-c. harmony. The same can be said about improvisation in jazz, despite all the obvious differences between these types of music.

What is true of music is also true of the *commedia dell'arte* and of extemporization in shorter verse genres. Despite a certain amount of spontaneity, varying according to form and tradition, improvisation is in each case controlled by conventions and rules, which furnish the

---

[3]Scholes 1970: 510. See also Apel 1969: 404-405 (s.v. "Improvisation, extemporization"); Sadie 1981: IX, 31-56 (s.v. "Improvisation").

perfomer with a matrix for his extemporizations. Pantalone in the *commedia dell'arte* will talk and act as befits a duped husband, and Scaramuccio will strut across the stage in the manner of a braggadocio; the stereotyped character of the *dramatis personae* as well as of the plot doubtless constrain the actor's performance and thus help him to act without a fixed text. Furthermore, the so-called scenarios, which set down the plot, were comparatively detailed and left only the minutiae of the dialogues and comic effects to improvisation. In fact, a need for help with the improvisations was apparently felt by the actors, which explains the emergence of the *zibaldoni*, collections of serious or comical scenes, written out for memorization.[4] Similar constraints exist for the shorter lyric. The *Schnadahüpfel*, for instance, are improvised songs from the Bavarian and Austrian Alps, which consist of four lines in a definite meter and are sung to a particular (but varying) melodic line. The singer has a certain store of ideas, images, and rhyme-patterns at his disposal, which he uses to compose an *ad hoc* poem. Very often a "new" *Schnadahüpfel* is almost identical to other already existing lyrics, just exchanging a name for a different one or replacing a line or phrase with a new one. As K. Beitl puts it in his survey of this lyric form: "Because of the dominantly formulaic nature of images and words, improvisation [in the *Schnadahüpfel*] moves in well-regulated tracks."[5] A conventional patterning is also typical of other forms of improvised shorter poetry. The extempore spontaneity of much improvised poetry is on closer analysis cast in a sometimes fairly rigorous mold, which largely determines the shape of the creation.

Without pursuing the question of improvisation in general any further, the few examples adduced suggest that the notions of creativity, spontaneity, and novelty often associated with improvisation are somewhat misleading. Equally misleading is, however, the idea that improvisation consists basically in the mechanical manipulation of pre-fabricated material. Improvisation is based on a technique and its mastery; it exists within a well-defined, rule-governed framework, but it depends also on the presence of mind and the inspiration of the artist. It ranges, to come back to improvisation in classical music, from the embellishments and ornaments introduced by a competent player into

---

[4]See Kindermann 1967: 270-271; Krömer 1990: 41-44.

[5]Beitl 1973-75: 643.

the performance of Baroque music to the improvisations and extemporizations on a keyboard instrument by composers like Bach, Mozart, or Liszt. The same extent and variety is found among the singers of Turkic oral epic poetry.

Radloff compares the Kirghiz singer to the Greek *aoidós*, while the Kazakh *aqïn* is likened to the Greek *rhapsōdós*, "who does not compose in the act of singing, but recites the poems of others, which he has heard."[6] Two things are interesting in Radloff's view, first that he sees a dichotomy among Turkic singers comparable to the situation in Ancient Greece, and secondly that he equates improvising with composing in performance. The Greek parallel, although suggestive, should not be pressed too far. It is generally thought that the *aoidós* as portrayed in Homeric figures like Demodocus or Phemius was a "creative singer," while the rhapsode, familiar from Plato's *Ion*, was a mere performer and reciter. The distinction between these two types of singers is, however, less clear-cut than one would wish. Phemius is called an *aoidós* in the *Odyssey* — Penelope addresses him as "divine singer" (θεῖος ἀοιδός, I.336), but he is referred to as a *rhapsōdós* in Plato's *Ion* (533c).[7] Radloff's application of these two Greek terms to Turkic oral epic poetry must in view of the difficulties encountered in their definition not be taken too seriously. A clearly recognizable opposition between two types of Turkic singers, as posited by Radloff, is, as I hope to show in this chapter, an unacceptable simplification.

As to composition in performance, it is according to Radloff on the one hand spontaneous (a good singer "improvises his songs according to the inspiration of the moment, so that he is incapable of reciting his poem twice in an absolutely identical manner"), but this spontaneity is on the other hand of a fairly restricted kind: "One should not believe, however, that this improvising means a new composing every time."[8] The expression "composition in performance" might hence be somewhat misleading: the epic is not actually composed in performance, it is rather *re*-composed in performance. The following examples will help to make this clear.

[6] Radloff 1885: xxi. It should be noted that Radloff's view of the Kazakh *aqïn* does not agree with that commonly held today; see Chapter Three, pp. 75ff.

[7] See Hammond, Scullard 1970: 919-920 (s.v "Rhapsodes").

[8] Radloff 1885: xvi.

In this chapter my main focus will be on singers whom I have myself interviewed and recorded; I shall start with Kirghiz singers. Of these the place of honor is due to Džüsüp Mamay of Xinjiang (see Chapter Three, pp. 85f.). Mamay's version of the *Manas*-cycle runs to over 200,000 lines. While the *Manas*-trilogy has been collected from many singers, Mamay is, in his own opinion, the only singer alive who is able to continue the trilogy into succeeding generations. According to Mamay's information, only one other singer, called Ibraim, also knew the eight epics of which his version is composed.[9] Mamay started to learn the epic at the age of eight, under the supervision of his father and brother Balbay. He was made to learn a portion of the epic every day. His father and brother, using the material Balbay had collected, would examine him, expecting him to make "no mistakes." This was the beginning of his career as a singer. He has, in his own words, "apart from eating and sleeping done nothing but learn and memorize since the age of eight." Mamay sees his main contribution to the preservation of the *Manas*-cycle in having changed the prose-parts of "branches" 4 to 8 (which he had learned in prosimetric form) into verse. "Changing prose into verse" is his way of describing his creativity as a poet. Asked whether he could make an epic of a story I would tell him, he answered that he was certainly capable of "changing prose into verse." By the same token, he is able to lengthen or shorten his performance, depending on the wishes of his audience. Lengthening and shortening, however, is different from changing prose into verse: while the former can be done by any good singer, the latter is something rare and special.

The vastness and diversity of Mamay's repertory leaves no doubt that he is one of the major Kirghiz singers of this century. To treat his art in detail would require a book-length study; I can only bring one example from his repertory to illustrate his position in Kirghiz oral tradition. I have chosen an episode from *Semetey*, the second epic of the *Manas*-trilogy, an episode I was able to record independently from another Kirghiz singer in 1985, the singer Abdurahman Düney (see Chapter Three, p. 86). *Semetey* celebrates the deeds of Manas' son Semetey. In his *Proben* Radloff published two poems on Semetey, one

---

[9]I have unfortunately not been able to trace this singer and obtain more information about him. On the eight epic poems of Mamay's version of *Manas* see Chapter Three, p. 85, note 79.

entitled "Semetey's Birth" (1,078 lines), the other simply "Semetey" (1,927 lines).[10] The first of these epics tells of Semetey's birth after the death of his father; of the persecution which Qanïkey, Manas' wife, has to suffer from Abeke and Köböš, Manas' younger brothers; of the treacherous behavior of Džaqïp, Manas' father, towards his own offspring; of Qanïkey's, Semetey's, and Čaqan's (Manas' mother's) flight to Qanïkey's father; and finally of Semetey's return as an avenger, when Qanïkey kills Abeke and Köböš, and Čaqan her own husband.[11] The second epic is devoted to the warlike deeds and death of Semetey and to the birth and coming of age of his son Seytek. An important role in this poem is played by Semetey's companions Kül-čoro and Qan-čoro; they are the sons of two of Manas' companions, Adžïbay and Almambet, respectively. While Kül-čoro, the "flower-companion," is a faithful friend of both Semetey and his wife, Qan-čoro, the "blood-companion," betrays Semetey and is instrumental in his death. One of the episodes in this epic treats of the winning of a bride for Semetey (ll. 255-354). Ay-čürök, the daughter of Aqïn-khan, is engaged to Ümütöy, Kökčö's son (Kökčö being one of Manas' Noghay adversaries). Semetey, who has heard of Ay-čürök's accomplishments (some of them magical), decides to marry her himself. Together with his companions Kül-čoro and Qan-čoro Semetey sets out on a bride-winning expedition and Kül-čoro succeeds in persuading the girl to flee with Semetey.[12]

Although Ay-čürök plays an important role in this poem, the bride-winning episode is comparatively short and obviously undeveloped. When Kül-čoro arrives at Aqïn-khan's abode, he hardly needs to tell Ay-čürök of his mission before she is ready to go with him:

> Oyndo džürgön Ay-čürök
> küdörüdöy bïlqïldap,
> 340 küčügüttöy čïŋqïldap...
> Anda keldiŋ, Kül-čoro!
> "Semetey čunaq keldi!" dep,
> qulaġïna saldï deyt.
> Ay-čürök čïġïp keldi deyt,

---

[10]These poems have been critically re-edited and translated into English in Hatto 1990: 305-395.

[11]For a detailed analysis see Hatto 1973.

[12]For a detailed analysis see Hatto 1974; on *Semetey* see also Žirmunskij 1961b: 168-187.

345   Semetey čunaq aldï deyt,
      üyün köstöy čuġoydu.

> Ay-čürök was disporting herself, waggling like a musk-deer,
> squealing like a puppy. And there you came, Kül-čoro! Telling her
> "The Wretch Semetey has come!", he put in a good word for him.
> Ay-čürök came out and away. The Wretch Semetey took her and
> urged his horse homewards with shouts of "Čü!"[13]

In later recorded versions of *Semetey* the bride-winning part of the epic
has been much expanded.[14] Ay-čürök is a swan-maiden, as is also clear
from Radloff's text, when she later threatens to put on her swan-dress
and fly away to her father (l. 1478). In the composite version of the
Manas-cycle published between 1958 and 1960, Manas and Aqun-khan
(Aqïn-khan in Radloff's text) promise to wed their children to one
another, should the one have a daughter and the other a son; they
perform what is called a *bel quda* in Kirghiz. When Čïnqodžo and
Toltoy threaten to take Aqun-khan's daughter by force, Ay-čürök dons
her white swan-clothes (*aq quu kep*) and flies to seek Semetey. Semetey
has, however, already been married to Čačïkey, Šaatemir's daughter,
who insults Ay-čürök, calling her a devil-faced blackface (*Šaytan süröt
qarabet*), and opposes her wish to marry Semetey. Ay-čürök vows to
steal Semetey's white falcon (*aq šumqar*) by transforming herself into a
ball of white silk (*aq bula*), a white fish (*aq balïq* or *aq čabaq*), and a
swan (*aq quu*). Čačïkey warns Kül-čoro of the imminent danger when
Semetey sets out on a hunting expedition with his companions. Kül-
čoro manages to keep Semetey from touching the silk and from
capturing the fish, but Semetey is not to be hindered from sending his
falcon after the swan. To his surprise, a storm arises and the swan
disappears with the falcon.[15] Semetey then sets out to recover his
falcon; when, with his companions' help, he finally finds his falcon and
meets Ay-čürök, he is informed by her of the *bel quda* binding them and

---

[13]Text and translation from Hatto 1990: 348/349; for consistency's sake I have
adapted Hatto's transcription of Kirghiz to the system used here.

[14]*Semetey* has been recorded from the singers Sayaqbay Qaralaev, Šapaq
Rïsmendeev, Moldobasan Musulmanqulov and others; more than ten variants have
been written down in Kirghizia. The publication of Qaralaev's version is in progress;
see Qïrbašev, Sarïpbekov 1987ff.; on the Kirghiz versions see also Yunusaliev
[Junusaliev] 1961: 292-295.

[15]See Yunusaliev [Junusaliev] et al. 1958-60: III, 149-163.

marries her.[16] The first part of the intrigue, up to the stealing of Semetey's falcon, comprises about 1,100 lines in the composite edition, while the second part, up to Semetey's and Ay-čürök's union in marriage, comprises about 5,000 lines. This edition does not give the full text of any variant and is hence only an approximate guide to the actual form and length of this episode in the variants on which it is based. According to the information provided by the general editor of this edition, V. M. Yunusaliev, Sayaqbay Qaralaev's variant of *Semetey*, on which the edition is mainly, though not exclusively based, comprises 14,000 lines.[17]

Džüsüp Mamay's variant of this episode comprises about 5,500 lines and agrees in plot basically with the text of the composite version.[18] In order to compare the different variants I shall quote from one scene in this episode, Semetey's departure on a hunting expedition. In the composite edition we have the following sequence of events: after the altercation between Ay-čürök and Čačïkey, Semetey appears and gets his horse Taybuurul ready to go hunting. Čačïkey stops him, trying to persuade him to wait for three days. Semetey tells her to let go his horse's bridle and not to interfere with his affairs.

<pre>
        Dep, ošentip, er Semeŋ
        altï erkečtin terisin
        tasma qïlġan buldursun,
        asïy ögüz terisin
   5   özök qïlġan buldursun,
        özögün üč ay kerdirgen,
        džïlan boor ördürgön,
        qaq ïrġayġa saptaġan,
        qarïlar körüp maqtaġan,
  10   "Qolġo džumaq bolsun" dep,
        qoy maqmal menen qaptaġan,
        alaqanïn körkömdöp,
        asïl taštan oydurġan,
        qoy bašïnday qorġošun,
  15   tüškününö qoydurġan,
        qayaša qïlġan adamdï
        qaqïldatqan buldursun,
</pre>

[16]See Yunusaliev [Junusaliev] et al. 1958-60: III, 164-194.

[17]See Yunusaliev [Junusaliev] 1961: 293-295; other singers whose variants have been used are Toġoloq Moldo and Šapaq Rïsmendeev.

[18]See Mamay 1984ff.: 2(I), 228-474.

qoqo[ŋ]doğon[19] qodžonu
qoquylatqan[20] buldursun, —
20   buldursundu Semetey
bura qarmap aldï, deyt,
tizgindep turğan ayïmïn
džondon arï saldï, deyt.
Šaatemir qïzï Čačïkey
25   közünün džašï tögülüp,
qayïğa tereŋ čömülüp,
qozğolo albay qalğanda,
džürö berdi Semetey,
opol toodoy körünüp...
                    (Yunusaliev [Junusaliev] et al. 1958-60: III, 158)

Having said this, Er Semetey[21]
took the whip —
a whip that was made from the white tanned hide
of six gelded he-goats,
5   a whip whose lash was made
from the hide of young oxen,
whose lash had been stretched (to dry) for three months,
whose thong had been plaited,[22]
whose handle was made of *ïrğa*,[23]
10   a whip which the old men, when they see it, praise,
saying: "May it be supple for the hand,"
whose cover was of choice velvet,
whose *alaqan*[24] was decorated with ornaments,
carved from precious stone,
15   whose lash was knotted at the end
with a piece of lead as big as a sheep's head,
a whip which causes a man
who had dared to be rude to scream,

---

[19]The text has *qoqondoğon*, a word not recorded in the Kirghiz dictionaries available to me; I have emended to *qoqoŋdogon* from *qoqoŋdo-* "to tower; walk (proudly) with head erect"; see Judaxin 1985 [1965]: I, 395 (s.v. *qoqoŋdo-*).

[20]The text has *qoyquylatqan*; Professor A. T. Hatto suggests emending to *qoquylatqan*, "making scream."

[21]Lit. "Thy Semetey."

[22]Professor A. T. Hatto suggests to add "in snake-belly (?) pattern." Kirghiz *džïlan* means snake; *džïlan boor* is glossed as "a peculiar kind of thong-plaiting; whip" in Judaxin 1985 [1965]: I, 279 (s.v. *džïlan*).

[23]The *ïrğa* is a shrub with very hard wood.

[24]The *alaqan* is a strap of leather with which the lash is fastened to the wooden handle.

a whip which makes cry out
20   the khodja,[25] strutting with head erect —
Semetey seized and turned the whip, it is said,
and struck his wife, who was holding the bridle,
over the whole length of her back, it is said.
Čačïkey, Šaatemir's daughter,
25   shed tears from her eyes,
sank deep into woe,
unable to move,
when Semetey set off,
towering like a giant...

In Džüsüp Mamay's variant, Semetey also gets ready to go hunting after Ay-čürök has disappeared. His wife tries to detain him, saying that she had a portentous dream and begging him to postpone his hunting expedition to the following day. Semetey answers that her dream has nothing to do with him and becomes angry about her intervention.

Tolġomo saptuu buldursun,
tolġoy qarmap aldï emi.
Buldursundun qayïšïn,
sayġa džazïp kerdirgen;
5   kök torpoqtun terisin,
ašïn džaqšï berdirgen;
iyin džaqšï qandïrïp —
čeberlerge terdirgen;
on eki tildüü ördürüp,
10   önörün sonun keltirgen;
qas dušmanġa tiygende,
qanduu qamčï dedirgen.
Buldursun menen qaq ošol,
may sooruġa čaptï emi.
15   Čïŋïrïp ïylap Čačïkey,
aylanïp attuu qačtï emi.
Qaldïrqan ala köynögü,
qat-qatïnan bölündü.
Čačïkeydin taqïmdan,
20   quyulup qanï tögüldü.
(Mamay 1984ff.: 2(I), 305-306)

Now he seized and twirled
the whip with the notched handle.

[25]In Kirghiz, *qodžo*, "khodja," denotes, strictly speaking, a descendant of the first caliphs; it is, as in the present passage, often associated with negative connotations, due to officially promoted anticlerical feelings; see Judaxin 1985 [1965]: I, 392 (s.v. *qodžo*, 1.).

He had made the lash of the whip
stretch out (to dry) on the (boulders) of a dry riverbed.[26]
5　The lash was from the hide of the well-fed
grey calf.[27]
The hide was well-tanned;
he had it collected for the artisans.
He summoned the best of masters
10　to plait the twelve-tongued lash.
When the lash touched the enemy,
he made people call it a bloody whip.
With a whizzing sound he now let the whip
come down on (Čačïkey's) back.
15　Čačïkey gave a piercing cry,
while the rider now turned round and galloped off.
Her blouse, multicolored like a butterfly,[28]
split open with a snap.
From the hollow of Čačïkey's knee
20　the blood came streaming down.

Abdurahman Düney treats this scene very briefly. The extract recorded (on tape) begins with Semetey calling to his companions to saddle his horse Taybuurul. His wife Čačïkey tries to stay him by holding on to his horse's neck, whereupon Semetey strikes her with his whip. The first lines of the quotation, describing the whip, are spoken with extreme rapidity by the singer, while the last six lines are sung.

Qoš qaraġay saptatqan,
tïšïnï qara körpö menen qaptatqan,
qamčï menen qoy sïndïrġan,[29]
qoy soyturġan buldursun,
5　qayaša aytqan qatïndï
qaqïldatqan buldursun,
qamčï menen čaptï, deyt.
Atiles iš ïlas köynök

---

[26]For this interpretation of line 4 (with *say* meaning "riverbed"; see Judaxin 1985 [1965]: II, 122, s.v. *say* II) I am grateful to Professor A. T. Hatto.

[27]The precise color and hue of *kök* is difficult to pin down; on the meaning of *kök at*, "grey horse," in Kirghiz see Laude-Cirtautas 1961: 79.

[28]The semantics of the color term *ala* is like that of other color terms in the Turkic languages complex; on the meaning "multicolored, variegated" in Kirghiz see Laude-Cirtautas 1961: 73.

[29]The extreme rapidity and indistinctness of the singer's performance makes it difficult to be certain about the second half of this line; *sïndïrġan* is not entirely clearly audible. For help with the transcription of my tape I am grateful to Mämbet Turdu-uulu of the *Manas* Research Group in Urumchi.

džik-džiginen bölündü,
10   qara qanï tögülüp,
ayal qatïn Čačïgey
tizisi menen tik tüšüp,
töbösü menen üp tüšüp.

The whip with a handle made from two pines,
covered on the outside with black lambskin,
the whip with which he had killed sheep,
the whip with which he had caused sheep to be slaughtered,
5   the whip which makes
the nagging wife shriek,
with this whip he lashed out, it is said.
The blouse made of silk and satin
opened at the seams,
10   her black blood was shed,
Čačïkey, his wife,
fell straight down on her knees,
fell crashing down on her head.

When we compare these three passages, the similarities between them leave no doubt that this scene is traditional. The word for whip, *buldursun*, is in fact a word only occurring in epic poetry; Judaxin quotes in his Kirghiz-Russian dictionary under the lemma *buldursun* the phrase "*asïy ögüz terisinen örüm qïlgan buldursun*," "a whip, plaited from the (complete) hide of a three-year-old ox," a phrase which is found also in lines 4-5 of the composite text.[30] The three variants, which I will designate C (composite text edited by Yunusaliev [Junusaliev] et al.), M (Mamay's variant), and D (Düney's variant), are equally traditional, although D is obviously much shortened. If we take the description of the whip first, we can see that this description consists of a number of definite concepts as well as of particular lexemes, occurring preferably (but not exclusively) in rhyme-position. The concepts are distributed in the following way:

Concepts	C	M	D
Whip made of ox/calf hide	+	+	—
Handle made of good wood	+	+	+
Handle covered in precious cloth	+	—	+
Plaited lash	+	+	—
Alaqan	+	—	—
Knot with lead	+	—	—
Whip is admired	+	—	—

[30]See Judaxin 1985 [1965]: I, 185.

	C	M	D
Whip punishes/injures opponent	+	+	−

Phrasing	C	M	D
kerdirgen (stretch)	+	+	−
sapta(t)ġan (with a handle)	+	−	+
qapta(t)ġan (covered)	+	−	+
ördürgön/ördürüp (plaited)	+	+	−
qaqïldatqan (whizzing)	+	−	+

Before discussing these tables, let us have a brief look at the concluding part of the scene. Here too we can distinguish between concepts and phrasing:

Concepts	C	M	D
Čačïkey is hit on the back	+	+	−
She cries	+	+	−
She sheds tears	+	−	−
She sheds blood	−	+	+
Her blouse rips	−	+	+
She falls down	(+)[31]	−	+

Phrasing	C	M	D
tögülüp (shed)	+	+	+
köynök (blouse)	−	+	+
bölündü (ripped)	−	+	+

It is interesting to note that all three variants agree with one another in some points, while in others two agree against the third. Thus on the level of lexemes *tögülüp* is shared by all three variants; while C and M agree against D in the case of *kerdirgen* and *ördürgön*, C and D against M in the case of *saptaġan*, *qaptaġan*, and *qaqïldatqan*, and M and D agree against C in the case of *köynök* and *bölündü*. Similar groupings can be found on the level of concepts. While concepts or lexemes which are found in only one variant might be innovations of that variant, concepts, and in particular lexemes, which are common to two or more variants are most likely traditional. It is interesting to note that despite its shortness D preserves a number of traditional elements either with C against M or with M against C, thus helping to determine the quality of Mamay's variant.

---

[31]In C Čačïkey falls into grief, rather than on the ground; see l. 26.

Mamay's text is fairly conservative. He does not innovate in a modernizing way, substituting for instance some modern piece of outfit or clothing for the traditional gear and garment of the protagonists, modernizations that are known from some epic traditions. He does, however, as far as we can judge from this extract, innovate in the sense of expanding and "embroidering" the tradition. In this there is a similarity to the technique of "ornamentation" described by A. B. Lord, in particular with reference to Avdo Međedović's *Wedding of Smailagić Meho*.[32] The clearest case in our extract is the addition of further rhymes to *kerdirgen*, which occurs in final position in line 6 of C, expanding the description of the whip by several lines (*berdirgen, terdirgen, keltirgen,* and *dedirgen*; ll. 5-12). A similar picture is presented by other epics in his repertory. The variant of *Qurmanbek* recorded from the Kirghiz singer Qalïq Akiev of Kirgizia in the 1930s comprises in the printed edition almost exactly 5,000 verse-lines.[33] The epic is basically in octosyllabic or heptasyllabic verse-lines, organized in laisse-type sections, but there are short prose-passages introducing and connecting the verse. Mamay's variant is only in verse and comprises about 8,500 verse-lines.[34] The variant of *Qurmanbek* I recorded from the Kirghiz singer Mämbet Sart in 1989, finally, comprises about 1,750 verse-lines; it is like Qalïq Akiev's variant, interspersed with short prose passages (see Chapter Three, pp. 86f.). The latter singer's variant is fairly close to that of Qalïq Akiev, while Mamay's variant, although traditional both in plot and diction, expands and embroiders in the manner illustrated above.

The formulaic and patterned character of the "whipping-scene" emerges by only looking at three variants of one passage in *Semetey*. Both the description of the *buldursun* and the hero's whipping whoever opposes his riding away (in particular his wife) are, however, more widely spread in Kirghiz epic poetry and clearly traditional.[35] In the *Memorial Feast for Kökötöy-Khan* Manas seethes with anger when he sees the Kalmuck feast:

[32]See Lord 1960: 88.

[33]See Akiev 1957.

[34]See Mamay 1984.

[35]Professor A. T. Hatto has kindly drawn my attention to the following examples.

asïy atnïŋ terisin
örmö qïlǵan buldursun,
qunan ögüz terisin
özök qïlǵan buldursun,
1285   tel boz uyduŋ terisin
büldürgö qïlǵan bulsursun,
qayaša bergen qatïndï
qayqaŋdatqan buldursun,
qonoq bermes saraynï
1290   qoquylatqan buldursun,
"džaba" degen Qalmaqnïŋ
džaǵïn ayra čaptï; — dedi
"möndü" degen Qalmaqnïŋ
bašïn ayra čaptï; — dedi

He brought down his great lash plaited from the hide of a five-year-old
horse, his lash with its core made from the hide of a three-year-old ox,
with its hand-loop made of the hide of a dun calf that sucked two
mothers — the lash which makes a snappish woman cringe, makes
courts that turn away the guest lament! — brought his great lash down
and cut open the sides of the Kalmak that gabble "Jaba!", cut open the
heads of the Kalmak that jabber "Möndü!"[36]

It hardly needs pointing out that the description of the whip in this
passage agrees in many points with the text-extracts quoted above.
With the lash plaited "from the hide of a five-year-old horse and its core
made from the hide of a three-year-old ox" we can compare the lash
made from the white tanned hide of six gelded he-goats and the hide of
young oxen in C or from the hide of the well-fed grey calf in M; with the
lash "which makes a snappish woman cringe" we can compare the whip
which makes the nagging wife shriek in D. The latter motif is further
elaborated in a second occurrence of this "theme" in *Kökötöy-Khan*:

on ekiden örgön buldursun
čapsa qulaq tundursun,
qayaša bergen qatïnnï
1560   qayqaŋdatqan buldursun,
köz salmaǵan qatïnnï
"közülüm!" degizgen buldursun,
til almaǵan qatïnnï
tilinen süydürgön buldursun,
1565   qol bermegen qatïnnï
qučaqlatqan buldursun,
qaršï čïqmaǵan qatïnnï
qaltïratqan buldursun,

[36]Text and translation from Hatto 1977: 36/37.

könmöy džürgön qatïnnï
1570 küldürüp qoyġon buldursun,
džandamay džürgön qatïnnï
"džanïm!" degizgen buldursun,
sïr bermegen qatïnnï
sïrdaš qïlġan buldursun —
1575 bu sözdördü aytïp bolġon soŋ,
buldursun-menen Er Manas
šondo turġan kepirderdi
džaġïn ayra čaptï: — dedi
musulmannïŋ džinnen
1580 tegerene qačtï. — dedi

> And now Er Manas with his great lash plaited from twelve thongs
> that deafens the ear as it falls, that makes a snappish woman cringe,
> that makes a neglectful woman say "My hero!", that makes a fractious
> woman dote on all one says, makes a woman who does not give a hand
> embrace you, who does not come to meet you tremble, who disagrees
> smile sweetly, who does not caress you say "Darling!", that makes a
> secretive woman confiding — with his great lash Er Manas struck the
> Unbelievers standing there and cut open their sides, at which they fled
> reeling from this devil of the Muslims.[37]

Apart from the general description of the whip as a "wife-beater," we
might compare line 1557 *on ekiden örgön buldursun,* a "lash plaited
from twelve thongs," with line 9 in M *on eki tildüü ördürüp,* "caused to
be plaited from twelve thongs," a formula also found in other passages,
as in line 1214 of *Boq-murun* (of the *Manas*-cycle) in the version
recorded by Radloff.[38] The ripping of the woman's clothes as in D is
paralleled in a passage from *Semetey* (in Radloff's version):

Asïï ögüstün teräsinän
örüm qïlġan buldursun
qoluna aldï Semetey,
975 anda turġan Ay-čüröktü
buldursun-minän čaptï'la! —
Daraysï dal-dalïnan bölündü,
qabïrġa 'Tom!' etip üzüldü!
Džaqšï tuuġan Ay-čürök
980 džerdä džatïp qaldï deyt!

> And he [Semetey] laid hold of his horse-lash made of plaited thongs
> from the hide of an ox in its fifth year and with it struck Ay-čürök
> standing there a mighty blow! Her silk was shredded to tatters, her

[37]Text and translation from Hatto 1977: 42/43-44/45.

[38]See Hatto 1990: 196/197.

ribs broke with a thud! The well-born Ay-čürök lay there on the ground![39]

In order to assess both the traditionality and the individuality of a scene like that of Semetey's departure in search of Ay-čürök, variants of the scene itself as well as other occurrences of the formulaic elements making up the scene have to be analysed. There can be no doubt that this scene is a highly patterned "topos," aptly named "Eulogy of the Lash" by A. T. Hatto.[40] While it consists of a number of formulaic elements, the singer is also free to use the traditional diction for elaboration as well as adaptation to his specific purposes. Mamay's "embroidering" of the *kerdirgen*-series is an example of this, as is the elaboration of the "wife-beating motif" by the bard of *Kökötöy-Khan* (lines 1557ff.). At the present stage of our knowledge of Kirghiz epic poetry, no definitive evaluation of traditional diction is possible; the analysis of the passages quoted above can therefore be no more than a preliminary discussion of what Radloff termed *Vortragsteile* in Kirghiz epic poetry.

Variation and Stability

In order to study the way a singer carries on a tradition — preserving, expanding, innovating, or corrupting it — it is instructive to compare his variant with that of other singers, preferably of different generations. As no two performances will be absolutely identical (although the degree of variation might differ from singer to singer and from tradition to tradition), one has ideally to compare several performed texts of these singers with one another. I am proposing to do this, at least to a limited degree, with a short extract from the Karakalpak *dastan Šaryar*.

This *dastan* is in plot closely related to the folktale of the Calumniated Wife and is particularly close, in its first part, to Pushkin's *Tale of Tsar Saltan*.[41] The *dastan* begins with the motif of the childless couple. Shah Darap (Darapša) has no children, although he has married

---

[39]Text and translation from Hatto 1990: 366/367.

[40]For a discussion of this topos with further references see Hatto 1977: 173.

[41]See AaTh 707; Nurmuxamedov 1983.

nine times. In desperation he leaves his throne and decides to wander
about in the garb of a dervish; on his wanderings he overhears three
girls boasting what they would do for the shah should he marry them:
the first promises to weave from one thread a tent holding forty
thousand soldiers, the second promises to provide food for forty thousand
soldiers and their horses from one seed of oats, while the third promises
to bear him a golden-haired boy and a silver-haired girl. After hearing
this the shah returns to his throne and sends his vizier Toman to woo
the girls. When Toman arrives at the girls' home, he asks their fathers,
three brothers by the names of Älibay, Dänebay, and Saribay, to come
out of their tents and negotiate with him. It is Toman's speech which
I wish to look at in the following comparative analysis of four texts.
Although the vizier is addressing the three brothers and will take back
all three girls, in his speech the addressee is generally in the singular
and he talks of just one girl.

The first text comes from the singer Qulamet-žïraw Übbi-ulï (1872-
1954). Qulamet-žïraw learned the *dastan Šaryar* from his teacher
Nurabulla-žïraw.[42] The second text comes from the singer Öteniyaz-
žïraw Iyimbetov (1874-1970); Öteniyaz-žïraw was a pupil of Erpolat-
žïraw, who was in turn one of Nurabulla's pupils.[43] The third text
comes from Žumabay-žïraw Bazarov; it was taken down in 1951.[44] The
fourth text comes also from Žumabay-žïraw; it was recorded by me in

[42]Qulamet's variant was taken down in 1939 by Ämet Šamuratov. This variant
has been edited twice; see Paxratdinov 1959 [the text quoted here is found on pp. 14-
16]; Maqsetov 1984: 133-221 [the text quoted here is found on pp. 137-139]. On the
singer see Maqsetov 1983: 109-121; Maqsetov 1984: 226-231.

[43]Öteniyaz's variant of *Šaryar* was taken down in 1959 by Qabïl Maqsetov; on
this singer see Maqsetov 1984: 231-234; Ayïmbetov 1988: 84. His variant is edited in
Maqsetov 1984: 11-131; the text quoted here is found on pp. 17-18. This edition
preserves the dialect features of the singer's text (*yaš* instead of *žas*, *dağ* instead of
taw, *tilläš* instead of *tiŋläš* etc.).

[44]This variant is preserved in MS R 373 (Inventory No. 127575) of the Archives
of the Literature Department of the Karakalpak Branch of the Uzbek Academy of
Sciences in Nukus. The manuscript comprises 52 pages; the text quoted here is found
on pp. 9-11. This passage is edited in Reichl 1985b: 639-40; I have left the manuscript
spelling (*ekki* for *eki* etc.), but adapted the transcription to the system used here. —
On further manuscript variants of *Šaryar* preserved in the Karakalpak Branch of the
Uzbek Academy of Sciences in Nukus see Maqsetov [Maksetov] et al. 1977: 79.

Nukus on June 24 and 25, 1981.[45] This singer is a pupil of Esemurat-žïraw, who in turn was a pupil of Nurabulla-žïraw. The affiliation between Nurabulla, Qulamet, Öteniyaz and Žumabay in terms of teacher-pupil relationships is hence the following:

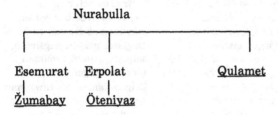

[45]As the result of a recent stay with the singer I have been able to emend some mistakes in the text; I have also corrected some printing mistakes and adapted the transcription system to the one used here. The text is in the singer's dialect; I have left the extra syllables at the end of a line (*ay* etc.); these are generally omitted in the printed editions of Karakalpak and other Turkic epic poetry. The following translation is based on my earlier translation in Reichl 1985b: 634-37.

Text 1: Qulamet-žïraw	Text 2: Öteniyaz-žïraw
Atlardï šaptïm qïyadaš,[46]	Araladïm qïyadaš,
aqpay ma közden selli žas,	ağïzdïm közden selli yaš,
boz üyde žanlar bar bolsaŋ,	bay baba üyde bar bolsaŋ,
šïqqïl maydanġa, xabarlas.	šïğïp maydanġa xabarlaš.
Eldi gezgen elšimen, 5	Araladïm qïyadaš,
tawdï gezgen tawšïman,	batïr erde bolur sawaš,
qusïmdï salġan awšïman.	bay baba üyde bar bolsaŋ,
Bay baba šïqqïl, xabarlas,	maydanġa šïğïp sen tilläš.
uldayïn körgen qïzïŋa,	Dağlardï gezgen dağšïman,
xannan kelgen žawšïman, 10	salġan qusïmnï awšïman,
xannïn žayï datqa[47] žay,	uldayïn körgen qïzïŋa,
körinisi ġana keŋ saray,	kelgen xanlardan žawšïman.
boz üyde žanlar bar bolsa,	Qarağay nayza qom baylap,
Älibay menen Dänebay,	qïyïstïrmağa kelgenmen,
eŋ kišisi Sarïbay, 15	aq girewke[48] sawïttï,
qarağay nayza qum[49] baylap,	seplemege kelgenmen.
quwantpağa kelgenmen,	Eki qoydïŋ balasïn,
aq girewke bek sawït,	telitiwge kelgenmen.
seplemege kelgenmen.	Eki qošqardïŋ balasïn,
Eki ġanïm,[50] müsäpir 20	dügistirmege kelgenmen.
eplemege kelgenmen.	Sizler temir, biz kömir,
Bizde ul bar, sizde qïz,	eritmege kelgenmen,
bizdi žibergen xanïmïz,	sizde qïz bar, bizde ul,
xannan kelgen žawšïmïz;	eki birdey mohmindi,
bizler kömir, siz temir, 25	emlemege kelgenmen.
eritpege kelgenbiz,	Ašïlġan bağdïŋ lalasï,

[46]This word is not recorded in the Karakalpak dictionaries; it is a compound of *qïya*, "mountain slope; expanse of land," and Persian *dašt*, "plain, field."

[47]A *datqa* (from Persian *dādxı‍‍ɣāh*, "a petitioner for justice") is a high official at the khan's palace who takes petitions to the khan. See Qalenderov et al. 1982ff.: II, 59 (s.v. *datqa*). Here the word is used as an attribute ("of high position").

[48]This word is not to be found in the Karakalpak dictionaries; for its meaning compare Kazakh *kirewke*, "coat of mail"; see Keŋesbaev et al. 1959-61: I, 335 (s.v. *kirewke*). Professor A. T. Hatto draws my attention to Kirghiz *aq küröökö soot*; see Judaxin 1985 [1965]: I, 471 (s.v. *küröökö*).

[49]Karakalpak *qum* means "sand, sandy desert"; Text 2 has *qom*, "saddle (of a camel)," which gives a better reading.

[50]This word is a crux; the first edition has *xannïŋ* instead of *ġanïm*. In Uzbek *ġanim* (from Arabic via Persian) means "enemy," a word which does not make much sense here. In view of the following comparison of the two people to be married with rams, I interpret *ġanïm* as a loanword from Persian/Tajik (and ultimately Arabic) *ġanam*, "sheep."

Text 3: Žumabay 1951

Text 4: Žumabay 1981

Atlar šaptïm qïyadan,		Taw-tawšïman, tawšïman,
közden aġar tatlï yaš.		qusïmnï salġan awšïman,
Aq boz üydiŋ išinde		ulday häm körgen qïzïŋa, ay,
bar bolsaŋ žandar xabarlaš!		patšadan kelgen yawšïman, öy.
Taw-tawšïman, tawšïman,	5	Atlanïp elden kelermen,
qusumnï salġan awšïman,		qädir-izzetin berermen,
ulday häm körgen qïzïŋa		beglerden körgen töremen.
patšadan kelgen yawšïman.		Ol ol bolsin, ol bolsïn!
Er žetkende ulïŋdï		Sorasaŋ bizden žol bolsïn!
üylendirmek parïzdï,	10	Bay-aġa üyde bar bolsaŋ, ay,
er žete ġoysa qïzïŋïz,		šïq maydanġa, xabarlaš, öy!
anïŋ eŋsesin aġartïp,		Žawlastïrmaq yawšïdan
qatarnï qosmaqlïq,		yawlasqanlarġa kelgenmen.
ata-anaġa parïzdï		Ellestirmek elšiden
bul išlerde etmeklik.	15	elleslerge kelgenmen.
Yada bizden, ya sizden		Eki mohmin[51] sawdasïn,[52] ay,
qalġan emes,		
burunġï ötken ata-babadan		eplemege kelgenmen, öy.
miyras qalġan žol eken.		Er žetken qïznï ayttïrmaq,
Žawlastarmaq yawšïdan,		er žetkendi üylentip,
ellestirmek elšiden	20	oŋ žaqta otaw tikmeklik
elleserlerge kelgenmen.		quda rahmat kelmeklik:
Ekki mömin sawdasïn		Bizden, sizden emes, ay,
eplemege kelgenmen.		ötken ata-babadan
Sizder sawït, biz usta,		qalġan bizge yol etken, oy.
seplemege kelgenmen.	25	Sizler sabït, biz usta,
Ekki mömin sawdasïn		seplemege kelgenmen.

[51]For the colloquial meaning "God-fearing" of *mohmin* (from Arabic *mo'min*) see Baskakov 1958: 463.

[52]Karakalpak *sawda* means "goods" and figuratively "cares"; see Baskakov 1958: 568 (s.v. *sawda*). In the latter sense the word is derived from Arabic *sawdā'*, "melancholy, desire"; the sense "love-desire, love," as in Uzbek *sawdā* and Turkish *sevda*, seems best suited for the present context.

240   *Composition in Performance and the Art of Memory*

Text 1: Qulamet-žïraw	Text 2: Öteniyaz-žïraw

<table>
<tr><td>

eki qošqar balasïn,
telitpege kelgenbiz,
lalï-maržan sädepti,
xïzmette baġrïm käbaptï,[53] 30
arada žawšï žürmeklik,
žawšï ayttïrïp kelmeklik,
bizden emes bay baba,
burïnġïlardan sebepti.
Mingen bedew želgendi,   35
haqtan[56] pärman bolġandï,
arada žawšï žürmeklik,
žawšï ayttïrïp kelmeklik,
bizden emes bay aġa,
Adam Ata, Hawa Ene,   40
payġambarlardan qalġandï.
At kekilin öreseŋ,
azdan däwran süreseŋ,
uldayïn körgen qïzïŋdï,
aq bilekten alasaŋ,   45
xannïŋ žayï datqa žay,
datqa žayġa barasaŋ,
xan aldïnda turasaŋ,
tärezini quradï,
zerge basïn ölšep aladï,   50
qïzïŋdï xanġa beresen,
sadaq tolġan žalġïz oq,
qadaldïq, bizge qaytpaq žoq,
xannan kelgen žawšïġa,
äžel žetpey ölmek žoq.   55

</td><td>

tilinde xalïqtïŋ sänasï,
uldayïn körgen qïzïŋa,
giriptar boldï, bay baba,
Emenniŋ ullï paššasï.
Ellestirmek elšiden,
žawlastïrmaq žawšïdan,[54]
qamïstan salġan say sadaq[55]
qadaldïq oġan qaytpaq žoq.
Qïz ayttïrġan žawšïġa,
arada žürgen elšige,
bay baba härgiz ölim žoq.
Lalï maržanlar sädepti,
hïzmette baġrïm käbaptï,
arada elši žürmeklik,
bizlerden emes, bay baba,
perištelerden sebepti.
Bul dünya degen yalġandï,
bay baba basïm amandï,
arada elši žürmeklik,
bizlerden emes, bay baba,
burïnġïdan qalġandï.
Erteŋ erte turasaŋ,
atqa eriŋ qoyasaŋ,
uldayïn körgen qïzïŋdi,
Šahidarap paššaġa,
aparïp öziŋ beresen,
bay baba qalay köresen?

</td></tr>
</table>

[53]Karakalpak *sädep* means "button (made of mother-of-pearl)" (from Arabic *şadaf*, "mother-of-pearl"); *käbap*, lit. "meat roasted on a spit," has the figurative senses "sorrow, grief." The two lines are traditional; Qalenderov et al. 1982ff. give a quotation from the *dastan Mäspatša: Atqa taqtï sädepti,/ žürek-bawïrïm käbaptï,* "He fastened the button to the horse, my heart was filled with grief."

[54]Here *žawšï* does not mean matchmaker but denotes the person calling two individuals or two peoples together to settle their dispute by strife or negotiations; see Qalenderov et al. 1982ff.: II, 187, 188) (s.v. *žawlastïr-, žawšï*).

[55]Karakalpak *sadaq* means "quiver" or "bow"; here the meaning is that of *sadaq oġï,* "arrow."

[56]Karakalpak *haq* (from Arabic *ḥaqq*) means "justice; law; truth"; here I take it to mean "God" as in Persian, Uzbek, Turkish, and other "Islamic" languages.

Text 1: Qulamet-žïraw

Xannïŋ hämiri tez deydi[m],[57]
tezirek žuwap bereseŋ,
aytïp boldïm arzïmdï,
bay baba özïŋ bileseŋ.

Text 3: Žumabay 1951		Text 4: Žumabay 1981
eplemege kelgenmen.		Sizler ġana temir, biz kömir,
Sadaq tolï sarï oq		eritlerge kelgenmen.
qadaldï, bizge qaytmaq yoq.		Eki mohmin sawdasïn, ay,
Patšadan kelgen yawšïġa	30	eplemege kelgenmen.
äžil etmey ölmek yoq.		Sizler sabït, biz usta,
Awïz ayġaq, til tayġaq,		seplemege kelgenmen.
tiymesin tildiŋ bir ušï.		Eki mohmin sawdasïn
Žawšïlïqqa kelgenim		eplemege kelgenmen.
bul da patšanïŋ küši.	35	Ayttïrarlarġa kelgenmen,
Üšte birdey qïzïŋdï		dediyarlerge kelgenmen.
qan ayttïrdï bay-aġa.		Bay-aġa qalay körersen,
Bu sözimniŋ mänisin		šïq maydanġa, xabarlaš, öy!
žarïlqawšï bir Alla.		Ašïlġan baġda gülimdi,
Baġ išinde qïzïl gül,	40	sarġaytmasïn žüzimdi, ay.
sayrar šäminde bülbül.		Xannan kelgen elšiden
Aytïp boldum arzïmdï.		elleserlerge kelgenmen.
Gähiy bergil qïzïŋdi,		Eki mohmin sawdasïn
gähiy berme qïzïŋdï,		eplemege kelgenmen.
sahibiqïran bay-aġa,	45	Sadaq tolï sarï oq
ïqtïyarï özïŋ bil!		qadaldï, bizge qaytmaq yoq.
Siyseri šïġar ol gošïm,		Patšadan kelgen yawšïman, ay,
onseri keler bul bašïm,		äželġa žetpey ölmek yoq.
qabul bolsïn köz yašïm.		Ašïlġan baġda qïzïl gül,
Gäh yarïlqa, gä qarġa,	50	sayrar šämende bülbül.
endigisin özïŋ bil,		Aytïp boldïm arzïmdï:
qïz atasï, bay-aġa!		Gähi bergil qïzïŋdï,
		gähi berme qïzïŋdï.
		Sahibiqïran bay-aġa, ay,
	55	ïqtïyarï özïŋ bil, ay!
		Aytïp boldïm arzïmdï:
		Gähi bergil qïzïŋdï,
		gähi berme qïzïŋdï,
		sahibiqïran bay-aġa,
	60	ïqtïyarï özïŋ bil, ay!

---

[57]The editions have *deydi*, "he said," but the form *deydim*, "I said," is required here.

Text 1: Qulamet-žïraw   Text 2: Öteniyaz-žïraw

I have raced the horse over the steppe.
I have passed through the steppe.

Do not the tears stream in floods from
my eyes?
I have shed floods of tears from my
eyes.

If there is anybody in the grey yurt,
come out and hear the news![58]
Father Bay, if you are in the yurt,
come out and hear the news!

I am a messenger who has tra-   5
versed the land,
I have passed through the steppe.

I am a mountaineer who has climbed
over the mountains,
On the battlefield there will be
fighting.

I am a hunter who has let fly his falcon.
Father Bay, if you are in the yurt,

Father Bay, come out, hear the news!
come out and listen!

For your daughter, who is looked upon
as a son,
I am a mountaineer who has climbed
over the mountains,

I have come from the khan as a   10
matchmaker.
I am a hunter who has let fly his
falcon.

The khan's palace is a place of high
position,
For your daughter, who is looked
upon as a son,

in appearance a wide mansion.
I have come from the khan as a
matchmaker.

Is there anybody in the grey yurt,
Having bound the pine lance to the
the camel's saddle,

Älibay and Dänebay,
I have come to make things fast;

and the youngest one, Sarïbay?   15
I have come to link together

Having bound the pine lance to
the camel's saddle,
the white-ringed coat of mail.

I have come to give happiness.
I have come to put to a new ewe

I have come to link together
the two young sheep.

the white-ringed strong coat
of mail.
I have come to cause to sport
with one another

I have come to skillfully unite   20
the two young rams.

the two sheep, the poor strangers.
You are the iron, I am the coal:

We have a son, you a daughter.
I have come to melt.

Our khan has sent us;
You have a daughter, we a son.

we are a matchmaker come from the
khan.
I have come to make whole

We are the coal, you the iron: 25
the two God-fearing creatures.

we have come to melt.
The tulip opens its blossoms in
the garden;

the wisdom of the people lies in
its language.

We have come to put
With your daughter, who is looked
upon as a son,

the two young rams to a new ewe.
the great pasha of Yemen

The button is made of rubies
and corals;

---

[58]A more literal translation of *xabarlas* is "let us exchange our news."

Text 3: Žumabay 1951

I have raced the horses over
    the steppe,
from my eyes sweet tears are flowing.

If there are people in the grey yurt,

let them hear the news!

I am a mountaineer who has   5
    climbed over the mountains,
I am a hunter who has let fly his falcon.
For your daughter, who is looked
    upon as a son,
I have come from the padishah as a
    matchmaker.
It is a religious duty to marry

your son when he has come of age.10
When your daughter comes of age,
with white shoulders,[59]

she must be united to her companion.

It is a religious duty for father and
    mother
to do these things.   15
(This custom) stems from neither
    us nor you,
it is the heritage
of our forefathers.

Dispute is brought by the summoner,
peace is brought by the   20
    messenger:
I have come to bring about a union.
I have come to skillfully unite

the love of two God-fearing creatures.
You are the coat of mail, we are
    the master,
I have come to link together.   25

I have come to skillfully unite
the love of two God-fearing creatures.

Text 4: Žumabay 1981

I am a mountaineer who has climbed
    over the mountains,
I am a hunter who has let fly his
    falcon.
For your daughter, who is looked
    upon as a son,
I have come from the padishah
    as a matchmaker.
I am coming on my horse from (my)
    people,
I am bringing honor and esteem,
I am a lord who is respected by the
    begs.
May it be well, may it be well!

May you ask us the reason for our
    coming!
Bay-agha, if you are in the yurt,
come out and hear the news!
Dispute is brought by the
    summoner:
I have come to summon to
    marriage negotiations.
Peace is brought by the messenger:

I have come to bring about a union.
I have come to skillfully unite

the love of two God-fearing creatures.
I have come to engage the daughter
    who has come of age,
to marry her who has grown up,
to erect a marriage tent on the right
    side,
to give thanks to God.
(This custom) does not stem from
    us, from you,
it has come from our forefathers
and continues to this day.

You are the coat of mail, we are
    the master,
I have come to link together.
You are the iron, we are the coal:

---

[59]Lit. "having made white her shoulders."

Text 1: Qulamet-žïraw   Text 2: Öteniyaz-žïraw

in doing my duty I am afflicted   30
     with grief.
I am walking about as a match-
     maker,
I have come doing the match-
     making.
(This custom) does not stem from
     us, Father Bay,
its origin lies in the past.

The racer I had mounted galloped 35
     along;
from God an order has come.
I am walking about as a match-
     maker,
I have come doing the match-
     making.
(This custom) does not stem from
     us, Father Bay,
it goes back to Father Adam and 40
     Mother Eve,
and to the Prophets.

May you plait the horse's locks,
may you lead the life of a lord,
may you take by her white hand
your daughter, who has been   45
     looked upon as a son.
The khan's palace is a place of
     high position;
may you go to the rich palace,
may you stand before the khan:
he will put up his scales
and weigh her head in gold   50
if you give your daughter to
     the khan.
Like a solitary arrow from a full
     quiver
we have stuck fast and do not
     return.
The matchmaker who has come from
     the khan
incurs neither death nor destruction.55
I have said the khan's command
     quickly,
may you give a quick answer!
I have said my wish,
may you, Father Bay, know yourself (what to do)!

has fallen in love, Father Bay.

Peace is brought by the messenger,

dispute is brought by the summoner.

Like the unfailing arrow sent from
     the reeds
we have fastened on her and do not
     return.
The matchmaker wooing a girl,

the messenger walking about
does not incur death, Father Bay.

The button is made of rubies
     and corals;
In doing my duty I am afflicted
     with grief.
I am walking about as a
     messenger.
(This custom) does not stem
     from us, Father Bay,
its origin goes back to the angels.
This world is transitory;
Father Bay, my head is in safety.
I am walking about as a
     messenger.
(This custom) does not stem,
     from us, Father Bay,
it goes back to the past.
If you get up tomorrow morning,
if you put your saddle on the horse,
if you yourself bring
your daughter, who has been
     looked upon as a son,
to Shah Darap, the pasha,

Father Bay, how do you feel
     about this?

Text 3: Žumabay 1951

The yellow arrow from the full quiver
has stuck fast, we will not return.
The matchmaker coming from the   30
        padishah
will incur neither death nor
        destruction.
The mouth denounces, the tongue
        is slippery:
may the tongue give no offense![60]
I have come as a matchmaker,

as the support of the padishah.   35

The khan, bay-agha, demanded
        in marriage
your three daughters together.
The meaning of these my words
may be blessed by the one God!

In the garden is the red rose,   40
in the flower garden the nightingale
        is singing.
I have spoken my wish.
Either you give your daughter
or you don't give your daughter.

Most honored bay-agha,   45

know your own wishes!
My flesh will amount to six *seri*,

my head will come to ten *seri*.[61]

May the tears from my eyes be
        welcome!
Bless or curse,   50

know the task at hand,

Text 4: Žumabay 1981

I have come to melt.
I have come to skillfully unite
the love of two God-fearing
        creatures.
You are the coat of mail, we are
        the master,
I have come to link together.

I have come to skillfully unite
the love of two God-fearing
        creatures.
I have come to make an engage-
        ment,
I have come to enter into talks.

Bay-agha, if you have an opinion,
come out and hear the news!
In the garden my rose has opened
        its blossom,
may my face be never made yellow!
As a messenger coming from the
        khan
I have come to bring about a union.
I have come to skillfully unite
the love of two God-fearing
        creatures.
From the full quiver the yellow
        arrow
has stuck fast, we will not return.
As a messenger coming from the
        padishah
I will incur neither death nor
        destruction.
In the garden the red rose has
        opened its blossoms,
the nightingale is singing in the
        flower garden.
I have said my wish:

[60]Karakalpak *ayğaq* means "witness"; the sense "informer" is suggested by Kirghiz *ayğaq*; see Judaxin 1985 [1965]: I, 29 (s.v. *ayğaq*). Line 33 may be translated literally as: "may the tip of the tongue not touch"; *tiy-* has also the sense "offend."

[61]A *seri* is the fourth of a *batman* (the latter a weight of between ca. 20 and 40 kg in Karakalpakistan). The meaning of these two lines is not entirely clear. Is the vizier saying that his head weighs more than his body, i.e. is of more worth and importance than his body? Or (as Professor A. T. Hatto suggests) is he saying that this will be the weight and value of his head and body if he is killed?

Text 3: Žumabay 1951

Text 4: Žumabay 1981

father of the girl, bay-agha!

either you give your daughter
or you don't give your daughter.
Powerful bay-agha,
55 you must know yourself what
            you want!
I have said my wish:
either you give your daughter
or you don't give your daughter.
Powerful bay-agha,
60 you must know yourself what
            you want!

The variation among these four texts is fairly limited. Let us look at the first ten lines of Text 1. These lines are composed of three groups of verses: the introductory lines 1-2, the vizier's request to come out of the yurt to negotiate with him in lines 3-4 (with a repetition in l. 8), and his self-introduction in lines 5-7 and 9-10 with the rhyme-words *elšimen* ("I am a messenger"), *tawšïman* ("I am a mountaineer"), *awšïman* ("I am a hunter"), and *žawšïman* ("I am a matchmaker"). The correspondence between the four texts can be tabulated in the following way:

Text 1	Text 2	Text 3	Text 4
1-2	1-2, 5	1-2	omitted
3-4, 8	3-4, 7-8	3-4	10-11
5-7, 9-10	9-12	5-8	1-4

The variations of the first two lines in Texts 1 to 3 are the following:

Text 1	Text 2	Text 3
Atlardï šaptïm qïyadaš,	Araladïm qïyadaš,	Atlar šaptïm qïyadan,
aqpay ma közden selli žas	agïzdïm közden selli yaš	közden agar tatlï yaš

If we take the various appellations of the vizier in this passage we get the following correspondences:

	Text 1	Text 2	Text 3	Text 4
elšimen	+	−	−	−
tawšïman	+	+	+	+
awšïman	+	+	+	+
žawšïman	+	+	+	+

Basing our analysis just on this short passage and on the three tables above, we can distinguish various kinds of variation: (1) Lines may be put in a different order in different variants; (2) lines may be repeated or (3) omitted altogether; (4) new lines may be added; and (5) lines may have the same rhyme-word in different texts but variations line-internally. Types (1) and (2) need no comment. Types (3) and (4) presuppose the notion of a traditional text (not just a story) being passed on from one singer to another, or, to put it even more pointedly, of an original. Lord has repeatedly emphasized that such a notion is incompatible with an oral tradition:

> Our real difficulty arises from the fact that, unlike the oral poet, we are not accustomed to thinking in terms of fluidity. We find it difficult to grasp something that is multiform. It seems to us necessary to construct an ideal text or to seek an original, and we remain dissatisfied with an ever-changing phenomenon. I believe that once we know the facts of oral composition we must cease trying to find an original of any traditional song. From one point of view each performance is an original. From another point of view it is impossible to retrace the work of generations of singers to that moment when some singer first sang a particular song.
>
> (Lord 1960: 100)

As to our example, we know that all three singers acquired their variant either directly or indirectly from one and the same singer. This means that we cannot be very wrong in assuming that those passages in which the singers' texts agree with one another are "original" in the sense that they were also part of Nurabulla's variant. This is not to say that Nurabulla's *Šaryar* is the *Ur-Šaryar*. As has been pointed out earlier (see Chapter Three, p. 67), Nurabulla first learned this *dastan* from Erman-žïraw, but later became also acquainted with Qazaqbay-žïraw's variant when he stayed with the latter in Bukhara. The *dastan* was probably composed some time in the 18th century, possibly influenced by written literature.[62] It is Nurabulla's variant, rather

---

[62]See Maqsetov [Maksetov] et al. 1977: 79.

than an original, which serves as point of reference for "preservation" and "change" in the four texts.

The absence of lines 1-2 in Text 4 is certainly an omission (especially as the singer has these lines in his earlier variant), while the absence of an equivalent to line 5 in Text 1 (*elšimen*) in the other texts could be interpreted either as an omission on the part of Öteniyaz-žïraw and Žumabay-žïraw or as an innovation on the part of Qulamet-žïraw; other variants would be needed to settle this question. But despite these difficulties — familiar to editors of medieval texts, who have to weigh the manuscript evidence to decide between preservation, interpolation, and textual corruption when establishing a critical text — the variation between the texts is such that the outlines of a traditional text are clearly visible. The first two lines are certainly part of this text. On metrical grounds *qïyadan* in Text 3 can be rated as a textual corruption. To go even further in the analysis of the two first lines, as one would if we were dealing with a written tradition, is probably not feasible. It seems reasonable to suppose that *selli žas/yaš* ("floods of tears") in Texts 1 and 2 is closer to Nurabulla's variant than Žumabay's *tatlï yaš* ("sweet tears"), but the first part of a line is generally more variable than the rhyme-word and hence less easy to interpret in terms of change or preservation.

Lines 5 to 9 in Text 4 are clearly an interpolation, not only when compared with Texts 1 and 2, but also when compared to Žumabay's earlier Text 3. If we were to establish a critical text these lines would have to be eliminated. Such a procedure would, however, be most questionable. Here Lord's remarks on the misguided nature of a search for the original are appropriate. Although we can see how a text changes from singer to singer and although we can interpret at least some of the changes as deviations from the tradition and even corruptions of the tradition (*Zersingen*), each text, each performance must also be judged on its own.[63] Lines 5 to 9 in Text 4 fit perfectly in their individual context; they are well-constructed and successfully enhance the ceremonial character of the vizier's speech. We might feel less happy with the frequent repetitions in Text 4. Here the printed text gives a somewhat distorted impression, however; what looks like redundancy in cold print is of an entirely different nature in a live

---

[63]On the notions "*Zersingen*" as a form of corruptive change and "*Umsingen*" (lit. "re-singing") as a form of adaptive change see Bausinger 1980: 268f.

performance. Repetition helps to drive home a point, to set the key of a passage, or simply to delight by prolonging the singing. The listener does not, as the reader may, find repetition tedious; indeed he needs a certain amount of redundancy in order to be able to follow what is sung.[64]

What has been said about the first ten lines (of Text 1) is confirmed by the rest of this passage. There is no need for a detailed analysis; the translations alone will have made the reader aware of the degree and nature of variation encountered in these texts. It is to be noted, however, that textual stability is not only found in the rhyme-words. There is a series of words and phrases associated with a series of ideas, all standing for the matchmaker's endeavors to wed two people: uniting two God-fearing creatures (*eplemege*), linking the chains of the coat of mail (*seplemege*), giving two sheep to a ewe to suckle (*telitpege*), melting iron (*eritpege*); these words occur in line-initial position and are constructed with an invariable *kelgenbiz*, "we have come" (lit. "for the linking etc. we have come").

The passage quoted here is neither a typical scene of Karakalpak oral epic poetry nor is it unusually high in formulas. Although some lines or even pairs of lines are formulaic — such as lines 29-30 in Text 1 — the passage as a whole does not consist of simply a string of formulas. If the texts agree as closely with one another as they do, the explanation for this does not only and primarily lie in their formulaic nature but rather in the way these *dastans* are learned and passed on from singer to singer. Before addressing the issue of learning and transmission, however, I wish to give one more example, which illustrates an even higher degree of textual stability.

The following texts come from the *dastan Qïrmandäli*, which was discussed in Chapter Six (see pp. 157ff.). I have chosen the first dialogue between Göruǵlï and Qïrmandäli. Göruǵlï asks the girl to give him a drink of water, but Qïrmandäli, in the spirit of verbal contest-poems (*aytïs*), refuses and requests Göruǵlï to come and get his drink himself. The first two texts are from Karakalpak *baqsï*s, Text 1 from Mädireyim Mätžanov and Text 2 from the *baqsï* Bekmurat-baqsï

---

[64]On this point see Ong 1982: 39ff.

Žumaniyazov. The third text is from the Turkmen singer Pelwan-
baxšï.[65]

Text 1

I
Göruġlï:
Suw boyïnda turġan qïzlar,
nazlïlar suw ber išeli?
Söylegen tilli zibanlar,
žananlar suw ber išeli?

II
Qïrmandäli:
Suwdïŋ boyïnda qayïr bolmas,
tüš öziŋ suwdan iše ber,
här kelgen tülki-šer bolmas,
kel öziŋ suwdan iše ber.

III
Göruġlï:
Äl mudam därbent saqladïm,
boyïŋa özim šaqladïm,
men bir nazlï qïz žoqladïm,
qïyalïm suw ber išeli?

IV
Qïrmandäli:
Suwïmdï bermeymen yada,
seniŋdey köpti dünyada,
haslïŋ türik seniŋ bala,
tüš öziŋ suwdan iše ber.

V
Göruġlï:
Uzïn-uzïn obaŋïzġa,
qonaq bolsam ordaŋïzġa,
qul bolayïn babaŋïzġa,
nazlïm bir suw ber išeli?

VI
Qïrmandäli:
Uzïn-uzïn obam žoqtï,
qonaq qonar ordam žoqtï,
qul bolarġa babam žoqtï,
tüš öziŋ suwdan išever.

Text 2

I
Göruġlï:
Suw boyïnda turġan gözzal,
nazlï yar suw ber išeli,
qašï-közin süzgen gözzal,
nazlï yar suw ber išeli.

II
Qïrmandäli:
Suwïmdï bermesmen yada,
düš öziŋ suwdan išever.
Seniŋdey köp dur dünyada,
düš öziŋ suwdan iše ber.

V
Göruġlï:
Uzïn-uzïn obaŋïzġa,
miyman bolsam ordaŋïzġa,
qul bolayïn babaŋïzġa,
nazanin suw ber išeli.

VI
Qïrmandäli:
Uzïn-uzïn obam žoqdur,
miyman alar ordam žoqdur,
qul bolarġa babam žoqdur,
düš öziŋ suwdan iše ber.

[65]Text 1: Maqsetov, Karimov 1986: 160-162; Text 2: Maqsetov, Mämbetnazarov,
Erpolatov 1963: 38-40; Text 3: Karryev 1983: 329-330.

Text 3

I
Köroğlï:
Howuz bašïnda duranlar,
näzlim, bir suw ber, ičeyli.
Sözlešip manï berenler,
Gïz oğlan, suw ber, ičeyli!

II
Harman Däli:
Howuz bašïnda hayïr olmaz,
düš, özüŋ suwdan ičewer.
Her tilki-šaġal šir olmaz,
düš, özüŋ suwdan ičewer.

III
Köroğlï:
Elmïdam derbent saqladïm,
mundan ganïmï oqladïm.
Seniŋ dek näzlim yoqladïm,
näzlim, bir suw ber, ičeyli.

IV
Harman Däli:
Suwumnï bermenem yada,
seniŋ kimin köp dünyäde.
Aslïŋ türkmen, haramzada!
Düš, özüŋ suwdan ičewer.

V
Köroğlï:
Uzaq-uzaq ordaŋïza,
gonaq bolsam obaŋïza.
Yetim bolayïn babaŋïza,
näzlim, bir suw ber, ičeyli.

VI
Harman Däli:
Uzaq-uzaq ordam yoqdur,
gonaq bolsaŋ obam yoqdur.
Men bir yetim, babam yoqdur.
Düš, özüŋ suwdan ičewer.

Text 1	Text 2
VII Görüġlï: Bälent daġdan aša bilmen, düšmana uġraša bilmen, men bir kesel tuša bilmen, nazlïm bir suw ber išeli?	**III** Görüġlï: Oža daġdan aša bilmen, ġanim körsem yoša bilmen, men bir qäste tüše bilmen, nazlï yar suw ber išeli.
VIII Qïrmandäli: Kesel bolġan üyde žatar, yardïŋ šiyrin läbin tatar, ašïq bolġan kännen öter, tüš öziŋ suwdan išeber.	**IV** Qïrmandäli: Ašïq bolġan känden öter, yardïŋ šiyrin läbin tatar, qäste bolġan üyde žatar, düš öziŋ suwdan iše ber.
IX Görüġlï: Görüġlï keldi mästana, sorsam läbiŋ qana-qana, irkilip qïlmaŋ bahana, nazlïm bir suw ber išeli?	**VII** Görüġlï: Bizdur Görüġlï märdana, emsem läbiŋ qana-qana, sendey yar tapsam bahana, nazlï yar suw ber išeli.
X Qïrmandäli: Bizni Qïrmandäli derler, göštiŋni qamlay žiyerler, eki köziŋni häm oyarlar, atïŋdï burda qaša ber!	**VIII** Qïrmandäli: Qïrmandäli qïz diyarler. Eki köziŋni oyarlar, sizdi bul žerde soyarlar, turma, bul žerden qašaber.

Text 1	Text 2
I Görüġlï: Beautiful girls, standing at the edge of the water, coquettish girls, give us water, let us have a drink! Girls, who have spoken with eloquent tongues, sweet girls, give us water, let us have a drink!	**I** Görüġlï: Beautiful girl, standing at the edge of the water, coquettish girl, give us water, let us have a drink! Beautiful girl, darting flirtatious glances, coquettish girl, give water, let us have a drink!

Text 3

VII
Köroģlï:
Godža daġdan aša bilmen,
ganïm görsem, džoša bilmen.
Men bir hasta düše bilmen,
näzlim, bir suw ber, ičeyli.

VIII
Harman Däli:
Ašïk bolan känden öter,
yarïŋ qandï-lebin tutar,
hasta bolan öyde yatar,
düš, özüŋ suwdan ičewer.

IX
Köroģlï:
Köroģlï gezdim messana,
emsem lebiŋ gana-gana.
Nazlï yar, etme bahana,
näzlim, bir suw ber, ičeyli.

X
Harman Däli:
Bize Harman Däli diyrler,
iki gözüŋi oyarlar.
Etiŋ čigleyin iyerler,
atïŋ öwür-de gačawer!

Text 3

I
Köroģlï:
You who are standing at the edge of the pond,
my coquettish girls, give us water, let us have a drink!
You who say wise things when you talk with one another,
young girls, give us water, let us have a drink!

Text 1   Text 2

II
Qïrmandäli:
There are no alms to be had at the edge
    of the water.
Dismount, take yourself a drink from
    the water!
Not every fox approaching is a lion.
Come, take yourself a drink from the
    water!

III
Göruġlï:
I have always guarded the narrow passage
    over the mountains.
I fit well to your person.
I have been looking for a coquettish girl.
Girl of my dreams, give us water, let us
    have a drink!

IV   **II**
Qïrmandäli: Qïrmandäli:
I don't give my water to a stranger. I don't give my water to a stranger.
There are many like you in the world. Dismount, take yourself a drink
                                          from the water!
By birth you are a Turkmen youth.[66] There are many like you in the
                                          world.
Dismount, take yourself a drink from Dismount, take yourself a drink from
    the water!   the water!

V   **V**
Göruġlï: Göruġlï:
I would like to be a guest of your tribe I would like to be a guest of your
                                          tribe
in your large village;   in your large village;
I wish to be a slave to your father. I wish to be a slave to your father.
Coquettish girl, give us water, let   Beautiful girl, give us water, let
    us have a drink!   us have a drink!

[66]Karakalpak *türik* means according to Baskakov "rolled up (sleeves, trousers etc.); thick-lipped," meanings which do not make any sense here; see Baskakov 1968: 663 (s.v. *türik*); Kazakh *türik*, "prudent," would give a better sense. When comparing this line to the Turkmen text, however, it becomes clear that the singer means "Turk" in the sense of "Turkmen," a description which fits Göruġlï.

Text 3

II
Harman Däli:
There are no alms to be had at the edge of the pond.
Dismount, take yourself a drink from the water!
Not every fox and jackal is a lion.
Dismount, take yourself a drink from the water!

III
Köroğlï:
I have always guarded the narrow passage through the
      mountains;
from there I shot my arrows at the enemy.
I have been looking for a coquettish girl like you.
My coquettish girl, give us water, let us have a drink!

IV
Harman Däli:
I don't give my water to a stranger.
There are many like you in the world.
By birth you are a Turkmen, you rogue!
Dismount, take yourself a drink from the water!

V
Köroğlï:
I would like to be a guest of your tribe
in your large village;
I would like to be like an orphan for your father.
My coquettish girl, give us water, let us have a drink!

Text 1	Text 2
VI	VI
Qïrmandäli:	Qïrmandäli:
I don't have a large village;	I don't have a large village;
I don't have a tribe which puts up guests;	I don't have a tribe which takes guests;
I don't have a father whose slave you could be.	I don't have a father whose slave you could be.
Dismount, take yourself a drink from the water!	Dismount, take yourself a drink from the water!
VII	III
Göruġlï:	Göruġlï:
I can't climb over the high mountains;	I can't climb over the high mountains;
	when I see the enemy, I can't get into a battle rage.
I can't encounter the enemy.	
I have fallen ill, I can't dismount.	I have fallen ill, I can't dismount.
Coquettish girl, give us water, let us have a drink!	Coquettish girl, give us water, let us have a drink!
VIII	IV
Qïrmandäli:	Qïrmandäli:
The man who is ill lies at home.	The man who is in love overcomes many things.
He kisses the sweet lips of his beloved.	He kisses the sweet lips of his beloved.
The man who is in love overcomes many things.	The man who is ill lies at home.
Dismount, take yourself a drink from the water!	Dismount, take yourself a drink from the water!
IX	VII
Göruġlï:	Göruġlï:
Göruġli has come, love-drunken.	We are Göruġlï the brave!
I want to kiss your lips again and again.	I want to kiss your lips again and again.
Don't hesitate and don't find some pretext!	The reason for this is that I want to find a sweetheart like you.
Coquettish girl, give us water, let us have a drink!	Coquettish sweetheart, give us water, let us have a drink!
X	VIII
Qïrmandäli:	Qïrmandäli:
We are called Qïrmandäli.	I am called the girl Qïrmandäli.
Your flesh will be eaten raw,	Your two eyes will be gouged out,
your two eyes will also be gouged out.	you will be cut to pieces here.
Turn your horse and flee!	Don't stay, flee from here!

Text 3

VI
Harman Däli:
I don't have a large tribe;
I don't have a village where you could be a guest;
I am myself an orphan, I don't have a father.
Dismount, take yourself a drink from the water!

VII
Köroǧlï:
I can't climb over the high mountains;
when I see the enemy, I can't get into a battle rage.
I have fallen ill, I can't dismount.
My coquettish girl, give us water, let us have a drink!

VIII
Harman Däli:
The man who is in love overcomes many things.
He kisses the sweet lips of his beloved.
The man who is ill lies at home.
Dismount, take yourself a drink from the water!

IX
Köroǧlï:
I, Köroǧlï, have walked about love-drunken.
I want to kiss your lips again and again.
Coquettish sweetheart, don't find a pretext!
My coquettish girl, give us water, let us have a drink!

X
Harman Däli:
We are called Harman Däli.
Your two eyes will be gouged out,
your flesh will be eaten raw.
Turn your horse and flee!

Comparing these texts to the extracts from *Semetey* and to the
parallel passages from *Šaryar* given above, we notice that there is far
less variation in the variants of this poem from *Qïrmandäli*. The
greatest difference between the three texts lies in the order of stanzas
and the loss of stanzas in Text 2. By comparison to Texts 1 and 3, Text
2 must be judged as not only missing two stanzas but also as having
changed the order of stanzas:

Texts 1/3:   I – II – III – IV – V – VI – VII – VIII – IX – X

Text 2:   I – 0 – 0   – II – V – VI – III – IV   – VII – VIII

This is a common enough phenomenon of folk poetry, where we find, as
in the present poem, regular stanzas rather than a laisse-like division
into irregular segments. It is in particular *aytïs*-poetry with which this
passage shows great similarity. Every "answer"-stanza takes up the
ideas, if not the words of the previous "demand"-stanza, refuting,
rebuffing, or simply making fun of the wooer.

Within the stanza, the variations are on the whole restricted to the
substitution of synonyms or the addition of extra syllables for metrical
reasons. Occasionally, whole lines are different in wording, though
often synonymous or at least related in meaning. The first stanza shows
more variations than most of the others, but even here we can see how
"conservative" the texts are:

l. 1   Text 1   Suw boyïnda turġan   qïzlar
        Text 2   (Suw boyïnda turġan)   gözzal
        Text 3   Howuz bašïnda   duranlar

l. 2   Text 1   nazlïlar   suw   ber   išeli
        Text 2   nazlï yar   (suw   ber   išeli)
        Text 3   nazlïm   bir suw   (ber   ičeyli)

l. 3   Text 1   söylegen tilli zibanlar
        Text 2   qašï-közin süzgen gözzal
        Text 3   sözlešip manï berenler

l. 4   Text 1   žananlar   suw   ber   išeli
        Text 2   nazlï yar   (suw   ber   išeli)
        Text 3   qïz oġlan   (suw   ber   ičeyli)

In lines 2 and 4 the variations are restricted to the substitution of
synonyms (as in l. 4) or grammatical categories (as in l. 2: singular vs.
plural, attributive adjective vs. nominalized adjective, possessive vs.
non-possessive). The variations in line 1 are of an equally minimal

nature: the semantic relationship between *suw boyïnda*, lit. "water-at-its-side," and *howuz bašïnda*, lit. "pond-at-its-head," is again that of synonymy; equally substitutable in the context of popular love-poetry are nouns like *gözzal*, "beautiful (one)," and *qïzlar*, "girls." The variation between Turkmen *duranlar*, "standing ones," and Karakalpak *turǧan gözzal/qïzlar*, "standing beauty (or beauties)/girls," is due to metrical reasons: the first half of the line in the Karakalpak texts demands an extra syllable (*turǧanlar*, mirroring Turkmen *duranlar*, would have been one syllable short), or, to put it the other way round, the first half of the line in the Turkmen text did not allow an extra syllable (*duran qïzlar*, mirroring Karakalpak *turǧan qïzlar*, would have had one syllable too many). Finally, in line 3, Texts 2 and 3 are clearly related in meaning, sharing a common lexeme (*söyle-*, *sözle(š)-*), while Text 2 has a different line, suitable for the different rhyme-pattern of the first stanza in this variant.

A similar picture is presented by the other stanzas of the extract as well as by the other verse-parts of the *dastan*. It would be tedious to give a list of variant readings here; the following table of the verse-passages in the three texts and their correspondence to one another will give an indication of the close relationship between these three variants (the verse-passage quoted above is no. 5 in the list):

Text 1	Text 2	Text 3	Text 1	Text 2	Text 3
1	1	1	15	16	16
2	2	2	16	17	17
3	3	3	17	0	18
4	4	4	18	18	19
5	5	5	0	0	20
6	6	6	19	20	21
7	7	7	20	19	22
8	8	8	21	0	23
9	9	9	22	0	24
10	11	10	23	0	25
11	10	11	24	0	26
12	12	12	25	0	27
0	13	13	26	0	28
13	14	14	27	0	29
14	15	15	28	0	30

As can be seen from these figures, the Turkmen variant is the most complete version, while Text 2 has omitted a number of stanzas. Once again the question of completeness and omission presupposes a fairly stable textual tradition with a clear relatedness between the various

texts in terms of singer-pupil relationships. In this particular case it is
incontestable that the Karakalpak *baqsï*s learned this *dastan* from
Turkmen singers. The most convincing proof of this is afforded by the
language of the Karakalpak texts. While some linguistic features of
Texts 1 and 2 shared with Text 3 (such as initial /y/ instead of /ž/ as in
yar, "beloved") can be explained as Karakalpak dialectal traits, others
are clear Turkmenisms.[67] Among the latter are forms like *išeli*, "let us
drink" (Turkmen *ičeyli*; Karakalpak *išeyik*); *bilmen*, "I can't" (dialectal
in Turkmen; Karakalpak *bilmeymin*); *yada*, "to the stranger" (Turkmen
yat + Dative suffix *-a* > *yada*; Karakalpak *žat* + Dative suffix *-qa* >
žatqa); or *oža daǧlar*, "high mountains," lit. "old mountains" (Turkmen
qodža daǧlar, Karakalpak *uša tawlar*) and others.

Apart from the textual evidence we know from the singers themselves
that they were greatly influenced by Turkmen *baxšï*s. The most
important Turkmen singer for the transmission of Turkmen versions
of *dastan* poetry to Karakalpak singers was a *baxšï* by the name of
Süyew-baqsï (d. around 1914). He is reputed to have known twelve
branches of the *Köroǧlu/Göroǧlï*-cycle and had a number of Karakalpak
as well as Turkmen pupils.[68] This Turkmen *baxšï* also performed
together and in competition with the Karakalpak singer Muwsa-baqsï
(1836-1907), from whom most contemporary Karakalpak *baqsï*s trace
their lineage. Ämet-baqsï Tariyxanov (b. 1923), from whom one of the
Karakalpak variants of *Qïrmandäli* has been recorded, learned this
dastan from Qurbaniyaz-baqsï, who was a pupil of Eščan-baqsï (1901-
1952); the latter was in turn a pupil of Muwsa-baqsï.[69] Bekmurat-baqsï
(b. 1902), the singer of Text 1, was at first a pupil of Qudaybergen-
baqsï, who also stood in direct descent from Muwsa-baqsï, but learned
Qïrmandäli later from another Karakalpak baqsï named Qïdïrniyaz-
baqsï.[70] The striking similarities between the three texts cannot be
explained only in terms of a close teacher-pupil relationship. They are
also due to the particular form of these *dastans*, the *baqsï*'s conception

[67]On initial /y/ instead of /(d)ž/ in Karakalpak see Nasyrov 1983: 75.

[68]See Ayïmbetov 1988: 131-133.

[69]On the Karakalpak *baqsï*s and their lineage see also Chapter Three, pp. 68f.
On Eščan-baqsï see Ayïmbetov 1988: 145; Maqsetov 1983: 140-158; on Ämet-baqsï see
Maqsetov 1983: 170-187.

[70]See Maqsetov, Mämbetnazarov, Erpolatov 1963: 129-130.

of his art and the influence of written texts on the oral transmission of epic poetry.

The Art of Memory

The three passages discussed in the previous sections — an extract from *Semetey* in three variants from different Kirghiz *manasčї*s and *semeteyči*s, a verse-passage from *Šaryar* as recorded from three Karakal-pak *žïraw*s, and an *aytïs*-like verse-dialogue from *Qïrmandäli* as performed by two Karakalpak *baqsï*s and one Turkmen *baxšï* — have shown different ways of continuing and changing a tradition. These ways of carrying on a tradition and the types of singers associated with these ways can be thought of as lying on a scale, at one end of which we have a singer like Džüsüp Mamay, who creatively enlarges the tradition, not only in size but also in artistic elaboration, and at the other a singer like Bekmurat-baqsï, who keeps so closely to the traditional text that one might suspect some kind of memorization process at work to ensure verbatim transmission. On this scale many intermediate and transitional positions are possible.

In some traditions a distinction is made between singers who are able to master a vast repertory, which they have acquired in the course of an extended apprenticeship from a master-singer, and singers who are able to perform only one epic or extracts, which they have learned from a brief stay with a singer or perhaps just from listening repeatedly as aficionados to the singing of epic poetry. In this way the Kirghiz distinguish between a *čoŋ manasčї*, a "big *manasčї*," who knows a whole epic of the cycle or even the whole cycle, and a *kičik manasčї*, a "little *manasčї*," who knows only extracts; or between a *džomoqču*, a singer who creatively carries on the tradition, and an *ïrčï*, a singer who is far more text-oriented and strives to preserve the text he knows with as few changes as possible. In the Kazakh tradition of oral epic poetry the two ends of the scale are generally denoted by the terms *aqïn* for the "creative singer" and *žïršï* (also *öleŋši*) for the "repro-ductive singer"; but, as E. Ismailov has pointed out, some singers combine the two functions in one person, making the distinction between the two types somewhat tenuous and hence giving rise to many intermediate types (see p. 78).

This wide range of possibilities is also found in non-Turkic traditions. Among *bylina*-singers some singers who stand in a teacher-pupil relation, often members of the same family, show little verbal change in the course of transmitting a *bylina* from one generation to the next, while other "schools" of singers are famous for their alterations and innovations. V. I. Čičerov wrote a pioneering dissertation on these "schools" of *bylina*-singers on the shores of Lake Onega, a line of study which has been taken up again in recent years and also applied to other traditions.[71] The Russian example makes it clear that both a creative and a conservative, "text-oriented" tradition are genuine traditions of oral epic poetry.

C. M. Bowra gives the singer Ryabinin's version of *Ilya of Murom and Kalin Tsar* as an example of a creative, innovative tradition:

> When Ryabinin sang of Ilya of Murom and Tsar Kalin to Rybnikov he gave quite a different story from that which he sang later to Gilferding. The first version has 289 verses, and the second 616, and the difference of scale is to be explained by more than a mere expansion of common themes. The second poem has different episodes and almost a different temper. What is true of Ryabinin is true of other bards from the same district whose poems were recorded by Rybnikov and Gilferding, and the evidence is conclusive that here at least the bard does not repeat himself exactly but improvises afresh on each occasion.
>
> (Bowra 1952: 217)

The Serbo-Croatian singers as described by M. Murko, M. Parry, and A. B. Lord are basically of this type. Lord has stressed the technical skill of the Yugoslav singer, enabling him to "compose in performance." This composition in perfomance is, as Lord underlines, not an extemporization, a creation *ex nihilo* — ideas associated with the term "improvisation" rejected by Lord — but rather the outcome of the mastery of traditional diction, theme-development, and story-patterning. Two performances by the same singer will differ, but there are definite limits to the extent one variant will deviate from another. After a careful analysis of variants and variation in Serbo-Croatian epic poetry, Lord reaches the following conclusion:

---

[71]Čičerov's dissertation from 1941 has only recently (and posthumously) been published; see Čičerov 1982. His work has been taken up, among others, by V. M Gacak, who has written a detailed analysis of textual variation in the Russian *byliny* and in the Romanian epic songs; see Gacak 1989. For the "schools" of *bylina*-singers see also Bowra 1952: 443ff.; compare also the discussion in Chadwick 1932-40: II, 238ff.

When we look back over these examples of transmission, we are, I believe, struck by the conservativeness of the tradition. The basic story is carefully preserved. Moreover, the changes fall into certain clear categories, of which the following emerge: (1) saying the same thing in fewer or more lines, because of singers' methods of line composition and of linking lines together, (2) expansion of ornamentation, adding of details of description (that may not be without significance), (3) changes of order in a sequence (this may arise from a different sense of balance on the part of the learner, or even from what might be called a chiastic arrangement where one singer reverses the order given by the other), (4) addition of material not in a given text of the teacher, but found in texts of other singers in the district, (5) omission of material, and (6) substitution of one theme for another, in a story configuration held together by inner tensions.

(Lord 1960: 123)

The word "conservativeness" is worth taking note of in this quotation. It underlines the fact that even in a creative, innovative tradition like that of Yugoslavia, changes and transformations are subject to a set of rules and constraints. Lord's list of categories tallies very well with the illustrations given in this chapter, in particular with the extract from *Semetey*. Although there is only minimal variation in the example given from *Qïrmandäli*, categories like "omission," "substitution," "changing the sequence," and "addition" also apply, restricted, however, to the level of the line, stanza, and verse-passage. This fundamental similarity between variation in a tradition like that of the Kirghiz *manasčï* and in a tradition like that of the Karakalpak *baqsï* suggests that both traditions are indeed on the same typological scale, despite the obvious and important differences between them.

One factor which accounts for the similarities among the different Turkic traditions is the emphasis placed on memory in the training of a singer. The singers I have talked to have repeatedly stressed both their good memory and the fact that they started learning epic poetry early in life, when their capacity for retaining what they had heard was best. They also talked of learning from a teacher, sometimes their father or a relative, often another singer. Mamay in particular stressed the fact that he had to apply himself to reproduce correctly what his father and brother told him. Žumabay-žïraw also emphasized his apprenticeship. He only sings the *dastans* which he learned from his teacher. Everything he knows he attributes to his three-year stay with Esemurat-žïraw Nurabullaev in Kungrad.

Having been an apprentice to a teacher means that the future singer learns the art of performing epic poetry by learning specific epic poems.

It is like learning the violin not by practicing scales and exercises but by following the Suzuki method of playing individual songs and melodies from memory. This leads, it should be stressed, to a definite textual awareness on the part of the singer. Even if a singer admits, or boasts, of adapting his performance to audience and circumstance, he will usually stress that in any case he performs the epic as he has learned it from his teacher. When I recorded *Qoblan* from Žumbabay-žïraw in 1990, the singer at first started to sing a shortened version of the epic, thinking that we would not have enough time for the performance of the complete epic. When it turned out that it was possible to spend several days together for the recording of the *dastan*, the singer insisted on singing a fuller version of the first part again, as this was the epic in the form it had been handed down to him by his teacher.

Although the conscious effort on the part of the apprentice singer to "memorize" and reproduce what he has heard "without mistakes" forms the basis of his training, the "qualified singer" is not a mere "memorizer." We associate with memorization learning by rote, as when an actor learns his part, a student a poem assigned by his teacher, or a Moslem the Koran. Lord's parallel to the acquistion of natural language is illuminating in this context:

> When we speak a language, our native language, we do not repeat words and phrases that we have memorized consciously, but the words and sentences emerge from habitual usage. This is true of the singer of tales working in his specialized grammar. He does not "memorize" formulas, any more than we as children "memorize" language. He learns them by hearing them in other singers' songs, and by habitual usage they become part of his singing as well. Memorization is a conscious act of making one's own, and repeating, something that one regards as fixed and not one's own. The learning of an oral poetic language follows the same principles as the learning of language itself, not by the conscious schematization of elementary grammars but by the natural oral method.
>
> (Lord 1960: 36)

Only in an oral tradition where a text or a corpus of texts has been preserved without alteration or changes from generation to generation, as is alleged of the Old Indic *Vedas*, is memorization in the strict sense a meaningful concept.[72] If there are no manuscripts with a fixed text

---

[72]On the role of memorization in the *Vedas* compare M. B. Emeneau's remarks in his study of the Toda oral poets: "More important than the details is the tradition that the whole immense corpus of Vedic literature was both composed and transmitted

to which the singer can refer, the epic poetry he has heard will itself have been variable. Even if it is the singer's concern not to stray from the tradition, he invariably deviates from it when he adapts his performance to his audience. To have learned epic poetry in the traditional way enables a singer to have his repertory at his fingertips. When I asked Žumabay-žïraw which of the three *dastans* in his repertory he would prefer to perform, he replied: "For me singing the three *dastans* is like eating bread!" ("Üš dästannï aytuw maġan pätir žegendey!"). He is able to begin and continue at any place in any epic poem of his repertory. The same is true of the performance of *Qurman-bek* by Mämbet Sart. After an interruption of several hours in the course of the recording session, the singer started again where he had left off without hesitation or indecision.

Somewhat different is, however, the case of the singer who is not in "complete control" of his repertory. The story of the Karakalpak singer Žaqsïlïq-žïraw Sïrïmbetov is also interesting in this connection. Žaqsïlïq (b. 1945) is a famous *qobïz*-player in Karakalpakistan. He performs regularly extracts from heroic poetry, but is not regarded as a fully traditional singer. Žaqsïlïq became first interested in becoming a singer when, as a ten-year-old shepherd boy, he heard a singer called Erežip-žïraw sing in his village. In 1961, sixteen years old, Žaqsïlïq took part in a singing competition in Nukus. At that time a famous singer, Qïyaz-žïraw Qayratdinov (1903-1983), noticed the boy and allowed him to study with him. Qïyaz-žïraw is famous for his version of *Edige*, which has only recently been edited.[73] Studying in this case meant, however, that Žaqsïlïq, who was still in school, could only stay for two and a half months with the singer. Over the following years he kept going back to Qïyaz-žïraw, staying with him for a period of one to two months at a time. Žaqsïlïq learned the musical side of the profession from his teacher, i.e. the art of playing the *qobïz* and of singing in the *žïraw*-manner, but owing to the curtailed stays with Qïyaz-žïraw he never learned a complete epic poem. Žaqsïlïq, however, possesses a

without any recourse to writing. Oral transmission down to the present day by memorization is undoubted — but at the same time suspect, since it is clear that there has at times been recourse to good old manuscripts to correct corrupted oral tradition." Emeneau 1964: 331. On the role of memorizing in modern Indian oral traditions see Smith 1977. On the "memorizing singer" see also Lord 1987b.

[73]See Bayniyazov, Maqsetov 1990.

manuscript, in which he recorded extracts from his teacher's version of *Edige*. It is this manuscript together with what he learned from his teacher which serves as the basis of his performance.

Similar cases are singers whose memory fails them. The Kazakh *aqïn* Müslimbek Sarqïtbay-ulï was unwilling to perform the *dastan Qïz Žibek* in 1989, because he had not sung it for a long time and hence had forgotten many lines. The Kazakh *aqïn* Šeryazdan Soltanbay-ulï regretted that there was no more interest in his art in Urumchi and that he was consequently out of practice and had forgotten a great deal. The variant of *Bögenbay* I recorded from him differs indeed from his earlier published variant mostly in the omission of lines and whole stanzas. The Karakalpak *baqsï* Genžebay-baqsï, from whom I had recorded extracts in 1983, was incapable of performing a complete *dastan* in 1990, giving his forgetfulness as an excuse for his refusal to sing.

"Remembering" and "forgetting" are, however, not the only differences between a singer like Žumabay-žïraw and Genžebay-baqsï. While the former is a fully traditional singer in that his repertory is entirely dependent on oral tradition, the latter has also been influenced by written tradition. Like Žaqsïlïq-žïraw, Genžebay has manuscript versions in his possession of the *dastans* he can perform. Manuscripts are also repeatedly mentioned by other singers. When asked how he learned *Bögenbay*, Šeriyazdan Soltanbay-ulï replied that as a boy of between ten and twelve years he lived with a teacher, Muallim Näžip-qan, to help him with his work in the house. This teacher loved Kazakh oral poetry and gave Šeriyazdan a manuscript of *Bögenbay* to read. He was given this manuscript in 1948/49, an old manuscript, whose last pages were missing. In the August of 1951 he sang the whole epic, all four parts, to about two hundred listeners. It took him about eight hours, with two intervals for drinking tea.[74] Mämbet Sart mentioned that his own pupils use manuscript versions and even tape-recordings of his variant of *Qurmanbek*.

The influence of a written tradition on a singer is certainly a major force in the shaping of a tradition where the singers endeavor to

---

[74]*Bögenbay* is an epic poem on an 18th-c. hero. Šeriyazdan Soltanbay-ulï's version comprises about 4,000 verse-lines and 213 pages in print; see Balïqšï-ulï et al. 1984: 74-287. As far as the singer was aware, he was the only singer in the Altay region who knew this poem. When the government sent scholars to collect oral epic poetry in 1962, they were referred to him as a well-known singer.

preserve the transmitted poetry as closely as possible. The awareness of textual identity is enhanced by the existence of written texts (whether in manuscript form or as printed editions). Written texts could also influence illiterate singers by being read out aloud to them; the popular narrator, called *qïssa-xan* in Central Asia, was one of the main channels for the spread of the knowledge of written texts. Singers, in particular Kazakh *aqïns*, have also been influenced by popular editions of Turkic epics from Central Asia, which were printed in Kazan in the 19th c. These editions are comparable to European chapbooks or 19th-c. lithographic editions of Turkish romances, reprinted as popular books to this day. In Khorezm the influence of written texts has been particularly strong, fostering the rise of singers in whom oral and written traditions are inextricably combined. One of the reasons for the textual closeness between the variants of *Qïrmandäli* discussed above is undeniably the existence of manuscript versions, guaranteeing as it were the conservative nature of textual transmission.[75]

Exclusive reliance on written material will lead to a singer who is no more than a "memorizing actor." It is difficult to draw the line, however, between such a "memorizing singer" and a "reproductive," "text-oriented" singer, whose art has been heavily influenced by written tradition. What separates these two singers is neither the "reproductive" quality of their poetry nor their having recourse to manuscripts or otherwise fixed texts. The criteria for distinguishing the singer from the actor seem to me to be: (1) the way an epic poem is learned and (2) the setting in which it is performed. As long as a singer learns his repertory in the traditional way, i.e. from a teacher, he stands in an oral tradition, even if his training has been imperfect (as in the case of Žaqsïlïq-žïraw), has been supported by manuscripts (as in the case of Genžebay-baqsï) or uses modern methods like tape-recordings (as in the case of Mämbet Sart's pupils). Of equal importance is the setting of the singer's performance. As a living art, the performance of oral epic poetry — in all its forms — presupposes an appreciative audience, appreciative not only of the singer's skill as a narrator and performer,

---

[75]On the influence of Kazan editions of Kazakh epic poems on their transmission see Reichl 1989c; on the influence of written tradition on Turkmen and Uzbek romances see Mirbadaleva 1975. For a discussion of the mixture of oral and written forms of transmission in many "oral literatures" see Finnegan 1974; the influence of written texts on Yugoslav singers has also been discussed by Lord; see Lord 1960: 124ff.; Lord 1967.

but also of the tales and, particularly in the case of the heroic epic, of the ethos with which it is imbued. When a singer limits his performance to events of a purely folkloristic nature, such as performances on the stage, the link with oral tradition has definitely been severed.

Textual closeness between variants as in *Qïrmandäli* cannot be simply explained as the result of written influence. The very structure of this type of epic poetry encourages a conservative transmission. As we have seen in an earlier chapter (see p. 159), the poetic appeal of this *dastan* lies in the songs, in particular in the song-contests. Similarly the art of the *baqsï* consists not only in telling a tale, but also, and even primarily, in singing the songs that make up the *dastan*. He is as much musician as storyteller, if not more so. These songs are often transmitted independently of their narrative context. An audience might not have time or leisure to listen to a whole *dastan* when a *baqsï* is present, but they will certainly have time and interest to listen to his singing of lyric songs and songs from the love-romances. The verse-parts of the *dastan*s are hence often performed and transmitted either as individual songs or as a sequence of songs. The situation is comparable to the oral transmission of lyric poetry or shorter narrative poetry, where the degree of textual stability is usually far greater than in longer narrative poetry.

This does not mean that romances, *dastan*s with lyrical verse-passages, are invariably transmitted more or less verbatim, while heroic epics, where a laisse-type verse arrangement predominates, are transmitted with less verbal accuracy and constancy. While in the Khorezm tradition Uzbek romances such as the *dastan Bazirgan* from the *Köroğlu/Göroğlï*-cycle are textually very close to corresponding Karakalpak and Turkmen versions, in the southern Uzbek tradition comparable love-romances such as *Kuntuğmiš* vary far more radically from variant to variant.[76] The influence of written textual transmission in Khorezm is one of the reasons for the differences between these two Uzbek traditions, but the conception of the singer differs also. In Khorezm the Uzbek *baxši* is, like the Karakalpak *baqsï*, in the first place a musician and it is his musical performance which is prized most highly; a manifestation of this shift from the singer of tales to the singer pure and simple is also the presence of other musicians at the *baxši*'s

---

[76]On *Bazirgan* see Reichl 1985b: 626ff.; on *Kuntuğmiš* see Reichl (forthcoming).

performance; the same can be said about the performance of the Karakalpak *baqsï*.

The conservative nature of textual variation is, as we have seen, not restricted to the transmission of romances like *Qïrmandäli* but is also found in the transmission of *dastan*s like *Šaryar* and even of Kirghiz epics like the various parts of the *Manas*-cycle. This conservativeness is explainable by the singers' training and it is possible through the development of what might be called the art of memory. Techniques of remembering are not only typical of oral societies. Frances Yates has devoted a study to the art of memory in Classical Antiquity, in the Middle Ages, and in the Renaissance, showing the manifold ways of structuring knowledge to make it easily remembered.[77] A great number of investigations carried out in the framework of oral-formulaic theory have revealed the mechanics of this art. The last chapter showed that the metrical structure of Turkic oral epic poetry, formulaic diction, parallelism, thematic patterning, and "runs," all contribute to make this type of poetry memorizable. For the Turkic singer of tales, just like his colleague in Yugoslavia, the plot and its various narrative divisions are also important elements for the process of storing an epic tale in his mind.[78] When I was recording *Qoblan* from Žumabay-žïraw on several noncontiguous occasions, the singer would go over the incidents we had already recorded by counting them out with his fingers and then proceed to enumerate the incidents still to come in order to calculate the length of the remaining recording time. The singer is helped in his awareness of the structural units of an epic poem by the structure of the epic itself, in which scenes of high tension and drama stand out as memorable events, "epic moments."[79]

The texts quoted above have also shown that one further way of ensuring a conservative oral transmission of an epic is by structuring the various passages in a clearly identifiable way. In the extract from *Semetey* we found a definite succession of events and, even more

[77]See Yates 1966.

[78]Compare Lord 1960: 94ff.

[79]This term was coined by A. T. Hatto in his introduction to the first volume of Hatto, Hainsworth 1980-89: "Epic poetry is apt to condense long-drawn tensions into brief scenes of dramatic power enhanced by visual magnificence..." (p. 4); compare also Hatto 1989b: 178ff.

surprising, verbal echoes between all three variants. These parallels were seen to consist in particular lexemes, strung together in the passage (*kerdirgen, sapta(t)ġan, qapta(t)ġan, ördürgön, qaqïldatqan*). These words are partly linked by similarities in sound, partly by an identical morphological structure (causative suffixes *-dir-/-dür-* and *-t-*, past participle in *-gen/-ġan/-gön*). The same phenomenon is found in the extract quoted from *Šaryar*; attention has been drawn in the analysis of this excerpt to the series *elšimen, tawšïman, awšïman, žawšïman* and *eplemege, seplemege, telitpege, eritpege*. In particular the last group of lexemes is fairly uncommon, almost manneristic, endowing this passage with a striking "verbal skeleton" to be "fleshed out" by an appropriate verbal context.

A different, but equally text-oriented, aid to memory is the technique found in the third illustration. Here the structural pattern of the contest-poem demands an "antiphonal" composition. Every stanza A calls for a counterpart stanza B, which means that the singer can learn this verse-passage as a sequence of mirror poems. Many dialogues in Turkic heroic epics and romances are structured on this model. Similar formal arrangements found in Turkic oral epic poetry are enumerations. When Rawšan in the Uzbek *dastan* of the same name comes to the town of Širwān, he asks for the hat-bazar where he knows his beloved is selling embroidered caps. The verse-passage consists virtually in stringing together stanzas on the model of "Here is the X-bazar, there is the Y-bazar, where is the hat-bazar?"[80] Type-scenes such as the arming of the hero, his ride through the desert etc. are generally structured by an enumeration of fixed elements, often expressed in specific lexemes or morphological forms (such as the *-ïllab*-series discussed on pp. 213ff.).

This list of devices is far from exhausting the singers' art of memory. Formulaic diction in its widest sense is clearly the main key to an understanding of this art. The discussion of the varieties of formulaic diction in the last chapter was introduced by a quotation from Nilsson's book on *Homer and Mycenae*, in which precisely this aspect of formulaic patterning was stressed. Formulaic diction has, however, also a poetic function. It is to the poetics of formulaic diction we must now turn in order to gain a fuller understanding of the singer's art.

---

[80]See Reichl 1985a: 94-99.

Chapter Nine

Rhetoric, Style, Narrative Technique

"Formulaic Rhetoric"

In a recent book on the interpretation of Older Germanic, in particular Old English, poetry in the light of "oral-formulaic theory," Alain
Renoir has coined the term "oral formulaic rhetoric" to convey both the
conventional nature and the stylistic effect of poetic diction. Renoir
argues that the shift in emphasis from composition to style frees the
study of earlier poetry from the controversial debate about its origin in
either writing or oral performance: "...prospective interpreters of such
ancient and mediaeval verse as reveals clearly oral-formulaic features
might often do well to disregard the obviously tantalizing question of
the actual mode of composition and to concentrate on the interpretation
of the text within the context of attested rhetorical practices of the oral-
formulaic tradition regardless of whether the lines on the page were
originally written in solitude or spoken before an audience."[1]   As
regards orally performed Turkic epic poetry, its origin in an oral milieu
is incontestable, although, as we saw in the last chapter, influences from
written forms of the epics must be taken into account. When interpreting Turkic oral epic poetry we do not need to establish its orality on the
basis of its formulaic nature. Unlike the situation in medieval or
classical literature, there is no "tantalizing question" about the mode
of composition of this type of poetry, even if we would wish to have more
detailed information on the composition and transmission of Turkic epic
poetry than is at present available. It is reasonable to suppose that the
presence of formulaic diction in Turkic oral epic poetry can be explained,
as in other traditions, in terms of its oral composition and transmis-

---

[1]Renoir 1988: 63.

sion. The various forms and levels of formulaic diction are certainly part of a singer's "art of memory." Formulaic diction is, however, not only a means to an end, but also an end in itself; whatever the original motivation for its genesis, it is the most salient stylistic trait of the epics as we have them. As a stylistic trait formulaic diction is an important element of textual structure; it is part of the conventions governing the oral epic and hence also part of the expectations the listeners bring to an epic performance. An understanding of Turkic oral epics as poetry would therefore be incomplete if attention were paid only to the functional aspect of formulaic diction, and its poetic effect as a stylistic phenomenon ignored.

Although we are justified in characterizing Turkic oral epic poetry as formulaic, "highly patterned" is probably a somewhat better term of description. As the patterning of language is one of the most fundamental characteristics of poetry in general, it is not surprising to find many similarities between Turkic oral epic poetry and other poetries, both oral and written. Parallelism, discussed earlier (see pp. 177ff.), is one of the patterns Turkic oral poetry shares with a wide variety of poetic traditions. Parallelistic structures, while found in all Turkic traditions, are a hallmark in particular of Kirghiz, Altaian, and Yakut epic poetry. I have quoted earlier the beginning of the Altaian epic *Kögütöy* (see p. 180); with this we might compare the first lines of another Altaian epic, *Altay-Buučay*. In one of the variants of this epic poem the hero (here called "Altay-Bučïy") is introduced as follows:

```
      Altï üyelü aq tayğanïŋ
      ayaŋ bolğon qoltïğïnda,
      d'ïlar-d'ïlbas kök talaydïŋ
      keen bolğon d'aqazïnda
5     attu-čuulu Altay-Bučïy d'urtap d'attï.
      Odorluğa malïn salğan,
      odïnduğa d'urtïn salğan,
      tebeelüge malïn salğan,
      tergeelüge d'urtïn salğan.
10    Ulaazïnaŋ uylar ičken,
      ulu-d'aan baatïr boldï,
      edžigineŋ elder ičken,
      erlu-d'aan kezer boldï.
                        (Surazakov 1961: 79)
```

On the glade at the foot
of the six-topped, white wooded mountain,
on the shore of the beautiful,

	evenly flowing blue sea,
5	there lived famous Altay-Bučïy.
	He put his cattle on the rich pasture,
	he erected his yurt on a place abounding in firewood,
	he put his cattle on the winter pasture,
	he erected his yurt on a place suitable for a *terge*.[2]
10	He was a great hero (*baatïr*),
	around whose yurt-base the cows drank;
	he was a mighty warrior (*kezer*),[3]
	at whose door the people drank.

This passage consists of three parallel series: lines 1 to 4 give the setting, lines 6 to 9 elaborate the geographical location, and lines 10 to 13 characterize the hero as rich in possessions, the lord and provider of his people. Each series contains two pairs, exhibiting strict grammatical parallelism. Where, as in this epic poem, longer stretches of text are built on parallelistic principles, there is a pronounced tension between movement and rest, flowing and halting. The idea expressed in the first half of the parallel structure is repeated and varied in the second half. In lines 6 to 7, for instance, Altay-Buučay (Bučïy) puts his cattle on a rich pasture and his yurt on a place abounding in firewood. The two following lines add nothing new to this: they take up the notion of the rich pasture again, varying it to a pasture suitable as winter pasture, whilst the place where the yurt is erected is now characterized as a place suitable for the erection of a palace-yurt. The effect of this "flowing and halting" is perhaps best understood by the reader familiar with the Old English stylistic device of variation. In *Beowulf* the narrative proceeds in a curiously forward and backward movement; instead of a steady forward flow, words and phrases are replaced by synonymous expressions, varying the semantic content of what has been said previously.[4] Two lines will illustrate this:

> Him ðā Scyld gewāt   tō gescæpwhīle
> felahrōr fēran   on Frēan wǣre.
> > (*Beowulf*, ll. 26-27)

> Then Scyld departed   to his destiny,
> the bold one set out to go   into the Lord's keeping.

---

[2] A *terge* is a palace or a palace-yurt.

[3] *Kezer* is literally "Caesar."

[4] On variation in *Beowulf* see Brodeur 1959: 39ff.

Scyld is taken up by *felahrōr, gewāt* by *fēran*, and *to gescœpwhīle* by *on Frēan wǣre*, resulting in a virtually parallelistic structure.

In the passage quoted from *Altay-Buučay* rhyme, alliteration, and parallelism interact to create an intricate pattern of sound and meaning. Vertical alliteration is found in lines 1-2 (*altï/ayaŋ*), 6-7 (*odorluġa/ odïnduġa*), 8-9 (*tebeelüge/tergeelüge*), 10-11 (*ulaazïnaŋ/ulu-d'aan*), and 12-13 (*edžiginen/erlu-d'aan*). The rhyming scheme is a—b—a—b—x—c—c—c—c—d—e—d—e, where the three rhyming groups agree with the three parallelistic sections of the passage. Rhyme and parallelism interact also in poetic traditions in which rigorous parallelism like that illustrated above is rare. The following two stanzas provide an example of strict patterning in Uzbek epic poetry. They come from a verse-passage in Ergaš Džumanbulbul-oġli's variant of *Rawšan*. Rawšan, one of Goroġli's grandsons, is setting out on his journey to Širwān to seek his beloved Zulxumār. When he arrives at the town-gate, he is questioned by his father Hasan:

Umrimga bahārim, senga yol bolsin?
Tālpingan šunqārim, senga yol bolsin?
Bir qozi, qočqārim, senga yol bolsin?
Nāwda osgan činārim, senga yol bolsin?
5   Sāġinsam xumārim, senga yol bolsin?

Bāġimda anārim, senga yol bolsin?
Qatārdagi nārim, senga yol bolsin?
Isfihān xandžarim, senga yol bolsin?
Elga e'tibārim, senga yol bolsin?
10   Sersāwda bāzārim, senga yol bolsin?[5]

Spring of my life, where are you going?
My falcon, beating your wings, where are you going?
My only lamb, my wether, where are you going?
My plane tree with sprouting branches, where are you going?
5   My most ardent desire, where are you going?

Pomegranate of my garden, where are you going?
My camel, walking in a caravan, where are you going?
My poniard, made in Isfahan, where are you going?
My honor among the people, where are you going?
10   My busy bazar, where are you going?

In this type of patterning we have a fixed part of the line, typically the second half, and a "middle rhyme." The "middle rhyme" is in *-ārim*,

---

[5]Zarif 1971: 68; for a translation of the whole passage see Reichl 1985a: 62-64.

i.e. a word ending in *-ār* (e.g. *bahār*, "garden") plus the suffix of the first person singular of the possessive pronoun (*-im*, "my"). The first part of the line is only loosely parallelistic (*umrimga*, "for my life," *bāġimda* "in my garden," *elga*, "for the people").

More common in Uzbek *dastans* is a different use of variation, repetition, and parallelism. This can be seen in the opening stanzas of Rawšan's ride to Širwān taken from the same *dastan*:

> Parwardigār panādi,
> hālin bilgan dānādi.
> Ātasidan duā ālib,
> Rawšan pālwān džonadi.

> 5   Mardni tuqqan enadi,
> enadan yagānadi.
> Ābro ber, deb yāš bačča,
> Širwān qarab džonadi.

> Kolda suqsur sonadi,
> 10   kattakolga qonadi.
> Ābro ber, deb bek Rawšan,
> yolga tušib džonadi.

> Kuysa yurak yānadi,
> sāwuq suwga qānadi.
> 15   Ābro ber, deb bek Rawšan
> Xumārni izlab džonadi.

> Mehtaraga suw ālib,
> čaqmāġiga quw ālib,
> yolga tušdi bek Rawšan,
> 20   ātasidan duā ālib.[6]

> The Creator is one's protector;
> he who knows his own condition is wise.
> After he had received his father's blessing,
> Rawšan the Strong set out on his journey.

> 5   His mother has given birth to a hero;
> he is his mother's only child.
> For the sake of honor,[7] the young child
> set out towards Širwān.

---

[6]Zarif 1971: 76; the whole verse-passage is translated in Reichl 1985a: 70-73.

[7]Lit. "Saying: 'Give honor!'"

       The wild duck swims on the lake,
10   settles on the big lake.
       For the sake of honor, Beg Rawšan
       set out on his way.

       If one burns (with love), the heart is in flames;
       one quenches thirst with cold water.
15   For the sake of honor, Beg Rawšan
       set out to look for Xumār.

       After he had poured water into his water pipe,
       after he had taken flint and tinder,
       Beg Rawšan set out on his way,
20   after he had received his father's blessing.

These stanzas, which have the rhyme-pattern a—a—b—a, fall into
halves; the first two lines differ from stanza to stanza, while lines 3 and
4 remain basically the same. In the second half of the stanza three facts
are stated: Rawšan has received his father's blessing; he sets out on his
journey; and he is eager to earn honor. These facts are both literally
repeated and varied in the passage quoted. Line 3 is repeated in line
20, line 11 in line 15. Line 11 is also varied in line 8, with *yāš bačča*,
"the young child," substituted for *bek Rawšan*, so that stanzas II, III,
and IV all have a virtually identical third line. In stanza V the rhyme
of the three previous stanzas is taken up, but the idea expressed by the
line is that of setting out on a journey rather than that of earning
honor: *yolga tušdi bek Rawšan*. The expression *yolga tušdi* is itself a
varied repetition of an earlier line, l. 12 *yolga tušib džonadi*, lit. "setting
out on his way he journeys." The rhyme-word *džonadi* is identical in
stanzas I to IV, thus enhancing the rondo-like character of this type of
verse-passage: as in a rondo a musical phrase is repeated, often with
variations, in the course of the piece, so here the same set of ideas are
expressed repeatedly, both with and without variations.[8]
     In a number of stanzas the introductory lines formulate a general
truth or present a nature image (I, III, IV). The interspersing of Uzbek
oral epic poetry with gnomic sayings and nature images has been
remarked upon earlier (see pp. 203f.). In particular the nature images

[8]A similar kind of repetitive patterning is found in one of the Serbo-Croatian
junačke pjesme in Vuk Karadžić's collection, *Marko pije uz ramazan vino*, "Marko
drinks wine on Ramazan"; see Đurić 1977: 318-320; translated in Ćurčija-Prodanović
1963: 68-70. M. Braun has aptly characterized this heroic song as a "kind of rondo in
words"; Braun 1961: 67.

— the rose opening up in the garden, the rose withering in autumn etc.
— are suggestive of the mood of a passage and reflect the emotional
state of the hero or heroine. Nature imagery (as e.g. in ll. 9-10) and
images like the fire of love (as in ll. 13-14) connect the *dastan* also to the
love-lyric. For the comparison of the lover with the nightingale and the
beloved with the rose, of the tears streaming from the eyes with a rain-
shower in spring, of the beautiful girl with a cypress and so on, parallels
can be found in both oral and Classical (Chaghatay and Persian) love-
poetry and love-romance.[9] Not all nature images derive from love-
poetry, however. Typical of Uzbek oral epic poetry are lines like the
following, all found in *Rawšan: Āt čāpilar baland tāġniŋ pastiga*, "The
horse gallops at the foot of the high mountain"; *Har hil isli bolar tāġniŋ
āġāči*, "The mountain tree has many kinds of scent"; *Qārli tāġda qalin
bitgan arčadi*, "On the snow-capped mountain the juniper grows
densely"; *Tāġlarniŋ bāši tuman*, "The mountain top is covered in mist";
Qirġiy degan qušlar bolar qiyāda, "The sparrow-hawk lives on the steep
cliff"; *Bahārda salqinli sāwuq tāġ yaxši*, "In spring a shadowy, cool
mountain is pleasant."[10] Nature images like these might not be
directly connected to the narrative, but they enrich the poetic texture
of the narrative by their appeal to the listener's own experience of
nature. It *is* pleasant to sit in the cool shade of a mountain when it is
hot, it *is* delightful to smell the scent of a mountain tree. The galloping
horse, the wild duck, and the sparrow hawk are all suggestive of the
heroic milieu of the tale: the hero riding on his horse on a mission or
into battle, the hero hunting the wild duck, the hero likened in his
strength and agility to a wild animal. It is probably not too far-fetched
to compare the poetic effect of these lines to the nature images in
medieval poetry like the *Chanson de Roland*. Evocative lines like "*Halt
sunt li pui e li val tenebrus,/ les roches bises, les destreiz merveillus*" (The
mountains are high and the valleys dark,/ the rocks are greyish-brown,
the narrow mountain passes awesome) come to mind, which appear, with
variations, at three points in the narrative, where they adumbrate

[9]For examples see Reichl 1985a: 39ff.

[10]See Reichl 1985a: 41.

imminent disaster.[11] The use of parallel stanzas is another technique the *Chanson de Roland* shares with Uzbek *dāstān*-poetry.[12]

Repetitive and parallelistic devices like the ones illustrated so far are, as Victor Šklovskij and other Russian formalists have convincingly argued, moments of retardation in the flow of the narrative.[13] Strict parallelism as in the Altaian example creates mirror-like structures which endow the narrative with a measured, quasi-ceremonial pace. Refrain-like repetitions as illustrated by the last quotation from *Rawšan* create a circular structure, comparable to the musical form of the rondo or a *tema con variazioni*. In Uzbek romance the stanzaic verse-passages often have regular refrains, which enhance the lyrical nature of these passages. Refrain-like lines are, however, also found in nonstanzaic passages. An example from *Alpāmiš* was given earlier (see p. 202 on refrain-like lines like "Give advice!" in the council scene); their occurrence in Karakalpak epic poetry has also been noted (see p. 246 on refrain-like lines like "I am a matchmaker come from the khan").

The extract from the Karakalpak *dastan Šaryar* cited in Chapter Eight (pp. 238ff.) is also an example of a third type of repetition and variation, of what one might term "additive" or "embroidering" variation. When discussing the vizier's speech in the last chapter, I drew attention to a series of lines built on the formula "I have come to link/bring together etc." (*seplemege/ eplemege ... kelgenmen*). Here the successive images — linking together the rings of a coat of mail, uniting two sheep, melting iron, putting two lambs to a ewe etc. — can be seen as images for one and the same idea, union in wedlock. An idea, a situation is unfolded by various images and paraphrases. Under the same headings of "unfolding" and "embroidering" other instances of an additive style can be listed. In a type-scene from Fāzil Yoldāš-oġli's variant of *Alpāmiš* quoted in Chapter Seven, the following (largely parallelistic) lines occurred (see pp. 213f.):

---

[11]Lines 814-15, 1830-31, 2271-72; compare Le Gentil 1955: 153f.

[12]On parallel laisses in the *Chanson de Roland* compare Rychner 1955: 82ff. Repetition and parallel structures in the *Chanson de Roland* were studied as early as 1897 by A. N. Veselovskij; see Veselovskij 1940 [1897].

[13]Šklovskij acknowledges his debt to Veselovskij's study of psychological parallelism, Veselovskij 1940 [1898]; see Šklovskij 1969: 52/53ff. On the function of repetition in poetry see also Lotman 1972: 158ff.

Qir kelsa qilpillatdi,
arna kelsa irǵitdi,
or kelsa omganlatdi,
šuytip Hakim yol tārtdi.

(Zarif, Mirzaev 1979: 83)

When he came to a mountain, he made his horse jump over,
when he came to a river, he made him jump across,
when he came to a slope, he made him gallop.
In this manner Hakim went his way.

Objectively three different situations are described, but these three
situations add up to a description of one single event, the hero's ride
through the steppe.

Addition and "summation" are widespread stylistic traits of Turkic
oral epic poetry.[14] They underlie the composition of type-scenes such as
the arming of the hero and the saddling of his horse, where point after
point is enumerated and described (see pp. 205ff.). One form of summation is the cataloguing description, in particular the description of the
hero's horse (*ta'rif*; see below) and the description of a beautiful woman,
the *blason*, as in the "beauty-catalogue" quoted from the *Book of Dede
Qorqut* in Chapter Two (p. 49). An example from *Alpāmiš* is the
portrayal of Barčin's beauty:

Barčin turur hurday bolib,
tiši gawhar durday bolib,
džamāllari āyday bolib,
misli asāw tāyday bolib,
5   bir miŋ qoyli bāyday bolib,
kozi quralayday bolib,
korganlarniŋ koŋli tolib....

(Zarif, Mirzaev 1979: 57)

Barčin is standing there like a houri:
her teeth are like gems and pearls,
her beauty is like that of the moon,
she is like an untamed filly,
5   she is like a rich man with a thousand sheep,
her eyes are like those of the young fallow deer;
those who see her rejoice in their hearts....

Similar descriptions can be found in most Turkic epics. In *Rawšan*
Zulxumār's beauty is like that of the moon; she has languishing
narcissus eyes, almond-shaped eyelids, poniard-curved eyebrows, pearl-

---

[14]On addition, variation, and summation as stylistic devices see Killy 1972: 35ff.

like teeth etc.[15]   In *Qambar* Nazïm is elaborately described in the
following terms:

      Tawïs qustay türlenip,
      qoŋïrawday altïn küŋrenip,
      erteli-keš serwenge
      šïġadï maylap šašïn da.
45   Žännetten šïqqan xorlarday
      forïmïna qarasaŋ,
      qïzïqpastay qay adam
      ol Nazïmnïŋ našïna?
      Süyegi asïl dür edi,
50   qudaydïŋ özi biledi,
      on törtinši ayday bop
      tüsedi kimniŋ qasïna?
      Alpïs somdïq är kezi
      üstine asïl kiygizdi,
55   žorġadan žegip qara kök
      küymeli arba mingizdi.
      Közi tüsken bendeniŋ
      žüregin ottay küygizdi.
      Ašïlġan güldey nurlanïp
60   qïlïġïmen süygizdi.
                  (Äwezov [Auezov], Smironova 1959: 37)

      Showing a play of colors like a peacock,
      resounding like a golden bell,
      she promenaded in the mornings and in the evenings,
      her hair made shiny with pomade.
45   What man, looking at her figure,
      resembling that of a houri come from paradise,
      will not become intoxicated
      by Nazïm's opiate?
      Her bones are made of precious pearls,
50   God himself knows it.
      Having become like the moon in its fourteenth day,
      on whose brow will (her glance) settle?
      She was dressed in a precious robe,
      made of cloth, at sixty rubles the ell,
55   and seated in a coach,
      to which a black-grey ambling horse was harnessed.
      Whenever someone cast a glance at her,
      She made his heart go up in flames.
      Shining like a rose in bloom,
60   she made everybody fall in love with her.

---

[15]See Reichl 1985a: 39f.

A description telescoped into an attribute becomes an *epitheton ornans*. Many of these epithets occuring in Turkic oral epic poetry are as in Ancient Greek and Old Germanic epic poetry "static." As Hector is κορυθαίολος ("with a shining helmet") and Beowulf *sigor-ēadig* ("victorious") so Qambar is *arïstan tuwġan* ("lion-born") or Manas *qabïlan tuuġan* ("tiger-born"). There is a difference, however, between the use of static epithets in Greek and Old English epic poetry: in Old English the epithet is not uniquely linked to a particular character, as is generally the case in the Homeric epics, but rather to a person's function, as hero, king, enemy, beloved and so on.[16] In the various traditions of Turkic oral epic poetry both uses are found. While many epithets in Kirghiz epic poetry, in particular in the 19th-century versions of the *Manas*-trilogy, are as in the Homeric epics linked to particular characters, epithets found in other traditions, as in Uzbek, Karakalpak, or Kazakh epic poetry, are predominantly of the "functional" kind as in *Beowulf*. For all its traditionality, formulaic diction in Turkic oral epic poetry is both varied and multiform. John Smith characterizes the Rajasthani oral epic of *Pābūjī* as extremely stylized:

> Whenever similar events occur, they are described in the same formulaic words; and similar events occur all the time. Allowing for substitution of proper names as appropriate, every battle in *Pābūjī* is the same battle, every journey the same journey, every meeting the same meeting.
>
> (Smith 1987: 598)

Although the characters in a Turkic epic are often types and their actions and feelings prototypal — Rawšan's love is the love of an ideal lover, Alpāmiš's valor is the valor of an ideal hero — stylization to such an extreme degree is certainly not typical of Turkic oral epic poetry. The highly patterned style, of which some elements have been described in the foregoing paragraphs, leaves enough room for variation and idiosyncrasy, both from the standpoint of the singer and that of the tradition.

---

[16]On some epithets see above pp. 185ff.; on the difference in the use of epithets between *Beowulf* and the Homeric poems see Whallon 1969: 95ff.

Characters

To characterize Rawšan as the ideal lover and Alpāmiš as the ideal hero is not to say that the protagonists in Turkic oral epic poetry are by definition idealized figures. Alpāmiš is different from Qambar, both are quite unlike Manas, and all three have little in common with Altay-Buučay. These various heroes represent different conceptions of the heroic and they exhibit idiosyncratic character traits, positive and negative, which mark them off from other heroes in other epics and other traditions. The heroes of the *Manas*-cycle, especially of the older versions from the 19th century, reflect the ethos of a (still) heroic society; they are of different stature from the heroes of epic traditions for which heroism is no longer a reality of life:

> The episodes of the *Manas*-cycle constitute a mode of heroic epic poetry that deserves the term 'existential' in the highest degree. The extreme precariousness of Manas's line symbolises the extreme precariousness of the Kirghiz tribes, hemmed in in their lofty mountains as they were by vastly superior enemies: by the Kalmak, then by the latters' conquerors, the Chinese; by the Kazakh hordes; by the Central Asian Khanates, in particular Kokand; and lastly by the Russians of the White Padishah.
>
> (Hatto 1979: 108)

While keeping these differences in mind, we can nevertheless also see similarities in the way the heroes are presented in different Turkic traditions of oral epic poetry. Although the protagonists are neither simply idealizations nor mere abstractions, they are generally types rather than individual characters. Heroes like Alpāmiš or Manas, heroines like Barčin or Qanïkey, companions like Qaradžān or Almambet, adversaries like Tāyči-xān or Qoŋurbay are essentially what E. M. Forster has called "flat characters":

> Flat characters were called "humours" in the seventeenth century, and are sometimes called types, and sometimes caricatures. In their purest form, they are constructed round a single idea or quality: when there is more than one factor in them, we get the beginning of the curve towards the round. The really flat character can be expressed in one sentence such as "I never will desert Mr Micawber." There is Mrs

Micawber — she says she won't desert Mr Micawber; she doesn't, and there she is.[17]

When we look at Alpāmiš or Manas, at Barčin or Qanïkey we can certainly see "the beginning of the curve towards the round," but their one-dimensionality is nevertheless their most distinguishing trait.[18]

One of the signs of a "flat character" is his functionality. In Turkic oral epics we find a particular configuration of characters. The relationship between the various *dramatis personae* can be likened to that between the figures in a game of chess. Every figure has its clearly defined function — the hero, the opponent, the helper, the heroine — and every move is prescribed by the rules of the game: the hero wins the bride and overcomes the aggressor; his companion acts as helper; his opponent resorts to the help of traitors and witches; the heroine is courageous and faithful to the hero. In this the characters of Turkic oral epic poetry resemble those of the folktale. Like these they never become insane, because "they have no depth, only surface."[19] This can be illustrated by some of the major protagonists in the epics summarized in Chapter Six.

If we look at a hero like Qambar we find that very little is said about him. He is of noble origin (his father Älimbay was a mighty khan), but his tribe has become impoverished through circumstances we are not told.[20] The longest description of his physical appearance is that in ll. 251ff., quoted in Chapter Six, from which it emerges that he had a

---

[17]Forster 1962: 75. For a discussion of Forster's distinction between "flat" and "round characters" in structuralist terms see Chatman 1978: 131ff. On character in narrative compare also Scholes, Kellogg 1966: 160ff.

[18]In the following the discussion is mainly focused on the characters of the epics summarized in Chapter Six, i.e. on figures such as Qambar, Alpāmiš, and Göroğlï. In comparing these figures to the protagonists of other epics and epic traditions my intention is to underline the typical; a careful interpretation of individual epics will, of course, also reveal many features which are unique to one epic or to one epic tradition only. The singular character of older Kirghiz epic poetry has been repeatedly stressed by A. T. Hatto; on plot and character in mid-nineteenth-century Kirghiz epic poetry see especially Hatto 1979.

[19]Lüthi 1981: 17.

[20]This lack of information might be partly due to Divaev's text, which shows a number of lacunae. Qambar says during his first meeting with Nazïm that his older brother had squandered all his possessions and left him nothing but his black horse with the white spot on its forehead (*qara qasqa at*); ll. 550-51; Äwezov [Auerzov], Smirnova 1959: 48.

golden forelock and that his character was more tender than that of a
girl (see pp. 148f.). Nothing is related of his birth and youth, nor of his
life after his marriage to Nazïm. He appears in five scenes in Divaev's
variant of *Qambar*. After having been described as a skillful hunter
and beneficial provider of food for his clan, Qambar's courage is first put
to the test in a dangerous hunting expedition, when he encounters and
successfully shoots a tiger. In the scene immediately following the tiger
hunt, Qambar and Nazïm meet for the first time, their interview being
brought to an abrupt end by Nazïm's older brothers. Qambar recedes
then into the background of the narrative, when the Kalmuck khan
asks for Nazïm's hand and lays siege to her father Äzimbay's encampment. The hero reappears in three scenes towards the end of the epic
poem, first when Äzimbay sends a delegation to ask for his help, then
when Kelmembet, the Kalmuck khan's messenger, summons Qambar
to his master, and finally when Qambar fights against the Kalmuck
khan and his men. During his tête-à-tête with Nazïm, Qambar shows
singular restraint, both in refusing to accept Nazïm's invitation to stay
with her and in not stooping to the level of her brothers' degrading
insults. When the delegation from Äzimbay arrives at Qambar's *awïl*,
the hero receives them courteously, generously offering them his
hospitality despite the straitened circumstances in which he lives.
When Qambar realizes the intent of their embassy, he not only forgives
the insult he had suffered from Äzimbay's sons, but is immediately
ready to come to their rescue. Only when Kelmembet appears as a
messenger from the Kalmuck khan and, without getting down from his
horse, commands Qambar to hasten to the khan, does the hero lose his
calm and composed frame of mind:

> Bul sözdi esitip Qambardïŋ
> 1495 qayratï suwday tasadï,
> žolbarïstay ïŋranïp,
> šïbïqtay beli buralïp,
> qaharmen žerdi basadï.
>   (Äwezov [Auezov], Smirnova 1959: 70)

> When Qambar heard these words,
> 1495 his mettle began to overflow like (boiling) water;
> roaring like a tiger,
> twisting his waist like a twig,
> he stamped the ground in anger.

When Qambar arrives at the khan's yurt, he requests Qaraman to return to his homeland. On the khan's refusal Qambar challenges him to single combat, not without first boasting of his courage in true heroic manner. Qambar and Qaraman fight with one another fiercely like two camel stallions; when the khan tumbles down from his horse, Qambar's battle rage gets the better of him and he pursues the khan's soldiers mercilessly:

Arïstan tuwġan Qambar-bek
1745   aš böridey žalaqtap
       araladï qonïstï.
                    (Äwezov [Auezov], Smirnova 1959: 75)

Greedy like a hungry wolf
1745   Beg Qambar, born as a lion,
       traversed the encampment.

Only after his bloodthirst has been satiated does he sit down to rest:

1770   Qalmaqtï qïrïp-žoydï qanïn šašïp,
       dušpandï men-mensigen qoydï basïp.
       Awlïna Äzimbaydïŋ keldi qaytïp
       mïsalï darïyaday köŋili tasïp.
       Dem alïp aq ordada otïr edi
1775   üstine Nazïm kirdi amandasïp.
                    (Äwezov [Auezov], Smirnova 1959: 76)

1770   He cut down and massacred the Kalmucks and shed their blood,
       he threw down the bragging enemy.
       When he came back to Äzimbay's encampment,
       his heart was full like an overflowing river.
       He sat down in the white *orda* (palace-yurt) to take a rest,
1775   when Nazïm entered and greeted him.

At this point the love-theme from the beginning of the epic is taken up again, and Qambar is finally described as a lover:

1782   Otïrdï sonda Qambar-bek šattanïp,
       ašïqtïq žügerinde ottay žanïp.
                    (Äwezov [Auezov], Smirnova 1959: 76)

1782   Then Beg Qambar was sitting there, filled with joy,
       the love in his heart burning like a fire.

Feelings such as anger, battle rage, and love are briefly described, and traits of character such as valor, honesty, and reliability mentioned, but for all that there is little psychological complexity in the portrayal of the hero. He comes to life not in scenes of reflexion and introspection but

of action and spirited dialogue. Qambar is basically a type and has the
effect on the listener (and reader) that E. M. Forster ascribes to a "flat
character": as his psychological make-up is clearly structured by a small
number of distinctive features he is easily recognized and easily
remembered.[21]

The same is true of heroes such as Alpāmiš/Alpamïs/Alpamïš or
Köroğlu/Göroğlï. Alpāmiš, in Fāzil's version of the *dastan*, grows to
somewhat fuller stature than Qambar, simply on account of the greater
complexity of the plot. We have the beginning of a heroic biography
when the hero's miraculous conception, his heroic strength in childhood,
and the circumstances of receiving his name are described; but as in
Qambar the hero's life after he has successfully completed his tasks is
not related. The double structure of the narrative creates a greater
variety of situations in which the hero is put to the test, but there is
never a shadow of doubt that Alpāmiš will behave in a way worthy of
a hero and that he will succeed in the end. Alpāmiš does, however, at
one stage let himself be deceived by the hag Surxayil. This leads to
the destruction of his companions and to his own imprisonment. As the
incident is presented in the *dastan*, the success of Surxayil's machina-
tions is entirely due to her skill as a sorcerer and does not reflect
negatively on Alpāmiš; there is no flaw involved in the hero's character,
nor is his capture the result of *hubris* or an excess of courage. As the
plot of *Alpāmiš* is more complicated than that of *Qambar*, Alpāmiš's
feelings are somewhat more varied than Qambar's. The hero is not only
depicted as a valiant and invulnerable warrior, but also as a lover and
a "man of feeling." When Alpāmiš returns, he is moved by the
miserable condition his relatives are forced to live in. On meeting his
son Yādgār, abused and tormented by the usurper Ultāntāz, Alpāmiš
is not ashamed to show his tears. Disguised as "Grandfather" Qultāy
he tells his son:

> Kozdan yāšim munčāq-munčāq tizildi,
> ustixān emranib, bağrim ezildi,
> xafa qildim, qaytay, senday qozimdi,
> ātam dema, menïŋ koŋlim buzildi....
> (Zarif, Mirzaev 1979: 341)

> The tears are flowing from my eyes like beads,
> my limbs are trembling, my heart is aching;

---

[21]See Forster 1962: 75ff.

I made you sad, my lamb, what can I do?
Don't say: "My father," else my heart will break in two....

There is pathos in the singer's elaboration of the hero's reunion with his
family, but there are also humorous traits, in particular in Alpāmiš's
scoffing song-dialogue with the usurper's mother Bādām.

The hero's biography is complete in the *Köroğlu/Göroğlï*-cycle.
Although not all singers know all the branches of this cycle and
although the recording of the cycle is fragmentary in the case of some
traditions, the cycle as such encompasses Köroğlu's/Göroğlï's complete
life, from birth to death, reaches even beyond the hero's life into that of
his adoptive sons and their children. The hero's miraculous birth is
typical of the eastern versions, where we also find a transformation of
the hero from a noble bandit-minstrel to a Central Asian feudal lord,
ruling in splendor and luxury (see pp. 322ff.). Due to the multiplicity
of variants recorded from a great number of Turkic as well as non-
Turkic traditions, the figure of Köroğlu/Göroğlï has many faces. He
impresses by his heroic deeds, his strength and valor, but he can also be
found in embarrassing situations which are not always to his credit. In
Qïrmandäli Göruğlï has to cede the prize to another singer and his
pupil, and he cuts a sorry figure when he tries to cover up his failure by
lying to his wife (see above pp. 157ff.). In another incident, Köroğlu is
surprised by his enemy Reyhan Arab and his confederates, while he is
attempting to abduct Perizade, the daughter of Ahmed Pasha of Kars.
He flees to the top of a church and is only saved from his predicament
when Awaz arrives to do battle with the Turks besieging Köroğlu and
kills Reyhan Arab.[22] In another branch of the cycle, "Köroğlu and
Princess Dünya," Köroğlu is treacherously captured and thrown into a
dungeon in Scutari. When his liberators arrive, they find that he has
eaten so heartily that rescuing him from the pit is no easy matter:

> They lowered into the well some dozen ropes tied together, which
> cracked more than once under the enormous weight, which was slowly
> hoisted up by some forty hands. Issa-Bally and even Dunah Pasha
> [Princess Dünya] were obliged to lend their aid, because Kurroglou, fed
> so liberally, had got as fat as a buffalo. Great was their joy when first
> his huge head appeared, and afterwards his giant elbows leaned upon
> the brink of the well. Issa kissed his master's hands. They brought

[22]See Meeting VIII in Chodzko 1842: 195-218.

immediately Kyrat and his arms, and with the greatest difficulty
buckled the armour upon the fattened limbs of the robber.

(Chodzko 1842: 330)

Humorous situations and grotesque traits, here applied to the hero
himself, are fairly common in Turkic epic poetry. They are often
connected with particular personages, such as the *köse*, a man with
little or no beard. Aldar-köse, "the deceitful *köse*," is a stock figure in
Kazakh folktales, also found in Karakalpak and Kirghiz folklore, whose
pranks are similar to those of Hodža Nasreddin and similar characters
in Turkish, Persian, Uzbek etc. anecdotes. In the Uzbek *dastan*
Rawšan, the hero encounters such a *köse* (Uzbek *kosa*) when he is on his
way to his beloved:

> Rawšanxān qarasa, bir kosa: džuda kohna bolib ketgan pir kosa, uč
> yuzdan āšgan, tort yuzga yānašgan, džuda qari kosa, yā baččaġar
> yildan adašgan, balki beš yuzga kirgan, daqyānus korgan, džami el-
> xalqqa firib bergan; dāim džuwānbāzlik, bedanabāzlik bilan umrini
> otkazgan uyiŋ kuygur. Čekkasidan tarlān āčgan, iyaginiŋ gošti qāčgan,
> qāšlari osgan, kozini bāsgan; iyaginiŋ ortasida bitta tuki bār ekan, u
> ham bir qarič bolib osgan, bu yālġiz sāqālga neča qimmat bahā tāš-
> lardan tešib āsgan. Burniniŋ suwi šorġalab, mingan āti yorġalab,
> Rawšanbekniŋ āldidan čiqa keldi.

(Zarif 1971: 115-116)

Rawšanxān saw that (the man on the horse) was a *köse*. He was a
very ancient, venerably old *köse*. He was an extremely aged *köse*, who
had passed three hundred years and was nearing his four hundredth
year. Maybe the scoundrel had made a mistake in reckoning his age
and he was already approaching five hundred. He was as old as
Methuselah[23] and played his tricks on all and sundry. May he be
cursed who had spent his whole life receiving pleasure from young boys
and quail fights! He had blotchy temples, a chin with hardly any flesh,
bushy eyebrows, and squinting eyes. There was one single hair in the
middle of his chin, which had grown one span; on this one-haired beard
he had threaded a number of valuable gems. With a running nose, his
horse in an ambling pace, he appeared before Rawšanbek.

The *köse* demands money from the hero and, as Rawšan is not willing
to give him any, deceitfully puts a lasso around the hero's neck and
pulls him along. Rawšan manages to get hold of the *köse*'s saber, cuts
off his head, and throws it into the air. The *köse*'s head lands in the
oven of a baker, who, frightened to death, runs away from home
together with his wife. The grotesque traits of the figure of the *köse*

---

[23]Lit. "he had seen Diocletian."

are, as can be seen from this short summary, embedded in an equally
bizarre episode.[24]

Other fantastic and often humorous figures are the various old women
in Turkic epic poetry. Some of them are benevolent and merely
somewhat ridiculous in their appearance or behavior, such as the hag
Köroğlu stays with in "Köroğlu and Princess Nighara" summarized in
Chapter Six (see pp. 153ff.). The old women in *Rawšan* are also
basically of this type; one of them has only a stump of a tongue and
cannot pronounce certain sounds. The same speech defect is used to
ridicule the usurper's mother in some versions of *Alpamïš*.[25] Many of
these hags are, however, malevolent, such as Surxayil in Fāzil's variant
of *Alpāmiš*. Surxayil is called a *mastān*, a word which occurs for the
same type of figure also in other Turkic languages, as for instance in
Kazakh (*mïstan kempir*) or in some dialects of Tatar.[26] Rawšan is
warned of the *mastāns* in Širwān by his father at his departure to the
land of his beloved:

Xabardār bol, Širwānniŋ kop mastāni,
mastānlardan xabardār bol, Rawšandžān!
(Zarif 1971: 75)

Beware of the many *mastāns* in Širwān,
beware of the *mastāns*, dear Rawšan!

Even more dangerous than the *mastān* is, however, the *yalmāğiz*.
This type of witch appears mostly in folktales, but is also encountered
in epics which are in plot closely connected to folktales. In the Uighur
dastan Čin Tömür Batur the hero's sister, Mäxtumsula, leaves the
house against her brother's orders to get embers to rekindle the extin-
guished fire in the hearth. When she enters a house to which a light,
shining in the dark, has guided her, she realizes with terror that she
has fallen into the hands of a "seven-headed *yalmawuz*" (*yette bašliq*

[24]On humorous traits in Uzbek *dastans* see Ašurov 1971.

[25]As e.g. in Fāzil's Uzbek variant (see Zarif, Mirzaev 1979: 373ff.) and the Kazakh
variant recorded from Mayköt Sandïbaev and Sultanqul Aqqožaev (see Äwezov
[Auezov], Smirnova 1961: 97ff.).

[26]See Tokarev et al. 1980-82: II, 189 (article "Mystán Kempír").

yalmawuz).[27] The *yalmāğiz* — this is the Uzbek form; the Uighur forms
are *yalmawuz* or *yälmüŋüč* — is a man-eating monster who is often
represented as a seven-headed ogress. This figure plays a prominent
role in the Kirghiz epic *Er Töštük* and the corresponding Kazkah
folktale *Er Töstük*, where her flight leads the hero on to his underworld
journey (see above pp. 136f.). Close parallels to this figure are the
*mangus*es of Mongolian folklore, many-headed monsters, with which the
ogress not only shares form and function, but possibly also her name.[28]

Although monster-like figures are also found among the hero's
adversaries (Qaraman, the Kalmuck khan in *Qambar*, is called a *diw*,
"demon"; he is also compared to Rustam, the giant-sized hero of
Ferdowsi's *Book of Kings*[29]), in Turkic epic poetry the enemy and the
hero are not so much distinguished by physical as by moral traits of
character. Qoŋurbay, Manas' chief antagonist, for instance, is of as
heroic a stature as Manas; it is his perfidious and deceitful behavior
that characterizes him as a negative hero.[30] Giant size and exaggerated physical features enter into the portrayal of both hero and adversary.
These features are also typical of the hero's companions. In *Rawšan* the
protagonist is helped by four scabby-headed brothers, of whom Aynāq,
the oldest, is so heavy that no horse or camel can carry him. The
scabby-headed men — called *kal* in Uzbek, *kel* in Turkish — derive in
this case from the extraordinary companions in the folktale and are
presented in the *dastan* as basically comical figures.[31] We might
compare with figures like these a comic character in the Serbo-Croatian

[27]Raxman et al. 1981: 27; for a translation of this folktale/*dastan* see Reichl 1986:
82-100; compare also Wingate 1930: 809-813; see *Motifs* G113 *Cannibal witch* and
G451 *Following witch's fire into her power*.

[28]On the *mangus* in Mongolian folklore (generally of male sex) see Lőrincz 1970;
Tokarev et al. 1980-82: II, 99-100 (article "Mángus"). The second element of Uzbek
yalmāğiz, Uighur *yälmawuz*, Kirghiz *džalmoğuz*, Kazakh and Karakalpak *žalmawïz*
etc. goes back to Common Turkic *-mağuz*, which might be related to Khalkha
Mongolian *maŋas*, Buryat *maŋad* etc. On the Turkic *yalmāğiz* see Tokarev et al.
1980-82: I, 439 (article "Žalmawïz Kempír").

[29]In l. 856; see Äwezov [Auezov], Smirnova 1959: 55.

[30]Compare Musaev 1979: 173ff. On the blurred line between protagonist and
antagonist in heroic epic poetry see Hatto 1989b: 243ff.

[31]Compare *Motif* F601 *Extraordinary companions*; on these comical figures in the
Uzbek *dastan* see Imāmov 1971.

Characters 291

heroic songs such as Tale of Orašac in Avdo Međedović's *Wedding of Smailagić Meho*. Tale of Orašac rides into battle in a fantastical outfit of tattered clothes and in the company of a standard-bearer who carries the standard upside down and a man in clerical garments carrying in one hand an enormous wine flask and in the other the Koran.[32]

Caricature and humor characterize the presentation of a number of figures in Turkic oral epic poetry. The description of Zulxumār's servant-girl Āqqiz (see the quotation on pp. 129f.) has a comical effect in the contrasts it evokes. Nazïm's brothers are described as thought-less hotspurs (Kazakh *tentek*), with the exception of Alšïoraz, her youngest brother, who speaks in favor of Qambar and later helps him in his fight against the Kalmucks. In a similar vein Surxayïl's seven sons are caricatured when they attempt to win Barčin's hand; again the youngest brother, Qāradžān, turns away from the others and sides with the hero. Of a more subtle nature are comic contrasts within one character such as that between Āzimbay's self-assured bearing when Kelmembet, the Kalmuck messenger, arrives for the first time, and his fainthearted subservience when the messenger returns in the role of a besieger:

```
        Ayağïn žerge paŋ basïp,
        manawrap közin zorğa ašïp,
765     Āzimbay šïqtï dalağa,
        turğanday bolïp uyqïdan.
        Āzimbay sonda söyleydi,
        ašuwï kelip azïraq.
        Beti ottay qabïnïp;
770     omïrawïn köterip
        nar buwraday šabïnïp....
                    (Äwezov [Auezov], Smirnova 1959: 53)
```

```
        Arrogantly treading the ground,
        hardly opening his eyes from indolence,
765     as if he had got up from sleep,
        Āzimbay came outside.
        Āzimbay then spoke.
        He flew into a rage easily;
        his face flashed like fire,
770     he raised his chest,
        raged like a camel stallion....
```

[32]See Lord 1974: 198f.

1070   Sol waqïtta Äzimbay
       türegeldi ornïnan,
       kökiregi kirildep,
       köziniŋ aldï iriŋdep,
       qayrat berdi özine
1075   "Kötere kör pirim!" — dep;
       üš sürinip žïğïldï.
       Är buwïnï dirildep,
       eki qolïn quwsïrïp
       esikten šïqtï dalaġa.

                    (Äwezov [Auezov], Smirnova 1959: 60)

1070   At that time Äzimbay
       rose from his seat,
       his chest groaning,
       his eyes full of pus.
       He plucked up courage
1075   and said: "Give help, my *pir*!"
       Thrice stumbling he fell down.
       Trembling in every limb,
       twisting his hands,
       he came out through the door.

The description of anger, as in Äzimbay's "grand entrance," is also a
favorite element of "formulaic rhetoric." Qaraman's fit of rage on
hearing of the failure of Kelmembet's first mission is sketched in the
following terms:

986   Žolbarïstay ïŋranïp,
       Qaraman qïldï qaharïn,
       aydaharday ïsqïrïp,
       betine žaydï zaharïn.

                    (Äwezov [Auezov], Smirnova 1959: 58)

986   Roaring like a tiger,
       Qaraman gave way to his anger.
       Hissing like a dragon,
       he let his venom flush his face.

When Awaz in *Rawšan* becomes angry he wriggles like a dragon and his
eyes glint like fire ("*adždarday tolğanib, kozlari ālāwday yānib*"), while
his foster father Goroğli's moustache stiffens like a saber and his cheeks
puff up like big sacks ("*šāmurti šāpday, har urti bir katta qāpday
bolib*").[33] Later, when Rawšan is taunted by a group of young men, he
flies into a rage:

---

[33]Zarif 1971: 57, 59.

...šerday hurpayib, yolbarsday čirpinib, qāplanday džimiyib, xezlanib-tezlanib, qahri kelib, adždahār yilānday zahri kelib, bahādirliklari uyġānib, otday yānib, ālāwday qābinib, bir quti gugurtday bolib, ot ālib ketganday boldi.

(Zarif 1971: 95)

...strutting like a lion, puffing himself up like a tiger, scowling like a leopard, burning to fight, overcome by anger, filled with poison like a dragon and a snake, his heroism bursting forth, burning like a fire, flaring up like a blaze, becoming like a box of matches, he was transformed into someone who had been set on fire.

Similar details can be found in other Turkic epics,[34] but also in the Serbo-Croatian epic poems, as when Meho angrily enters the high judge's chamber in the *Wedding of Smailagić Meho*: "the hero's hair, bristling like a wolf's fur in December, had raised his plumed cap, and he gnashed his teeth in his jaws, even as a saw when men cut wood, and from his teeth living fire darted."[35]

Hyperbole is a stylistic trait closely associated with many traditions of heroic poetry and its presence in Turkic oral epic poetry is hence to be expected.[36] There is, however, a difference in degree between the epics of the "central" and "southwestern traditions" — Turks, Azerbaijanians, Turkmens, Kazakhs, Karakalpaks, Kirghiz, Uzbeks, and Uighurs — and the epics of the Turkic peoples living further east, such as the Altaians, Tuvinians, and Yakuts. The latter are much closer to the world of the Mongolian epic with its heroes endowed with shamanistic powers and its profusion of *mangus*-like adversaries. Altay-Buučay, who had been fatally deceived by his wife and sister, fights after his resurrection from the dead against three *mangus*es with their underworld host and wins the final victory by killing a giant who had a mole on his head as big as a three-year-old sheep.[37] There are no hard and fast dividing lines separating one tradition from another, and traits present in one tradition can also be found in another, but a basic

---

[34]Compare the quotation from *Manas* in which the hero's anger is described in Bowra 1952: 62.

[35]Lord 1974: 143.

[36]Compare the discussion of the hero in Bowra 1952: 91-131; Putilov 1988: 67-121; Hatto 1989b: 241-269. The hero of the heroic epic shares many characteristics with the hero of romance; on the latter see Stevens 1973: 72-95.

[37]See Surazakov 1961: 120.

difference between the conception of the hero in these two areas of Turkic oral poetry cannot be denied.

Qambar, Köroğlu/Göroğlï, and Alpāmiš are heroes as we expect them to be: brave, valiant, of mighty, superhuman strength. We do not doubt their ultimate success in contest and battle, although, as we have seen, the hero might be the losing party temporarily. Göroğlï must cede place to a holy man and minstrel in *Qïrmandäli*, and Alpāmiš succumbs to the lure of wine and enchantment provided by a malevolent witch. The heroes we meet in these epics are certainly of greater than human stature, but their heroic aggrandizement and idealization stays within the limits of what we expect as readers of the *Iliad* or *Beowulf*, of the *Chanson de Roland* or the *Nibelungenlied*. Matters change, however, when we compare the Altaian version of the Alpamïš-story with Fāzil's variant; here the hero's breathing when asleep uproots trees and grinds rocks into sand, and his sneezing carries the seven-headed monster D'elbegen over ten mountains and a hundred lakes. It is true that hyperbole of this kind is not unknown to the reader of medieval oral narrative, in particular when we go to the western fringes of Europe. The principal hero of the Old Irish Ulster cycle of heroic tales, Cú-chulainn, can fully rival the Altaian Alïp-Manaš in heroic stature. Even as a boy his bloodlust could only be quenched after the women of Emain Macha had bared their breasts and he was plunged into three vats of water, and his battle frenzy was strange and awful, as we hear in the *Cattle-Raid of Cooley*:

> The first war-spasm seized Cúchulainn, and made him into a monstrous thing, hideous and shapeless, unheard of. His shanks and his joints, every knuckle and angle and organ from head to foot, shook like a tree in the flood or a reed in the stream. His body made a furious twist inside his skin, so that his feet and shins and knees switched to the rear and his heels and calves switched to the front of his shins, each big knot the size of a warrior's bunched fist. On his head the temple-sinews stretched to the nape of his neck, each mighty, immense, measureless knob as big as the head of a month-old child. His face and features became a red bowl: he sucked one eye so deep into his head that a wild crane couldn't probe it onto his cheek out of the depths of his skull; the other eye fell out along his cheek.
>
> (Kinsella 1970: 150)

When Alïp-Manaš, however, transforms himself into a fly, qualities other than heroic, however hyperbolically presented, are at stake: with the power to change shapes the hero disposes not only of heroic strength but also of supernatural faculties; he wields forces that lie in the realm of magic and witchcraft.[38]

This conception of the hero is widespread. Magic transformations are also found in the Irish sagas and are characteristic of the Finnish *runos*. Instead of the heroic outlook which, in Bowra's words, "admires man for doing his utmost with his actual, human gifts," we find here "a more primitive outlook which admires any attempt to pass beyond man's proper state by magical, non-human means."[39] Bowra continues by giving examples for this "more primitive outlook," among them the Altaian epic poem (*čörčök*) *Kögütöy*:

> In *Kogutei*, a traditional poem of the Altai Tatars, it is again super-natural powers which count. The hero is not the man Kogutei but a beaver whose life he spares and whom he takes home. The beaver duly marries a human bride and behaves very like a man, but though he is a great hunter and performs many feats of valour, he is not a human being and does not reflect a heroic outlook. His final triumphs come through magic, and it is clear that he has much of the *shaman* in him when he escapes death at the hands of his brothers-in-law, lays a curse on their whole family, returns to Kogutei, and enriches him by his magical arts.[40]

Shape-shifting and other shamanistic traits can be found in the epic poetry of the "central" and "southwestern traditions," but they are normally confined to the periphery of heroic action rather than forming its center. Köroğlu's horse, for instance, can change its appearance in the Azerbaijanian version translated by Chodzko, though not quite as radically as Alïp-Manaš's horse, which transforms itself into a star:

> That wonderful horse [i.e. Köroğlu's Qïrat] possessed also this peculiarity, that whenever he came to any strange city, he dropped his ears like an ass, made his bristles stand up on end, and with his mane

[38]On the hero as shaman in Turkic and Mongolian epic poetry compare Lipec 1984: 52ff.

[39]Bowra 1952: 5; see Chapter Five, p. 123.

[40]Bowra 1952: 6. This *čörčök* is also mentioned in the third volume of the Chadwicks' *Growth of Literature*, where it is praised as "the most outstanding poem of the Altai Tatars in respect of length and excellence of style," and where, after a short summary and discussion, it is favorably compared to the Russian *byliny*: "The daring hyperboles, the relevance and significance of the racy narrative, resemble the Russian *byliny*. But *Kogutei* shows equally with the poems of the *Manas* Cycle that even the Russian *skazitely* must yield to the Tatar minstrel as an artist in sustained narrative poetry." Chadwick 1932-40: III, 99, 101.

dishevelled, his tail thrust between his legs, walked along like a jade, in order that none of the passers-by might covet him, or throw a spell on him.

(Chodzko 1842: 97)

Although the shape-shifting power of the horse might belong to the periphery of epic poetry, the horse itself is in many epics one of the principal characters. The importance of the horse is reflected in its description, termed *ta'rif* (from Arabic *taʕrīf*, "definition").[41] Chodzko relates that the descriptions of the hero's horse in the *Köroglu/Görogli*-cycle "are considered, by the best judges of horses in Persia, as the surest authority to depend upon in hippological questions."[42] In the *Book of Dede Qorqut* Bamsï Beyrek addresses his horse in terms of praise and affection:

> Ačuq ačuq meydana beŋzer senüŋ alïnčuǵuŋ,
> iki šeb čïraǵa beŋzer senüŋ gözčügezüŋ,
> ibrišime beŋzer senüŋ yiličügün,
> iki qoša qardaša beŋzer senüŋ qulačuǵuŋ,
> eri muradïna yetürür senüŋ arxačuǵuŋ.
> At dimezem saŋa qartaš direm qartašumdan yig,
> bašuma iš geldi yoldaš direm yoldašumdan yig.
> (Ergin 1958-63: I, 136)

> Your dear forehead resembles the wide, open field,
> your dear eyes resemble two gems, shining in the night,
> your dear mane resembles silk thread,
> your dear ears resemble twin brothers,
> your dear back brings a man to the fulfillment of his wishes.
> I shall not call you horse, I shall call you brother, better than a brother;
> when there is a task at hand, I shall call you companion, better than a companion.

A similar passage is found in *Qambar*. Here the hero both describes and praises his horse, comparing the horse's neck to a golden staff, its ears to two reeds, its legs to four strong posts, and its hoofs to teacups turned upside down, and calling it his winged Pïraq (in Islamic legend, the name of Mohammed's horse on which he ascended into heaven), his

[41]See also Chapter Seven, pp. 197ff., on "horse-epithets."

[42]Chodzko 1842: 12; compare the description of the hero's horse *ibid.*: 23-24.

older and younger brother, and his companion in need.[43] In Fāzil's
variant of *Alpāmiš* a Kalmuck *sinči*, an expert on horses, describes the
hero's horse Bāyčibār in 40 lines, of which I quote the beginning:

Yilqičinda ozi kelgan sinlidir,
tobišqān tuyāqli, marāl bellidir,
arāsat kuninda adžab hāllidir,
qimmatbahā ekan ozbakniŋ āti,
5   minganlarniŋ haqdin yetar maqsadi,
qoltiġida tort yarim gaz qanāti,
asil tulpār ekan ozbakniŋ āti.
Ozi šunday kelgan ekan čāwkar kok,
quyruġidan berisinda kiri yoq,
10   qanday bolsa minganlarga koŋil toq,
men bilaman ildamlikda mini yoq.

            (Zarif, Mirzaev 1979: 116)

The horse approaching is of good stature in the herd,
with fleet hoofs[44] and loins like a maral deer.
On the Day of Judgement it will be in a wonderful state.
The Uzbek's horse is most valuable;
5   God fulfills the wishes of those who mount it.
It has wings on its shoulders, four and a half ells long;
the Uzbek's horse is a true *tulpār* (winged horse).
The horse approaching is a dappled grey.
It is without blemish from head to tail.
10   Whoever mounts it, his heart is overjoyed.
I do not know any shortcomings in its speed.

    In epic poetry the horse often has the power of speech like a human
being, advising the hero of what to do or warning him of imminent
danger. It has also a name, often based on its color and appearance.
Köroğlu/Göroğli's horse is called "Qïrat," "Grey-Horse"; Rawšan's
"Džiyrānquš," "Chestnut-Bird"; Alpāmiš's "Bāy-Čibār," "Bay-Dappled";
Manas' horse is called "Aqqula," "Light-Bay"; Semetey's "Taybuurïl,"

[43]"Qanattï tuwġan pïraġïm,/ aġa-ini sen ediŋ./ Tar žerde žoldas šïraġïm,/ moynïŋ altïn tayaqtay,/ qamïstay eki qulaġïŋ,/ tört ayaġïŋ qazïqtay,/ töŋkergen kese tuyaġïŋ...." *Qambar* (Divaev's version), ll. 318ff.; Āwezov [Auezov], Smirnova 1959: 43.

[44]*Tobišqān* is not recorded in the Uzbek dictionaries; Pen'kovskij's Russian translation has "hoofs like diamonds"; an Uighur translation has "big hoofs"; see Pen'kovskij, Mirzaev 1982: 145; Sadiri, Ābāydulla 1987: 155. I take the word to be a form of dialectal *tāwušqān*, "hare," and interpret hare-hoofs as fleet hoofs; see Šāabdurahmānov 1971: 253 (s.v. *tāwušxān*); Ma'rufov et al. 1981: II, 196 (s.v. *tāwušqān*).

"Foal-Piebald"; Er Töštük's "Čalquyruq," "Grey-Tail"; and Qambar's horse is simply described as *qara qasqa at*, "the black horse with the white mark on its forehead."[45] Like the hero, the horse grows not by years but by days. In the Tuvinian heroic tale *Möge Bayan-Toolay*, the horse grows as it is saddled: when the headgear and bridle are put on, it becomes a two-year-old foal, when the saddlecloth is put on, it becomes a three-year-old foal, and when the saddle is put on, it becomes a fully grown horse.[46] It is often the horse that saves the hero; Alpāmiš can be pulled out from the dungeon only by Bāy-Čibār, when the horse's tail miraculously lengthens;[47] in *Altay-Buučay* the hero is brought back to life by the heavenly Teŋeri-khan's daughter, who is fetched to earth by one of the hero's horses, which had flown up into the sky in the form of an eagle.[48] The horse is sometimes born at the same time as the hero, as Kamar-tay and Hasan in the Turkish variant of "Köroğlu and Princess Nighara" (see p. 155); it is also specially chosen by the hero, as Bāy-Čibār in *Alpāmiš*.[49] If it is a winged horse (*tulpar*), it has to be specially treated for its wings to grow, as is elaborately described in some of the Köroğlu/Göroğlï variants.[50] The importance of the horse as the hero's companion and helper in Turkic oral epic poetry is doubtless a reflection of the nomadic lifestyle which forms the historical and societal background to this type of poetry. This is true not only of Turkic, but also of Mongolian epic poetry, where it has been argued that the horse performs the role of an *alter ego* of the hero.[51]

Before concluding this section on character, at least a few words must be said about the heroines in Turkic epic poetry. The heroine is

[45] On the various types of horses in terms of color and appearance compare Radloff 1893: I, 440-452; Keŋesbaev 1977: 514-8; Grebnev 1960: 70-76.

[46] See Grebnev 1975: 357; compare also Grebnev 1960: 35.

[47] See Zarif, Mirzaev 1979: 281.

[48] See Surazakov 1961: 111ff.

[49] See p. 162; on the motif of the hero choosing his horse see also Urmančeev 1980a: 52-55.

[50] See Chodzko 1842: 20ff; Kaplan, Akalın, Bali 1973: 6ff. — For the motif of the winged horse giving his life for his rider see Hatto 1977: 156f.

[51] See Veit 1985; for a detailed discussion of the figure and role of the horse in Turkic and Mongolian epic poetry see Lipec 1984: 124ff.

generally defined in relation to the hero — she is his beloved, his bride, his wife, also his sister — and hence often has a complementary role in an epic. A notable exception is the Karakalpak epic *Qïrïq Qïz* (Forty Maidens). In this epic the main protagonist is Gülayïm, the daughter of a rich bay, who, together with her forty maidens, trains to become a formidable warrior on the island of Miywalï. Although there is a subplot involving the Khorezmian hero Arïslan (a hero to whom Gülayïm is married in the end) and his sister Altïnay, the action focuses primarily on her heroic deeds.[52] A. T. Hatto's comments on heroines in epic poetry in general apply also to the heroines of Turkic oral epic poetry:

> The heroines of heroic/epic poetry appear more stereotyped than the heroes. There are fewer of them, and the place they are allotted in what by definition are male-dominated societies is more restricted. Yet the heroines seem to range more widely between their extremes, for they comprise at one pole passive women skilled in domestic arts, such as weaving and embroidery, like (apparently) Penelope and Cú Chulainn's wife Emer, and at the other pole active battle-maidens skilled in the arts of war and featuring even as the tutors of male warriors, like Scáthach, who gave Cú Chulainn and Fergus weapon-training.
>
> (Hatto 1989b: 256-7)

Nazïm in *Qambar* can be placed at one end of the scale. She is not only beautiful, but also tries to entice the hero by her specifically feminine qualities. When preparing to persuade Qambar to stay with her at their first meeting she sets up a loom and spreads out her yarn and she prepares *qïmïz* and *araq* (brandy). Barčin in *Alpāmiš* or Gülayïm in *Qïrïq Qïz* are at the other end of the scale, representing the type of the heroic maiden who in physical prowess cedes the place to none except her future husband. Barčin, it is to be noted however, loses her quality of heroic maiden in the second part of the *dastan*, where she is, like Penelope, the suffering widow, who almost meekly agrees to marry once again. In a number of epics not only the hero's bride or wife plays an important role, but also his sister. In Fāzil's variant of *Alpāmiš* it is Qaldirġač, the hero's sister, who receives Barčin's message calling for help and who urges the hero to come to the

---

[52]*Qïrïq Qïz* is considered the main epic of the Karakalpaks; no other variants of the epic outside the Karakalpak tradition have been found. It was recorded between 1938 and 1944 from the Karakalpak *žïraw* Qurbanbay Tāžibaev. See Chadwick, Zhirmunsky 1969: 282f.

rescue of his beloved. Her admonishing words have the occasional barb in them, not unlike the *hvöt* ("instigation speech") of her Old Nordic sisters.[53] But there is also the figure of the obedient, though shrewd wife. Qanïkey, in *Manas*, is such a heroine:

> Kanıkey, of Manas' several wives the only one acquired through regular marriage with matchmaker and bride-wealth, and daughter of a khan, made her bid on the nuptial couch for independence-within-dependence. Her praises as a possible bride dwell more on her delicate upbringing and spotless reputation than on her skill in the domestic arts, which subsequently prove to be distinguished. But if her needle is as yet not mentioned, her dagger is. For on being roughly surprised on the nuptial couch by Manas she draws blood for blood, indeed double, with stabs to her lover's arm and leg. In the sequel Kanıkey was a perfect wife. She served Manas and his interests in every way, counselling him for his good against his desires, ever sweet-tempered, even under his lash, a preserver of his line, free in the Schillerian sense of the full discharge of duty, heroically, when called upon to act, though not as a warrior-woman.
>
> (Hatto 1989b: 263)

She is also the loving mother when she is forced to flee with her son Semetey from Köböš's and Abeke's persecution, and she is the merciless avenger when she mutilates and kills Abeke and Köböš with her own hands.[54]

There are, finally, also the figures of the unfaithful wife and of the treacherous sister as in the Altaian epic poem *Altay-Buučay*. When Altay-Buučay does not return from his hunting expedition, his sister sends a message to two brothers, Arnay-khan and Čarnay-khan, asking them to help the hero's wife and sister. When the brothers arrive they are made welcome and told that, should Altay-Buučay be still alive, it is their duty to kill him. Altay-Buučay does indeed return and is received by his wife with a poisoned drink. As the hero does not die from this potion, the women call on the brothers to kill Altay-Buučay. In a fight lasting for seven days they are, however, unable to get the better of the hero. Only when Altay-Buučay asks his wife and sister to throw peas and flour under his adversaries' feet and they throw the peas and flour under his own feet instead, can the brothers subdue the hero. They are still unable to kill him, as he has an external soul, the

---

[53]See Zarif, Mirzaev 1979: 67ff. On the function of sisters, especially as shaman-esses, in Yakut epic poetry see Hatto 1989b: 263.

[54]See above Chapter Eight, p. 224.

whereabouts of which are unknown to them. Altay-Buučay's wife extricates the necessary information from her husband and the hero is finally killed with cruelty.[55] The figures of the unfaithful wife and of the treacherous sister and the motifs combined with these figures as in *Altay-Buučay* are of frequent occurrence in Altaian, Tuvinian, but also in Tungus folklore. In the Tuvinian heroic tale *Xan-Šilgi a'ttïg̣ Xan-Xülük*, "Xan-Xülük on his horse Xan-Šilgi," the hero is in a similar way deceived by his wife and his sister and killed by his opponent Alday-Mergen.[56] In the Tungus heroic tale of Altaney, two brothers are betrayed by their sister, who calls on a hostile hero to kill them.[57] Meletinskij has noted the archaic character of these figures in Turkic and Mongolian epic poetry and seen in the betrayal of the hero by his sister a clear trace of a breaking with an endogamous marriage alliance system.[58] It is possible that there is a level of meaning in these narratives which allows us to see them as rationalizations of social norms and patterns. Although an interpretation of these tales in the spirit of Claude Lévy-Strauss' analysis of myth might hence be feasible, such an interpretation lies outside the scope of this chapter, which is more narrowly focused on questions of style and narrative technique.

Composition and Narrative Technique

At the beginning of the preceding section the characters of Turkic oral epic poetry were compared to the figures in a game of chess. The presence of the protagonist requires that of the antagonist; a move in one direction entails a countermove in another direction. Turkic epic poetry belongs, with the *Odyssey*, the *Arabian Nights* and the *Decameron*, to a literary tradition "où les actions ne sont pas là pour servir d' 'illustration' au personnage mais où, au contraire, les person-

---

[55]This is a summary of the first part of Kalkin's variant (up to l. 609); see Surazakov 1961: 83-97.

[56]See Quular, Sarïg̣-ool 1963: 194-238. There are also Tuvinian variants of *Altay-Buučay*; see Grebnev 1960: 17-20.

[57]For a discussion of the Tungus variants as well as of a Mongolian variant of this story see Kőhalmi 1985: 115ff.

[58]See Meletinskij 1963: 290; he cites further examples *ibid*: 270f., 290f.

nages sont soumis à l'action."[59]   As in the folktale, the narrative
structure of Turkic epic poetry can be viewed as a sequence of choices
from a finite and fairly limited number of options. A systematic survey
of story-patterns would yield a comparatively small list of *actants*, who
engage in a predictable and rigorously circumscribed set of actions.[60]
Once a plot like that of winning a bride has been chosen, a certain
range of possible patterns in the development of the story together with
a group of obligatory and optional figures is almost automatically
implied. Similarly, if the hero's biography is to begin with his birth,
there is a choice between a relatively small list of motifs with which to
commence his life-story: presence or absence of the motif of miraculous
conception (e.g. by eating an apple given by a dervish etc.); presence or
absence of the motif of miraculous birth (e.g. birth in a grave etc.);
presence or absence of heroic deeds in childhood (e.g. herding cattle as
a newborn infant etc.); and in the absence of heroic deeds, presence or
absence of the motif of the unpromising youth (unpromising because of
being e.g. scabby-headed etc.).[61] Although the actual plot of a narrative
might be fairly complex, complexity and variability are principally
determinate and firmly rooted in the conventions governing plot and
character.

Plot and character refer to one aspect of narrative; other elements are
composition and narrative technique. The composition of a Turkic epic
can be outlined as follows:

A Formulaic introduction/Introductory formula(s)
B Narration
C Scene I
D Connecting Narration/Transitional formula(s)

[59]Todorov 1978: 33.

[60]See for instance Claude Bremond's sketch of a logic of narrative in Bremond
1973; his classification of different narrative roles such as *patient, agent volontaire,
agent involontaire, obstructeur, améliorateur* etc. could easily be applied to Turkic oral
epic poetry, elevating narrative analysis to a more abstract level than the one chosen
in this book.

[61]On the motifs of the childless couple and miraculous conception/miraculous birth
see above pp. 164f.; on the motif of heroic deeds in childhood see pp. 37f. On the motif
of the unpromising youth in Mongolian and Turkic epics and folktales see Laude-
Cirtautas 1981; see in particular *Motifs* L101 *Unpromising hero*, L112 *Hero (heroine)
of unpromising appearance*, and L114.1 *Lazy hero*.

E Scene II

...

Y Final Scene

Z Formulaic conclusion/Concluding formula(s)

The beginning of an epic is as a rule formulaic. Russian scholars, when studying the composition of the *bylina* and also that of the Serbo-Croatian heroic lay, distinguish between *zapev*, "pre-song," and *začin*, "beginning." According to N. I. Kravcov, a *zapev* represents a lyrico-narrative passage which expresses the singer's attitude to the story or his relationship to the audience, while the *začin* is directly connected to the tale to be related.[62] The function of a *zapev* in Kravcov's sense is in many Turkic traditions fulfilled by improvised songs (*terme*), which are sung before the recitation of an epic commences (compare Chapter Four, pp. 97ff.). Azerbaijanian *dastans* are generally introduced by three poems called *ustadnamä*, "master-composition," in which observations on love and life are made and much proverbial lore is expressed.[63] The *zapev*-like call on the audience to listen to the singer's words, a common introductory formula in medieval narrative,[64] is also found in Turkic epic poetry, as for instance at the beginning of *Qambar* (Divaev's variant):

> Žaqsïlar dastan aytayïn,
> äweli Alla sïyïnïp,
> ekinši kämil pirime.
> Qulaq salïp tïŋdağan
> 5 žamandïq körme tiride.
> (Äwezov [Auezov], Smirnova 1959: 36)

---

[62]See Kravcov 1985: 247 and his classification and discussion of beginnings in Serbo-Croatian heroic lays.

[63]For examples see for instance the collection of love-romances in Tähmasib et al. 1979. — For a detailed account of the formulaic beginnings in Turkic and Mongolian folktales and epics see Laude-Cirtautas 1983.

[64]From many possible examples I quote the beginning of a Middle English popular romance, a Middle High German minstrel romance and an Old French *chanson de geste*: "Lytyll and mykyll, olde and yonge,/ Lystenyth now to my talkynge, /Of whome Y wyll you [klythe..." (*Octavian*; Mills 1973: 75); "nu ruochet hœren mîne bete/ daz ir swîget dar zuo,/ daz ich iu daz kunt getuo" (now be so kind as to hear my request, /namely that you be quiet,/ so that I can tell you this [story]) (*Biterolf und Dietleib*; Jänicke 1866: 1); "Qui veust oïr chançon de beau semblant,/ Si face paiz, si se traie en avant..." (Those who would like to listen to a well-turned song/ should hold their peace and come forward...) (*Otinel*; Guessard, Michelant 1859: 1).

> Good people, I want to narrate a *dastan*,
> putting my hope first in God,
> second in my *pir*, who has reached perfection.
> May he who lends me an ear and listens
> experience no ills in his lifetime!

Other forms of formulaic beginning are the introduction of the narrative by a proverb or maxim, as for instance the opening of the *Memorial Feast for Kökötöy-Khan* quoted in Chapter Seven (p. 181), and what Vsevolod Miller termed *geografičeskij začin* and *xronologičeskij začin*, the setting of the story in place and time. The geographical and chronological elements are often combined; typical examples of such epic beginnings have been quoted earlier, from the *Köroğlu/Göroğlï*-cycle (see Chapter Five, p. 128) and from the Karakalpak *dastan Qïrïq Qïz* (see Chapter Seven, p. 180). For the sake of convenience, I will repeat the last-named quotation as an example of this type of beginning:

> Burïnği ötken zamanda,
> sol zamannïŋ qädiminde,
> qaraqalpaq xalqïnda,
> ata žurtï Turkstanda,
> 5 Sarkop degen qalada,
> az noğaylï elatïnda....
> (Maqsetov, Žapaqov, Niyemullaev 1980: 42)

> In the days of old,
> in the days of yore,
> among the Karakalpaks,
> in the homeland of Turkestan,
> 5 in a town called Sarkop,
> in the small Noghay tribe....

The scene of action differs according to epic tale and epic tradition. While the epics of the *Köroğlu/Göroğlï*-cycle situate the action in a more or less fabulous land Čambïl, Çamlıbel etc., a number of Kazakh, Kirghiz, and Karakalpak epics, such as *Qambar* or *Qïrïq Qïz*, place the events to be related among the Noghays at the time of the breakup of the Golden Horde. Other historical or pseudo-historical chronological and geographical qualifications are given; *Alpāmiš* in Fāzil Yoldāš-oğli's variant, for instance, is placed among the Qonğïrāt in the period of the Kalmuck wars. There is an aura of historicity especially in the heroic epics of the "central traditions," even if the narrative as such cannot be termed historical. In this they differ significantly from more easterly traditions such as the Altaian or Yakut traditions, where, as in the passage quoted from the Yakut *oloŋxo Quruubay Xaannaax Qulun Qullustuur* (Qulun Qullustuur of Rough Character) in Chapter Seven (pp. 199f.), the action is often placed at the Beginning of Time. Earthly action can also be embedded in a timeless, mythological framework, as in the Tuvinian epic tale *Pagay D'ürü*:

> Üstü Purxan par turu,
> Xaan Qurbustu Täŋkäräkäy,
> Küd'ü Purxan Paqšï,
> aldï oranda
> 5 Qara san attïg Xaan,
> Talay Xaan.
>
> (Radloff 1866b: 399-400)

> Above (in heaven) there lived Purxan,
> Khan Qurbustu Täŋkäräkäy,
> Küd'ü Purxan Paqšï.
> Below (on earth) there lived
> 5 the khan with the horse Qara-san,
> Talay-khan.

The dawn of history is, however, also invoked in other traditions. A part of the *Manas*-cycle, entitled "Almambet, Er Kökčö and Aq-erkeč," begins in Radloff's version:

> Džer džer bolgondo,
> suu suu bolgondo,
> altï atanïn uulu Qapïr bar ekän,
> üč atanïn uulu Busurman bar ekän.
> 5 Tört arïštuu Oirottun —
> qïl džaqaluu Oirotton —
> altïn aydar, čoq belbäü
> Qara-qandïn balasï,
> qabïlan tuugan Almambet,
> 10 top ooliya džïïlïp,
> top oozïnan bütüptü,
> bar ooliya džïïlïp,
> batasïnan bütüptü,
> Arčaluu Mazar azrät
> 15 Aldasïnan bütüptü!

When land became land, and water water, there were the Infidels, Sons of six Fathers, and the Muslims, Sons of Three. The son of Kara-khan — Khan of the Oirot of the Four Regions, of the Oirot of the horse-hair collars, of him with the golden forelock and tasseled sash — to wit tiger-born Almambet, had been conceived from the word of the

> many Elders gathered together, from the blessings of all the assembled
> Elders, from the Lord Allah of Arčaluu Mazar![65]

The Bashkir epic *Ural-batïr* (Hero Ural) commences with a comparable
formulaic passage:

> Boron-boron borondan,
> keše-maðar kilmägän,
> kilep ayaq baθmaǧan,
> ul tirälä qoro yer
> 5 barlïǧïn his kem belmägän,
> dürt yaǧïn dingeð uratqan
> bulǧan, ti, ber urïn.
>
> (Säǧitov [Sagitov], Xarisov et al. 1977: 55)

> In the days of yore,
> when no man had yet appeared,
> when no foot had yet trod the earth,
> when dry land was around there,
> 5 of which nobody knew,
> when the four sides were surrounded by sea,
> there was, it is said, some place.

The formulaic beginning of the Tuvinian heroic tale, on the other hand,
has become reduced to the formula *š ïyaan am*, translatable as "Lo and
behold!" (see p. 57).

In a number of traditions, the introductory formulas stress the
authenticity of the stories by referring to their transmission from storyteller to storyteller and from singer to singer. Turkish *hikâye*s are often
prefixed by the formula *"Ravıyan-ı ahbar ve nâkilân-ı âsar şöyle rivayet
ederler ki...,"* "The narrators of stories and the tellers of legends narrate
that..."[66] One of the Uighur variants of *Göroǧlï* begins with a similar
formula:

> Qedimqi äsärlärdin näqil kältürüp riwayät qilǧuči söz ustiliri, söz
> kanliridin ünčä-märwayitqa oxšaš yaltirap nur čečip turidiǧan
> ibarilärni elip čiqip, töwändiki dastanni riwayät qilidu...
>
> (Tatliq et al. 1986: 3)

> The masters of speech, who from olden times transmit stories and tell
> tales, have from the store of words preserved expressions which radiate
> and shine like gems and precious stones, and narrate the following
> *dastan...*

---

[65]Text and translation from Hatto 1990: 14/15.

[66]See Spies 1929: 50; Boratav 1946: 42.

Other formulas underline the mixture of truth and falsehood in the story, as in the quotations from *Manas* and *Alpāmiš* given in Chapter Five (see pp. 125f.). In *Alpāmiš* the "truth/falsehood-formula" occurs at the end of the *dastan* and is hence an example of a formulaic conclusion. The concluding lines of an epic are on the whole less elaborate than the opening lines. Many epic poems simply end with the statement that the hero and heroine have reached their goal, much in the way folktales are concluded. Chodzko notes that at the end of a performance the singer requests the audience in a song to show their appreciation of his art by tangible means:

> Thus ends the tale of Kurroglou, which, when an aushik [ašïq] has recounted, he never forgets to sing a poetical eulogy of his own or of anybody else's composition, praising the person who is to pay him for his trouble. He complains against the persecutions of coquetish [sic] fate; recommends wisdom and abstinence; and, at last, wishes you to live one thousand nine hundred and ninety-nine years, that is to say, as long as lived the patriarch Noah, — of course, on condition that the cloud of your liberality pour a golden shower upon the parched lips of the aushik's empty and yawning pocket.
>
> (Chodzko 1842: 344)

Similar good wishes are found at the end of Divaev's variant of *Qambar*:

> Äweli aytqan, ekinši tïŋdaġandar,
> žetissin muradïna barša žandar.
> Düniyege kelip ketti ne asïl zat,
> 1845 žamannan dat, žaqsïdan qaladï at;
> bir duġa oqïŋïzdar arwaġïna
> Qambardïŋ bolïp žatsïn köŋili šat,
> ayaġï bul dastannïŋ boldï tämäm,
> kelmeydi köp aytuwġa meniŋ šamam.
> 1850 Qudaya žaqsïlarġa xuzïr bolġay
> osïnša beynetpenen boldï tämäm.
>
> (Äwezov [Auezov], Smirnova 1959: 78)

> May in the first place the narrator, in the second place the listeners,
> may all living beings reach the goal of their wishes.
> Many noble creatures have lived in this world;
> 1845 enmity remains from the bad man, a good name from the good man.
> Read a prayer for Qambar's soul:
> may his heart live in bliss.
> This *dastan* has reached its conclusion;
> I have no more strength to say much more.
> 1850 May God give all good men peace.
> Having exerted our strength we have thus come to an end.

The Turkish *aşık* Müdami is more down-to-earth with his good wishes at the end of his performance, when he hopes that his audience will have a good night and a lot of fun in bed.[67] In the *Book of Dede Qorqut* the various branches of the cycle also have formulaic endings. Dede Qorqut appears, plays his *qopuz*, and makes a tale of the adventures which have just been related, and the narrative finishes with Dede Qorqut's moral reflections and admonitions.

While introductory formulas are the rule and concluding formulas fairly common, there is more variety in the presence or absence of transitional formulas. In many epics and epic traditions a change of scene is explicitly introduced. Sometimes it is only marked by particles, such as the adverb *alqissa*, "in short" (from Arabic), in the Uzbek *dastan*s of the Khorezmian "school," also found in other traditions, or in Karakalpak *dastan*s the adverb *äne*, "now," signifying that a new section in the narrative is beginning. Sometimes, as for instance in Divaev's variant of *Qambar*, references to the segmentation of the narrative can be altogether missing. In Turkmen epic poetry the formula "*Habarï kimden al?*", "Whom are we going to talk about?" (lit. "Take the news from whom?"), is commonly employed both at the beginning of a new scene and a new branch in the *Göroğlï*-cycle. *Harman Däli*, for instance, begins with the formula: "*Hayïr, yağšï, habarï kimden al?*", "Good, fine, whom are we going to talk about?", and has at the first change of scene the formula: "*Habarï kimden al? — Köroğlïdan!*", "Whom are we going to talk about? — Köroğlï!" Corresponding formulas occur in other epic traditions. When the Turkish singer Behçet Mahir, in his version of *Köroğlu*, switches to a new scene or topic, he uses similar expressions:

> Şimdi bu, hizmette olsun, haberi nerden verelim Bolu Beylerinden.
> (Kaplan, Akalı, Bali 1973: 7)

> Now, let this one be at his work! From whom shall we get news?
> From the Bey of Bolu!

In *Rawšan* the audience is frequently requested, as in the quotation just given, to leave protagonist A with whatever he or she is engaged in and see what protagonist B is doing; compare for instance:

---

[67] See Başgöz 1975: 202-203 (English translation); Başgöz 1986b: 136-137 (Turkish text).

— Sen bilmaysan... sen bilmaysan, — deb āta-bāla bir-biriniŋ gapini
bekār čiqarišib, "ha, seni koraman-da," — deyišib tura bersin, endi
gapni Rawšanbekdan ešitiŋ.

(Zarif 1971: 60)

Let father and son say to one another: "You don't know... you don't
know...", let them exchange useless words and say: "Ha, I can see
through you!", and hear now from Beg Rawšan!

In the *Book of Dede Qorqut* the formula:

At ayaǧï külüg,
ozan dili čevük olur.

The horse's feet are fleet,
the *ozan*'s tongue is swift.

occurs repeatedly to mark the passage of time.[68]

In a number of these formulaic expressions the narrator turns to the
listeners, inviting them to follow him to a new scene or event. The
singer includes the audience also in formulas like "And then X said this
and that. Let us see what he or she said!" Several examples have been
cited in Chapter Two in connection with the occurrence of this formulaic
expression in the *Book of Dede Qorqut* (see p. 50). In *Rawšan* the
listeners are at various stages asked to hear or even to see what is
taking place, for instance in the final battle:

Endi koriŋ Aynāqni...
...
Endi koriŋ, mard Hasan...

(Zarif 1971: 211, 215)

Look now at Aynāq...
...
Look now, Hasan the hero...

A singer might also comment on the action or add his reflections to the
story. While extensive comments from a singer are generally rare in
the epic poetry of the Turkic peoples, some singers are more prone to
giving an opinion or commentary than others. Behçet Mahir interrupts
his narrative frequently to explain certain passages or simply indulge
in moralizing observations. In the branch "Köroğlu and Han Nigâr,"

[68]This formula occurs five times (in the text of the Dresden manuscript); see
Ergin 1958-63: I, 81, 90, 110, 186, 239; Lewis 1974: 30, 37, 53, 118, 176. On the
meaning "quick" of *külüg* see Rossi 1952: 342 (s.v. *külük*).

discussed in Chapter Six, Köroğlu falls in love with Han Nigâr when he sees her picture shown him by a dervish. At this stage the singer explains:

> O zaman kalemdar devrişler, bir insanın gittiği yerden, yahut geldiği yerden, tasvirini alırdı, ki o adamın haberi hiç olmazdı. Neden? Öyle kalemdar dervişler var idi eskiden. Bir adamı da tasviri kalem ile, ya camekan üstüne, ya da kağıt üstüne alınırdı. Şimdi de tasvirler makineler ile alınıyor. Her bir şey kolaylık olmuş.
>
> (Kaplan, Akalın, Bali 1973: 78)

> At that time dervishes wielding the pen took the picture of some person wherever he came or went, without this person noticing it. How come? In the old days there were such dervishes wielding the pen. The picture of a person was taken either on glass or on paper. Now pictures are taken with cameras. Everything has become easy.

The narrator is physically present at the moment of performance, relying on the interaction with his audience. In this, oral epic poetry differs significantly from written narrative, where we have instead of the narrator the author, who is present in the tale in many different guises: as a seemingly neutral narrating voice, barely intruding into the narrative; as a clearly articulate author-narrator, commenting on the action; as an "I" narrating the story from his or her point of view; or in the guise of a fictitious narrator relating the story.[69] Although a singer can, as we have seen, comment on the action, he does this as a person, not as a persona in the way the implied author in, for instance, Thackeray's *Vanity Fair* offers his observations on the follies and vices of his age. Furthermore, the singer does not comment on his own story, but on a story he has inherited from the tradition. Even in those cases where the singer is creative, he is creative within the context of his tradition and does not compose a work which is his only. Other singers will sing the same work and it will then be as much their property as his. When talking of the role of the narrator in oral epic poetry, it has thus to be kept in mind that the distinctions elaborated in literary criticism relative to the novel do not automatically apply to oral narrative.

If we look, for instance, at the various Turkic epics which were summarized in Chapter Six, we can see that the story is basically narrated from what in art criticism is called a "parallel perspective."

---

[69]The "narrating voice" in the novel has been extensively analysed in literary criticism; see for instance Lämmert 1955: 67ff.; Scholes, Kellogg 1966: 240ff.

In this type of perspective there is no vanishing point; parallel perspective is best known from East Asian painting, where the scene of a picture is viewed from an exalted position with all the lines drawn as parallels which never meet. The narrator of an epic "objectively" surveys the action like a Chinese or Japanese painter, without introducing his point of view, with a vanishing point somewhere within the "picture." The actors in the epics, too, do not impose their point of view on the events related. When Alpāmiš summarizes in his own words what has happened to him during his seven-year imprisonment, his first-person account does not differ in point of view from that given earlier in the narrative. This "neutral point of view" is one of the most noticeable features which distinguishes the oral epic from the novel. This is not to say that the singer and the audience do not take sides. There is never any doubt as to where right and wrong lie. "Our side" is right and "the other side" is wrong, or, as the *Chanson de Roland* puts it, "*Paien unt tort e chrestiens unt dreit,*" "the pagans are in the wrong and the Christians are in the right" (l. 1015). This does not exclude the possibility of one or the other person on "the other side," such as Qāradžān or Almambet, coming over to "our side"; but there is no serious attempt to represent any postion other than one's own with the eyes of the other.

In telling his tale, the singer proceeds in a linear progression. Flashbacks and anticipations are unusual, although dreams and visions, as in Fāzil's *Alpāmiš*, occur. Information which has been omitted at an earlier stage but is necessary for the understanding of some later event is filled in at that point in the narrative. When Ultantāz ousts Alpāmiš's and his own father Bayböri in the hero's absence, we are told that Bayböri had Ultantāz by a slave-woman; we are not told about this bastard son when he was born, presumably around the time the hero himself was born. There is no flashback here, but simply a short explanation of how this situation arose. The singer concentrates on one thing at a time; there was no need to talk about Ultantāz when he did not yet figure in the narrative.[70] The linearity of the narrative also excludes digressions. There are, as I have mentioned, lengthy narrative comments in Behçet Mahir's version of *Köroğlu*; these comments are the closest parallels to what we might call digressions. But they are not of

---

[70]Compare what Hatto calls "limelighting technique" in Kirghiz epic poetry; Hatto 1979: 111.

the nature of the digressions for instance in *Beowulf*, which mirror and supplement the main narrative in many ways.

In his linear progression, the singer changes the scene frequently. There are usually two realms of action between which he switches: "home" and "abroad." In Fāzil's *Alpāmiš*, "home" is the land of the Qoṇġïrāt tribe and "abroad" the land of the Kalmucks. The scene changes from one to the other, focusing mainly on Alpāmiš and Barčin, but also on the other protagonists and antagonists. This change of scene entails a contemporaneity of two lines of action — while Alpāmiš is at home, Barčin is sought after by Kalmuck suitors abroad; while Alpāmiš is in prison abroad, his family are subjugated at home. Having two things happening at the same time does not mean, however, that we have a double plot or a plot and a subplot. In *Alpāmiš*, *Qambar*, the various branches of the *Köroğlu/Göroğlï*-cycle and other epics summarized, the two story lines do not lead an independent existence but are closely related to one another, with the focus on the hero and his deeds. A double plot as we know it from the novel is rare; something like a double plot is, for instance, found in the Karakalpak epic *Qïrïq Qïz*, where the fortunes of the heroine and the hero form each a comparatively independent plot, which are only in the course of the epic interwoven and finally connected with one another.

The narrative is generally told from "beginning to end," but not everything is told. The story does not unfold in a slow and even pace in third-person narrative, but moves from dramatic scene to dramatic scene. To illustrate this, I want to look at the beginning of the Uzbek *dastan Rawšan*. After the introductory passage, the drama begins with Goroğli's visit to his adoptive son Awaz, trying to arrange a wedding between Gulanār, Awaz's daughter, and Rawšan, Hasan's son (Hasan is Goroğli's second adoptive son). After the exchange of courteous greetings, the dialogue between father and son becomes more and more heated, resulting in a full-fledged quarrel (verse-passages I to IV).[71] The fourteen-year-old Rawšan has been listening and runs away in tears to Goroğli's wife Āġa Yunus, who comforts him by giving him a magic ring. On this ring Rawšan sees the image of Zulxumār, with whom he falls in love immediately. The dialogue (in prose) between Rawšan and his grandmother is followed by a typical scene (in verse), that of the

[71]The numbering of the verse-passages agrees with that in my translation; Reichl 1985a.

hero saddling his horse and getting his armor ready (verse-passage V). The departure of the hero is once again a dramatic scene. Hasan is sitting with the gatekeeper at the town-gate, when Rawšan appears, unrecognized in his warlike splendor by his father. There is a lively dialogue between the gatekeeper, Hasan, and Rawšan, culminating in the father's blessing (verse-passages VI to XI; see above p. 274). The hero then rides to Širwān. The hero's ride is another type-scene of Uzbek epic poetry, related in third-person narrative in a verse-passage of heptasyllabic or octosyllabic lines (XII; see pp. 214f.). It occurs again in the *dastan* at two later points in the story. Once in Širwān, Rawšan puts his armor and horse in hiding. He then encounters an old woman, who takes him into her house. This scene starts with Rawšan asking the birds and flowers in the crone's garden after Zulxumār (verse-passage XIII), continues with a dialogue between the old woman and the hero, who has climbed on top of a tree to hide (XIV), and the woman's offer to take the boy into her house (XV), and concludes with another dialogue between the two, in the course of which the story of the woman's sons is told (XVI). Before Rawšan has his first interview with his beloved, he has several more adventures, among them his meeting with the *köse* mentioned earlier (p. 288), all of which are represented as dramatic scenes in which the protagonists engage in lively dialogues. The *dastan* proceeds in this manner till the final battle-scene is reached (verse-passage LX) and the happy end is narrated in the concluding passage.

A similar composition is characteristic of other epics as well. *Alpāmiš* begins equally dramatically with a council scene (see above pp. 201f.) and moves like *Rawšan* from scene to scene. In *Qambar* the focus is first on the heroine, who is seen seated at the top of her tower with the suitors parading before her (see pp. 145f.); the focus then shifts to Qambar, who is introduced in a hunting-scene full of dramatic tension. When they first meet, the narrator presents a scene full of contrasts and conflicts: Nazïm, disappointed with Qambar's lack of attention, chiding her servant-women; then her cajoling words and Qambar's restrained reply; the boisterous appearance of Nazïm's older brothers with their foul language; and finally the appeal to reason by Nazïm's youngest brother Alšïoraz.

When comparing the narrator's point of view with the parallel perspective of East Asian painting, my intention was to emphasize the "objectivity" of the narrative and the lack of a specific figure, either the narrator or one of the protagonists, through whose eyes we are made to see the action. This does not mean, however, that the story is viewed from a distance. On the contrary, the narrative proceeds from scene to scene, focusing on one individual event at a time, which is enacted in monologues and dialogues, not unlike a play. There is a further dimension to these scenes in prosimetric *dastans*. The change from prose to verse, from recitation to singing, is often co-occurrent with a change from third-person "linking" narration to a scene, either a type-scene (hero's ride, battle etc.) or a dramatic scene in direct speech. In some of these scenes the action may become accelerated or reach a turning point, in others events have come to a standstill: we have "static" monologues or dialogues in which the various actors express their feelings, similar to the arias of classical opera. Musical styles can bring out these differences in Uzbek epic poetry, with songlike melodies for stanzaic, lyrical passages, and stichic melodies for nonstanzaic, descriptive verse-passages. At the end of *Alpāmiš* we have a singing contest between various figures, in which both metrically and musically marriage-songs (*yār-yār*) are imitated. The incorporation of lyric songs, not only textually but also musically, into epic is also found in other versions. When the Kazakh *aqïn* Muqaš Baybatïrov comes to this part of his variant, he changes his stichic tune to that of lyrical songs.[72]

* * * * *

In summary it can be said that there are two stylistic processes at work in the epics we have looked at: a process which can be captured by the term "formulaic rhetoric" and a process which we might call "scenic elaboration." Turkic epic poetry is on the one hand rigorously governed by conventions of genre and is hence highly predictable in its form and structure. Diction is formulaic, the plot determines to a large extent the development of the story, and the figures appearing in the epic are (with some notable exceptions) "flat" rather than "round" characters, comparable in their patterned relationships to one another to the figures in a game of chess. When it comes, on the other hand, to the telling of

---

[72]Compare the record produced by Melodija, *Alpamïs. Qazaqtïŋ xalïq eposï* ['A.' A Kazakh folk epic]. Sung by Muqaš Baybatïrov and read by Tanat Žaylibekov. Tashkent, Melodija D-026293-96.

the story, the emphasis shifts, so to speak, from the general to the particular. The rhetorical devices available to the singer are now put to effect to create a dramatic scene which captivates the audience by its imaginative detail and immediacy. The protagonists are still types rather than individuals, the diction is still formulaic, and a particular scene like that of the hero departing is still a type-scene. But by scenic elaboration the listener (and derivatively the reader) is put into the scene and made part of the drama. This involvement of the listener by making him a spectator is encapsulated in the singer's invitation to look and see (*koriŋ*), an invitation which is actually superfluous in a good performance. The oral epic, like drama, is only then successful when the audience is attentive and lets itself become enchanted; scenic elaboration is the most prominent technique for achieving this goal.

Chapter Ten

Transformations in Space and Time

> Ffele romaunses men maken newe,
> Off goode knyghtes, stronge and trewe;
> Off here dedys men rede romaunce,
> Bothe in Engeland and in Ffraunce:
> Off Rowelond, and off Olyuer,
> And off euery Doseper;
> Off Alisaundre, and Charlemayn;
> Off kyng Arthour, and off Gawayn,
> How they were knyghtes goode and curteys....
> *Richard Cœur de Lyon*, ll. 7-15[1]

As the poet of the 13th-century Middle English romance *Richard Cœur de Lyon* points out, the *chansons de geste*, the *romans antiques*, and the Arthurian cycle were equally popular in England and France. He could have added Germany and Italy, the Scandinavian countries and the Iberian Peninsula. Although the "matter of France, the matter of Rome, and the matter of England" have not found the same favor with all literary traditions, the vogue these tales and tale-cycles enjoyed in medieval Europe from Iceland and Ireland to Central and Southern Europe is a remarkable phenomenon. Change, however, is a concomitant of diffusion. The Old French *Chanson de Roland* is as different from its retelling in prose in the Old Norse *Karlamagnús saga* as are Chrétien's *romans courtois* from Malory's *Morte d'Arthur*. The study of these adaptations, translations and re-compositions has provided valuable insights into the interdependence of textual transmission, literary fashion and poetic creation. While the *chansons de geste*

---

[1]Brunner 1913: 81. — "Men make many new romances/ of good knights, strong and true./ People read romances of their deeds,/ both in England and in France:/ of Roland and of Oliver,/ and of everyone of the Twelve Peers of Charlemagne;/ of Alexander and Charlemagne;/ of King Arthur and of Gawain,/ how they were good and courtly knights...."

found only sporadic imitations in medieval Germany, Arthurian romances of the courtly type were the major influence on the development of the Middle High German courtly romances. The "national character" of the *chansons de geste* prevented their adoption in medieval Germany, where epic poetry based on the Germanic legends was still popular in noncourtly circles. In England, on the other hand, only a few Middle English Arthurian romances can be described as courtly; when courtly literature in English arose in the late 14th century, Italian poetry had become more fashionable than the Arthurian *romans courtois*.

Turkic oral epic poetry has also been influenced by foreign models. The prestige French courtly literature had in medieval Europe is comparable to the role Classical Persian literature played for the diffusion of "romantic stories" and the development of lyricism in the love-*dastans*. Much of this influence has been exerted through the medium of written literature, but, as in medieval England, bilingualism helped spread stories across linguistic boundaries. In particular in southern Uzbekistan, in Tajikistan, and in northern Afghanistan a number of singers are bilingual, a fact which accounts not only for the presence of Iranian influences in Turkic oral poetry but also for the popularity of originally Turkic epic poetry among speakers of Iranian languages. The changes encountered in different versions of the same tale in different traditions tell us something about the way oral epic poetry is cultivated in a different linguistic and cultural milieu. Some of these differences are, as in the case of medieval literature, also indicative of historical development and changes in time as well as in place. Both of these processes, transformations in space and in time, will be illustrated in this chapter. I will first discuss variation and diffusion with reference to the *Köroğlu/Göroğlï*-cycle and then questions of historical development with reference to the Alpamïš-story.

Köroğlu/Göroğlï: Variation and Diffusion

No epic tale is as widely spread among Turkic peoples as that of Köroğlu/Göroğlï.[2] It also provides a good example of how tales can cross

---

[2] A general survey is given in Karryev 1968; compare also Boratav 1964: 24-28; Boratav 1967; Boratav 1984.

linguistic and ethnic boundaries. Tales of Köroğlu/Göroğlï are known among a variety of non-Turkic peoples; among the Tajiks and Kurds, who are speakers of Iranian languages; among the Central Asian Arabs; and among the Georgians and the Armenians. Most scholars see the historical nucleus of this cycle in the Jalali movement in Turkey and Azerbaijan at the end of the 16th century. Among the rebels (Turkish *celâlî*) against the Ottoman sultan and the Persian shah there is said to have been one Köroğlu (in Turkish spelling; Azerbaijanian: Koroğlu), who was according to the Armenian historian Arakel of Tabriz (17th c.) both a military leader and a singer.[3]

The oldest published version of the *Köroğlu/Göroğlï*-cycle is A. Chodzko's English translation of an Azerbaijanian version (1842).[4] Recently a manuscript from the middle of the 19th century has come to light in the Manuscript Department of the Georgian Academy of Sciences in Tbilisi; this variant contains 28 branches and is fairly close to Chodzko's text.[5] Verse-portions from the cycle have, however, been preserved from an earlier time. In the first half of the 18th century an Armenian merchant, called Eljas Mušegjan, on a mission from the Persian shah to the Russian tsar, was arrested in Astrakhan. In his possession a collection of Azerbaijanian songs with short prose commentaries from the *Köroğlu*-cycle were found, which were written down in Armenian script in 1721. These songs are in wording surprisingly close to some of the contemporary Azerbaijanian variants.[6]

From Azerbaijan the stories spread east and west. The main representatives of the western version are the Turkish and Azerbaijanian *dastan*s. Other Turkic texts which belong to the western version are the tale of Kürulï written down by Radloff among the Tobol

---

[3]See Boratav 1984: 92-97; Karryev 1968: 8ff.; Korogly 1983: 169ff.; see also Klimovič 1959; on the Jalali movement see Kinross 1977: 286f.

[4]According to Boratav the original of this translation is a manuscript in the Bibliothèque Nationale in Paris, in which the prose-parts are in Persian and the verse-parts in Azerbaijanian; see Boratav 1984: 21, 230, 255; this manuscript is not listed in Blochet's catalogue (1932-33).

[5]See Korogly 1983: 182-247. — On the Azerbaijanian version of the cycle see Karryev 1968: 45-63; Tähmasib 1972: 130-176.

[6]See Karryev 1968: 10ff.; Tähmasib 1959: 468-475.

Tatars and the Crimean Tatar *destan* of Kör-oğlu.[7] According to
Chodzko's variant Köroğlu/Koroğlu was a Turkmen from the Teke tribe.
His father was the "master of the stud" of Sultan Murad, "ruler of one
of the provinces of Turkestan."[8] The equerry falls into disgrace one day
when he chooses two ungainly foals for his master. In a fit of rage the
sultan has his equerry blinded, but condescends to present the grey foal
to the latter's son. From that time onward the boy calls himself Köroğlu (Kor-oğlu), "the son of the blind man" (Turkish *kör*, Azerbaijanian
kor, "blind"). He vows to avenge his father's mutilation, gathers a
retinue of brave men around him and builds a fort on Čamlïbel, the
pine-wooded mountain pass. From there he rides out on his numerous
expeditions on his *tulpar* (winged horse) Qïrat (or *Kïrat* in Turkish
spelling, "grey horse").

The Azerbaijanian and the Turkish versions are very similar, both as
regards the explanation of the hero's name and his characterization as
a daring and brave brigand. In the Turkish variants Köroğlu fights
against the bey of Bolu and is not a Turkmen. The specification that
the hero is a Turkmen is not generally found in the western version of
the cycle; it is typical of the eastern version and is among the Azerbaijanian variants restricted to Chodzko's text. One of the earliest
Turkish variants of the cycle was published by I. Kúnos in the eighth
volume of Radloff's *Proben*. Kúnos edits a 19th-c. lithograph of the
Köroğlu-story. This chapbook-version contains the main episodes of the
cycle: the blinding of Köroğlu's father, the acquisition of his horse Kïrat
and the formation of his band of warriors, among whom Ayvaz and
Kenan play a prominent role. It ends with a love-romance between
Hasan, Köroğlu's son, and Benli Hanım, which is brought to a happy
end through the help of Köroğlu and his men.[9]

Only comparatively few variants have been taken down from Turkish
*aşık*s, of which many are fragmentary. Among the longer ones is a
version lasting for more than ten hours, which W. Eberhard recorded (on

[7]On the Tobol Tatar text see Chapter Six, pp. 155f.; on a Crimean Tatar variant
see Bekirov 1980: 49-63.

[8]Chodzko 1842: 17.

[9]See Radloff 1899: 1-27; this text is still available in contemporary Latin script as
a popular booklet in Turkey. For a summary of this variant see also Boratav 1984:
30-33.

tape) in 1951 from the singer Hasan Devren in Gaziantep in south-eastern Turkey.[10] The most "complete" Turkish variant of *Köroğlu* is that recorded from Behçet Mahir in Erzerum in eastern Anatolia in 1958. This singer is illiterate; he is a peddler and tells the story of Köroğlu in the coffeehouses during the month of Ramazan. His version contains fifteen branches of the cycle and comprises about 600 pages in print. It is characterized by its lively, colloquial prose, interlarded with the narrator's comments and asides (see pp. 309f.). His narration proceeds at a leisurely pace and comes up to the expectations his opening remarks raise:

> Şimdi Köroğlunun esas neden Köroğlu olduğundan, babasından ve kendisinden, esasen başından konuşacağım. Baştan ahiri gideceğim, konuşa konuşa izahat vereceğim, bu kol kol ve kafile kafile. Çünkü her yemeğin lezzeti ayrı ayrı malum a.
>
> (Kaplan, Akalın, Bali 1973: 1)

> Now I will tell about Köroğlu, why he was called Köroğlu, about his father and himself, from the very beginning. I will go from beginning to end, I will narrate and give explanations, branch by branch and episode by episode. For, as everybody knows, every dish has its own separate flavor.

The prose-parts predominate over the verse-portions. According to Eberhard, a singer would sing during a stretch of 30 to 45 minutes an evening; each such session would on average contain one song.[11] The songs are comparatively stable, while individual minstrels differ from one another mainly in the prose-parts of the cycle.[12] This explains why there is a world of difference between the factual, condensed prose of the chapbooks and the vivid and somewhat meandering prose-style of a narrator like Behçet Mahir. The comparative stability of the verse-parts is an indication of their constitutive role in the cycle. They form as it were the nucleus of the individual tales, around which the narrative is constructed. Köroğlu himself is presented not only as a

---

[10] See Eberhard 1955: 31 (Text C); this version is, however, incomplete and has never been edited. See his analysis *ibid.*: 31-44. For a summary of a Turkish version which was published in Bulgaria see Karryev 1968: 77-99.

[11] Eberhard 1955: 49.

[12] *Ibid.*

courageous outlaw but also as a talented minstrel, whose songs are quite naturally incorporated into the tales.[13]

The composition of the tale-cycle is very similar to that of the *Book of Dede Qorqut*. The initial motif of the blinding of Köroğlu's father determines the course of action insofar as Köroğlu becomes an outlaw and gathers a band of valorous companions around him. But apart from this general structure of the cycle, the individual branches are independent of one another and strung together in an open-ended series of episodes and adventures. These consist of bride-winning expeditions (see Chapter Six), rescues from captivity, and military campaigns against the bey of Bolu and other enemies. Although *Köroğlu* is extended into the second generation with Köroğlu's son Hasan, whose love-adventure forms a separate branch, the cycle as a whole comes to an end with Köroğlu's death, which is often told as occurring when the old weapons were replaced by firearms.[14]

In the eastern versions of the cycle the protagonist is called Göroğlï, Goroğli, Göruğlï or Guroğlu, "the son of the grave" (from Persian *gūr*, "grave"). The difference in name is connected to a difference in plot. In the Uzbek and Uighur *dastan*s we are told that the hero was miraculously born in the grave. According to an Uighur variant, Zülpär-ayim, the sister of Ähmäd-xan, ruler over Čämbil, becomes unwittingly pregnant when the prophet Ali rides past her garden and desires her. When she finds out her condition she asks God to be merciful to her and cover up her shame by letting her die. Zülpär-ayim dies, but her child, a boy, is born in the grave and nursed by a dappled mare. When the boy is discovered, he is adopted by Ähmäd-xan and given the name "Göroğli."[15] The Turkmen version forms a bridge between the western and the eastern versions in that both the motif of the birth of the hero in a grave and of the blinding of his father are found here.[16] This

---

[13] According to Boratav a poet of the 16th c. by name of Köroğlu is identical with a Jalali captain by the same name; see Boratav 1964: 26.

[14] See Boratav 1964: 25f.

[15] See Tatliq et al. 1986: 3ff.

[16] See Karryev 1968: 140ff.; Karryev 1983: 11ff. Pelwan-baxšï calls his hero Köroğlï and not, as is usual in the Turkmen variants, Göroğlï. As the word for "grave" in Kazakh is *kör* with a voiceless initial consonant, the hero is also called Köruğlï (with /k/) in the Kazakh variants of the cycle. The motif of the blinding of the hero's father is also found in some Kazakh branches of the cycle as well as in some

change in name and plot goes hand in hand with a different conception of the hero. The rebel has become a feudal lord, who holds a sumptuous court with his retinue. Often he leaves it to his companions, adoptive sons, grandsons, and even great-grandsons to perform heroic deeds. By the same token, fabulous and fantastic traits begin to predominate, in particular in the Uzbek and Tajik (Iranian) versions:

> The Uzbek Gorogli is not a "noble bandit," but the Bek of the Turkmens and Uzbeks, of noble birth, ruler of the city and the land of Chambil, similar to the famous rulers of epic provenance — Charlemagne, King Arthur, Prince Vladimir of Kiev, the Kirghiz Manas or the Kalmuck Jangar. He is a wise and powerful sovereign and epic hero as well, the protector of his people against foreign invaders, alien khans and beks. In accordance with the democratic character of the tale, the figure of Gorogli becomes the embodiment of the popular ideal of patriarchal authority looking after the good of the people and in particular after the oppressed and unfortunate, while the legendary "Age of Gorogli" and his state Chambil come to resemble a popular Utopia — a land where under the authority of a wise ruler the eternal popular dream of social justice comes true.
>
> (Chadwick, Zhirmunsky 1969: 302-302)

The degree of popularity of the cycle differs from tradition to tradition. While from Karakalpak singers only few *dastans* have been recorded, other traditions, such as the Uzbek one, are particularly rich. Over sixty branches of the cycle are known in Uzbek; the *baxšis* of Khorezm needed seventeen days for the performance of the *Köroğlu/Göroğlï*-cycle.[17] As I have mentioned earlier, the *Köroğlu/Göroğlï*-cycle was (and is) also cultivated among the Uzbeks living in southern Tajikistan; it consists in some regions of no less than sixty-four branches.[18] The Karakalpak branches of the cycle, such as *Qïrmandäli*, are comparatively short (comprising between ten and somewhat over one hundred pages in print), while some of the Uzbek *dastans* are of great length: Ergaš Džumanbulbul-oğli's variant of

Uzbek *dastans* of Goroğli; in the Khorezmian branches the hero is is called Köroğli rather than Goroğli; see Žirmunskij, Zarifov 1947: 192ff., 197.

[17] See Mirzaev 1979: 19; compare Chapter Four, p. 97. On the Uzbek variants see Žirmunskij, Zarifov 1947: 165-279.

[18] See p. 71. Some branches of the cycle are only known from southern Tajikistan.

324   *Transformations in Space and Time*

Xāldārxān, for instance, runs to over 400 pages in the printed edition.[19]
The Uzbek branches of the cycle are, like other Uzbek *dastans*,
composed in verse and prose, with passages in rhymed prose and long,
elaborate verse-portions, differing markedly in style and narrative scope
from the Turkish *hikâyes*. As has been pointed out in Chapter Eight,
the Karakalpak branches of the cycle have been strongly influenced by
Turkmen and Khorezmian versions of the *Köroğlu/Göroğlï*-epic (see p.
260). Although similar influences have been exerted on the Kazakh
variants of the cycle, these form a distinct group among the eastern
Köroğlu/Göroğlï-dastans. Some of the Kazakh variants recorded are in
verse and prose and are both formally and stylistically comparable to
the shorter Karakalpak and Uzbek *dastans* of the Khorezmian tradition.
The majority of the Kazakh branches of the cycle are, however, pure
verse-epics, some in laisses of octosyllabic lines, some in (generally four-
lined) stanzas of endecasyllabic lines, and some in a mixture of both.[20]
This is to say that the Kazakh *žïraws* and *aqïns* sing the tales of
Köroğlu/Göroğlï in the form customary for Kazakh epic poetry rather
than in the prosimetric form in which the *dastans* are performed among
the Turkmens, from whom the *Köroğlu/Göroğlï*-cycle has spread to the
Kazakhs. This greater independence from neighboring traditions is also
shown by many idiosyncracies in the contents of the Kazakh branches
of the cycle, where more prominence is given to Köroğlu/Göroğlï (also to
his father Rawšan) than in most eastern versions.

The non-Turkic versions of the story of Köroğlu/Göroğlï fall like the
Turkic versions into two groups, a western and an eastern group. In the
western version the hero is "the son of the blind man," who, together
with his companions, sets out on various adventurous expeditions.
While the Armenian texts of the cycle are in verse, the other non-
Turkic western variants are either in prose or in prose with interspersed
verses. The Kurdish and Georgian tales which have been recorded are
all fairly short. It is interesting to note that in as far as they have
verse-passages these are in a Turkic language (generally Azer-

---

[19]See Zarif 1981. — On the Karakalpak variants of the cycle see Maqsetov
[Maksetov] et al. 1977: 49-58; see also the edition by Maqsetov, Karimov 1986.

[20]See the edition by Ġumarova, Äbišev 1989; on the Kazakh variants compare also
Karryev 1968: 235-249; Qoŋïratbaev 1987: 128-139. The latter attempts in a
somewhat speculative manner to link the Kazakh branches of the cycle with an earlier
period than is normally posited for the *Köroğlu/Göroğlï*-epic.

baijanian).[21]   The eastern version of non-Turkic variants comprises two hardly comparable groups of texts: tales in Arabic and *dastans* in Tajik.

The tales collected among the Arabs of Bukhara are short narratives in prose without a single line of verse.[22]   These texts retell, in bare outlines, five branches, the hero's birth in the grave (he is hence called "Gūroglī," "son of the grave"); his first heroic deed, the abduction of Rayhan-Arab's daughter; Gūroglī's capturing and adoption of Awaz; his finding a bride for his adoptive son; and Awaz's rescue from hanging by Gūroglī.

> Gūroglī is the son of a Turkmen married to the sister of a man called Gaždum. The hero is born after the death of his mother in the grave and, after his father has also died, is brought up by his uncle. In Gaždum's absence, Rayxān-Arab comes to abduct Gaždum's wife. Gūroglī unwittingly helps in this when he agrees to persuade his aunt to offer Rayxān-Arab a glass of water. In exchange for arranging this tête-à-tête, Gūroglī is allowed to mate his mare with the Arab's stallion. Gūroglī's horse has a foal, which in turn is covered by Xodža Xidir's (Hïzïr's) stallion. Xidir looks after the foal born from this union for three years. When he returns with this tulpār for the hero, he prophesies that Gūroglī will have no children and marry a peri. Then Gūroglī sets out to bring his aunt back from Rayxān-Arab's country. When he manages to see his aunt during the Arab's nap, she advises him to take back to her husband the Arab's daughter instead of herself, as she has grown too old. Gūroglī steals Rayxān-Arab's daughter in the same manner the latter had earlier abducted Gaždum's wife. When Rayxān-Arab, only scantily dressed in a bed-sheet, pursues Gūroglī, his horse is unable to jump across a river and the Arab falls into the water. Gaždum is content to marry the girl instead of recovering his wife.
>
> Gūroglī gathers forty companions around him and marries two peris from the land of Džambul. One day he is told of the beauty of Awiz-xān, the son of a butcher, who serves the emir of an unnamed town as a scribe. On approaching the town, Gūroglī binds the emir's shepherd and drives 400 of his sheep into town. He poses as Awiz-xān's uncle and declares that he is selling the sheep for his brother-in-law, the butcher. The butcher sends for his son to help Gūroglī drive the rest of the sheep into town. When Awiz-xān leaves town with Gūroglī, he is carried away by the hero. Awiz-xān is adopted by Gūroglī and

[21]On the Armenian version see Karryev 1968: 64-67; on the Kurdish version see *ibid.*: 67-71; on the Georgian version see *ibid.*: 71-76. Twelve short Georgian texts with Russian translations are edited in Člajdze 1978; of these texts only one contains verse-passages.

[22]See Cereteli 1956: 89-94 (text), 253-259 (translation); Vinnikov 1969: 179-184 (text), 184-190 (translation). On the "Arabic version" compare also Karryev 1968: 222-226.

develops into a skillful hunter. On a hunting expedition, Awiz-xān comes across a Kazakh encampment and falls in love with Axmad-bātïr's daughter. Gūroglī woos the girl for Awiz-xān, and as both Gūroglī and Axmad-bātïr are mighty heroes, they both agree to the marriage without fight or quarrel.

One day Awiz-xān decides to visit his parents. When his presence in his native town is made known, however, the emir has Awiz-xān imprisoned. Gūroglī arrives just in time before Awiz-xān is to be hanged and rescues his adopted son from the gallows. After his return to Džambul, Gūroglī goes out hunting. When he comes back, he tells his companions that he has lived long enough, having been married to two peris but having had no children, whereupon he lies down and dies.[23]

These texts are no more than summaries of five episodes treated at much greater length in other versions of the *Köroğlu/Göroğlï*-cycle. In content they agree closely with the Uzbek version of the cycle, with only small changes (such as the role of Xidir/Hïzïr in the begetting and training of the hero's horse Qïrat) and obviously drastic simplifications in plot and narrative structure.[24]

Of a quite different nature are the Tajik branches of the *Köroğlu/Göroğlï*-cycle. Tajik is a dialect of Persian which is mostly spoken by the Iranian population of northern Afghanistan, Tajikistan and Uzbekistan, but is also found in the neighboring Central Asian republics. The Tajiks live in close contact with speakers of Turkic languages, especially with speakers of Uzbek, which explains the marked Turkic influence on the lexicon and structure of the Tajik language as well as the diffusion of the *Köroğlu/Göroğlï*-cycle among the Tajiks. The recording of Tajik oral epic poetry only began in the 1930s; by the 1980s a rich corpus of texts had been collected, comprising ca. 360,000 verse-lines.[25] The main

---

[23]These are basically the contents of the text published by Cereteli. The text published by Vinnikov is very similar; the end is slightly different in that Gūroglī meets an old woman in a cave on his last hunting expedition. When she asks him what he is doing in the cave, Gūroglī answers that he has grown old and, despite being married to two peris, is leaving the world without children. He then returns and dies.

[24]On the corresponding branches of the Uzbek cycle see Žirmunskij, Zarifov 1947: 192ff.; Karryev 1968: 209ff. Göroğlï's marriage to the peris, the subject of several branches, is only mentioned in the Arabic texts.

[25]This is the number given in Braginskij, Nazarov, Šermuxammedov 1987: 671. For general information on the Tajik *Köroğlu/Göroğlï*-cycle see Boldyrev 1939; Braginskij 1958; Karryev 1958: 227-234; Cejpek 1959: 487-492; Braginskij 1987.

protagonist of the cycle is called "Gūrūġlī" (also "Gūrġūlī"), and the singers are hence called *gūrūġlīxān* ("reader of *Gūrūġlī*"), *gūrūġlīguy* ("narrator of *Gūrūġlī*") or *gūrūġlīsarā* ("singer of *Gūrūġlī*").

The branches of the cycle are in verse, ranging from ca. 200 to ca. 2,500 lines.[26] The metrical analysis of the verse is still a matter of dispute. The lines have on average ten to twelve syllables, which are arranged in rhythmic groups of three syllables, somewhat in the manner of a dactylic foot.[27] The verse-lines are grouped into laisses, as can be seen from the illustrations quoted below. Tales about Gūrūġlī have, however, also been recorded in prose, both as folktales and as a prose-cycle of eight *dastans*, told by Madžid Šarifov, a narrator from northern Tajikistan.[28] From some singers only short texts have been recorded, while from others the complete cycle has been taken down. The longest variant of the cycle is that by Hikmat Rizā, which comprises 34 *dastans*, running to over 100,000 lines. The *dastans* are performed to the accompaniment of the *dutar*. The singer uses different melodies for his performance; over thirty such melodies are known to exist. A performance might last from six to twelve hours. It normally takes place at night. To the singer's repertory belongs not only epic poetry; he also performs songs, lyric poetry, and extracts from Classical Persian poetry. The *Gūrūġlī*-cycle is mainly found in southwestern Tajikistan, where two "singer-schools" can be distinguished; of these that of Kulyab (Kulāb) is considered the cradle of the Tajik version of *Köroġlu/Göroġlī*.

The Tajik *Gūrūġlī*-cycle has a kernel of six episodes: Gūrūġlī's birth and the founding of Čambul; his adoption of Awaz; the hostility between Awaz and Ahmad; Awaz's marriage to Ahmad's daughter; Awaz's fight against the enemies of Čambul; and the adventures of Awaz's sons Nuralī and Šeralī.[29] In order to give an impression of the Tajik

[26]Of the twenty branches published in Braginskij, Nazarov, Šermuxammedov 1987 the shortest comprises 156 lines, the longest 1,738 lines; the majority of the branches are between 300 and 600 lines. Among the variants of the cycle recorded from Qabud Haqnazarov the longest published in Amānov 1976 comprises ca. 2,500 lines.

[27]See Beliaev 1975: 211f.; Braginskij 1987: 43f.; compare also the musical example in Braginskij, Nazarov, Šermuxammedov 1987: 688-695.

[28]For a folktale on Awaz see Amānov 1980: 97-102; for Šarifov's text see Amānov 1960: 271-409. This prose-cycle is also listed in Braginskij, Nazarov, Šermuxammedov 1987: 682, where it is erroneously said to consist of seven branches.

[29]See the analysis in Braginskij, Nazarov, Šermuxammedov 1987: 671-683.

Gūrūġlī, I will give a summary of the first branch of the cycle according to the variant taken down from Qurbān Džalil (d. 1946).[30] This singer's version consists of nine *dastans* of a total of 8,000 lines; the first branch is 460 lines long.

> Rayhānarab, a mighty padishah, hears through his soothsayer about Ahmad, the ruler of the Turkmens, his wife Dalla and his beautiful sister Hilāl. Rayhānarab sends a magician to Ahmad to bring Hilāl's portrait back to him. Overcome by the girl's beauty, Rayhānarab sends a delegation to Ahmad to woo Hilāl for him. Ahmad agrees, but Hilāl, who has led the life of a Cinderella in her brother's household, flees into the desert, where she dies. Ahmad sends his daughter, disguised as Hilāl, to Rayhānarab. Rayhānarab, who is unaware of the substitution, presents a mare by the name of Qullā to Ahmad as a return gift. One day this mare reaches Hilāl's tomb. Unknown to anybody a boy has been born in the tomb, whom the mare feeds and thus keeps alive. When the child is detected by Ahmad's tribesmen, the boy is brought to Ahmad and called Gūrūġlī, "son of the grave."
>
> One day Gūrūġlī chases away Ahmad's forty herdsmen and drives the horses into the desert. When Ahmad arrives to punish the boy, he realizes that Gūrūġlī has found an excellent grazing pasture. Ahmad allows Gūrūġlī to choose a horse for himself, whereupon Gūrūġlī takes Qullā, saying that he is only taking what is his rightful due. Gūrūġlī's behavior is considered insolent by Ahmad, and uncle and nephew part company.
>
> The news of Gūrūġlī's prowess reaches the ears of Rayhānarab, who realizes that as Gūrūġlī is Hilāl's son he was tricked by Ahmad. In order to take revenge he abducts Ahmad's wife Dalla. Gūrūġlī helps Rayhānarab in this expedition, in exchange for Rayhānarab's permission to let the latter's stallion mount Gūrūġlī's Qullā. From this union a foal, worthy of a hero like Gūrūġlī, is born. Ahmad promises Gūrūġlī to present him with a harness for his horse if he brings him Rayhānarab's daughter. Gūrūġlī disguises himself as a dervish, reaches Rayhānarab's castle, and with Dalla's help carries off the girl. Rayhānarab pursues the violator of his honor but is unable to catch up with Gūrūġlī when the latter jumps across a river on his fabulous horse.
>
> Gūrūġlī, having become famous, builds himself a fortress called "Čambuli-mastān." Two peris in the garden of Iram (the earthly paradise), Aġāyunus and Širmā, hear of Gūrūġlī and fly in the likeness of doves to his fortress to become his wives. As Gūrūġlī has no children of his own, he disguises himself as a *qalandar* (dervish) and goes to Isfahan to abduct Hasan, the son of a weaver; later he goes to Qipčāq to bring Šādmān as an adoptive son to Čambul.

---

[30]On this variant see Braginskij, Nazarov, Šermuxammedov 1987: 679; for the text see Braginskij, Nazarov, Šermuxammedov 1987: 47-57; for a Russian translation see *ibid.*: 357-368; compare also the translation in Petrosjan 1975: II, 353-363.

The course of events is similar to that of the Arabic texts summarized above and agrees basically with the Uzbek and Uighur versions: Gürüġlī is born in a grave and raised by his uncle; he is instrumental in his aunt's abduction by Rayhānarab (although unintentionally so in other versions), in the course of which Gürüġlī's horse is covered by Rayhānarab's steed; and he abducts in turn the latter's daughter for his uncle to wed. There are also differences such as Rayhānarab's wish to marry Hilāl, and Hilāl's pregnancy, which remains unexplained. The story of Gürüġlī's birth up to his stealing Rayhānarab's daughter takes up the greater part of the *dastan* (ll. 1-386). The foundation of Čambul, Gürüġlī's marriage to two peris, and his adoption of Hasan and Šādmān are narrated in summary fashion only (ll. 387-460). In the first lines the setting is given:

> Rayhānarab bud pādšāhi kalān,
> hukmrānī mekard ba džahān,
> qizu qirqin dāšt čandinta āydžān,
> Xirmangul guftagī duxtar dāšt — māhi džān,
> 5   tilismgar dāst sehrxān,
> qur'azan dāšt, qur'a mezad; mekard bayān;
> xāh dust medid, xāh dušman,
> dar Rayhān mekard bayān.
> Qur'a zad, did xalqi turkamān,
> 10   ābādišān dar tuqai Naistān.
>   (Braginskij, Nazarov, Šermuxammedov 1987: 47)

> Rayhānarab was a great padishah,
> who ruled over the earth.
> He had many beautiful servant-girls and slave-girls,
> and he had a daughter by the name of Xirmangul, who was beautiful
>   as the moon.
> 5   He had a magician and a sorcerer,
> as well as a soothsayer, who cast the lots and read them;
> he could see both friend and enemy
> and revealed these to Rayhān.
> He cast the lots and saw the people of the Turkmens,
> 10   who lived prosperously in the *tuqay* (an area covered by reeds) of
>   Naistān (Nowhere).

The singer proceeds to name the ruler of the Turkmens, his advisers and family and continues with Rayhānarab's wish to have Hilāl's portrait. Although direct speech is introduced into the narrative, long dialogues or monologues are absent. There is little dramatization and there are

no lyrical passages as in the Uzbek *dastans*.[31] As can be inferred from
the shortness of the *dastan*, the narrative pace is swift; the singer moves
from event to event without indulging in detailed descriptions or
elaborating on individual scenes. Only rarely does the narrator enlarge
on a point, as when Gūrūġlī feeds his foal:

> Kuluni nar kard baytalašān,
> 325 az āčaš burda mānd kirān.
> Zārī kard, girift širi insān,
> širi ādam bixurānd, girift aqli insān.
> Ba čul xamid peši ušturbān,
> girift šir az ušturbān,
> 330 dādaš širi farāwān,
> baland šud qāmati tallān.
> Ba čul raft peši gusfandbān,
> dādaš širi farāwān,
> az quwwati xudaš gašt kard ba čulhā.
> 335 Širi rubah xurāndaš, dawand šud dar maydān.
> Širi zarguš xurāndaš, az dur mekard gumān.
> Yapāġu tāy šud, tāi kalān,
> sawāri kardaš dar aylāqi kalān...
>
> (Braginskij, Nazarov, Šermuxammedov 1987: 54)

> Gūrūġlī's mare gave birth to a foal.
> 325 It was taken from its mother's side.
> When it complained, he took human milk,
> gave human milk to his foal, and so it acquired human intelligence.
> He went into the desert in search of the camel herdsman,
> took milk from the camel herdsman,
> 330 and gave his foal milk in abundance.
> It grew tall in stature, with a dapple-grey hide.
> He went into the desert in search of the shepherd,
> and gave his foal sheep milk in abundance.
> Strengthened by it, the foal began to run about in the steppe.
> 335 He gave his foal fox's milk, and it began to gallop around on the field.
> He gave it hare's milk, and it began to scent from afar.
> The one-year-old foal grew into a big foal;
> Gūrūġlī rode it on the wide summer pastures...

Although some variants of the Tajik *Gūrūġlī*-cycle are longer and
somewhat more circumstantial in their narrative development, the
various branches of the cycle are basically short epic poems, which do
not achieve the "epic breadth" of some of the longer Uzbek *dastans*. In
subject matter the Tajik *Gūrūġlī*-poems are similar to the Uzbek

---

[31]Some Tajik singers do, however, incorporate lyrical passages into their *dastans*;
see Braginskij 1987: 39.

branches of the cycle, in particular as regards the prominence given to Gūrūġlī's adoptive son Awaz and to Awaz's son Nuralī.[32] Differences do, however, exist, both in the details of the various plots and in their *dramatis personae*. Among the latter the figure of Sāqī is unique to the Tajik *dastans*. He is introduced in the last lines of the branch summarized above as a singer who sings about the heroic deeds of Gūrūġlī and his retinue:

> Nāmi Sāqī šud bābā, tambur dādaš az tillā,
> xāniš mekard az dunyā,
> 460 bayān mekard az qahramāniyā.

(Braginskij, Nazarov, Šermuxammedov 1987: 57)

> Sāqī was called "Grandfather" and given a *tanbur* made of gold.
> He sang about (what happened in) the world,
> 460 he told stories about heroic deeds.

In this function Sāqī reappears in various *dastans*, not unlike Grandfather Qorqut in the *Book of Dede Qorqut*.

To sum up: the *Köroğlu/Göroğli*-cycle most likely originated in Azerbaijan at the end of the 16th century, from where it spread north, east, and west. Kúnos, the editor of an early Turkish chapbook, remarks that the story of Köroğlu has spread to Turkey from Azerbaijan and adds that the basis of the popular prints in which the story circulates is in oral tradition:

> Even the contemporary chapbooks have been written down by people of Azerbaijanian origin. An indication of this is the language of the popular prints, which has preserved many Azerbaijanian characteristics. There can be no doubt that these chapbooks are of popular origin. The various songs of the tale are sung separately, and I have heard and recorded such Anatolian songs in various parts where the popular prints are unknown.

(Kúnos in Radloff 1899: ix-x)

From northern Azerbaijan the tale-cycle spread to other Transcaucasian peoples, also to those speaking non-Turkic languages such as the Georgians, Kurds, and Armenians. From there the story spread to the

---

[32]See Boldyrev 1939: 303f.; Karryev 1968: 230f. For an edition of Uzbek *dastans* on Nurali see Imāmov et al. 1989; for a French translation of Uzbek *dastans* on Nurali see Dor 1991; compare also Žirmunskij, Zarifov 1947: 265-270.

Crimean Tatars, the Tobol Tatars, and the Karaims.[33] In the southern
Azerbaijanian version translated by Chodzko Köroğlu is a Turkmen, a
circumstance which points to a possible Turkmen influence on this
version. Be that as it may be, the Turkmen version certainly plays a
central role in the transformation of the story and its diffusion to the
east. The motif of the hero's birth in a grave characterizes all eastern
versions, even if many of them also contain the motif of the blinding of
the hero's father. From the Turkmens the cycle reached other peoples
by different paths. It has been noted that the version of *Köroğlu/Gör-
oğlï* current among the Turkmens of Stavropol (north of the Caucasus)
is similar to that of the Kazakhs. Some of these Turkmens fled to the
Maŋqïstaw region in the province of Mangyshlak (on the eastern shore
of the Caspian Sea) in the 17th century. It is from these Turkmens that
Kazakh singers seem to have learned the cycle.[34] The Karakalpaks and
Khorezmian Uzbeks, on the other hand, were influenced by the
Turkmens with whom they live in close contact in the oasis of Khorezm.
Uzbek *baxšis* became familiar with the repertory of Turkmen singers
also in other parts of Uzbekistan. Islām-šāir, for instance, learned the
dastan Xirmān-Dali (of the *Goroğli*-cycle) from a Turkmen singer in the
Bukhara region.[35] From the Uzbeks the story traveled to the Uighurs,
as well as to the Arabs of Bukhara and to the Tajiks. In the course of
its diffusion the story-cycle changed not only in the conception of the
hero, transforming an outlaw and minstrel into a Central Asian padishah, but also in size and scope. The cycle was extended not only to
Köroğlu's/ Göroğlï's adoptive sons, but also to his grandsons and, in the
Uzbek version, even to his great-grandson Džahāngir, Nurali's son.[36]

The story-cycle did not, of course, spread in straight lines. The
Karakalpak tradition, for instance, has not only been under the
influence of the Turkmen but also of the Uzbek *dastans*. Mutual
influences can be discerned, as for instance of the Uzbek on the Tajik
tradition, but also vice versa of the Tajik *dastans* on the version of the

---

[33]Klimovič mentions an unedited Karaim version of the *Köroğlu/Göroğlï*-cycle; see
Klimovič 1959: 185, note 1.

[34]See Ġumarova, Äbišev 1989: 7.

[35]See Mirzaev 1979: 49.

[36]See Žirmunskij, Zarifov 1947: 276-278.

Uzbek-Laqays in southern Tajikistan.[37]   Each ethnic and linguistic group incorporated the epic cycle into its own tradition. The prose-tale with occasional interspersed poems is prevalent in some traditions, the verse-epic in others, the prosimetric *dastan* in yet others. It speaks for the popularity of the story-cycle that in multilingual and multicultural settings like those found in the Caucasus it also became diffused across linguistic boundaries. Bilingual singers were the carriers of this diffusion, made all the easier in a bilingual context such as that prevalent in southern Uzbekistan and Tajikistan.

Alpamïš: Variation and Chronology

The diffusion of the *Köroglu/Göroglï*-cycle among speakers of Turkic and non-Turkic languages offers a good example of how not only folktales but also epic and narrative poetry spreads across language-boundaries in situations of linguistic and cultural contact. Other Turkic epics are more restricted in their diffusion. The epic of Alpamïš is, with few exceptions, only found in the Turkic world; outside of the Turkic-speaking peoples variants have been recorded only from the Tajiks and, in the form of the folktale, from the Arabs of Central Asia.[38] What is interesting about the Alpamïš-story is its dissemination not so much in terms of geography as in terms of chronology. The different variants and versions that have been transmitted and recorded vary considerably as to their historical depth. The situation here is similar to that familiar from medieval literature where for instance the legend of the Nibelungs is extant in different versions which were not only composed at different times but also suggest different stages in the development of the legend:

> ...the abundant traditions handed down in both Old Norse and Middle High German and the intricacies of relating these traditions to one another with the tempting prospect of establishing some ancestral prototype have made the Nibelung question into the North European

---

[37]See Karryev 1968: 233; Mirzaev 1979: 55f.

[38]Four Tajik variants are edited in Amānov, Demidčik 1959; of these two are in verse (comprising ca. 350 lines each) and two in prose. Compare also Žirmunskij 1960: 30-35. — I will generally use the form "Alpamïš" for the hero's name, unless I refer to a specific variant (Uzbek "Alpāmiš," Kazakh, Karakalpak "Alpamïs" etc.).

equivalent of the Homeric question and have engaged scholars in
exceptionally subtle and detailed debates.

(Andersson 1980: 15)

So far only one variant of the Alpamïš-story has been discussed, that
taken down from the Uzbek *baxši* Fāzil Yoldāš-oġli (see Chapter Six, pp.
161ff.). Fāzil's *Alpāmiš* is, however, just one of many Uzbek variants of
the epic. Tora Mirzaev has studied and compared these variants in
detail, listing 28 *baxšis* from whom the *dastan* has been recorded.[39]
Although there is considerable diversity between these variants, they
are in plot structure, motif sequence, but also style and narrative
technique, so similar to one another that there can be no doubt about
their belonging together. It is useful to group the Uzbek *Alpāmiš-
dastans* together into one class, denoting this class as the "Uzbek
version" of the epic of Alpamïš. In a similar manner the Karakalpak
variants of the epic can be classified as the "Karakalpak version" and
the Kazakh variants as the "Kazakh version." The term "version" here
signifies a group of variants of the same epic which all share the same
language as well as the peculiarities — stylistic, musical or otherwise
— of their respective traditions.[40]   Some of the variants within a
particular "language version" will be related more closely to one
another than others, owing to contacts between singers, singer-pupil
relationships, the influence of written texts, or simply the caprice of
transmission (missing links in the chain of transmission, incomplete
recordings etc.). Just as an editor of a classical or medieval text which
has been transmitted in various manuscripts tries to make sense of the
manuscript tradition by classifying and arranging the texts in a
stemma, the scholar in the field of oral epic poetry will want to compare
the various recordings of an epic in order to assess the growth and
transformation of the epic in the course of its oral transmission. Like
the classicist and medievalist, the folklorist can attempt to arrange his
data in some kind of stemma, although the form of oral transmission

[39]See Mirzaev 1968; for a list of singers see *ibid.*: 161-169. In his edition of Berdi
Baxši's variant, Mirzaev lists 33 texts (both fragmentary and complete) of the *dastan*;
see Mirzaev 1969: 108-110. On the Uzbek variants see also Afzalov 1959.

[40]As pointed out earlier (see p. 6), I do not generally differentiate between
"version" and "variant" in the way these terms are often distinguished in Russian and
Central Asian scholarship. In this section, I will, however, use the term "variant"
with reference to one singer only (as in "Fāzil's variant of the epic of Alpamïš") and
reserve the term "version" for a group of texts/variants or a group of versions.

does not permit inferences of a stringency such as is possible in the textual criticism of literature transmitted purely in writing.[41]

In his detailed study of the Alpamïš-story, V. Žirmunskij has shown that a comparison and classification of the various variants of the story helps to understand diffusion both in place and in time. On closer analysis, the Uzbek, Karakalpak, and Kazakh versions agree so closely with one another that they can be grouped together into a higher group, termed "Kungrat version" by Žirmunskij.[42] When compared to other versions and variants of the Alpamïš-story, the "Kungrat version" is characterized by placing the story in the world of the nomadic Turks, more particularly the Qoṇġïrāt or Qoṇïrat tribe, who, according to the various texts recorded, live in the land of Žideli Baysïn and are engaged in warfare against the Kalmucks. Fāzil's variant begins with the words:

Burungi otgan zamānda, on āltï uruġ Qoṇġïrāt elida Dābānbiy degan otdi.

(Zarif, Mirzaev 1979: 5)

In the days of yore, among the Qoṇġïrāt people of the sixteen clans there lived a man by name of Dābānbiy.

In Berdi-baxši's Uzbek variant Dābānbiy divides his realm among his two sons, giving Baysïn to Bāysarï, Qoṇġïrāt to Bāybori.[43] Similarly, the Kazakh variant recorded from Äbdrayïm Baytursïnov begins:

Burïngï ötken zamanda,
din musïlman amanda,
Žideli Baysïn žerinde
Qoṇïrat degen elinde,
Bayböri degen bolïptï.

(Äwezov [Auezov], Smirnova 1961: 106)

In the days of yore,
when the faith of Moslems was flourishing,

---

[41]The chronological study and interpretation of variants of epic poetry has been successfully applied to the Russian *byliny* and the Romanian heroic ballads in Anikin 1984 and Gacak 1989.

[42]For a comparision see Žirmunskij 1960: 15-62; Žirmunskij argues that the Tajik poems and prose tales on Alpamïš as well as folktales on Alpamïš recorded among the Central Asian Arabs also belong to this group. On the Karakalpak version see also Sagitov 1959; Maqsetov [Maksetov] et al. 1977: 15-19. The Kazakh version has been studied in detail by Sydykov 1975.

[43]See Mirzaev 1969: 8.

in a place called Žideli Baysïn,
among the people called Qoŋïrat,
there lived a man called Bayböri.

The same setting is found in the Karakalpak version; the opening lines
of the variant recorded from Niyaz-ulï Ögiz-žïraw read:

Ertedegi äyyem zamanda,
ol zamannïŋ qädiminde,
Žiydeli Baysïn xalqïnda,
Qoŋïrat degen el edi,
urïwï edi ïrġaqlï.

(Bayniyazov, Ayïmbetov 1981: 9)

In the days long past,
in the days of yore,
among the Žiydeli Baysïn people,
there was a tribe called Qoŋïrat,
and in it a clan called Ïrġaqlï.

As can be seen from these examples, there is some uncertainty among
the singers as to the exact geographical location and tribal affiliation of
Alpamïš and his forefathers. The Qoŋïrat (Qonġirāt) were together with
other tribes such as the Qïpčaq (Kipchak) and the Nayman part of the
Golden Horde (13th c.). It is believed that like other Turkic tribal
names "Qoŋïrat" (Qonġirāt) is of Mongolian origin.[44] As a Turkic tribal
unit the Qoŋïrat (Qonġirāt) entered later into the composition of the
Uzbeks, Karakalpaks, and Kazakhs; the Kazakh Qoŋïrat are part of the
Middle Horde; the Karakalpak Qoŋïrat form one the two tribal groups
(*arïs*) of the Karakalpaks, who lived in the past predominantly on the
southern shore of the Aral Sea and the western side of Amu-Darya. The
Ïrġaqlï mentioned in the Karakalpak *Alpamïs* are a clan belonging to
the Žawïnġïr, one of the two divisions of the Qoŋïrat.[45] Among the
Uzbeks, the greatest number of Qonġirāt was according to the 1924
census to be found in the Baysun-Darya valley in southern Uzbekistan
(*Surxandar'inskaja oblast'*).[46] Is this the region called Baysïn or Žiydeli
Baysïn, "Baysïn rich in *žiyde*-trees (oleaster, *elaeagnus*)"? While some
Turkologists have answered this question in the affirmative, others have

---

[44]See Ždanko 1950: 118-121.

[45]See Ždanko 1950: 51-62; Nasyrov 1983: 60f.; Mukanov 1974: 58ff.

[46]See Džabbarov 1971: 129.

suggested that the geographical term "Žiydeli Baysïn" originally denoted the area south of the Aral Sea.[47] According to Žirmunskij the epic of Alpamïš as known among the Uzbeks, Kazakhs, and Karakalpaks originated with the Uzbek tribe of the Qongïrāt. At the time of khan Muḥammad Šaibānī (early 16th century) this tribe had according to historical sources not yet moved to the Baysun-Darya valley but was to be found in the vicinity of Termez (on the border of present-day Afghanistan). This means that the "Kungrat version" of the epic must have been composed after their move further north to Baysïn (Baysun), i.e. not before the 16th century.[48] H. Zarif, on the other hand, while also asserting that the epic originated with the Qongïrāt, locates Baysïn on the shores of the Aral Sea.[49] For Zarif's hypothesis speaks the fact that groups of Uzbek Qongïrāts are found in Khorezm and that according to an old tradition Barčin's grave is to be found on the bank of the lower Syr-Darya.[50] Abu'l Ġazi mentions in his *Pedigree of the Turkmens* (*Šedžere-i terakime*; 17th c.) that for many years seven maidens ruled the Oghuz, one of whom was called Barčïn-Salor. She was Qarmïš-bay's daughter and married to Mamïš-bek. "Her grave is on the bank of the Syr-Darya and is widely known among the people."[51] Clearly, Barčïn-Salor is Barčin and Mamïš-bek is Alp-mamïš ("hero Mamïš") or, through assimilation of the initial /m/ in Mamïš, Alp-pamïš ≈ Alp-amïš; the hero of the Altaian version is still called "Alïp-Manaš" with initial /m/. Zarif believes that the "Kungrat version" originated in

[47]In a study of the flora in *Alpamïš* S. I. Sagitov has tried to prove the latter hypothesis; it is, however, doubtful that the botanical terms found in the extant variants of the epic can be interpreted as historical evidence. The famous hypothesis about the original habitat of the Indo-Europeans, based on the study of common plant-terms in the Indo-European languages, comes to mind, a hypothesis which has remained controversial. See Sagitov 1968.

[48]The tribal composition of the Uzbeks is a complicated matter. The settled population of what are today called Uzbeks was generally called "Sarts" in pre-revolutionary Russia. The semi-nomadic Uzbeks are composed of two groups, the Uzbek tribes, descended from the Dešt-i Qïpčaq, who moved into Transoxania in 16th century with Šaibānī-khan, and the descendants of an earlier Turkic population of the area. See Karmyševa 1960.

[49]See Žirmunskij 1960: 46ff.; Zarifov 1959: 8; Mirzaev 1968: 18-19.

[50]See Ždanko 1950: 119-120.

[51]Kononov 1958: 79 (text); 78 (translation).

this region before the Mongol invasion of the Dešt-i Qïpcaq south of the Aral Sea, i.e. before 1200.

Without detailed historical research any attempts at dating the origin of this version must rest on extremely shaky foundations. Historical investigations are, however, hampered by major obstacles. There are still many gaps in our knowledge of the history of the Central Asian Turks, some due to the lack of historical sources, some to their inadequacy and ambiguity, some to the confusing use of tribal names in historical documents, which are not always easy to match with one another. Furthermore, the historical interpretation of the names of persons and places we find in the epics is fraught with problems. Although a certain historicity of figures and places can be discerned in many heroic epics, the relationship between a historical fact and its reflection in literature is often more than tenuous. It is incontestable, for instance, that King Hygelac's raid of the Franks and subsequent death as alluded to in the Old English *Beowulf* refers to an event from around A.D. 521, which is recorded independently in Frankish historiographical works. But the fact that Hygelac's death can be dated into the 6th century does not make Beowulf, who is Hygelac's nephew, thane, and ultimately successor in the epic, into a 6th-century figure nor *Beowulf* into a 6th-century epic. As far as we can judge, Beowulf is an entirely legendary figure, and the Old English epic as we have it cannot have been composed much earlier than the 8th century, maybe even as late as the 10th century.

Although it might not be possible to reach agreement and certainty on the dating of the "Kungrat version," it is undeniable that the plot of the Alpamïš-story was already known to the Turkic peoples of Central Asia before the Oghuz moved west from Dešt-i Qïpčaq into Iran and ultimately Anatolia. Otherwise the closeness between the *Tale of Bamsï Beyrek* in the *Book of Dede Qorqut* and the Central Asian versions of *Alpamïš* could only be explained through borrowing from medieval Anatolia into Central Asia, a hypothesis which is not very likely. The correspondences between the "Kungrat" and the "Oghuz version" are indeed so remarkable that there can be little doubt that they represent developments of the same story.[52]

___

[52]See Ergin 1958-63: I, 116-153 (text); for an English translation see Sümer, Uysal, Walker 1972: 40-69; Lewis 1974: 59-87.

Among the Oghuz, Bay Büre Beg and Bay Bidžan Beg have no children, but their prayers are fulfilled and Bay Büre gets a son, Bay Bidžan a daughter. The two children are promised to one another in their cradles. Merchants are sent out to buy presents for Bay Büre's son Beyrek. When they return after sixteen years with a sea-born grey stallion foal (*deŋiz qulunï boz aygïr*), a mighty bow with a white grip (*ağ tozlu qatï yay*), and a mace with six sides (*altï perlü gürz*), their encampment is raided. Beyrek comes to their rescue without revealing his identity. At his father's tent the merchants pay homage to their rescuer when they see him, and his first heroic deed is thus made known. Now that heads have been cut the young man can according to Oghuz custom receive a name, and Dede Qorqut ceremonially names him Bamsï Beyrek of the grey stallion (*boz aygïrlu Bamsï Beyrek*).

Bamsï Beyrek encounters his betrothed, Banï Čiček, for the first time when he is out hunting. He comes upon her tent, not knowing who she is, and is challenged to a three-fold contest, a bow-shooting contest, a horse-race, and a wrestling match. Beyrek is victorious, but is impressed by Banï Čiček's skill and strength. Before he can marry the girl, her brother Deli Qarčar has to be satisfied. He demands from Dede Qorqut, who is sent as matchmaker, one thousand male camels, stallions and rams which have never seen a female, one thousand dogs without tails and ears, and one thousand huge fleas. Dede Qorqut manages to find the animals, but has to employ deceit when it comes to bringing the fleas. He locks Čiček's brother Deli Qarčar into a flea-infested sheep-fold, where he gets more than his fair share of the bride-price he demanded. A marriage-feast is prepared, but in the night Bamsï Beyrek is attacked by the infidels — the king of Bayburt also wants to marry Banï Čiček — and led away as prisoner together with thirty-nine of his companions.

Sixteen years later still no news of Beyrek's fate has reached the Oghuz. Yartačuq, who was once given a shirt by Beyrek, takes this, dips it in blood and declares that Beyrek is dead, asserting in this way his right to Banï Čiček's hand. When he is about to be married to Beyrek's wife, Beyrek hears of what has happened from merchants who have gone out to look for him. The king of Bayburt's daughter, having fallen in love with Beyrek, frees the prisoner. Beyrek is let down the castle wall by a rope, finds his horse and rides back home. On the way he exchanges clothes with an *ozan*, a singer. Before he reaches the marriage feast, he meets with shepherds loyal to him, with his youngest sister, and with his other sisters, who are all lamenting for their brother. At the feast he is given his own bow to prove his skill; Beyrek shoots through the mark, the bridegroom's ring, and breaks it into pieces. He then addresses songs to Bayïndir Khan and the ladies of his court, exchanges songs with his faithful wife and is finally recognized by everybody. The ultimate proof of his identity is given when he smears his blood on his blind father's eyes, who miraculously regains his eyesight by this treatment. The story ends with the liberation of Beyrek's companions and the destruction of Bayburt, and with Beyrek giving his seven sisters to his companions and himself taking the king of Bayburt's daughter as his second wife.

There is no need to enumerate the points this tale of the *Book of Dede Qorqut* has in common with the epic of Alpamïš as represented for instance in Fāzil's variant summarized in Chapter Six. The names of the hero and his father are also identical; Bay Büre clearly corresponds to Bay Böri, and in the name "Bamsï" the name-form "Bamïš" or "Mamïš" can be recognized which, on the evidence of Abu'l Ġazi, must be thought to be the basis for "Alp-amïš."[53]   The only noticeable difference between the "Oghuz" and the "Kungrat version" lies in the historical setting of the story: instead of the Qoŋïrat we have the Oghuz, instead of the infidel (Buddhist-Lamaist) khan of the Kalmucks the infidel (Christian) king of Bayburt.   Both the Christians and the Kalmucks are later adaptations of the Oghuz and the Uzbeks, Kazakhs and Karakalpaks to their respective world, and neither can have been original to the story from which their versions ultimately derive. This story (in whatever form) cannot have been composed any later than the 11th century, the time when Oghuz tribes started moving westwards from the lower reaches of the Syr-Darya.[54]   It was then like the other tales in the *Book of Dede Qorqut* reset in an Anatolian milieu.   The story of Bamsï Beyrek lived on in Turkish folklore in the *hikâyes* of Bey Böyrek, which attest to the vitality of the Alpamïš-story not only in Central Asia but also in Turkey.[55]

Although there is no space here to give extensive illustrations from the various versions and variants of the Alpamïš-story, I will give two examples of what Žirmunskij termed the "Kipchak version" in order to demonstrate both the similarity between these versions and their respective differences.   I will take one of the Bashkir variants of the Alpamïš-story, which was recorded in 1968 from a 76-year-old Bashkir woman, Ömmöxayat Qoldäwlätova. This variant is comparatively short; it comprises 15 pages in manuscript, 11 pages in print; it is a prosimetric tale, containing 134 verse-lines.[56]   Over twenty Bashkir variants

---

[53]On the "Oghuz version" of the Alpamïš-story see Žirmunskij 1960: 63-84; compare also Žirmunskij 1974 [1962]: 584-589.

[54]On the date see Žirmunskij 1974 [1962]: 526-532; Boratav 1982-83 [1958].

[55]See Boratav 1982-83 [1939]; for a comparative analysis of the tale of Bamsï Beyrek see also Ruben 1944: 206-227; Rossi 1952: 58ff.; Korogly 1976: 112-122.

[56]Sägitov [Sagitov], Xarisov 1973: 26-36 (text); Sägitov [Sagitov], Zaripov, Sulejmanov 1987: 227-239 (translation); on the informant see Sägitov [Sagitov], Xarisov

have been recorded, all short tales, some prosimetric.[57] This is not to say that the Bashkirs do not also possess longer epic poems; their most famous epic, *Ural-batïr*, is predominantly in verse and comprises over 4,000 verse-lines.[58] Qoldäwlätova's variant can be summarized briefly as follows:

> Äylär and Aqkübäk, two neighboring khans, are childless. When Aq-kübäk's wife gives birth to a son, Äylär's wife has a daughter, called Barsïnhïlïw.[59] Aqkübäk's son grows at such a miraculous speed that the khan's *hïnsï* (soothsayer) calls him "Alpamïša," as he is obviously destined to become an *alïp* (hero). Aqkübäk's wife gives also birth to a daughter, called Qarluġas; not long afterwards Aqkübäk dies.
>
> As Alpamïša and Barsïnhïlïw grow older, both acquire heroic strength and Barsïnhïlïw announces that she will only marry a suitor who is able to defeat her in a wrestling match. Alpamïša catches a horse for himself from a herd of horses, jealously guarded by Qoltaba, and, on his horse Qolyerän, he sets out on his journey to Barsïnhïlïw. Alpamïša defeats Barsïnhïlïw and lives with her in a tent till she conceives, when the two marry and move to Alpamïša's home-land.
>
> Büðär-khan, who earlier wooed Barsïnhïlïw but was rejected, invades Alpamïša's country; he is, however, defeated. But Alpamïša lies down to sleep for six days and six nights and Büðär-khan is able to capture the hero, whom he then locks into an underground prison. One day Alpamïša sends a letter to his wife by a wild goose. His son Ayðar shoots down the goose, and the letter reaches Qoltaba instead, the guardian of horses, who had in Alpamïša's absence made Qarluġas his slave and set his eyes on Barsïnhïlïw. Alpamïša's wife, however, had made it a condition that whoever wanted to marry her had to be able to draw Alpamïša's bow and shoot through a ring. So far no one had been able to perform this feat.
>
> In his prison, Alpamïša makes himself a *kuray*.[60] His playing attracts Büðär-khan's three daughters, the youngest of whom has a tunnel dug to his prison, through which she provides him with food.

1973: 325.

[57]See Säġitov [Sagitov], Xarisov 1973: 325-332; Säġitov [Sagitov], Zaripov, Sulej-manov 1987: 507-508. On the Bashkir variants compare also Žirmunskij 1960: 85-96; Žirmunskij bases his analysis on five Bashkir variants.

[58]Edited in Säġitov [Sagitov], Xarisov et al. 1977.

[59]Bashkir *-hïlïw* corresponds to Kazakh *-suluw*, "beauty."

[60]"The Bashkirs have a characteristic flute *kuray* with four front fingerholes and one rear thumbhole. It is made from the reeds of a grass called *kuray*. The kuray player is a respected citizen without whom — and naturally, too, without the folk singer — no celebration used to be complete." Buchner 1971: 200; compare also Sachs 1913: 235 (s.v. *Kuraj*).

She brings Alpamïša his sword and finally his horse, to whose tail a rope is fastened, which allows Alpamïša to pull himself from his prison. On his way home, the hero punishes two disloyal shepherds and exchanges his clothes with those of his son. He arrives at where Qoltaba sits in state on his throne, takes his own bow, shoots through the ring and, with his second arrow, kills the fleeing usurper. He is reunited with his wife and family and celebrates his return with a magnificent feast.

Once again the similarity to the Uzbek variant summarized in Chapter Six is striking. There are clearly two parts to the story, and the plot of each part is characterized by the same series of motifs. It is particularly noteworthy that the figure of Qoltaba is a conflation of Qultāy the guardian of horses and Ultāntāz the usurper. In view of Qultāy's reluctance to let Alpamïš choose a horse for himself in the Uzbek version, a trait which is otherwise out of character with the figure of Qultāy, it is possible that Qultāy was originally a negative figure and that the unity of the two functions in one figure as in the Bashkir variant might be the older form of the story.[61] This variant shares with the "Kungrat version" the figure of a usurper, while the *Tale of Bamsï Beyrek* has instead the motif of the hero's clothes dipped in blood by a treacherous villain to pretend he has died (see also the Altaian version). On the other hand, the "Oghuz" and the "Kipchak" versions lack the figure of the hero's blood brother, although good and bad friends appear in the Tatar folktale, and a loyal brother-in-law in the Altaian version. The figure of Qāradžān might have been introduced later into the "Kungrat version" in accordance with the conventions of the heroic epic of the "central" Turkic traditions. As has been pointed out earlier, a character like Qāradžān belongs to the inventory of heroic epic poetry and is best understood in comparison with similar figures like that of Almambet in *Manas* (see pp. 165f.). Unlike the "Oghuz" and "Kungrat version," the Bashkir version makes no references to a historical setting. Although some names in the narrative can be connected to those of Bashkir tribes, the action basically takes place in a timeless fairy-tale world.[62]

---

[61]See Žirmunskij 1960: 88-89.

[62]Kireev points out that names like "Äylär" can be linked with Bashkir tribal names; he also notes that in one Bashkir variant a Kungrat-khan, obviously harking back to the Qoŋïrat, appears. See Kireev 1959.

Shorter but clearly related to the Bashkir version is the Tatar folktale of Alpamša.[63]

> Alpamša is a shepherd. One day he finds an orphaned wild gosling, for which he cares till the animal grows into a goose and flies away. When an old man tells him that the beautiful Sanduġač will marry the man who is able to carry three millstones to the top of a hill and put them down at the padisha's feet, Alpamša is persuaded to take part in the contest. He is the only suitor who is able to perform this feat of strength and wins Sanduġač's hand.
>
> The padishah Qïltap also woos Sanduġač and threatens to take her by force. To repulse his attack, Alpamša and Sanduġač choose horses for themselves and set out on a war-expedition at the head of their army. When they reach Qïltap's realm, Alpamša proceeds on his own to steal Qïltap's Aqbüz (white-grey horse) in order to win the victory over Qïltap. Alpamša finds Qïltap asleep and whispers into his ear:

> Qïltap aġay,
> Qïltap aġay,
> Aqbüz atïŋ birsäŋ, aġay,
> Sanduġačïŋ üzeŋä bulsïn.

> Grandfather Qïltap,
> Grandfather Qïltap,
> if you give your horse Aqbüz, grandfather,
> Sanduġač will be yours.

> In his sleep Qïltap reveals the secret of where to find Aqbüz. Alpamša catches Aqbüz and together with Sanduġač awaits Qïltap's attack. While waiting, Alpamša becomes tired and lies down to fall into a deep "heroic sleep." Meanwhile Qïltap's host attacks and is defeated by Sanduġač, who has put on her armor and mounted Aqbüz. Qïltap returns with his army, defeats Alpamša's men, who are able to flee with Sanduġač, captures Alpamša, who is still asleep in his tent, together with his horse Aqbüz, and has Alpamša thrown into a dungeon. Qïltap asks again for Sanduġač's hand but is put off by her father.
>
> After twenty-four days Alpamša wakes up and finds himself in prison. When he sees a flock of wild geese fly by he calls out to them:

> Qïyġaq qazlar,
> qïyġaq qazlar,
> barmïysïzmï
> beznen yaqqa?

---

[63]See Gatina, Jarmi 1977: 268-276; on the Tatar variants of this narrative see *ibid.*: 396f.; for a Russian translation see Jarmuxametov 1957: 220-235; compare also Žirmunskij 1960: 96-103; on the Tatar narrative see also Urmančeev 1980b.

Äger barsaŋ bezneŋ yaqqa,
xat yazayem qanatïŋa.

You geese with your shrill cries,
you geese with your shrill cries,
wouldn't you like to come
to my side?
If you came to my side,
I would write a letter on your wing.

Among the geese is the orphaned goose which was reared by Alpamša, and the goose carries a message to Sanduġač. Sanduġač sends for one of Alpamša's friends, who has received one hundred rubles from her husband, but he refuses to bring help to Alpamša. She then calls another of Alpamša's friends, who was given an awl for the making of bast-shoes by Alpamša, and this friend agrees to bring food to the imprisoned hero. When Alpamša hears steps approaching his dungeon he calls out:

Döp itken,
döp-döp itken
ayu miken, büre miken?
Älle minem
yöz sum birgen
dustïm miken,
dustïm miken?

Is it a bear, is it a wolf
who approaches with heavy steps,
tock-tock?
Or is it
my friend
to whom I gave one hundred rubles,
is it my friend?

When Alpamša receives no answer, he asks again:

Döp itken,
döp-döp itken
ayu miken, büre miken?
Älle minem
šöšle birgen
dustïm miken,
dustïm miken?

Is it a bear, is it a wolf
who approaches with heavy steps,
tock-tock?
Or is it
my friend

to whom I gave an awl,
is it my friend?

This time Alpamša is given an answer and provided with the food Sanduġač has sent him. When his friend leaves, Alpamša asks him to tell Sanduġač to wait for him for five years before she marries again.

One day Qïltap sends his daughter and his wife to Alpamša's dungeon to pour poison on him. When they approach, they hear the prisoner playing a fiddle. He is singing:

Aldan kilä,
aldan kilä,
aldaġïsï kölä kilä,
artaġïsï džïrlïy kilä;
bu nindi ġadžäp
ešlär bu,
bu nindi ġadžäp
ešlär bu?

Coming from the front,
coming from the front,
the one in front comes smiling,
the one behind comes crying.
What strange things
are these,
what strange things
are these?

Qïltap's daughter pours the poison into a ditch instead of into Alpamša's dungeon and the women return to the palace, assuring the padishah that the prisoner has been poisoned. The girl takes pity on Alpamša and brings him a miraculous sword which is kept in her father's chest. Alpamša succeeds in freeing himself with the help of the sword, regains his horse Aqbüz and rides back to Sanduġač.

When he arrives in his home town, he disguises himself as a poor man and takes up quarters with an old woman. He is told that Sanduġač is to be married the following day. Alpamša makes his appearance at her wedding-feast, where Sanduġač's sister recognizes him despite his beggarly garb. In order to be certain of his identity, Sanduġač lets a loaf of bread, destined for the beggar, roll on the ground, and her sister flings off his cap when Alpamša bends down to pick it up. Alpamša's birthmark on his head becomes visible and he is also recognized by his wife. When he is taken to the seat of honor, the padishah demands that he prove his identity. Alpamša whistles for his horse Aqbüz, rides on it in splendor, picks up his flintlock (which thirty or forty men were unable to lift from the ground), and shoots with it while the people are shouting hurrah. The new bridegroom flees in terror and Alpamša is happily reunited with his wife.

As the story stands it is clearly a folktale, comparable to other Tatar folktales with similar motifs. The form of the narrative should not deceive us, however, as to its origin. Quite apart from the name of the hero and the outline of the story, the folktale reveals through a number of traits its close relationship to the epic of Alpamïš. Much is made of Alpamša's and Sanduġač's first choosing a horse for themselves and then capturing Aqbüz. Here one and the same motif, that of the hero choosing his horse against the oppostion of the guardian of horses, has been split into two elements, where the first element (choosing a horse at home) remains undeveloped, while the second element is elaborated (Aqbüz as the enemy's horse). Qoltaba, the guardian of horses and subsequent oppressor, and Büdär-khan, Barsïnhïlïw's suitor, of the Bashkir version have become conflated in the figure of Qïltap, whose name is obviously a variant of Qoltaba. Somewhat inconsequentially, he does not reappear as Sanduġač's husband-to-be when Alpamša returns, but some otherwise unknown "new bridegroom" is introduced instead. Other motifs such as the flintlock (*mïltïq*; a bow in other variants) are superfluous in the context of the present folktale since Alpamša has already been recognized by his birthmark; the motif has clearly been incorporated because it is part of the traditional story.

Another indication of the close connection between folktale and epic are the verses in the story. On first sight, these verses are not any different from verses commonly introduced into folktales; when Alpamša senses the approach of people he expresses himself in verses which remind one of the verse the giant utters on smelling a human in "Jack and the Beanstalk." When looking at the Bashkir variants of the Alpamïš-story, which are characterized by longer verse-passages and where the relationship to epic poetry is more patent, similar verses are found, as when Alpamïša addresses the wild geese:

> Qïrasay qaðïm, qïrasay qaðïm,
> kilse, qaðïm, kilse, qaðïm,
> qanatïŋa xat yaðayïm,
> tïwġan ilgä, käläšemä
> kitheŋse alïp, kitheŋse alïp.
> (Sägitov [Sagitov], Xarisov 1973: 32)

> My wild goose, my wild goose,
> come, my goose, come, my goose,
> I will write a letter on your wing.
> To my homeland, to my bride,
> take it, take it.

When Alpamïša in the Bashkir tale tries to get the horse Qolyerän from Qoltaba, and the latter refuses the various gifts Alpamïša promises in return, he finally offers his sister Qarluġas. These verse-lines are very similar to those whispered by Alpamša in the Tatar folktale into Qïltap's ear while he is asleep. Compare:

> Qoltaba aġay, Qoltaba aġay,
> Qolyerändi birse, aġay, birse, aġay,
> mine tapqan qart äsämde,
> qarïndašïm Qarluġastï
> hiŋä fiða qïlam, aġay, qïlam, aġay, — ti.
> (Säġitov [Sagitov], Xarisov 1973: 30)

> Grandfather Qoltaba, Grandfather Qoltaba,
> if you give Qolyerän, grandfather, if you give it, grandfather,
> then both my old mother who bore me
> and my sister Qarluġas
> I will sacrifice to you, grandfather, I will sacrifice to you,
> grandfather, he said.

In the Bashkir variants these verses are sung in the manner typical of the singing of Bashkir epic poetry.[64]

Žirmunskij groups the Bashkir and Tatar variants together as the "Kipchak version" of the Alpamïš-story. Tatar and Bashkir descend like Kazakh and Karakalpak from the language of the Kipchaks, who are found in the steppes between the Caspian and the Aral Seas from the 11th century onwards (see p. 20). By using the term "Kipchak version" Žirmunksij signalizes that in his view the Tatars and Bashkirs share the Alpamïš-story with the Karakalpaks and Kazakhs (as well as the Kipchak-Uzbeks) from the time when they were together in the Kipchak tribal confederation, that is before the "Kungrat version" was developed. Other scholars have assumed a later origin of the "Kipchak version" under the influence of the Central Asian epic of Alpamïš.[65] Support for the "Kipchak hypothesis" comes from the Altaian version of Alpamïš, to which I will turn in concluding my survey of versions.

Although the story of Alpamïš is popular among the Altaians, only one variant has been recorded, from the famous Altaian singer N. U.

---

[64]See the musical notations of extracts from *Alpamïša* in Säġitov [Sagitov], Xarisov 1973: 362-369. On the importance of the verse-passages in the Bashkir variants for the interpretation of these variants as epic poetry rather than prose-retellings of epics see Kireev 1959: 191ff.

[65]See Kireev 1959.

Ulagašev (1861-1946) in 1939.[66] The summary of his variant is briefly the following:

> In the Altai there lives a hero by the name of Baybaraq. He is married to the beautiful Ermen-Čečen (Ermen-the-Sweet-Tongued), by whom he has a daughter, called Erke-Qoo (Erke-the-Beautiful), and a son, called Alïp-Manaš. When Alïp-Manaš has grown up, he is married to Kümüdžek-Aru (Kümüdžek-the-Pure).
>
> One day Alïp-Manaš reads in a book of prophecy that Aq-qaan has a beautiful daughter, called Erke-Qaraqčï (Erke-the-Sharp-Eyed). A great number of suitors have already requested her in marriage, but in vain; instead of her hand they have received death. Despite the entreaties of his wife, Alïp-Manaš departs on his light-grey horse (*aq-boro*) to woo Erke-Qaraqčï. After a long journey he reaches a river, which he has to cross on a ferry. The old ferryman is sorry for Alïp-Manaš and laments his fate. Upon this, the hero gives him a nine-sided copper arrow (*toğus qïrlu d'es soğoon*) as a life-token: as long as the arrow does not rust the hero can be assumed to be alive.
>
> On nearing Aq-qaan's territory, Alïp-Manaš's horse Aq-Boro stops and warns the hero. Alïp-Manaš pays no heed and hits his horse with a whip, whereupon the white-grey horse flies away into the clouds and is transformed into a star on the sky. As Alïp-Manaš proceeds on his journey, he becomes sleepy and lies down to rest. When Aq-qaan is informed by his frightened shepherds of the sleeping hero of gigantic size, he sends a seven-headed ogre (*d'elbegen*) to capture him. When the ogre approaches on his blue buffalo, he takes fright and flees back to the khan. An army attacks the sleeping hero, but it turns out that Alïp-Manaš is invulnerable. Aq-qaan has a ninety-fathom-deep hole dug out and has Alïp-Manaš laid in chains and thrown into it.
>
> After nine months Alïp-Manaš finally wakes up and realizes his situation. One day he manages to send a message to his parents, his sister, and his wife on the wing of a wild goose. When the message reaches his home, his relatives send the hero Aq-Köböŋ (White-Cotton), loved by Alïp-Manaš as a brother (*qarïndaštardïy süüšken*), to his rescue. Aq-Köböŋ is equipped with ample provisions for Alïp-Manaš, but when he reaches the captive he reproaches Alïp-Manaš that he had sent greetings to his parents, wife and sister, but not to him. He therefore refuses to help the hero in captivity, eats the provisions himself, thus doubling his strength, and leaves Alïp-Manaš to his fate. Aq-Köböŋ collects the bones of the men slain by Aq-qaan, intending to prove Alïp-Manaš's death by them and hoping to gain Kümüdžek-Aru's

---

[66]This variant was first edited in 1940 and then reprinted in the series *Altay baatïrlar*; see Surazakov 1985: 245, No. 41(2); Surazakov et al. 1959: 28-67. A full Russian translation of the Altaian text first appeared in 1941 and a shortened prose translation in 1939; for the former see Koptelov 1961: 24-67; the latter has been recently reprinted in Taksami 1988: 60-68. For a summary see Žirmunskij 1960: 140-144.

hand. He tells the ferryman on his return journey that Alïp-Manaš
has died, but the life-token belies Aq-Köböŋ's words.

After Aq-Köböŋ's refusal to rescue Alïp-Manaš, his horse Aq-Boro
comes down from heaven to pull him out of the pit. His tail is,
however, not strong enough, and the hero has to be saved by other
means. In a dream, Aq-boro is told of a miraculous foam to be found in
Külerbay-qaan's realm, which alone can give Alïp-Manaš enough
strength to break his chains. The horse transforms himself into a thin
hair and flies unnoticed by Külerbay-qaan, his horse, hawks, dogs, and
men to the spring-lake where he swallows a big gulp of the miraculous
golden foam. The horse returns to his master, shares the miraculous
foam with Alïp-Manaš, which invests him with the necessary strength
to shake off his chains and climb out of the pit. Alïp-Manaš kills the
d'elbegen as well as Aq-Qaan and his daughter, who had been
responsible for the loss of so many lives, and starts his journey home.

On his way Alïp-Manaš changes himself into a *tastaraqay* (a scabby,
bald-headed man) and his Aq-boro into a plain and inconspicuous horse.
When he reaches the river, the ferryman is overjoyed when he
recognizes the hero, his identity being verified by the shining arrow,
and informs him of Aq-Köböŋ's evil designs on his wife. Farther on his
way, Alïp-Manaš meets Qan-Čüreŋkey, his sister's husband, who is on
the way to Aq-Köböŋ's and Kümüdžek-Aru's wedding-feast; the traitor
had been successful in deceiving Alïp-Manaš's relatives. Qan-Čüreŋkey
proves his loyalty to his brother-in-law by his reluctance to go to the
toy. When Alïp-Manaš arrives at the marriage yurt, he sees Aq-Köböŋ
sitting in the seat of honor and eight servant girls combing Kümüdžek-
Aru's silver hair. Alïp-Manaš exchanges lyrical songs (*qodžoŋ*) with
his wife, in which he probes her fidelity and she expresses her unbroken
love to her husband. When he asks her what she would do if Alïp-
Manaš and his horse were outside, she rushes to the threshold and
says:

> "Aq-boro čaqïžïna kelze,
> altïn tügin sïymaar edim.
> Alïp-Manaš d'anïp kelze,
> altïn erdin oqšoor edim!"

> "If Aq-boro had come to his horse-post,
> I would curry his golden hair.
> If Alïp-Manaš had come back,
> I would kiss his golden lips."

On hearing this Aq-Köböŋ transforms himself into a crane and flies
away through the smoke-hole of the yurt. Alïp-Manaš sends an arrow
from his iron bow after the fugitive and the arrow grazes the crane's
head and leaves a mark there. Then a huge *toy* is prepared to celebrate
the return of the hero.

The basic plot of the Alpamïš-story is clearly recognizable. The
beginning of the Altaian variant differs from the other versions in that

Alïp-Manaš is already married before he sets out on his *Brautwerbung*.
Erke-Qaraqčï, who corresponds to Barčïn (Barsïnhïlïw, Banï Čiček,
Sanduġač) in the other versions, is here the type of the warlike, man-
slaying maiden who has to be overcome before she can be married. In
the Altaian version this figure is only negatively presented, and Erke-
Qaraqčï is hence doomed to perish in the end. Other elements of the
story are very close to the versions discussed so far: the hero's capture
in his sleep; the message sent on the wing of a wild goose; the treacherous behavior of the hero's friend (as in the "Oghuz version"); the horse
as companion and helper (as in the "Kungrat version"); the test of
friends and wife on the hero's return and the exchange of songs (as in
the "Oghuz" and "Kungrat version"). On the other hand, a number of
traits bring the Altaian *čörčök* of Alïp-Manaš in line with the stylistic
and narrative conventions of Altaian epic poetry. The motif of the hero
reading about his future in the *sudur bičig*, the book of prophecy (*sudur*
deriving from Sanskrit *sūtra*, "sutra, Buddhist narrative") is common in
Altaian narrative. Similarly the hyperbolic style of Altaian (and
Mongolian) epic poetry is also present in this tale, as when Alïp-
Manaš's gigantic stature and the terrifying effect it has on the
inhabitants of Aq-qaan's realm is described (see above p. 294). The
seven-headed *d'elbegen* is also a stock-figure of the Altaian *čörčök*; in
function and appearance this ogre corresponds to the witch-figures of
other epic traditions (see pp. 289f.), in particular to Surxayil in the
Uzbek version of the Alpamïš-story. Shape-shifting, which generally
points to a shamanistic background (see pp. 295f.), plays an important
role in the epic; not only the hero's horse is capable of changing shape
but also Alïp-Manaš's adversary Köböŋ, who attempts to flee by
transforming himself into a crane. Other elements, which are not found
in the non-Altaian versions, might have come into Ulagašev's variant
from folktales, such as the figure of the ferryman and the motif of the
life-token. In its entirety, however, the Altaian version is strikingly
close to the other versions of the Alpamïš-story.

Žirmunskij tried to explain this similarity in historical terms.
According to his hypothesis the Alpamïš-story first developed among
Turkic peoples in the form of a heroic tale on the southern foothills of
the Altai Mountains between the 6th and the 8th century (the period of
the Second East Turkic Empire; see p. 14). The story reached the lower
reaches of the Syr-Darya with the Oghuz and spread from there among
the Kipchaks before the time of the Mongolian invasions. The "Kungrat

version" of the story in the form of a heroic epic was developed only later among the Uzbek tribe of the Qoṅġirāt some time in the 16th century. Žirmunskij's explanation of the relationship between the "Oghuz" and the "Kungrat version" has been generally accepted. The similarities between the story of Bamsï Beyrek in the *Book of Dede Qorqut* and the various Uzbek, Kazakh, and Karakalpak *Alpamïš*-epics certainly point to a common source, which must antedate the Oghuz' migration to the West from the 11th c. onwards. The Kipchaks were doubtless instrumental in the dissemination of the Alpamïš-story among the Central Asian Turks. It has been pointed out that the Kipchaks are still today an important tribe of the Altaians and that the Alpamïš-story could hence have reached the Altaians through the Kipchaks.[67] This would make the Altaian version younger than Žirmunskij proposed; rather than seeing it as an archaic survival, it can be viewed on a par with the other versions of the story. Later contacts and influences can, of course, not be ruled out, but it seems safe to postulate the crystallization of a common Turkic version of the Alpamïš-story not later (and perhaps also not much earlier) than the 11th c. It stands to reason that the story was not created *ex nihilo* at that moment. The close parallels between the Alpamïš-story and other tales of the return of the hero, and in particular the striking similarities between the Alpamïš-story and the *Odyssey*, show that the tale is based on a widespread story-pattern (see Chapter Six, pp. 169ff.). It is possible that this story-pattern reached Central Asia from the West, but there is no evidence to allow tracing the path of migration from the Greeks to the Turks. The prehistory of the Alpamïš-story remains shrouded in darkness.

* * * * *

The discussion of variation with reference to the *Köroğlu/Görogli̇*-cycle and the story of Alpamïs has revealed both the unity and the diversity of Turkic oral poetry. A great number of Turkic peoples share the same narratives. This common core of their epic traditions has either spread from one part of the Turkic-speaking world to another, as in the case of the *Köroğlu/Görogli̇*-cycle, or, as with the Alpamïš-story, it has been inherited from the time when Turkic peoples which are separated today lived not only in close contact with one another but

[67]See Surazakov 1959.

were in many cases also part of the same tribe or tribal grouping (like that of the Kipchaks). The physical mobility of the nomad as well as the continual remaking of tribal confederations has helped to spread stories over a vast area. Cultural contact, as that between the Turkic-speaking and the Iranian-speaking populations of Central Asia or that between the various peoples of the Caucasus, has created a symbiosis of traditions where ethnic and linguistic boundaries are easily crossed in all directions. Nevertheless, each tradition, whether Turkic or non-Turkic, has its own specific characteristics and gives its own individual shape to the stories shared with others. The Turkish *hikâye* of Köroğlu and the Uzbek *dastan* of Goroğli, the Kazakh epic of Alpamïs and the Altaian *čörčök* of Alïp-Manaš are as different from one another as the Middle English romance *Sir Tristrem* is from Gottfried von Straßburg's *Tristan* or the Old Norse *Atlakviða* is from the Middle High German *Nibelungenlied*.

Although we find the story of Alpamïs also among the Altaians, the plots, style, and structure of Altaian epic poetry and in particular the role shamanism plays in Altaian narratives set this tradition apart from that of the Central Asian Turks and the Turks of Azerbaijan and Turkey. Altaian oral narrative poetry is much closer to the Tuvinian, Yakut, and other East Siberian (Khakas, Shor etc.) traditions of epic poetry than to that of the Kazakhs or Uzbeks. This is not to say that there is no common heritage shared by all Turkic traditions. Parallelism, alliteration, formulaic diction, the mixture of verse and prose, the manner of performance and the originally close connection between singer and shaman are part of this heritage. On the other hand, there is a certain homogeneity in the "central traditions" of Turkic oral epic poetry — in particular as regards their conception of the heroic, which is doubtless a reflection of the nomadic past (and in some cases present) of these peoples on the steppes and mountains of Central Asia. While stressing a certain homogeneity of these "central traditions," their diversity should not be forgotten. From a historical point of view the Kirghiz epic tradition must be set apart from the Kipchak or Noghay epic tradition, which reflects the interior history of the Golden Horde (13th to 15th c.); and from a literary point of view Kirghiz epic poetry, in particular of the 19th century, is also in many ways unique.[68] It is the "central traditions" on which my discussion of Turkic oral epic poetry in this book has been focused. Not all of them have, however, been given the same amount of attention and none of them could be treated comprehensively; even where a tradition has been described in more detail, the choice of singers, texts, and of questions to be raised has inevitably been subjective. As long as the collecting and editing of Turkic oral epic poetry continues, no definitive study of any single tradition is possible. Many scholars, beginning with linguists and explorers of the 19th century such as W. Radloff or H. Vámbéry, have contributed to our knowledge of Turkic epic poetry. Nevertheless, a great number of blank areas remain on our map of Turkic epic poetry. Some of these — such as the question of origins — may never become charted, while others — such as the numerous problems connected with the transmission and performance of epic poetry — promise to become *terra cognita* after further exploration.

As this chapter has dealt with the *Köroğlu/Göroğlï*-cycle and with the Alpamïš-story, I will end it with two quotations from these tales, the final formula of Behçet Mahir's Turkish variant of *Köroğlu* and of N. U. Ulagašev's *Alïp-Manaš*:

> İşte burda tamam oluyor, hikâyemiz de son verdi. Böylece tarihler, gün bu günkü güne kadar söylemektedir.
>
> (Kaplan, Akalın, Bali 1973: 587)

> Here then we come to an end, our tale is finished. In this way the stories have been told up to the present day.

> Qïsqa bolġonïn uzatpadïm,
> uzun bolġonïn qïsqartpadïm.
> Albatïdaŋ uqqanïm bu edi.
> Artïq qožorïm d'oq turu.
>
> (Surazakov et al. 1959: 67)

> I did not lengthen what is short,
> I did not shorten what is long.
> This is what I heard from the people.
> There is nothing to add to this.

---

[68]See Borovkov 1958. Borovkov distinguishes three Turkic epic traditions from a historical point of view, the Kipchak, the Kirghiz, and the Oghuz-Turkmen epic traditions. The special status and quality of older Kirghiz epic poetry has been repeatedly stressed by A. T. Hatto.

Bibliography

Abbreviations

AaTh: see Aarne, Thompson 1961.
Motif: see Thompson 1955-58.

Aarne, A., S. Thompson (1961), *The Types of the Folktale*. FF Communications, 184. 2nd rev. ed. Helsinki.

Abdullaev, R. S. (1989), "Bytovanie dastanov v Uzbekistane" [The occurrence of dastans in Uzbekistan], in Zemcovskij 1989: 113-117.

Abrahams, R. D. (1976), "The Complex Relations of Simple Forms," in Ben-Amos 1976: 193-214.

Abylkasimov, B. Š. (1984), *Žanr tolgau v kazaxskoj ustnoj poèzii* [The genre of the tolǧaw in Kazakh oral poetry]. Alma-Ata.

Afzalov, M. I. (1959), "Uzbekskaja versija èposa 'Alpamyš'" [The Uzbek version of the epic 'A.'], in Čicerov, Zarifov 1959: 144-157.

Akiev, Q. (1957), *Qurmanbek* ['Q.']. Ed. S. Bayxodžoev. Frunze.

Albright, C. F. (1976), "The Azerbaijani ⁱÂshiq and His Performance of a *Dâstân*," *Iranian Studies*, 9, 220-247.

Alekseev, N. A. (1980), *Rannie formy religii tjurkojazyčnyx narodov Sibiri* [Early forms of religion of the Turkic-speaking peoples of Siberia]. Novosibirsk.

Alekseev, N. A. (1987), *Schamanismus der Türken Sibiriens. Versuch einer vergleichenden arealen Untersuchung*. Trans. R. Schletzer. Studia Eurasia, 1. Hamburg.

Alizade, H., ed. (1941), *Koroǧlu* ['K.']. Baku.

Almqvist, B., S. Ó Catháin, P. Ó Héalaí, eds. (1987), *The Heroic Process. Form, Function and Fantasy in Folk Epic. The Proceedings of the International Folk Epic Conference, University College Dublin, 2-6 September 1985*. Dublin.

Amānov, R., ed. (1960), *Fol'klori sākināni sargahi Zarafšān* [The folklore of the inhabitants of the upper Zarafšān-valley]. Stalinabad.

Amānov, R., ed. (1976), *Gūrūglī. Dāstāni bahādurāni Čambuli mastān* ['G.' Dastans of the heroes of Čambul]. Dushanbe.

Amānov, R., ed. (1980), *Afsānhāi xalqii tādžik* [Tajik folktales]. Dushanbe.

Amānov, R., ed., L. N. Demidčik, trans. (1959), *Alpāmiš* ['A.']. Stalinabad.

Andersson, T. M. (1980), *The Legend of Brynhild.* Islandica, 43. Ithaca, NY.

Anikin, V. P. (1984), *Byliny. Metod vyjasnenija istoričeskoj xronologii variantov* [Bylinas. The method of elucidating the historical chronology of variants]. Moscow.

Apel, W., comp. (1969), *Harvard Dictionary of Music.* 2nd ed., rev. and enlarged. Cambridge, MA.

Arend, W. (1933), *Die typischen Szenen bei Homer.* Berlin.

Arens, W. (1973), *Die anglonormannische und die englischen Fassungen des Hornstoffes. Ein historisch-genetischer Vergleich.* Frankfurt a. M.

Arsunar, F., ed. (1963), *Köroğlu* ['K.']. Ankara.

Asïlxan, B., ed. (1983), *Altïn saqa. Kazaqtïŋ qïyal-ğažayïp ertegileri* [The Golden Trunk. Kazakh folktales]. Alma-Ata.

Ašurov, T. (1971), "Yumor yaratiš wasitalariga dāir" [The stylistic means of creating humor], in Mominov et al. 1971: 97-102.

Astaxova, A. M. (1962), *Narodnye skazki o bogatyrjax russkogo éposa* [Folktales about the heroes of the Russian epic]. Moscow.

Äwezov [Auezov], M. (1961), "Kirgizskaja narodnaja geroičeskaja poéma 'Manas'" [The Kirghiz heroic folk epic 'M.'], in Bogdanova, Žirmunskij, Petrosjan 1961: 15-84.

Äwezov [Auezov], M. O., N. S. Smirnova, eds. (1959), *Qambar-batïr* ['The hero Q.']. Alma-Ata.

Äwezov [Auezov], M. O., N. S. Smirnova, eds. (1961), *Alpamïs-batïr* ['The hero A.']. Alma-Ata.

Äwezov [Auezov], M. O., N. S. Smirnova, eds. (1963), *Qïz Žibek* ['Q. Ž.']. Alma-Ata.

Ayïmbetov, Q. (1988), *Xalïq danalïğï. Ötken künlerden elesler. Qïylï-qïylï qïlwalar* [The wisdom of the people. Phantoms of past days. Various happenings]. Nukus. [*Xalïq danalïğï* was first published in 1960.]

Bajalieva, T. D. (1972), *Doislamskie verovanija i ix perežitki u kirgizov* [Pre-Islamic beliefs and their survivals among the Kirghiz]. Frunze.

Bajgaskina, A. (1973), "Évolucija stixotvornyx razmerov i logika razvitija muzykal'noj formy kazaxskoj narodnoj pesni" [The evolution of meter and the logic of the development of the musical form of Kazakh folk song], in *Problemy muzykal'nogo fol'klora narodov SSSR. Stat'i i materialy* [Problems of the musical folklore of the peoples of the USSR. Essays and documents]. Moscow, 126-146.

Bibliography

Balandin, A. I., ed. (1983), *Onežskie byliny zapisannye A. F. Gil'ferdingom letom 1871 goda* [Bylinas from Lake Onega, written down by A. F. Hilferding in the summer of 1871]. Arkhangelsk.

Balïqšï-ulï, Q., O. Egewbayew, collectors, Q. Arabin, ed.(1984), *Qazaq xïsalarï*. 2. *Batïrlar žïrï* [Kazakh xïssas. 2. The heroic epic]. Urumchi.

Bang, W., G. R. Rachmati, ed. and trans. (1932), "Die Legende von Oghuz Qaghan," in *Sitzungsberichte der Preußischen Akademie der Wiss., Phil.-hist. Kl.*, 25, 683-724.

Barthold, W. (1962), *Zwölf Vorlesungen über die Geschichte der Türken Mittelasiens.* 2nd ed. Hildesheim.

Başgöz, İ. (1952), "Turkish Folk Stories about the Lives of Minstrels," *Journal of American Folklore*, 65, 331-339.

Başgöz, İ. (1967), "Dream Motif in Turkish Folk Stories and Shamanistic Initiation," *Asian Folklore Studies*, 26, 1-18.

Başgöz, İ. (1975), "The Tale-Singer and His Audience. An Experiment to Determine the Effect of Different Audiences on a *Hikaye* Performance," in *Folklore. Performance and Communication*, ed. D. Ben-Amos, K. S. Goldstein. The Hague, 143-203.

Başgöz, İ. (1976), "The Structure of the Turkish Romances," in *Folklore Today. A Festschrift for Richard M. Dorson*, ed. L. Dégh, H. Glassie, F. J. Oinas. Bloomington, IN, 11-23.

Başgöz, İ. (1978a), "The Epic Tradition Among Turkic Peoples," in *Heroic Epic and Saga. An Introduction to the World's Great Folk Epics*, ed. F. J. Oinas. Bloomington, IN, 310-335.

Başgöz, İ. (1978b), "Epithet in a Prose Epic: The Book of My Grandfather Korkut," in *Studies in Turkish Folklore. In Honor of Pertev N. Boratav*, ed. İ. Başgöz. Indiana Univ. Turkish Studies, 1. Bloomington, IN, 25-45.

Başgöz, İ. (1986a), *Folklor Yazıları* [Writings on folklore]. Istanbul.

Başgöz, İ. (1986b), "Hikâye Anlatan Aşık ve Dinleyicisi" [The aşık telling a hikâye and his listeners], in Başgöz 1986a: 49-137. [For an English version see Başgöz 1975.]

Basilov, V. N., ed., M. F. Zirin, trans. (1989), *Nomads of Eurasia*. Seattle, WA.

Baskakov, N. A. (1958), *Karakalpaksko-russkij slovar'* [A Karakalpak-Russian dictionary]. Moscow.

Baskakov, N. A., et al. (1966), *Tjurkskie jazyki* [The Turkic languages], Jazyki narodov SSSR, 2. Moscow.

Baskakov, N. A. (1969), *Vvedenie v izučenie tjurkskix jazykov* [An introduction to the study of the Turkic languages]. 2nd ed. Moscow.

Bausinger, H. (1980), *Formen der "Volkspoesie."* Grundlagen der Germanistik, 6. 2nd rev. ed. Berlin.

Bayniyazov, Q., N. Ayïmbetov, eds. (1981), *Alpamïs (Dästan)* [The dastan 'A.'].
    Qaraqalpaq fol'klorï, 7. Nukus.

Bayniyazov, Q., Q. Maqsetov et al., eds. (1990), *Edige. Qaraqalpaq xalïq
    dästanï* ['E.' A Karakalpak folk epic]. Nukus.

Beaton, R. (1980), *Folk Poetry of Modern Greece.* Cambridge.

Becking, G. (1933), "Der musikalische Bau des montenegrinischen Volksepos,"
    Archives Néerlandaises de Phonétique Expérimentale, 8-9, 144-153.

Beitl, K. (1973-75), "Schnaderhüpfel," in *Handbuch des Volksliedes*, ed. R. W.
    Brednich, L. Röhrich, W. Suppan. 2 vols. München, I, 617-677.

Bekirov, Dž., ed. (1980), *Destanlar* [Dastans]. Tashkent.

Beliaev, V. M. (1975), *Central Asian Music. Essays in the History of the Music
    of the Peoples of the U.S.S.R.* Ed. M. Slobin. Middletown, CT.

Ben-Amos, D., ed. (1976), *Folklore Genres.* Publ. of the American Folklore Soc.,
    26. Austin, TX.

Benzing, J. (1959), "Das Hunnische, Donaubolgarische und Wolgabolgarische,"
    in Deny et al. 1959-64: I, 685-695.

Blochet, E. (1932-33), *Bibliothèque Nationale. Catalogue des Manuscrits Turcs.*
    2 vols. Paris.

Bogdanova, M. I., V. M. Žirmunskij, A. A. Petrosjan, eds. (1961), *Kirgizskij
    geroičeskij èpos Manas* [The Kirghiz heroic epic 'M.']. Moscow.

Boldyrev, A. N. (1939), "Ustnyj èpos Tadžikistana" [The oral epic of Taji-
    kistan], *Družba Narodov*, 1939.1, 299-304.

Bombaci, A. (1964), "The Turkic Literatures. Introductory Notes on the History
    and Style," in Deny et al. 1959-64: II, xi-lxxi.

Boratav, P. N. (1946), *Halk Hikâyeleri ve Halk Hikâyeciliği* [Popular hikâyes
    and the art of storytelling]. Istanbul.

Boratav, P. N. (1964), "L'épopée et la 'ḥikâye'," in Deny et al. 1959-64: II, 11-
    44.

Boratav, P. N., trans. (1965), *Aventures merveilleuses sous terre et ailleurs de
    Er-Töshtük le géant des steppes.* Paris.

Boratav, P. N. (1967), "Kör-Oğlu," *Islam Ansiklopedisi* [Encyclopedia of Islam],
    2nd ed. Istanbul, VI, 908-914.

Boratav, P. N. (1973), *100 Soruda Türk Halk Edebiyatı* [Turkish popular
    literature: One hundred questions]. 2nd ed. Istanbul.

Boratav, P. N. (1982-83), *Folklor ve Edebiyat (1982)* [Folklore and literature],
    2 vols. Istanbul.

Boratav, P. N. (1982-83 [1939]), "Bey Böyrek Hikâyesi Ait Metinler" [Texts
    concerning the tale of Bey Böyrek], in Boratav 1982-83: II, 141-210.

Boratav, P. N. (1982-83 [1958]), "Dede Korkut Hikâyelerindeki Tarihi Olaylar
    ve Kitabın Telif Tarihi" [Historical elements in the tales of Dede
    Korkut and the genesis of the book], in Boratav 1982-83: II, 109-140.

Boratav, P. N. (1984), *Köroğlu Destanı* [The destan 'K.']. 2nd ed. Istanbul [1st ed. 1931].

Borovkov, A. K. (1958), "Voprosy tjurkojazyčnogo ėposa narodov Srednej Azii i Kazaxstana" [Problems in the study of the Turkic epic of the peoples of Central Asia and Kazakhstan], in Braginskij, Petrosjan, Čičerov 1958: 55-100

Borovkov, A. K., et al. (1959), *Uzbeksko-russkij slovar'* [An Uzbek-Russian dictionary]. Moscow.

Bowra, C. M. (1945), *From Virgil to Milton*. London.

Bowra, C. M. (1952), *Heroic Poetry*. London.

Braginskij, I. S. (1958), "O tadžikskom ėpose 'Gurguli' i ego xudožestvennyx osobennostjax" [On the Tajik epic 'G.' and its poetic characteristics], in Braginskij, Petrosjan, Čičerov 1958: 126-148.

Braginskij, I. S. (1987), "Tadžikskij narodnyj ėpos 'Gurugli'" [The Tajik folk epic 'G.'], in Braginskij, Nazarov, Šermuxammedov 1987: 7-44.

Braginskij, I. S., A. A. Petrosjan, V. I Čičerov, eds. (1958), *Voprosy izučenija ėposa narodov SSSR* [Problems in the study of the epic of the peoples of the USSR]. Moscow.

Braginskij, I. S., X. Nazarov, V. Šermuxammedov, eds. and trans. (1987), *Gurugli. Tadžikskij narodnyj ėpos* ['G.' A Tajik folk epic]. Ėpos narodov SSSR. Moscow.

Braun, M. (1961), *Das serbokroatische Heldenlied*. Opera Slavica, 1. Göttingen.

Bremond, C. (1973), *Logique du récit*. Paris.

Brockelmann, C. (1923), "Altturkestanische Volkspoesie I," *Asia Major (Probeband)*, 1-22.

Brockelmann, C. (1924), "Altturkestanische Volkspoesie II," *Asia Major*, 1, 24-44.

Brodeur, A. G. (1959), *The Art of Beowulf*. Berkeley, CA.

Brunner, K., ed. (1913), *Der mittelenglische Versroman über Richard Löwenherz*. Wien, Leipzig.

Burrow, J. A. (1965), *A Reading of 'Sir Gawain and the Green Knight.'* London.

Buchner, A. (1971), *Folk Music Instruments*. Prague.

Bynum, D. E. (1976), "The Generic Nature of Oral Epic Poetry," in Ben-Amos 1976: 35-58.

Castagné, J. (1930), "Magie et exorcisme chez les Kazak-Kirghizes et autres peuples turks orientaux," *Revue des Études Islamiques*, 4, 53-151.

Cejpek, J. (1959), "Die iranische Volksdichtung," in *Iranische Literaturgeschichte* by J. Rypka et al. Leipzig, 461-551.

Cereteli, G. V. (1956), *Arabskie dialekty Srednej Azii. I. Buxarskij arabskij dialekt* [The Arabic dialects of Central Asia. I. The Bukhara Arabic dialect]. Tbilisi.

Chadwick, N. K., trans. (1932), *Russian Heroic Poetry.* Cambridge.

Chadwick, H. M. and N. K. (1932-40), *The Growth of Literature.* 3 vols. Cambridge.

Chadwick, N. K., V. Zhirmunsky (1969), *Oral Epics of Central Asia.* Cambridge.

Chatman, S. (1978), *Story and Discourse. Narrative Structure in Fiction and Film.* Ithaca, NY.

Child, F. J., ed. (1882-98), *The English and Scottish Popular Ballads.* 5 vols. Boston.

Chodzko, A., trans. (1842), *Specimens of the Popular Poetry of Persia, as Found in the Adventures and Improvisations of Kurroglou, the Bandit-Minstrel of Northern Persia; and in the Songs of the People Inhabiting the Shores of the Caspian Sea.* London.

Čičerov, V. I. (1982), *Školy skazitelej Zaonež"ja* [Schools of singers at Lake Onega]. Ed. V. P. Anikin. Moscow.

Čičerov, V. I., X. T. Zarifov, eds. (1959), *Ob épose 'Alpamyš.' Materialy po obsuždeniju éposa 'Alpamyš'* [On the epic 'A.' Material for the study of the epic 'A.']. Tashkent.

Cincius, V. I., et al. (1975-77), *Sravnitel'nyj slovar' tunguso-man'čžurskix jazykov. Materialy k étimologičeskomu slovarju* [A comparative dictionary of the Manchu-Tungus languages. Material for an etymological dictionary]. 2 vols. Leningrad.

Člajdze, L. G. (1978), *Gruzinskaja versija éposa "Ker-Ogly"* [The Georgian version of the epic 'K.']. Tbilisi.

Comrie, B. (1981), *The Languages of the Soviet Union.* Cambridge Language Surveys. Cambridge.

Ćurčija-Prodanović, N., trans. (1963), *Heroes of Serbia.* London.

Davkaraev, N. (1959), *Očerki po istorii dorevoljucionnoj karakalpakskoj literatury* [Sketches of the history of pre-Revolutionary Karakalpak literature]. Tashkent.

Dawson, C., ed. (1955), *The Mongol Mission. Narratives and Letters of the Franciscan Missionaries in Mongolia and China in the Thirteenth and Fourteenth Centuries.* Trans. by a Nun of Stanbrook Abbey. New York.

Deny, J., et al., eds. (1959-64), *Philologiae Turcicae Fundamenta.* 2 vols. Wiesbaden.

Dextjar', A. A. (1979), *Problemy poétiki dastanov urdu* [Problems of the poetics of Urdu dastans]. Moscow.

Dillon, M., ed. (1968), *Irish Sagas.* Cork.

Doerfer, G. (1963-75), *Türkische und mongolische Elemente im Neupersischen.* Ak. d. Wiss. u. d. Lit., Veröffentlichungen der Orientalischen Kommission, 16, 19-21. 4 vols. Wiesbaden.

Dor, R. (1975), *Contribution à l'étude des Kirghiz du Pamir Afghan.* Paris.

Dor, R. (1982), "Un Fragment Pamirien de *Manas*," *Central Asiatic Journal,* 26, 1-55.

Dor, R., trans. (1991), *Nourali ou les aventures lyriques d'un héros épique.* Paris.

Dor, R., G. M. Naumann (1978), *Die Kirghisen des afghanischen Pamir.* Graz.

Drerup, E. (1920), "Homer und die Volksepik," *Neophilologus,* 5, 257-273.

Duggan, J. J. (1973), *The Song of Roland. Formulaic Style and Poetic Craft.* Berkeley, CA.

Düysenbaev, I., ed. (1959), *Qozï Körpeš — Bayan Suluw* ['Q. K. and B. S.']. Alma-Ata.

Dunn, C. J. (1980), "Ainu," in Hatto, Hainsworth 1980-89: I, 328-344.

Durić, V., ed. (1977), *Antologija narodnih junačkih pesama* [An anthology of heroic songs]. 8th ed. Belgrade.

Džabbarov, I. M. (1971), "Nekotorye étnografičeskie materialy v uzbekskoj versii éposa 'Alpamyš'" [Ethnographical material in the Uzbek version of the epic 'A.'], *Sovetskaja Étnografija,* 1971.2, 128-133.

Džaynaqova, A., R. Qïdïrbaeva [Kydyrbaeva], eds. (1984ff.), *Manas. Epos. Sayaqbay Qaralaevdin variantï boyunča* ['M.' An epic. According to S. Qaralaev's version]. Iff. Frunze.

Džambul (1949), *Izbrannoe* [Selections]. Moscow.

Eberhard, W. (1955), *Minstrel Tales from Southeastern Turkey.* Berkeley, CA.

Eberhard, W., P. N. Boratav (1953), *Typen türkischer Volksmärchen.* Wiesbaden.

Egewbayew, O., ed. (1985), *Qazaq xïsalarï* [Kazakh xïssas]. Vol. IV. Urumchi.

Egewbayew, O., et al., eds. (1988), *Qazaqtïŋ ğašïqtïq žïrlarï* [Kazakh love epics]. Vol. II. Urumchi.

Elçin, Ş. (1967), "Wort und Begriff destan im Türkischen," in *Der Orient in der Forschung. Festschrift für Otto Spies,* ed. W. Hoenerbach. Wiesbaden, 147-157.

Eliade, M. (1964), *Shamanism. Archaic Techniques of Ecstasy.* Trans. by W. R. Trask. Bollinger Ser., 76. Princeton, NJ.

Emeneau, M. B. (1964), "Oral Poets of South India — The Todas," in *Language in Culture and Society. A Reader in Linguistics and Anthropology,* ed. D. Hymes. New York, 330-341 [originally published in 1958].

Emsheimer, E. (1956), "Singing Contests in Central Asia," *Journal of the International Folk Music Council,* 8, 26-29.

Ergin, M., ed. (1958-63), *Dede Korkut Kitabı* ['The Book of Dede Qorqut']. 2 vols. Türk Dil Kurumu Yayınları, 169, 219. Ankara.

Feldman, W. (1983), "The Motif-Line in the Uzbek Oral Epic," *Ural-Altaische Jahrbücher*, 55, 1-15.

Findeisen, H., H. Gehrts (1983), *Die Schamanen. Jagdhelfer und Ratgeber, Seelenfahrer, Künder und Heiler.* Köln.

Finnegan, Ruth (1974), "How Oral is Oral Literature?", *Bulletin of the School of Oriental and African Studies*, 37, 52-64.

Finnegan, R. (1977), *Oral Poetry. Its Nature, Significance and Social Context.* Cambridge.

Fitzhugh, W. W., A. Crowell, eds. (1988), *Crossroads of Continents. Cultures of Siberia and Alaska.* Washington, D.C.

Fleischer, H. L. (1888), "Über den türkischen Volksroman Sîreti Seijid Baṭṭâl," in *Kleinere Schriften. III.* Leipzig, 226-254.

Foley, J. M. (1981), "Tradition-Dependent and -Independent Features in Oral Literature: A Comparative View of the Formula," in *Oral Traditional Literature. A Festschrift for Albert Bates Lord*, ed. J. M. Foley. Columbus, OH, 262-281.

Foley, J. M. (1985), *Oral-Formulaic Theory and Research. An Introduction and Annotated Bibliography.* Garland Folklore Bibliographies, 6. New York.

Foley, J. M. (1987), "Formula in Yugoslav and Comparative Folk Epic: Structure and Function," in Almqvist, Ó Catháin, Ó Héalaí 1987: 485-503.

Foley, J. M. (1988), *The Theory of Oral Composition. History and Methodology.* Bloomington, IN.

Foley, J. M. (1990), *Traditional Oral Epic. The 'Odyssey', 'Beowulf', and the Serbo-Croatian Return Song.* Berkeley, CA.

Forster, E. M. (1962), *Aspects of the Novel.* Harmondsworth, Middlesex [originally published in 1927].

Fowler, A. (1982), *Kinds of Literature. An Introduction to the Theory of Genres and Modes.* Oxford.

Frenzel, E. (1980), *Vom Inhalt der Literatur. Stoff—Motiv—Thema.* Freiburg.

Frings, Th. (1939-40), "Die Entstehung der deutschen Spielmannsepen," *Zeitschrift für Deutsche Geisteswissenschaft*, 2, 306-321.

Frings, Th., M. Braun (1947), *Brautwerbung.* Leipzig.

Frye, N. (1957), *Anatomy of Criticism. Four Essays.* Princeton, NJ.

Gabain, A. von (1953), "Inhalt und magische Bedeutung der alttürkischen Inschriften," *Anthropos*, 48, 537-556.

Gabain, A. von, et al. (1963), *Turkologie.* Handbuch der Orientalistik, 1. Abtl., V.1. Leiden.

Gabain, A. von (1964), "Die alttürkische Literatur," in Deny et al. (1959-64): II, 211-243.

Gabain, A. von (1974), *Alttürkische Grammatik.* 3rd ed. Wiesbaden.

Ġabdullin, M. (1964), *Qazaq xalqïnïŋ awïz ädebiyeti* [The oral literature of the Kazakh people]. Alma-Ata.

Gacak, V. M., ed. (1975a), *Tipologija narodnogo éposa* [The typology of the folk epic]. Akademija Nauk SSR, Inst. Mirovoj Literatury. Moscow.

Gacak, V. M. (1975b), "Vostočnoromanskij vojnickij i južnoslavjanskij junackij épos" [East Romance and South Slavic heroic epic], in Gacak 1975a: 128-138.

Gacak, V. M. (1989), *Ustnaja épičeskaja tradicija vo vremeni. Istoričeskie issledovanije poètiki* [Oral epic tradition in the course of time. Studies in historical poetics]. Moscow.

Gandjeï, T. (1957), "Überblick über den vor- und frühislamischen türkischen Versbau," *Der Islam*, 33, 142-156.

Gatina, X. X., X. X. Jarmi, eds. (1977), *Tatar xalïk idžatï. Äkijatlär* [Tatar folk poetry. Folktales]. Vol. I. Kazan.

Geißler, F. (1955), *Brautwerbung in der Weltliteratur*. Halle.

Geng Shimin, T. Ayup, N. Doläti, eds. (1980), *Qädimqi Uyǧurlarniŋ tarixiy dastani Oǧuznamä* ['O.' A historical dastan of the Ancient Uighurs]. Beijing.

Geng Shimin, M. Ilekenow, M. Orazbay-uli (1986), *Turki ulttarnïŋ tarixi dastanï Oǧïznama* ['O.' A historical dastan of the Turkic peoples]. Beijing.

Geng Shimin, K. Reichl (1989), "Uigurische Vierzeiler aus Kuchar," *Materialia Turcica*, 15, 55-87.

Gerould, G. H. (1904), "Forerunners, Congeners, and Derivatives of the Eustace Legend," *Publications of the Modern Language Association*, 19, 335-448.

Godley, A. D., ed. and trans. (1920-25), *Herodotus*. Loeb Classical Library. 4 vols. London, Cambridge, MA.

Gökyay, O. Ş. (1973), *Dedem Korkudun Kitabı* ['The Book of Dede Qorqut']. Istanbul.

Grebnev, L. V. (1960), *Tuvinskij geroičeskij épos. Opyt istoriko-ètnografičes- kogo analiza* [The Tuvinian heroic epic. Sketch of a historico-ethno- graphic analysis]. Moscow.

Grebnev, L. V., trans. (1969), *Boktu-Kiriš i Bora-Šèèlej. Tuvinskoe narodnoe skazanie* ['B.-K. and B.-Š.' A Tuvinian folk narrative]. Kyzyl.

Grebnev, L. V., trans. (1975), "Möge Bayan-Toolay. Tuvinskij narodnyj épos" ['M. B.-T.' A Tuvinian folk epic], in Petrosjan 1975: I, 352-366.

Grimm, W. (1857), "Die Sage von Polyphem," *Abhandlungen der Königl. Akademie der Wissenschaften zu Berlin, Phil.-hist. Klasse*, 1857, 1-30.

Grousset, R. (1952), *L'empire des steppes. Attila, Gengis-Khan, Tamerlan*. 4th ed. Paris.

Guessard, F., H. Michelant, eds. (1859), *Otinel. Chanson de geste*. Paris.

Gumarova [Gumarova], M. (1956), "'Suranšy-batyr' v versii Džambula" ['S.' in Džambul's version], in *Tvorčestvo Džambula (Stat'i, zametki, materialy)* [Džambul's work (Essays, notes, documents)]. Akademija Nauk Kazaxskoj SSR, Trudy Otdela Narodnogo Tvorčestva Instituta Jazyka i Literatury, 2. Alma-Ata, 36-51.

Gumarova, M., Ž. Äbišev, eds. (1989), *Batïrlar žïrï. IV. Körugli* [Heroic epics. IV. 'K.']. Alma-Ata.

Gumilev, L. N. (1967), *Drevnie Tjurki* [The Ancient Turks]. Moscow.

Güney, E. C. (1964), *Aşık Garip* ['A. G.']. 2nd ed. Istanbul.

Hainsworth, J. B. (1991), *The Idea of the Epic.* Eidos, 3. Berkeley, CA.

Hambly, G., et al. (1969), *Central Asia.* The Weidenfeld and Nicolson Universal History, 16. London.

Hammond, N. G. L., H. H. Scullard, eds. (1970), *The Oxford Classical Dictionary.* 2nd ed. Oxford.

Harva, U. (1938), *Die religiösen Vorstellungen der altaischen Völker.* FF Communications, 125. Helsinki.

Harvilahti, L. (1987), "Zwei Fliegen mit einer Klappe: Zum Parallelismus der Sprichwörter," *Finnisch-Ugrische Forschungen,* 48, 27-38.

Hatto, A. T. (1965), "Ḥamâsa. iv. — Central Asia," *The Encyclopaedia of Islam.* New ed. Leiden, III, 115-119.

Hatto, A. T. (1973), "Semetey. Part I," *Asia Major,* N.S. 18, 154-180.

Hatto, A. T. (1974), "Semetey. Part II," *Asia Major,* N.S. 19, 1-36.

Hatto, A. T., ed. and trans. (1977), *The Memorial Feast for Kökötöy-Khan (Kökötöydün Ašı). A Kirghiz Epic Poem.* London Oriental Series, 33. Oxford.

Hatto, A. T. (1979), "Plot and Character in Mid-Nineteenth-Century Kirghiz Epic," in *Die mongolischen Epen. Bezüge, Sinndeutung und Überlieferung. (Ein Symposium),* ed. W. Heissig. Asiatische Forschungen, 68. Wiesbaden, 95-112.

Hatto, A. T. (1980 [1970]), "Shamanism and Epic Poetry in Northern Asia," in Hatto 1980: 117-138 [originally published in 1970].

Hatto, A. T. (1980), *Essays on Medieval German and Other Poetry.* Anglica Germanica Ser., 2. Cambridge.

Hatto, A. T. (1980-82), "The Marriage, Death and Return to Life of Manas: A Kirghiz Epic Poem of the Mid-Nineteenth Century," *Turcica. Revue d'Études Turques,* 12, 66-94 [Part I]; 14, 7-38 [Part II].

Hatto, A. T. (1987a), "Manas," *The Encyclopaedia of Islam.* New ed. Leiden, VI, 370-371.

Hatto, A. T. (1987b), "'Wife-Trouble' unter Helden," in Heissig 1987: 116-128.

Hatto, A. T. (1989a), "Epithets in Kirghiz Epic Poetry 1856-1869," in Hatto, Hainsworth 1980-89: II, 71-93.

Hatto, A. T. (1989b), "Towards an Anatomy of Heroic/Epic Poetry," in Hatto, Hainsworth 1980-89: II, 145-306.

Hatto, A. T., ed. and trans. (1990), *The Manas of Wilhelm Radloff.* Asiatische Forschungen, 110. Wiesbaden.

Hatto, A. T. (1991), *Eine allgemeine Theorie der Heldenepik.* Rheinisch-Westfälische Akademie der Wissenschaften, Vorträge, G 307. Opladen.

Hatto, A. T. (forthcoming), "What is an Heroic Lay? Some Reflections on the Germanic, Serbo-Croat and Fula," to appear in *Proceedings of the Symposium 'The Study of Oral Tradition and South Slavs.'* School of Slavonic and East European Studies, University of London.

Hatto, A. T., J. B. Hainsworth, eds. (1980-89), *Traditions of Heroic and Epic Poetry. I. The Traditions,* ed. A. T. Hatto. *II. Characteristics and Techniques,* ed. J. B. Hainsworth. 2 vols. London.

Heath, P. (1987-88), "Romance as Genre in *The Thousand and One Nights,*" *Journal of Arabic Literature,* 18, 1-21; 19, 1-26.

Hegel, G. W. F. (1955 [1842]), *Ästhetik.* Ed. F. Bassenge, with an introduction by G. Lukács. 2 vols. Berlin [originally published in 1842].

Heissig, W., ed. (1981a), *Fragen der mongolischen Heldendichtung. I.* Asiatische Forschungen, 72. Wiesbaden.

Heissig, W. (1981b), "Wiederbeleben und Heilen als Motiv im mongolischen Epos," in Heissig 1981a: 79-100.

Heissig, W., ed. (1985), *Fragen der mongolischen Heldendichtung. III.* Asiatische Forschungen, 91. Wiesbaden.

Heissig, W., ed. (1987), *Fragen der mongolischen Heldendichtung. IV.* Asiatische Forschungen, 101. Wiesbaden.

Herzog, G. (1951), "The Music of Yugoslav Heroic Epic Folk Poetry," *Journal of the International Folk Music Council,* 3, 62-64.

Heusler, A. (1905), *Lied und Epos in germanischer Sagendichtung.* Dortmund.

Heusler, A. (1943), *Die altgermanische Dichtung.* 2nd ed. Potsdam.

Holbeck, B. (1984), "Formelhaftigkeit, Formeltheorie," *Enzyklopädie des Märchens.* Berlin, IV, cols. 1416-40.

Holzapfel, O. (1990), "Heimkehr des Gatten (AaTh 974)," *Enzyklopädie des Märchens.* Berlin, VI, cols. 702-707.

Hu Zhen-Hua (1982), "Ke'erkezizu minjian wenxue gaikuang" [Survey of Kirghiz oral literature], *Xinjian minjian wenxue,* 2, 176-202.

Hu Djen-Hua [Zhen-Hua], R. Dor (1984), "*Manas* chez les Kirghiz du Xinjiang: Bref Aperçu," *Turcica. Revue d'Études Turques,* 16, 29-50.

Husainova, Z. (1971), "Ergaš Džumanbulbul Oġli. (Bibliograpfiya)" [E. Dž.-o. A bibliography], in Mominov et al 1971: 180-196.

Husainova, Z. (1976), "Muhammadqul Džänmuräd Oġli Polkan. (Bibliografiya)" [M. Dž.-o. P. A bibliography], in Mirzaev et al. 1976: 155-161.

Hymes, D. (1981), *"In Vain I Tried to Tell You."* Essays in Native American *Ethnopoetics.* University of Pennsylvania Publ. in Conduct and Communication. Philadelphia, PA.

Illarionov, V. V. (1982), *Iskusstvo jakutskix olonxosutov* [The art of the Yakut oloŋxohuts]. Yakutsk.

Imāmov, K. (1971), "Komik qahramān" [The comic hero], in Mominov et al. 1971: 103-109.

Imāmov, K., et al., eds. (1989), *Nurali. Dāstānlar* ['N.' Dastans]. Ozbek xalq idžādi. Tashkent.

Ismailov, E. (1957), *Akyny. Monografija o tvorčestve Džambula i drugix narodnyx akynov* [Aqïns. A study of the work of Džambul and other folk singers]. Trans. from Kazakh by X. Syzdykov, Ju. Dombrovskij. Alma-Ata.

Jacob, G. (1904), *Vorträge türkischer Meddâh's (mimischer Erzählkünstler).* Berlin.

Jahn, K., trans. (1969), *Die Geschichte der Oğuzen des Rašîd ad-Dîn. Mit 25 Miniaturen und 26 Facsimiles.* Forschungen zur islamischen Philologie u. Kulturgeschichte, 4; Österr. Akad. der Wiss., Philos.-hist. Kl., Denkschriften, 100. Wien.

Jakobson, R. (1966), "Grammatical Parallelism and its Russian Facet," *Language*, 40, 399-429.

Jänicke, O., ed. (1866), *Deutsches Heldenbuch. I. Biterolf und Dietleib. Laurin und Walberan.* Berlin.

Jarmuxametov, X. X., ed. (1957), *Tatarskie narodnye skazki* [Tatar folktales]. Moscow.

Jettmar, K., H. W. Haussig, B. Spuler, L. Petech (1966), *Geschichte Mittelasiens.* Handbuch der Orientalistik, 1. Abtl., V.5. Leiden.

Johansen, U. (1959), "Nordasien," in *Völkerkunde*, ed. H. Tischner. Frankfurt a. M., 148-162.

Judaxin, K. K. (1985 [1965]), *Kirgizsko-russkij slovar'* [A Kirghiz-Russian dictionary]. 2 vols. Moscow [repr. 1985].

Jungbauer, G., trans. (1923), *Märchen aus Turkestan und Tibet.* Jena.

Kaplan, M., M. Akalın, M. Bali, eds. (1973), *Köroğlu Destanı.* Anlatan B. Mahir [The destan 'K.' Narrated by B. Mahir]. Ankara.

Karmyševa, B. X. (1960), "Ètnografičeskaja gruppa 'Tjurk' v sostave Uzbekov" [The ethnographic group 'Turk' in the ethnic composition of the Uzbeks], *Sovetskaja Ètnografija*, 1960.1: 3-22.

Karomatov, F. (1972), *Uzbekskaja instrumental'naja muzyka. Nasledie* [Uzbek instrumental music. The cultural heritage]. Tashkent.

Karryev, B. A. (1968), *Èpičeskie skazanija o Ker-ogly u tjurko-jazyčnyx narodov* [Epic tales about 'K.' among the Turkic-speaking peoples]. Moscow.

Karryev, B. A., ed. and trans. (1983), *Gjor-Ogly. Turkmenskij geroičeskij èpos* ['G.' A Turkmen heroic epic]. Èpos narodov SSSR. Moscow.

Katašev, S. (1979), "Osnovnye ritmičeskie opredeliteli altajskix narodnyx pesen" [The basic rhythmic determinants of Altaic folk songs], in *Ulagaševskie čtenija* [Readings in memory of Ulagašev], I. Gorno-Altajsk, 112-133.

Kebekova, B. (1985), *Qïrgïz, Qazaq aqïndarïnïn čïgarmačïlïq baylanïšï* [The relationship between the works of the Kirghiz and the Kazakh singers]. Frunze.

Kebekova, B., A. Toqombaeva, eds. (1975), *Qïrgïz el džomoqtoru* [Kirghiz folktales]. Frunze.

Kenesbaev, S. K., et al. (1959-61), *Qazaq tilinin tüsindirme sözligi* [An encyclopedic dictionary of the Kazakh language]. 2 vols. Alma-Ata.

Kenesbaev, I. (1977), *Qazaq tilinin frazeologiyalïq sözdigi* [A phraseological dictionary of the Kazakh language]. Alma-Ata.

Ker, W. P. (1908), *Epic and Romance. Essays on Medieval Literature.* 2nd ed. London.

Kidajš-Pokrovskaja, N. V. (1975), "K probleme žanrovoj differenciacii èposa i skazki tjurkojazyčnyx narodov (Raznotipnye vploščenija sjužeta ob izgnanii)" [On the problem of genre differentiation between the epic and the folktale of the Turkic-speaking peoples (Genre-specific realizations of the theme of banishment)], in Gacak 1975a: 235-249.

Kidajš-Pokrovskaja, N. V., A. S. Mirbadaleva (1971), "Tradicionnye èlementy stilja v èpičeskom tekste" [Traditional elements of style in the epic text], in *Tekstologičeskoe izučenie èposa* [The textological analysis of the epic], ed. V. M. Gacak, A. A. Petrosjan. Moscow, 64-96.

Kidajš-Pokrovskaja, N. V., A. S. Mirbadaleva, eds. and trans. (1972), *Rustamxan. Uzbekskij geroiko-romaničeskij èpos* ['R.' An Uzbek heroico-romantic epic]. Èpos narodov SSSR. Moscow.

Kidajš-Pokrovskaja, N. V., O. A. Nurmagambetova, eds. and trans. (1975), *Koblandy-batyr. Kazaxskij geroičeskij èpos* ['The hero Q.' A Kazakh heroic epic]. Èpos narodov SSSR. Moscow.

Killy, W. (1972), *Elemente der Lyrik.* München.

Kindermann, H. (1967), *Theatergeschichte Europas. III. Das Theater der Barockzeit.* 2nd ed. Salzburg.

Kinross, Lord (1977), *The Ottoman Centuries. The Rise and Fall of the Turkish Empire.* London.

Kinsella, T., trans. (1970), *The Tain. Translated from the Irish Epic Táin Bó Cuailnge.* Dublin, London.

Kireev, A. N. (1959), "O baškirskoj skazke 'Alpamyša i Barsyn-Xylu'" [On the Bashkir tale 'A. and B.'], in Čičerov, Zarifov 1959: 187-196.

Kljaštornyj, S. G. (1964), *Dreventjurkskie runičeskie pamjatniki kak istočnik po istorii Srednej Azii* [The Old-Turkic runic inscriptions as a source for the history of Central Asia]. Moscow.

Klimovič, L. (1959), "K istorii izučenija èposa 'Kër-ogly'—'Gor-ogly'" [On the history of the study of the epic 'K.'—'G.'], in *Iz istorii literatur sovetskogo vostoka* [Pages from the history of the literatures of the Soviet East]. Moscow, 181-199.

Kőhalmi, K. U. (1985), "Die brave Schwester, die böse Schwester und der weiße Hase," in Heissig 1985: 112-124.

Köhnken, A. (1976), "Die Narbe des Odysseus. Ein Beitrag zur homerisch-epischen Erzähltechnik," *Antike und Abendland*, 22, 101-114.

Köksal, H. (1984), *Battalnâmelerde Tip ve Motif Yapışı* [Type- and Motif-Structure in the 'Battalnâmes']. Kültür ve Turizm Bakanlığı, Millî Folklor Araştırma Dairesi Yayınları, 59, Halk Edebiyatı Dizisi, 10. Ankara.

Kononov, A. N., ed. and trans. (1958), *Rodoslovnaja Turkmen. Sočinenie Abu-l-Gazi, xana xivinskogo* [The Pedigree of the Turkmens. A work of Abu'l Ġazi, khan of Khiva]. Akademija Nauk SSSR, Inst. Vostokovedenija. Moscow, Leningrad.

Kononov, A. N. (1960), *Grammatika sovremennogo uzbekskogo literaturnogo jazyka* [A grammar of modern literary Uzbek]. Tashkent.

Kononov, A. N. (1980), *Grammatika jazyka tjurkskix runičeskix pamjatnikov (VII — IX vv.)* [A grammar of the language of the Turkic runic inscriptions (VII — IX c.)]. Leningrad.

Köprülü, F. (1966 [1934]), "Ozan" [Ozan], in Köprülü 1966: 131-144.

Köprülü, F. (1966 [1942]), "Bahşı" [Baxšï], in Köprülü 1966: 145-156.

Köprülü, F. (1966), *Edebiyat Araştırmaları* [Literary studies]. Türk Tarih Kurumu Yayınları, VII. Dizi, 47a. Ankara.

Koptelov, A. L., ed. (1961), *Geroičeskie skazania. Zapisany ot narodnogo skazitelja N. U. Ulagaševa* [Heroic narratives. Recorded from the singer N. U. Ulagašev]. Gorno-Altajsk.

Korogly, X. (1974), "Iz vostočno-zapadnyx fol'klornyx svjazej. Temjaglaz (Depegëz) i Polifem" [On East-West relationships in folklore. Crown-eye (Depegöz) and Polyphemus], in *Tipologija i vzaimosvjazi srednevekovyx literatur Vostoka i Zapada* [Typology and relationships between the medieval literatures of East and West], ed. B. L. Riftin et al. Moscow, 275-288.

Korogly, X. (1975), "Oguzskij èpos (Sravnitel'nyj analiz)" [The Oghuz epic (A comparative analysis)], in Gacak 1975a: 64-81.

Korogly, X. (1976), *Oguzskij geroičeskij èpos* [The Oghuz heroic epic]. Akademija Nauk SSSR, Inst. Vostokovedenija, Inst. Mirovoj Literatury. Moscow.

Korogly, X. G. (1983), *Vzaimosvjazi èposa narodov Srednej Azii, Irana i Azerbajdžana* [Relationships between the epics of the peoples of Central Asia, Iran and Azerbaijan]. Moscow.

Kowalski, T. (1921), *Ze studjów nad formą poezji ludów tureckich. I* [Studies on the form of poetry of the Turkic peoples]. Prace komisji orjentalistycznej, 5. Warsaw.

Kravcov, N. I. (1985), *Serbskoxorvatskij èpos* [The Serbo-Croatian epic]. Moscow.

Krömer, W. (1990), *Die italienische Commedia dell'Arte.* Erträge der Forschung, 62. 2nd ed. Darmstadt.

Ksenofontov, G. V. (1928), *Legendy i rasskazy o šamanax u Jakutov, Burjat i Tungusov* [Legends and tales about the shamans among the Yakuts, Buryats, and Tungus]. Part I. Irkutsk.

Kunanbaeva, A. B. (1987), "Kazaxskij èpos segodnja: Skazitel' i skazanie" [The Kazakh epic today. Singer and narrative], *Sovetskaja Ètnografija,* 1987.4, 101-110.

Kwanten, L. (1979), *Imperial Nomads. A History of Central Asia, 500-1500.* Philadelphia, PA.

Kydyrbaeva, R. Z. (1984), *Skazitel'skoe masterstvo manasči* [The narrative art of the manasčï]. Frunze.

Lambertz, M. (1958), *Die Volksepik der Albaner.* Leipzig.

Lämmert, E. (1955), *Bauformen des Erzählens.* Stuttgart.

Laude-Cirtautas, I. (1961), *Der Gebrauch der Farbbezeichnungen in den Türkdialekten.* Ural-Altaische Bibliothek, 10. Wiesbaden.

Laude-Cirtautas, I. (1981), "Der Held in der Gestalt eines armseligen Jungen. (Zu einem Verwandlungsmotiv und seinen Ausformungen in den mongolischen und türkischen Epen und Märchen)," in Heissig 1981a: 1-12.

Laude-Cirtautas, I. (1983), "Zu den Einleitungsformeln in den Märchen und Epen der Mongolen und der Türkvölker Zentralasiens," *Central Asiatic Journal,* 27, 211-248.

Laude-Cirtautas, I., trans. (1984), *Märchen der Usbeken. Samarkand, Buchara, Taschkent.* Köln.

Laude-Cirtautas, I. (1987), "Kirgizskij poèt-skazitel' Sagymbaj Orozbakov (1867-1930) i èpos 'Manas'" [The Kirghiz poet-singer Sagïmbay Orozbaqov (1867-1930) and the epic 'M.'], *Sovetskaja Tjurkologija,* 1987.3, 74-82.

Le Gentil, P. (1955), *La Chanson de Roland.* Connaissance des Lettres, 43. Paris.

Lester, G. A. (1974), "The Cædmon Story and its Analogues," *Neophilologus,* 58, 225-237.

Levend, A. S. (1956), *Ġazavât-Nâmeler ve Mihaloğlu Ali Bey'in Ġazavât Nâmesi* [The 'Ġazâvat-Nâmes' and Mihaloğlu Ali Bey's 'Ġazâvat-Nâme']. Türk Tarih Kurumu Yayılarından, XI. Seri, 8. Ankara.

Lewis, C. S. (1942), *A Preface to Paradise Lost.* London.

Lewis, G., trans. (1974), *The Book of Dede Korkut.* Harmondsworth, Middlesex.

Lipec, R. S. (1984), *Obrazy batyra i ego konja v tjurko-mongol'skom épose* [The figure of the hero and his horse in the Turco-Mongolian epic]. Moscow.

Lord, A. B. (1960), *The Singer of Tales.* Cambridge, MA.

Lord, A. B. (1967), "The Influence of a Fixed Text," in *To Honor Roman Jakobson. Essays on the Occasion of His Seventieth Birthday.* 3 vols. Janua Linguarum, Ser. Maior, 31-33. The Hague, II, 1199-1206 [also in Lord 1991: 170-185].

Lord, A. B., trans. (1974), *The Wedding of Smailagić Meho. Avdo Međedović.* With a translation of conversations concerning the singer's life and times by D. E. Bynum. Serbo-Croatian Heroic Songs, 3. Cambridge, MA.

Lord, A. B. (1987a), "Central Asiatic and Balkan Epic," in Heissig 1987: 321-350 [also in Lord 1991: 211-244].

Lord, A. B. (1987b), "The Nature of Oral Poetry," in *Comparative Research on Oral Traditions. A Memorial for Milman Parry,* ed. J. M. Foley. Columbus, OH, 313-349.

Lord, A. B. (1991), *Epic Singers and Oral Tradition.* Myth and Poetics. Ithaca, NY.

Lőrincz, L. (1970), "Die Mangus-Schilderung in der mongolischen Volks-literatur," in *Mongolian Studies,* ed. L. Ligeti. Amsterdam, 309-340.

Lotman, Ju. M. (1972), *Die Struktur literarischer Texte.* Trans. by R.-D. Keil. München.

Lüthi, M. (1981), *Das europäische Volksmärchen.* 7th ed. Munich.

Magoun, F. P., Jr. (1955), "Bede's Story of Cædmon: The Case History of an Anglo-Saxon Oral Singer," *Speculum,* 30, 49-63.

Malinowski, B. (1926), *Myth in Primitive Society.* New York.

Malov, S. E. (1957), *Jazyk žёltyx ujgurov. Slovar' i grammatika* [The language of the Yellow Uighurs. A dictionary and grammar]. Alma-Ata.

Mamay, Džüsüp (1984), *Qurmanbek* ['Q.']. Ed. S. Ömür. Urumchi.

Mamay, Džüsüp (1984ff.), *Manas* ['M.']. Ed. A. Matïlï et al. 1(I)ff. Urumchi.

Mamay, Džüsüp (1985), *Toltoy. Qïrğïz elinin baatïrlïq dastanï* ['T.' A heroic epic of the Kirghiz people]. Ed. O. Qïdïrbay, Dž. Džaqïp. Urumchi.

Mamedov, T. A. (1984), *Pesni Köroglu* [The songs of Köroğlu]. Baku.

Maqsetov, Q. M. (1983), *Qaraqalpaq žïraw baqsïlarï* [The Karakalpak baqsïs and žïraws]. Nukus.

Maqsetov, Q. M., ed. (1984), *Šaryar* ['Š.']. Qaraqalpaq fol'klorï, 13. Nukus.

Maqsetov, Q. M., Q. Mämbetnazarov, Ö. Erpolatov, eds. (1963), *Göruǧlï* ['G.']. Nukus.

Maqsetov [Maksetov], Q. M., et al. (1977), *Očerki po istorii karakalpakskogo fol'klora* [Essays on the history of Karakalpak folklore]. Tashkent.

Maqsetov Q. M., A. Täžimuratov (1979), *Qaraqalpaq fol'klorï* [Karakalpak folklore]. Nukus.

Maqsetov, Q. M., N. Žapaqov, T. Niyemullaev, eds. (1980), *Qïrïq Qïz* ['Forty Maidens']. Qaraqalpaq fol'klorï, 6. Nukus.

Maqsetov, Q. M., A. K. Karimov, eds. (1985), *Ǧärip — Ašïq, Sayatxan — Hämra* ['Ašïq G.', 'S. and H.']. Qaraqalpaq fol'klorï, 14. Nukus.

Maqsetov, Q. M., A. K. Karimov, eds. (1986), *Göruǧlï* ['G.']. Qaraqalpaq fol'klorï, 15. Nukus.

Marcuse, S. (1964), *Musical Instruments. A Comprehensive Dictionary*. New York.

Martyncev, A. E. (1976), "O formax parallelizma v tjurkskom stixe" [On the forms of parallelism in Turkic verse], *Sovetskaja Tjurkologija*, 1976.5, 43-48.

Ma'rufov, Z. M., et al. (1981), *Ozbek tiliniŋ izāhli luǧati* [An encyclopedic dictionary of the Uzbek language]. 2 vols. Moscow.

Mehl, D. (1968), *The Middle English Romances of the Thirteenth and Fourteenth Centuries*. London.

Meletinskij, E. M. (1963), *Proisxoždenie geroičeskogo éposa. Rannie formy i arxaičeskie pamjatniki* [The origin of the heroic epic. Early forms and archaic documents]. Moscow.

Meletinskij, E. M. (1983), *Srednevekovyj roman. Proisxoždenie i klassičeskie formy* [Medieval romance. Its origin and classical forms]. Moscow.

Meletinskjij, E. M. (1986), *Vvedenie v istoričeskuju poétiku éposa i romana* [Introduction to the historical poetics of epic and romance]. Moscow.

Mélikoff, I., ed. and trans., (1960), *La Geste de Melik Dânişmend. Étude critique du Dânişmendnâme*. 2 vols. Bibliothèque Archéologique et Historique de l'Insitut Français d'Archéologie d'Istanbul, 10, 11. Paris.

Menges, K. H. (1947), *Qaraqalpaq Grammar. I. Phonology*. New York.

Menges, K. H. (1968), *The Turkic Languages and Peoples. An Introduction to Turkic Studies*. Ural-Altaische Bibliothek, 15. Wiesbaden.

Merchant, P. (1971), *The Epic*. The Critical Idiom, 17. London.

Meyer, R. M. (1889), *Die altgermanische Poesie nach ihren formelhaften Elementen beschrieben*. Berlin.

Miller, R. A. (1971), *Japanese and the Other Altaic Languages*. Chicago.

Mills, M., ed. (1973), *Six Middle English Romances*. London.

Minorsky, V. (1936), "Tât," in *Encyclopaedia of Islam*. Leiden, VIII, 697-700.

372   *Bibliography*

Mirbadaleva, A. S. (1975), "Obščie čerty i specifika turkmenskix i uzbekskix romaničeskix dastanov" [General traits and characteristics of the Turkmen and Uzbek love-dastans], in Gacak 1975a: 110-127.

Mirzaev, T. (1968), *Alpāmiš dāstāniniŋ ozbek variantlari* [The Uzbek variants of the epic 'A.']. Tashkent.

Mirzaev, T., ed. (1969), *Alpāmiš. Aytuwci Berdi baxši* ['A.' Narrated by Berdibaxši]. Tashkent.

Mirzaev, T. (1971), "'Yakka Ahmad' dāstāni toġrisida" [On the dastan 'Y. A.'], in Mominov et al. 1971: 51-59.

Mirzaev, T. (1979), *Xalq baxšilariniŋ epik repertuari* [The epic repertory of the folk singers]. Tashkent.

Mirzaev, T., et al., eds. (1976), *Polkan šāir* [Polkan-šāir]. Tashkent.

Mirzaev, T., et al., eds. (1978), *Islām šāir wa uniŋ xalq poeziyasida tutgan orni* [Islām-šāir and his place in folk poetry]. Tashkent.

Mirzaev, T., B. Sarimsāqov (1981), "Dāstān, uniŋ turlari wa tarixiy taraqqiyāti" [Subgenres and historical development of the dāstān], in *Ozbek fol'kloriniŋ epik žanrlari* [The epic genres of Uzbek folklore]. Tashkent, 9-61.

Mominov, I., et al., eds. (1971), *Ergaš Šāir wa uniŋ dāstānčilikdagi orni* [Ergaš-šāir and his place in the art of the singer]. Tashkent.

Mominov, I., et al., eds. (1975), *Širin bilan Šakar, Kuntuġmiš, Ārzigul. Dāstānlar* ['Š. and Š.', 'K.', 'Ā.' Dastans]. Ozbek xalq idžādi. Tashkent.

Moyle, N. K. (1990), *The Turkish Minstrel Tale Tradition*. Harvard Dissertations in Folklore and Oral Tradition. New York.

Mukanov, M. S. (1974), *Ètničeskij sostav i rasselenie kazaxov srednego žuza* [The ethnic composition and settlement of the Kazakhs of the Middle Horde]. Alma-Ata.

Mukanov, M. S. (1979), *Kazaxskaja jurta* [The Kazakh yurt]. Alma-Ata.

Muminov, I. M., et al. (1974), *Istorija karakalpakskoj ASSR* [The history of the Karakalpak ASSR]. 2 vols. Tashkent.

Mundy, C. S. (1956), "Polyphemus and Tepegöz," *Bulletin of the School of Oriental and African Studies*, 18, 279-302.

Musaev, S. (1979), *Èpos "Manas". Naučno-populjarnyj očerk* [The epic 'M.' An essay for the general reader]. Frunze.

Mutallibov, S. M., ed. and trans. (1960), *Mahmud Kāšġariy. Turkiy sozlar devāni (Devānu luġātit turk)* ['The Dīvān luġāt at-Turk' of Mahmūd of Kashgar]. 3 vols. Tashkent.

Mylius, K. (1983), *Geschichte der Literatur im alten Indien*. Leipzig.

Nasyrov, D. S. (1983), "Dialekty karakalpakskogo jazyka" [The dialects of the Karakalpak language], in *Voprosy karakalpakskogo jazykoznanija* [Problems of Karakalpak linguistics], ed. D. S. Nasyrov et al. Nukus, 56-113.

Nettl, B. (1964), *Theory and Method in Ethnomusicology*. New York.

Nilsson, M. P. (1933), *Homer and Mycenae*. London.

Nurmagambetova, O. (1988), *Kazaxskij geroičeskij èpos Koblandy-batyr* [The Kazakh heroic epic 'Q.']. Alma-Ata.

Nurmuxamedov, M. K. (1983), *Skazki A. S. Puškina i fol'klor narodov Srednej Azii* [Pushkin's tales and the folklore of the peoples of Central Asia]. Tashkent.

Nutku, Ö. (1976), *Meddahlık ve Meddah Hikâyeleri* [The art of the meddah and the meddah tales]. Ankara.

Olcott, M. B. (1987), *The Kazakhs*. Studies of Nationalities in the USSR. Stanford, CA.

Ong. W. J. (1982), *Orality and Literacy. The Technologizing of the Word.* London.

Oring, E., ed. (1989), *Folk Groups and Folklore Genres. A Reader.* Logan, UT.

Orozbaqov, S. (1978-82), *Manas* ['M.']. Ed. Č. T. Ajtmatov et al. 4 vols. Frunze.

Orudžov, Ä. Ä., et al. (1966-87), *Azärbaydžan diliniŋ izahlï luğäti* [An encyclopedic dictionary of the Azerbaijanian language]. 4 vols. Baku.

Paksoy, H. B. (1989), *Alpamysh. Central Asian Identity Under Russian Rule.* Hartford, CT.

Parry, M. (1971 [1930]), "Studies in the Epic Technique of Oral Verse-Making. I. Homer and Homeric Style," in Parry 1971: 266-324 [originally published in 1930].

Parry, M. (1971 [1932]), "Studies in the Epic Technique of Oral Verse-Making. II. The Homeric Language as the Language of an Oral Poetry," in Parry 1971: 325-364 [originally published in 1932].

Parry, M. (1971), *The Making of Homeric Verse*. Ed. A. Parry. London.

Parry, M., A. B. Lord, eds. (1953-54), *Serbocroatian Heroic Songs*. Collected by Milman Parry, ed. and trans. by A. B. Lord. 2 vols. Cambridge, MA., Belgrade.

Paxratdinov, A., ed. (1959), *Šaryar* ['Š.']. Nukus.

Pelliot, P. (1930), "Sur la légende d'Uğuz-Khan en écriture ouigoure," *T'oung Pao*, 25, 247-358.

Pen'kovskij, L. M., trans., T. Mirzaev, ed. (1982), *"Alpamyš"*. *Uzbekskij narodnyj èpos* ['A.' An Uzbek folk epic]. Leningrad.

Petrosjan, A. A., ed. (1975), *Geroičeskij èpos narodov SSSR* [The heroic epic of the peoples of the Soviet Union]. 2 vols. Moscow.

Philippi, D. L., trans. (1979), *Songs of Gods, Songs of Humans. The Epic Tradition of the Ainu.* Tokyo.

Phillips, N. (1981), *Sijobang. Sung Narrative Poetry of West Sumatra.* Cambridge Studies in Oral and Literate Culture, 1. Cambridge.

Poppe, N. (1958), "Der Parallelismus in der epischen Dichtung der Mongolen," *Ural-Altaische Jahrbücher*, 30, 195-228.

Poppe, N. (1960), *Vergleichende Grammatik der altaischen Sprachen. I. Vergleichende Lautlehre*. Porta Linguarum Orientalium, N.S., 4. Wiesbaden.

Poppe, N. (1965), *Introduction to Altaic Linguistics*. Ural-Altaische Bibliothek, 14. Wiesbaden.

Preminger, A., F. J. Warnke, O. B. Hardison, Jr., eds. (1974), *Princeton Encyclopedia of Poetry and Poetics*. Enlarged ed. Princeton, NJ.

Propp, V. Ja. (1955), *Russkij geroičeskij èpos* [The Russian heroic epic]. Leningrad.

Propp, V. Ja. (1964), "Principy klassificacii fol'klornyx žanrov" [The principles of the classification of folklore genres], *Sovetskaja Ètnografija*, 1964.4, 147-154.

Propp, V. [Ja.], (1968), *Morphology of the Folktale*. Trans. L. Scott, rev. L. A. Wagner. 2nd rev. ed. Bloomington, IN.

Propp, V. Ja. (1976 [1941]), "Motiv čudesnogo roždenija" [The motif of the miraculous birth], in *Fol'klor i dejstvitel'nost'. Izbrannye stat'i* [Folklore and reality. Selected articles]. Moscow, 205-240.

Putilov, B. N. (1988), *Geroičeskij èpos i dejstvitel'nost'* [Heroic epic and reality]. Leningrad.

Puxov, I. V. (1962), *Jakutskij geroičeskij èpos Olonxo. Osnovnye obrazy* [The Yakut heroic epic 'oloŋxo'. Its basic forms]. Moscow.

Qalenderov, M., et al. (1982ff.), *Qaraqalpaq tiliniŋ tüsindirme sözligi* [An encyclopedic dictionary of the Karakalpak language]. 4 vols. Nukus.

Qaralaev, S. (1956), *Er Töštük* ['E. T.']. Frunze.

Qarataev, M. Q., et al., eds. (1972-78), *Qazaq Sovet Enciklopediyasï* [Kazakh Soviet encyclopedia]. 12 vols. Alma-Ata.

Qasqabasov [Kaskabasov], S. A. (1972), *Kazaxskaja volšebnaja skazka* [The Kazakh fairy-tale]. Alma-Ata.

Qasqabasov, S. (1984), *Qazaqtïŋ xalïq prozasï* [Kazakh popular prose]. Alma-Ata.

Qïrbašev, K., R. Sarïpbekov, eds. (1987ff.), *Semetey. Epos. Sayaqbay Qaralaev-din variantï boyunča* ['S.' An epic. According to S. Qaralaev's variant]. Iff. Frunze.

Qoŋïratbaev, Ä. (1987), *Qazaq eposï žäne turkologija* [Kazakh epic and Turkology]. Alma-Ata.

Quular, D., S. Sarïg-ool, eds. (1963), *Tïwa tooldar* [Tuvinian tales]. Kyzyl.

Radloff, W. (1866a), "Über die Formen der gebundenen Rede bei den altaischen Tataren," *Zeitschrift für Völkerpsychologie und Sprachwissenschaft*, 4, 85-114.

Radloff, W., ed. and trans. (1866b), *Proben der Volkslitteratur der türkischen Stämme Süd-Sibiriens. I. Die Dialecte des eigentlichen Altai: der Altajer und Teleuten, Lebed-Tataren, Schoren und Sojonen.* St. Petersburg [text volume and translation volume].

Radloff, W., ed. and trans. (1870), *Proben der Volkslitteratur der türkischen Stämme Süd-Sibiriens. III. Kirgisische Mundarten.* St. Petersburg [text volume and translation volume].

Radloff, W., ed. and trans. (1872), *Proben der Volkslitteratur der türkischen Stämme Süd-Sibiriens. IV. Die Mundarten der Barabiner, Taraer, Toboler und Tümenischen Tataren.* St. Petersburg [text volume and translation volume].

Radloff, W., ed. and trans. (1885), *Proben der Volkslitteratur der nördlichen türkischen Stämme. V. Der Dialect der Kara-Kirgisen.* St. Petersburg [text volume and translation volume].

Radloff, W., ed. (1891), *Das Kudatku Bilik des Jusuf Chass-Hadschib aus Bälasagun. Theil 1. Der Text in Transcription.* St. Petersburg.

Radloff, W. (1893), *Aus Sibirien. Lose Blätter aus meinem Tagebuche.* 2nd ed. 2 vols. Leipzig.

Radloff, W. (1893-1911), *Versuch eines Wörterbuches der Türk-Dialecte.* 4 vols. St. Petersburg.

Radloff, W., ed. (1896), *Proben der Volkslitteratur der nördlichen türkischen Stämme. VII. Die Mundarten der Krym.* St. Petersburg [text volume only].

Radloff, W., ed. (1899), *Proben der Volkslitteratur der türkischen Stämme. VIII. Die Mundarten der Osmanen.* Ed. I. Kúnos. St. Petersburg [text volume only].

Radloff, W. (1990), "Samples of Folk Literature from the North Turkic Tribes. Preface to Volume V: *The Dialect of the Kara-Kirgiz.*" Trans. G. B. Sherman, A. B. Davis. *Oral Tradition*, 5, 73-90.

Raquette, G., ed. and trans. (1930), *Täji bilä Zohra. Eine osttürkische Variante der Sage von Tahir und Zohra.* Lunds Universitets Årsskrift, N.V. Avd. 1, 26.6. Lund, Leipzig.

Räsänen, M. (1969), *Versuch eines etymologischen Wörterbuchs der Türksprachen.* Helsinki.

Raxman, A., et al., eds. (1981), *Ujǧur xälq dastanliri* [Uighur popular dastans]. Urumchi.

Reichl, K., trans. (1985a), *Rawšan. Ein usbekisches mündliches Epos.* Asiatische Forschungen, 93. Wiesbaden.

Reichl, K. (1985b), "Oral Tradition and Performance of the Uzbek and Karakalpak Epic Singers," in Heissig 1985: 613-43.

Reichl, K., trans. (1986), *Märchen aus Sinkiang. Überlieferungen der Turkvölker Chinas.* Köln.

Reichl, K. (1987), "Beowulf, Er Töštük und das Bärensohnmärchen," in Heissig 1987: 321-350.

Reichl, K. (1989a), "Formulaic Diction in Old English Epic Poetry," in Hatto, Hainsworth 1980-1989: II, 42-70.

Reichl, K. (1989b), "Uzbek Epic Poetry: Tradition and Poetic Diction," in Hatto, Hainsworth 1980-1989: II, 94-120.

Reichl, K. (1989c), "Formulaic Diction in Kazakh Epic Poetry," *Oral Tradition*, 4, 360-381.

Reichl, K. (1990), "Nan silafu he tujue yingxiong shishi zhong de pingxing shi: Chengshi hua jufa de shixue tansuo" [Parallelism in South Slavic and Turkic epic poetry. Towards a poetics of formulaic diction], *Minzuwen xueyanjiu*, 1990.2, 85-91.

Reichl, K. (forthcoming), "*Octavian* and *Kuntuǧmiš*: Romance and Dāstān," in *Fragen der mongolischen Heldendichtung. V*, ed. W. Heissig. Asiatische Forschungen. Wiesbaden.

Reinhard, K. and U. (1984), *Musik der Türkei*. 2 vols. Taschenbücher zur Musikwissenschaft, 95, 96. Wilhelmshaven.

Renoir, A. (1988), *A Key to Old Poems. The Oral-Formulaic Approach to the Interpretation of West-Germanic Verse*. University Park, PA.

Riedinger, A. (1985), "The Old English Formula in Context," *Speculum*, 60, 294-317.

Rossi, E., trans. (1952), *Il "Kitāb-i Dede Qorqut". Racconti epico-cavallereschi dei Turchi Oǧuz tradotti e annotati con "facsimile" del MS. Vat. Turco 102*. Studi i Testi, 159. Città del Vaticano.

Ruben, W. (1944), *Ozean der Märchenströme. I. Die 25 Erzählungen des Dämons (Vetâlapancavimśati). Mit einem Anhang über die 12 Erzählungen des Dede Korkut*. FF Communications, 133. Helsinki.

Rychner, J. (1955), *La chanson de geste. Essai sur l'art épique des jongleurs*. Soc. de Publ. Romanes et Franç., 53. Geneva, Lille.

Šaabdurahmānov, Š. Š. (1971), *Ozbek xalq šewalari luǧati* [An Uzbek dialect dictionary]. Tashkent.

Šaabdurahmānov, Š., M. Afzalov, T. Mirzaev, eds. (1973), *Fāzil šāir* [Fāzil-šāir]. Tashkent.

Sachs, C. (1913), *Real-Lexikon der Musikinstrumente, zugleich ein Polyglossar für das gesamte Instrumentengebiet*. Berlin.

Sachs, C. (1930), *Handbuch der Musikinstrumentenkunde*. 2nd ed. Leipzig.

Sadie, S., ed. (1981), *The New Grove Dictionary of Music and Musicians*. 20 vols. London.

Šādieva, S., ed. (1965), *Āyparča* ['Ä.'] Tashkent.

Sadiri, S., N. Äbäydulla, trans. (1987), *Alpamiš. Xälq dastani* ['A.' A folk epic]. Urumchi.

Sa'dulla, Š., et al., eds. (1955), *Ozbek xalq ertaklari* [Uzbek folktales]. Tashkent.

Sadykov, A. S., S. M. Musaev, A. S. Mirbadaleva, B. M. Junusaliev, K. K. Kyrbašev, N. V. Kidaiš-Pokrovskaja, eds. and trans. (1984ff.), *Manas. Kirgizskij geroičeskij épos.* ['M.' A Kirghiz heroic epic]. Iff. Épos narodov SSSR. Moscow.

Sagitov, I. T. (1959), "Karakalpakskaja versija éposa 'Alpamys'" [The Karakalpak version of the epic 'A.'], in Čičerov, Zarifov 1959: 178-186.

Säġitov [Sagitov], M. M., Ä. I. Xarisov, eds. (1973), *Bašqort xalïq idžadï. Epos* [Bashkir folk literature. Epic]. Vol. II. Ufa.

Säġitov [Sagitov], M. M., Ä. I. Xarisov, et al., eds. and trans. (1977), *Baškirskij narodnyj épos* [The Bashkir folk epic]. Épos narodov SSSR. Moscow.

Säġitov [Sagitov], M. M ., N. T. Zaripov, A. M. Sulejmanov, eds. (1987), *Baškirskoe narodnoe tvorčestvo. I. Épos* [Bashkir folk literature. I. Epic]. Ufa.

Sagitov, S. I. (1968), "K voprosu o lokalizacii legendarnoj mestnosti Žideli-Bajsun po dannym botaniki" [On the question of the localization of the legendary place 'Ž.-B.' according to botany], *Sovetskaja Étnografija,* 1968.1, 130-133.

Salmin, A. K. (1987), "Dva čuvašskix termina, oboznačajuščix skazku" [Two Chuvash terms denoting the folktale], *Sovetskaja Tjurkologija,* 1987.2, 33-37.

Sarimsāqov, B. (1978), *Ozbek adabiyātida sadž^c* [Rhymed prose in Uzbek literature]. Tashkent.

Sarqïtbay-ulï, M. (1982), "Qïz Žibek" ['Q. Ž.'], *Mura,* 1982.1, 33-75.

Sarqïtbay-ulï, M., M. Šükiman-ulï, K. Žarïs-ulï (1983), "Äsilqan men Tänidiŋ aytïsï" [The aytïs between Äsilqan and Täni], *Mura,* 1983.2, 23-30.

Saville-Troike, M. (1989), *The Ethnography of Communication. An Introduction.* 2nd ed. Oxford.

Ščerbak, A. M. (1959), *Oguz-nāme. Muxabbat-nāme. Pamjatniki drevne-ujgurskoj i starouzbekskoj pis'menosti* ['O.' 'M.' Monuments of Old Uighur and Old Uzbek literature]. Moscow.

Ščerbak, A. M. (1961), "Sootnošenie alliteracii i rifmy v tjurkskom stixo-složenii" [The correlation between alliteration and rhyme in Turkic meter], *Narody Azii i Afriki,* 1961.2, 142-153.

Scherf, W. (1982), *Lexikon der Zaubermärchen.* Stuttgart.

Schlauch, M. (1927), *Chaucer's Constance and Accused Queens.* New York.

Schmaus, A. (1953), "Studie o krajinskoj epici" [Studies on the Moslem epic], *Rad Jugosl. Akademije,* 296. Zagreb.

Scholes, P. A. (1970), *The Oxford Companion of Music.* 10th rev. ed. Ed. J. O. Ward. London.

Scholes, R., R. Kellogg (1966), *The Nature of Narrative.* London.

Schröder, W. J. (1967), *Spielmannsepik*. 2nd ed. Stuttgart.

Sevortjan, Ė. V. (1974ff.), *Ėtimologičeskij slovar' tjurkskix jazykov* [An etymological dictionary of the Turkic languages], Iff. Moscow.

Seydou, C., ed. and trans. (1976), *La geste de Ham-Bodêdio ou Hama le Rouge*. Classiques Africains, 18. Paris.

Sinor, D., ed. (1990), *The Cambridge History of Early Inner Asia*. Cambridge.

Šklovskij, V. (1969), "Svjaz' priëmov sjužetosloženija s obščim priëmami stilja" [The connection between devices of plot-structuring and general stylistic devices], in *Russischer Formalismus. I. Texte zur allgemeinen Literaturtheorie und zur Theorie der Prosa*, ed. and trans. J. Striedter. München, 36-121.

Slobin, M. (1976), *Music in the Culture of Northern Afghanistan*. Tucson, AZ.

Smirnova, N. S., et al., eds. (1968), *Istorija kazaxskoj literatury. I. Kazaxskij fol'klor* [A history of Kazakh literature. I. Kazakh folk literature]. Alma-Ata.

Smirnova, N. S. (1968), "Očerk istorii kazaxskogo fol'klora" [A sketch of the history of Kazakh folklore], in Smirnova et al. 1968: 64-124.

Smith, J. D. (1977), *"The Singer or the Song?* A Reassessment of Lord's 'Oral Theory'," *Man*, N.S. 12, 141-153.

Smith, J. D. (1987), "Formulaic Language in the Epics of India," in Almqvist, Ó Catháin, Ó Héalaí 1987: 591-611.

Spies, O. (1929), *Türkische Volksbücher. Ein Beitrag zur vergleichenden Märchenkunde*. Form und Geist, 12. Leipzig.

Spuler, B. (1966), "Geschichte Mittelasiens seit dem Auftreten der Türken," in Jettmar et al. 1966: 123-310.

Stebleva, I. V. (1976), *Poėtika drevnetjurkskoj literatury i eë transformacija v ranne-klassičeskij period* [Poetics of Old Turkic literature and its transformation in the early Classical period]. Moscow.

Steinitz, W. (1934), *Der Parallelismus in der finnisch-karelischen Volksdichtung, untersucht an den Liedern des karelischen Sängers Arhippa Perttunen*. FF Communications, 115. Helsinki.

Stemmler, Th., ed. (1988), *Schöne Frauen — Schöne Männer. Literarische Schönheitsbeschreibungen. 2. Kolloquium der Forschungsstelle für europäische Literatur des Mittelalters*. Mannheim.

Šternberg, L. Ja. (1908), *Materialy po izučeniju giljackago jazyka i fol'klora. I. Obrazcy narodnoj slovesnosti. C. 1-aja. Ėpos* [Material for the study of the Gilyak language and folklore. I. Specimens of oral literature. Part I. Epic]. St. Petersburg.

Stevens, J. (1973), *Medieval Romance. Themes and Approaches*. London.

Stojanov, A. K. (1988), "Iskusstvo xakasskix xajdži" [The art of the Khakas xaydžïs], in *Altyn-Aryg. Xakasskij geroičeskij ėpos* ['A.-A.' A Khakas heroic epic], ed. and trans. V. E. Majnogaševa. Épos narodov SSSR. Moscow, 577-590.

Šukjurova, R. M., trans. (1987), *Fazlallax Rašid ad-Din: Oguz-Name* [The 'Oğuz-Näme' by F. Rašid ad-Din]. AN Az. SSR, Inst. Vostokovedenija, Istočniki po istorii Azerbajdžana. Baku.

Sulejmanov, X. S. (1959), "Tema družby i pobratimstva v dastane 'Alpamyš'" [The theme of friendship and brotherhood in the dastan 'A.'], in Čičerov, Zarifov 1959: 91-92.

Šul'gin, B. (1973), "Ob altajskom kae" [On the Altaian qay], in Surazakov et al. 1973: 454-460.

Sümer, F., A. E. Uysal, W. S. Walker, trans. (1972), *The Book of Dede Korkut. A Turkish Epic.* Austin, TX.

Surazakov, S. S. (1959), "Ob altajskom skazanii 'Alyp-Manaš'" [On the Altaian tale 'A.-M.'], in Čičerov, Zarifov 1959: 197-202.

Surazakov, S. S., et al., eds. (1958), *Altay baatïrlar. Altay albatïnïŋ at-nerelü čörčöktöri* [Altaian heroes. Altaian heroic epic poetry]. Vol. I. Gorno-Altajsk.

Surazakov, S. S., et al., eds. (1959), *Altay baatïrlar. Altay albatïnïŋ at-nerelü čörčöktöri* [Altaian heroes. Altaian heroic epic poetry]. Vol. II. Gorno-Altajsk.

Surazakov, S. S., ed. and trans. (1961), *Geroičeskoe skazanie o bogatyre Altaj-Buučae* [The heroic tale of the hero Altay-Buučay]. Gorno-Altajsk.

Surazakov, S. S. (1985), *Altajskij geroičeskij épos* [The Altaian heroic epic]. Moscow.

Surazakov, S. S., I. V. Puxov, N. A. Baskakov, eds. and trans. (1973), *Maadaj-Kara. Altajskij geroičeskij épos* ['M.' An Altaian heroic epic]. Épos narodov SSSR. Moscow.

Sydykov, T. (1975), *Glubokie korni* [Deep roots]. Alma-Ata.

Tähmasib, M. H., ed. (1959), *Koroğlu* ['K.']. Akademija Nauk Azerbajdžanskoj SSR, Inst. Literatury i Jazyka. Baku.

Tähmasib, M. H. (1972), *Azärbaydžan xalg dastanlarï (Orta äsrlär)* [Azerbaijanian popular dastans (Middle Ages)]. Baku.

Tähmasib, M. H., et al., eds. (1979), *Azärbaydžan mähäbbät dastanlarï* [Azerbaijanian love-romances]. Baku.

Taksami, Č. M., ed. (1988), *Skazanie o prostore* [Tales about the open spaces]. Leningrad.

Tatliq, Ä., et al., eds. (1986), *Emir Göroğli. Uyğur xälq dastanliridin.* ['Emir G.' Uighur popular dastans]. Vol. I. Urumchi.

Taube, E. (1973), "Baldžïn Xēr," *Wissenschaftliche Zeitschrift der Universität Halle*, 22.3, 59-66.

Taube, E., trans. (1978), *Tuwinische Volksmärchen.* Berlin.

380 *Bibliography*

Tekin, T. (1968), *A Grammar of Orkhon Turkic.* Ural and Altaic Ser., 69. Bloomington, IN, The Hague.

Tenišev, È, R., et al., eds. (1984), *Sravnitel'no-istoričeskaja grammatika tjurkskix jazykov. Fontetika* [A comparative-historical grammar of the Turkic languages. Phonetics]. Moscow.

Thompson, S. (1955-58), *Motif-Index of Folk-Literature.* 6 vols. Rev. ed. Copenhagen, Bloomington, IN.

Thurneysen, R. (1921), *Die irische Helden- und Königssage bis zum siebzehnten Jahrhundert.* Halle.

Timofeev-Teplouxov, I. G., narrator, V. N. Vasil'ev, transcriber, È. K. Pekarskij, G. U. Èrgis, eds., A. A. Popov, I. V. Puxov, trans. (1985), *Stroptivyj Kulun Kullustuur. Jakutskoe olonxo* ['Obstinate Qulun Qullustuur.' A Yakut epic]. With an introductory chapter by I. V. Puxov and G. U. Èrgis. Èpos narodov SSSR. Moscow.

Todorov, Tz. (1978), *Poétique de la prose (choix), suivi de Nouvelles recherches sur le récit.* Paris.

Tokarev, S. A., et al. (1980-82), *Mify narodov mira* [Myths of the peoples of the world]. 2 vols. Moscow.

Trojakov, P. A. (1969), "Promyslovaja i magičeskaja funkcija skazyvanija skazok u xakasov" [The venatorial and magic function of the telling of tales among the Khakas], *Sovetskaja Ètnografija*, 1969.2, 24-34.

Tursunov, E. D. (1975), "Tjurko-mongol'skie versii skazanija ob osleplenii ciklopa" [The Turko-Mongolian versions of the tale of the blinding of the Cyclops], *Sovetskaja Tjurkologija*, 1975.3, 36-43.

Uplegger, H. (1964), "Das Volksschauspiel," in Deny et al. (1959-1964), II, 147-170.

Urmančeev, F. I. (1980a), *Èpičeskie skazanija tatarskogo naroda. Sravnitel'no-istoričeskie očerki* [The epic tales of the Tatar people. Comparative-historical essays]. Kazan.

Urmančeev, F. I. (1980b), "Legendy o bulgarskix bogatyrjax i skazanie ob Alpamyše" [The legends on Bulgar heroes and the tale of A.], *Sovetskaja Tjurkologija*, 1980.2, 30-38.

Urmančeev, F. (1984), *Geroičeskij èpos tatarskogo naroda* [The heroic epic of the Tatar people]. Kazan.

Vajnštejn, S. I. (1976), "Problemy istorii žilišča stepnyx kočevnykov Evrazii" [Problems in the history of the dwellings of the nomads of the Eurasian steppes], *Sovetskaja Ètnografija*, 1976.4, 42-62.

Vajnštejn [Vainshtein], S. (1980), *Nomads of South Siberia. The Pastoral Economies of Tuva.* Ed. and with an introduction by C. Humphrey, trans. M. Colenso. Cambridge Studies in Social Anthropology, 25. Cambridge.

Vámbéry, H. (1865), *Reise in Mittelasien von Teheran durch die Turkmanische Wüste an der Ostküste des Kaspischen Meeres nach Chiwa, Bochara und Samarkand, ausgeführt im Jahr 1863.* Leipzig.

Vámbéry, H., ed. and trans. (1911), *Jusuf und Ahmed. Ein özbegisches Volksepos im Chiwaer Dialekte.* Budapest.

Veit, V. (1985), "Das Pferd — Alter Ego der Mongolen? Überlegungen zu einem zentralen Thema der mongolischen Geschichte und Kultur," in Heissig 1985: 58-88.

Veliev, K. N. (1987), "Tradicionnye formuly v tjurkojazyčnom épose. (Opyt lingvopoétičeskogo analiza)" [Traditional formulas in Turkic epic poetry. (An essay in linguistico-poetic analysis)], *Sovetskaja Tjurkologija*, 1987.3, 88-83.

Vertkov, K., G. Blagodatov, É. Jazovickaja (1963), *Atlas muzykal'nyx instrumentov narodov SSSR* [An atlas of the musical instruments of the peoples of the Soviet Union]. Moscow.

Veselovskij, A. N. (1940), *Istoričeskaja poétika* [Historical poetics]. Ed. V. M. Žirmunskij. Leningrad.

Veselovskij, A. N. (1940 [1897]), "Épičeskie povtorenija kak xronologičeskij moment" [Epic repetition as a chronological element], in Veselovskij 1940: 93-124.

Veselovskij, A. N. (1940 [1898]), "Psixologičeskij parallelizm i ego formy v otraženijax poétičeskogo stilja" [Psychological parallelism and its forms in the reflections of poetic style], in Veselovskij 1940: 125-199.

Vinnikov, I. N. (1969), *Jazyk i fol'klor Buxarskix arabov* [The language and folklore of the Bukhara Arabs]. Moscow.

Vinogradov, V. S. (1958), *Kirgizskaja nardonaja muzyka* [Kirghiz folk music]. Frunze.

Vinogradov, V. S. (1984), "Napevy 'Manasa'" [The melodies of 'M.'], in Sadykov et al. 1984: 492-509.

Voorwinden, N., M. de Haan, eds. (1979), *Oral Poetry. Das Problem der Mündlichkeit mittelalterlicher epischer Dichtung.* Wege der Forschung, 555. Darmstadt.

Watts, A. C. (1969), *The Lyre and the Harp. A Comparative Reconsideration of Oral Tradition in Homer and Old English Epic Poetry.* Yale Studies in English, 168. New Haven, CT.

Waxatov, B., et al., eds. (1963), *Aqïndar žïrï. Qazirgi xalïq poeziyasï* [The song of the aqïns. Contemporary folk poetry]. Alma-Ata.

Wensinck, A. J. (1978), "Al-Khaḍir (al-Khiḍr)," *The Encyclopaedia of Islam.* New ed. Leiden, IV, 902-905.

Whallon, W. (1969), *Formula, Character, and Context. Studies in Homeric, Old English, and Old Testament Poetry.* Cambridge, MA.

Wingate, R. O. (1930), "Children's Stories from Chinese Turkestan," *Bulletin of the School of Oriental and African Studies*, 5, 809-822.

Winner, T. G. (1958), *The Oral Art and Literature of the Kazakhs of Russian Central Asia*. Durham, NC.

Wünsch, W. (1934), *Die Geigentechnik der südslawischen Guslaren*. Brünn.

Xamraev, M. (1969), *Očerki teorii tjurkskogo stixa* [Outlines of a theory of Turkic verse]. Alma-Ata.

Yates, F. A. (1966), *The Art of Memory*. London.

Yolboldi, N., M. Qasim (1987), *Džuŋgudiki türkiy tillar* [The Turkic languages of China]. Urumchi.

Yunusaliev [Junusaliev], B. M., et al., eds. (1958-60), *Manas* ['M.']. 4 vols. Frunze.

Yunusaliev [Junusaliev], B. M. (1961), "Ob opyte sozdanija svobodnogo varianta éposa 'Manas'" [On the attempt to edit a free variant of the epic 'M.'], in Bogdanova, Žirmunskij, Petrosjan 1961: 282-297.

Žabaev, Žambïl (1955), *Üš tomdïq šïgarmalar žïynagï* [Complete works in three volumes]. Akademija Nauk Kazaxskoj SSR, Institut Jazyka i Literatury. 3 vols. Alma-Ata.

Zarif [Zarifov], H., ed. (1939), *Uzbekskij fol'klor. Xrestomatija dlja pedagogičeskix institutov* [Uzbek folklore. An anthology for Pedagogical Institutes]. Tashkent.

Zarif [Zarifov], H. [X. T.] (1959), "Osnovye motivy éposa 'Alpamyš'" [The basic motifs of the epic 'A.'], in Čičerov, Zarifov 1959: 6-25.

Zarif [Zarifov], H., ed. (1965), *Awazniŋ arazi. Gulixirāmān. Dāstānlar* ['Awaz insulted.' 'G.' Dastans]. Ozbek xalq idžādi. Tashkent.

Zarif [Zarifov], H. (1970), "Ulkan šāir" [A great singer], *Ozbek tili wa adabiyāti*, 1970.5, 38-42.

Zarif [Zarifov], H., ed. (1971), *Ergaš Džumanbulbul Oǧli. Tardžimai hāl, Rawšan, Qunduz bilan Yulduz* [Ergaš Džumanbulbul-oǧli. 'Autobiography.' 'R.' 'Q. and Y.'] Tashkent.

Zarif [Zarifov], H. (1973), "Fāzil šāir — mašhur dāstānči" [Fāzil-šāir, a famous singer], in Šāabdurahmānov, Afzalov, Mirzaev 1973: 5-29.

Zarif [Zarifov], H., ed. (1981), *Xāldārxān. Dāstān* ['X.' Dastan]. Ozbek xalq idžādi. Tashkent.

Zarif [Zarifov], H., T. Mirzaev, eds. (1979), *Alpāmiš. Dāstān* ['A'. Dastan]. Ozbek xalq idžādi. Tashkent.

Zataevič, A. V. (1971), *Kirgizskie instrumental'nye p'esy i napevy* [Kirghiz instrumental songs and melodies]. Ed. V. S. Vinogradov. Moscow.

Ždanko, T. A. (1950), *Očerki istoričeskoj étnografii Karakalpakov. Rodoplemennaja struktura i rasselenie v XIX — načale XX veka* [Essays on the historical ethnography of the Karakalpaks. Tribal structure and settlement in the 19th and early 20th c.]. Akademija Nauk SSSR,

Trudy Instituta Étnografii im. N. N. Mikluxo-Maklaja, Novaja Serija, 9. Moscow, Leningrad.

Ždanko, T. A., S. K. Kamalov, eds. (1980), *Étnografija Karakalpakov. XIX-načalo XX veka. (Materialy i issledovanija)* [The ethnography of the Karakalpaks. 19th c. to the beginning of the 20th c. (Documents and studies)]. Tashkent.

Zemcovskij, I. I., ed. (1989), *Muzyka éposa. Stat'i i materialy* [The music of the epic. Essays and documents]. Yoshkar-Ola.

Zenker, J. Th. (1866), *Türkisch-arabisch-persisches Handwörterbuch*. 2 vols. Leipzig.

Zguta, R. (1978), *Russian Minstrels. A History of the 'Skomorokhi'*. Oxford.

Žirmunskij, V. M. (1960), *Skazanie ob Alpamyše i bogatyrskaja skazka* [The tale of 'A.' and the heroic tale]. Moscow.

Žirmunskij [Schirmunski], V. [M.] (1961), *Vergleichende Epenforschung*. Berlin.

Žirmunskij, V. M. (1961), "Vvedenie v izučenie éposa 'Manas'" [Introduction to the study of the epic 'M.'], in Bogdanova, Žirmunskij, Petrosjan 1961: 85-196 [repr. with abbreviations in Žirmunskij 1974a: 23-116].

Žirmunskij, V. M. (1962), "Istoričeskie istočniki skazanija o razgrablenii doma Salor-Kazana" [Historical sources of the tale of the plundering of Salur Qazan's house], in *Drevnij mir. Sbornik statej* [The world of antiquity. A collection of essays], ed. N. V. Pigulvskaja et al. Leningrad, 377-85.

Žirmunskij [Zhirmunsky], V. M. (1967), "The Epic of 'Alpamysh' and the Return of Odysseus," *Proceedings of the British Academy*, 52, 1966. London, 267-286.

Žirmunskij, V. M. (1974 [1962]), "Oguzskij geroičeskij épos i 'Kniga Korkuta'" [The Oghuz heroic epic and 'The Book of Qorqut'], in Žirmunskij 1974a: 517-631 [originally published in 1962].

Žirmunskij, V. M. (1974 [1968], "O tjurkskom narodnom stixe. Nekotorye problemy teorii" [On the Turkic popular verse. Some theoretical problems], in Žirmunskij 1974a: 644-680 [originally published in 1968].

Žirmunskij, V. M. (1974a), *Tjurkskij geroičeskij épos* [The Turkic heroic epic]. Leningrad.

Žirmunskij, V. M. (1974b), "Épičeskie skazanija o nogajskix bogatyrjax v svete istoričeskix istočnikov" [Epic tales about the Noghay heroes in the light of the historical sources], in Žirmunskij 1974a: 387-516.

Žirmunskij, V. M. (1979 [1960]), "Legenda o prizvanii pevca" [The legend of the singer's calling], in *Sravnitel'noe literaturovedenie. Vostok i zapad* [Comparative literary criticism. East and West]. Leningrad, 397-407 [originally published in 1960].

Žirmunskij [Zhirmunsky], V. M. (1985 [1965]), "Rhythmico-Syntactic Parallelism as the Basis of Old Turkic Folk Epic Verse," in *Selected Writings. Linguistics, Poetics*. Moscow, 320-352 [originally published in 1965].

Žirmunskij, V. M., X. T. Zarifov (1947), *Uzbekskij narodnyj geroičeskij ėpos* [The Uzbek heroic folk epic]. Moscow.

Zlatkin, I. Ja. (1983), *Istorija džungarskogo xanstva 1635-1758* [A history of the Dzungarian khanate 1635-1758]. 2nd ed. Moscow.

Zonis, E. (1973), *Classical Persian Music. An Introduction.* Cambridge, MA.

Zunun, S., A. Momin, eds. (1982), *Uyğur xälq čöčekliri* [Uighur folktales]. Vol. IV. Urumchi.

Glossary of Terms*

Aġa (Agha)   older brother; term of respect

Aq saqal   lit. "white beard"; term of respect

Aqïn   singer; poet (Kazakh, Kirghiz) [see p. 64]

Ašïq (Turkish *Aşık*)   lit. "lover"; minstrel, singer (Turkish, Azerbaijanian [see pp. 65f.]

Aul (Awïl)   nomadic encampment; village (Kazakh, Karakalpak)

Aytïs   song-contest, contest-poem (Kazakh, Karakalpak) [see p. 77]

Baqsï   singer (Karakalpak); shaman, quack (Kazakh) [see p. 65]

Batïr   hero

Bātmān (Batman)   unit of weight, in Uzbekistan ranging from 30 to 200 kg, in Karakalpakistan from 20 to 40 kg, depending on the region

Baxši   singer (Uzbek) [see p. 65]

Baxšï   singer (Turkmen); shaman, quack (Kirghiz) [see pp. 65]

Bay   rich man

Beg   lord; term of respect (also *Bek*)

Bylina   Russian oral narrative poem

Čiltan   Forty Saints (also called *qïrqlar*), invisible saints who help those who by their piety deserve their assistance [see p. 162]

Čörčök   tale; heroic tale; epic (Altaian) [see p. 138]

Dāira   a kind of tambourine

Dastan   general term for longer narrative in verse or in verse and prose (Uzbek, Turkmen, Aserbaijanian, Uighur, Karakalpak, Kazakh, Kirghiz) [see pp. 124f.]

Diw   ogre, monster [see p.147]

---

*The glosses on the various terms are merely intended as a help for the reader and not as exhaustive definitions; for more information see the page-references in brackets. The meanings and languages specified for a term are those encountered in the book.

Dombira (Dombïra) plucked lute-type instrument without frets [see p. 107]

Dutar (Dutār) plucked lute-type instrument with frets [see pp. 105f.]

Džomoq heroic epic (Kirghiz) [see pp. 62f.]

Ġïdždžak a type of spike-fiddle [see p. 107]

Hikâye tale, minstrel tale (Turkish) [see p. 125]

Hïzïr Islamic saint [see p. 61]

Houri maiden of paradise

Ïrčï singer (Kirghiz) [see p. 82]

Jalali rebels against the Ottoman sultan and the Persian shah at the end of the 16th century [see p. 319]

Khodja descendant of the caliphs; Moslem teacher [see p. 228]

Köse beardless comical figure [see p. 288]

Kuray a type of flute (Bashkir) [see p. 341]

Manasčï singer, singer of *Manas* (Kirghiz) [see pp. 82ff.]

Meddah narrator (Turkish) [see pp. 88f.]

Öleŋši singer (Kazakh) [see p. 78]

Oloŋxo epic (Yakut) [see p. 62]

Oloŋxohut singer (Yakut) [see p. 62]

Orda palace, palace-yurt

Ozan singer (in *Dede Qorqut*) [see p. 64]

Peri fairy

Pilaw rice dish

Pir patron saint; leader of a religious order [see p. 157]

Qaġan ruler, khan

Qayčï singer (Altaian) [see pp. 62f.]

Qïmïz fermented mare's milk [see p. 17]

Qïssa story, narrative [see p. 89]

Qïssa-xān storyteller, narrator [see p. 89]

Qobïz horsehair fiddle (Karakalpak, Kazakh) [see p. 104]

Qomuz plucked lute-type instrument without frets (Kirghiz) [see p. 103]

Qopuz plucked lute-type instrument (in *Dede Qorqut*) [see pp. 103f.]

Sadžᶜ rhymed prose [see p. 129]

Šāir singer, poet (Uzbek) [see p.64]

Saz lute-type instrument (Turkish)

Semeteyči singer of *Semetey* (Kirghiz) [see pp. 81f.]

Sufi Islamic mystic

Tanbur   a type of lute [see p. 107]

Terma   improvised poem, shorter poem (Uzbek) [see p. 78]

Terme improvised poem, shorter poem (Kazakh, Karakalpak) [see p. 78]

Tolǧaw a type of poem (Karakalpak, Kazakh) [see p. 100]

Tool   tale, heroic tale, epic (Tuvinian) [see p. 62; 138]

Toolču   narrator, singer (Tuvinian) [see p. 62]

Topšuur   two-stringed plucked instrument (Altaian) [see p. 63]

Toy   feast

Tulpār   winged horse

Ustaz (Ustāz, Ustād)   master

Xïssa   narrative poem (from *qïssa*) (Kazakh) [see p. 125]

Žïraw   singer (Karakalpak, Kazakh) [see pp. 66ff.]

Žïršï   singer (Kazakh) [see p. 78]

Xalat   long coat; coat of honor

Yurt   felt-tent

Zakāt   alms-tax

Zindān   dungeon

Index

Printed in the United States
by Baker & Taylor Publisher Services

Printed in the United States
by Baker & Taylor Publisher Services